What's Eating You?

What's Eating You?

Food and Horror on Screen

EDITED BY

CYNTHIA J. MILLER AND
A. BOWDOIN VAN RIPER

BLOOMSBURY ACADEMIC
NEW YORK • LONDON • OXFORD • NEW DELHI • SYDNEY

BLOOMSBURY ACADEMIC
Bloomsbury Publishing Inc
1385 Broadway, New York, NY 10018, USA
50 Bedford Square, London, WC1B 3DP, UK

BLOOMSBURY, BLOOMSBURY ACADEMIC and the Diana logo are
trademarks of Bloomsbury Publishing Plc

First published in the United States of America 2017
Paperback edition first published 2018

Copyright © Cynthia J. Miller, A. Bowdoin Van Riper, and Contributors, 2017

Cover design: Catherine Wood
Cover image © Peter Jackson and WingNut Films

All rights reserved. No part of this publication may be reproduced or
transmitted in any form or by any means, electronic or mechanical,
including photocopying, recording, or any information storage or
retrieval system, without prior permission in writing from the publishers.

Bloomsbury Publishing Inc does not have any control over, or responsibility for,
any third-party websites referred to or in this book. All internet addresses given
in this book were correct at the time of going to press. The author and publisher
regret any inconvenience caused if addresses have changed or sites have ceased
to exist, but can accept no responsibility for any such changes.

Names: Miller, Cynthia J., 1958– editor. | Van Riper, A. Bowdoin editor.
Title: What's eating you? : food and horror on screen /
edited by Cynthia J. Miller and A. Bowdoin Van Riper.
Description: New York : Bloomsbury Academic, 2017. |
Includes bibliographical references and index.
Identifiers: LCCN 2016034482 (print) | LCCN 2016053036 (ebook) |
ISBN 9781501322389 (hardback : alk. paper) | ISBN 9781501322396 (ePDF) |
ISBN 9781501322419 (ePUB)
Subjects: LCSH: Horror films–History and criticism. |
Food in motion pictures. | Cannibalism in motion pictures.
Classification: LCC PN1995.9.H6 W435 2017 (print) |
LCC PN1995.9.H6 (ebook) | DDC 791.43/6564–dc23
LC record available at https://lccn.loc.gov/2016034482

ISBN: HB: 978-1-5013-2238-9
PB: 978-1-5013-4396-4
ePub: 978-1-5013-2241-9
ePDF: 978-1-5013-2239-6

Typeset by Newgen Knowledge Works (P) Ltd., Chennai, India

To find out more about our authors and books visit
www.bloomsbury.com and sign up for our newsletters.

*For everyone who's ever been bored by
eating the same old thing*

Tell me what you eat, and I will tell you what you are.

—ANTHELME BRILLAT-SAVARIN

Contents

Acknowledgments xi

Introduction 1
Cynthia J. Miller and A. Bowdoin Van Riper

PART ONE Let the Eater Beware 13

1. Death at the Drive-Thru: Fast Food Betrayal in *Bad Taste* and *Poultrygeist* 15
   Cynthia J. Miller

2. Let Them Eat Steak: Food and the Family Horror Film Cycle 31
   Hans Staats

3. Much Still Depends on Dinner: Cannibalism and Culinary Carnival in *Shaun of the Dead* and *Zombieland* 49
   Sue Matheson

4. *Dumplings*: The Commodification of Cannibalism and the Liminal Condition of Consumption 65
   Alex Pinar and Salvador Jiminez Murguia

5. The Goo in You: Food as Invader in *The Stuff* 81
   A. Bowdoin Van Riper

PART TWO Sins of the Flesh 97

6. Cannibalism as Cultural Critique: Peter Greenaway's *The Cook, The Thief, His Wife, and Her Lover* and Thatcherism 99
   Thomas Prasch

7. "The red gums were their own": Food, Flesh, and the Female in *Beloved* 123
   Bart Bishop

8   "Do I Look Tasty to You?": Cannibalism beyond Speech and the Limits of Food Capitalism in Park's *301/302*   137
    Tom Hertweck

9   Flesh and Blood in Claude Chabrol's *Le Boucher*   155
    Jennifer L. Holm

10 A Hunger for Dead Cakes: Visions of Abjection, Scapegoating, and the Sin-Eater   169
    Ralph Beliveau

PART THREE   The Extreme End of Consumption   187

11 Coprophagia as Class and Consumerism in the *Human Centipede* Films   189
    Mark Henderson

12 Eat, Kill, . . . Love? Courtship, Cannibalism, and Consumption in *Hannibal*   205
    Michael Fuchs and Michael Phillips

13 Catering to the Cult of Ishtar: *Blood Feast*   221
    Rob Weiner and A. Bowdoin Van Riper

14 From Gourmet to Gore: Jean-Pierre Jeunet's *Delicatessen*   237
    Karen A. Ritzenhoff and Cynthia J. Miller

15 Who Can Be Eaten? Consuming Animals and Humans in the Cannibal-Savage Horror Film   253
    Erin E. Wiegand

PART FOUR   You Are What You Eat   269

16 "You Are What Others Think You Eat": Food, Identity, and Subjectivity in Zombie Protagonist Narratives   271
    LuAnne Roth

17 From Sugar-Fueled Killer to Grotesque Gourmand: The Culinary Maturation of the Cinematic Serial Killer   293
    Mark Bernard

18 Consumption, Cannibalism, and Corruption in Jorge Michel Grau's *Somos lo que hay* 309
  Stacy Rusnak

19 Sinister Pastry: British "Meat" Pies in *Titus* and *Sweeney Todd* 325
  Vivian Halloran

20 All-Consuming Passions: Vampire Foodways in Contemporary Film and Television 339
  Alexandra C. Frank

About the Editors 355
Notes on Contributors 356
Index 361

Acknowledgments

This volume owes a great debt to so many scholars who have come before, and whose work has inspired and informed the essays that appear here. We would like to extend our thanks to all of them. Our deepest thanks also go to Peter Jackson and Wingnut Film Productions Ltd. for allowing us to use an absolutely ideal image from *Bad Taste* for our cover image. We would, of course, like to thank the wonderful Katie Gallof, Susan Krogulski, and Ellen Conlon at Bloomsbury for their enthusiasm and support of the project. Finally, to each of the individuals whose work provides the ingredients for this volume, thank you for your considerable skills in cooking up new perspectives, your willingness to tinker with your recipes, and your collegiality as the scholarly meal was being prepared. Our special thanks to Tom Hertweck, Salvador Murgulia, Alex Pinar, and Hans Staats for joining the party after the first course had already been served.

Introduction

Cynthia J. Miller and
A. Bowdoin Van Riper

Old adages tell us that we are what we eat or, more broadly, divide us into two categories: those who live to eat, and those who eat to live. Food creates and binds our relationships with others, even as it sustains our bodies. Preferences for certain dishes, beyond the homogenizing reach of mass media and national chains, mark out local and regional identities. Commitments to particular diets signal allegiance to larger systems of belief. Food, as a prepared offering or a shared indulgence, acts as a gateway to intimacy and a catalyst for romance. Linked so closely, in so many ways, to our identities, food and the act of eating bubble over with taboos, fears, morals, and hierarchies. To eat the wrong thing, or eat the wrong way, is to risk being Other—monstrous—"a figure on whom fears and anxieties can be projected."[1]

Cinematic portrayals of food and consumption, then, are part of an active and ongoing "dinner conversation"—a continually evolving dialogue that, nonetheless, remains firmly rooted in civilization's past—about what, when, how, and perhaps whom to eat. Tied to these discussions about, around, and over food are complex questions of meaning made visible on screen: How do our foodways help define our beliefs, values, and aspirations? How does consumption—as sustenance, violence, or performance—encapsulate the inner and outer struggles of our existence? Are we hunters or prey? Connoisseurs or cave dwellers? Pure or polluted?

Horror narratives routinely grasp these questions, both personal and social, and spin them into nightmares. Monstrous Others "personify terror and menace" as they dine on forbidden fare such as insects in *Bram Stoker's Dracula* (1992) or vomit in *Bad Taste* (1987).[2] The tables of consumption are turned in films like *Delicatessen* (1991) and *Cannibal Holocaust* (1980), and the consumer becomes—at the hands of the deranged, the vengeful, or the desperately hungry—the consumed, thus depicting, as Mark Bousquet suggests, "humanity's fear of finding itself on the menu."[3] Overindulgence, as *Le Grande Bouffe* (1973) and *Street Trash* (1987) warn, can kill us, and occasionally, as films like *The Stuff* (1985) and *Poultrygeist* (2006) illustrate, our food rises up from the plate or the kitchen counter and fights back. From *Blood Feast* (1963) to *Sweeney Todd* (2007), motion pictures have reminded us that we live in a world whose ultimate law is: eat, or be eaten.

To eat, or not to eat

In *Big Night* (1996), Tony Shalhoub's character Primo articulates the existential significance of food when he exclaims: "To eat good food is to be close to God." Implicit in that statement is the belief that other food—food that is in any number of ways "not good"—is the opposite of all that is divine, holy, revered, and pure. Such foods often become taboo; ineligible for consumption without violating cherished cultural norms and values.

Anthropologists such as Mary Douglas have long studied the nature, origins, and function of food taboos. Notions of purity and pollution are central here to the question "To eat, or not to eat?" Douglas's seminal work on eating habits contends that the complex system of rules and representations assigned to living things (and hence, the food that derives from them) support a given culture's vision of itself, creating and expressing a unity of experience.[4] The culinary, as James Keller notes, is

> highly suggestive of abstract cultural processes, such as class, race, gender, ethnicity, history, politics, geography, aesthetics, spirituality, and nationality, as well as more subjective conditions, such as obsession, indifference, depression, elation, rage, meditation, neurosis, psychosis, mental illness, mystical ecstasy, carnal desire, and love.[5]

Members often categorize cultural elements and transactions in oppositions such as "clean and unclean" or "pure and polluted." So, to designate a food as "taboo," either through the formal prohibition of laws or informal social sanctions such as discrimination, rejection, or fear, is to highlight what Blair Davis has referred to as "the civilizing role of food," where taboo foodways serve as a signal of danger, warning that harm—physical, social, or existential—will come to the eater.[6]

While the immediate physical hazards of rancid or infested food are readily apparent in both life and cinematic art, the social and existential perils require a bit more unpacking, and are often more subtly conveyed. Monstrous appetites—desires, passions, requirements or overindulgences—result in the eaters, as well as the substances they consume, becoming objects of horror. Some of these may take the form of addictions and obsessions, in films such as *Street Trash* and *The Stuff*, where death-by-ingestion becomes horrific spectacle, with narratives serving as morality tales about loss of control and excess. Others may take the form of consumption so repugnant and reviled that audiences avert their gaze, unwilling to even imagine the ingestion of forbidden fare, as in *Bad Taste* and *Human Centipede* (2009). And of course, the consumption of other human beings, either whole or in part, in genre traditions ranging from cannibal holocaust films to zombie and vampire foodways, signify the violation of the body by those so Other that not only culture, but human existence, is threatened.

Dangerous dishes

When Alfred Hitchcock, the Master of Suspense, hosted a "Ghost-Haunted House Party" for Warner Bros. executives and members of the press on March 7, 1953, the "Carte de Mort" on the tombstone-shaped invitations promised a menu of nauseating delicacies:

> Morbid morgue mussels, suicide suzettes, consommé de cobra, vicious-soise, home-fried homicide, ragout of reptile . . . corpse croquettes, barbecued banshee, opium omelette, stuffed stiffs with hard sauce, gibetted giblets, mobster thermidor, tormented tortillas, ghoulish goulash, blind bats en casserole, python pudding, fresh-cut lady fingers, Bloody Marys, Dead Grand-dad, formaldehyde frappe.[7]

While conceived for his own satirical amusement, this merger of the macabre with Hitchcock's renowned obsession with gastronomy demonstrated the evocative power of "dangerous dishes"—food that offends the sensibilities, creates culinary chaos, or threatens to devolve cultural norms of consumption. Hitchcock's menu articulates, by negative example, the unspoken agreement that food and horror—death, dismemberment, or creatures that, in Mary Douglas's words, "cross categories" and become, for many, objects of disgust—is an uncomfortable pairing. It creates, for some—such as those individuals drawn to pufferfish and absinthe—a point of fascination with the forbidden, but for most, it touches on fundamental fears of both the act and the consequences of taking the horrific into the body.

When brought to life on the silver screen, in films such as *Dumplings* (2004), *Blood Feast*, or *Sweeney Todd*, the power of dangerous dishes increases exponentially as we see, hear, and feel their threat to our physical, social, and psychological beings. We find such images "unsavory," in part, because they erase all of the transformative work that serves as an unacknowledged bridge between the worlds of nature and culture, between "the raw" and "the cooked."[8] We find such obvious connections between nature and "cuisine" exceedingly distasteful—capable of "ruining our appetites"—because, as Leon Rappoport suggests, eating "is as much or more a matter of the mind as it is of the body."[9] Our visceral revulsion at all manner of dangerous dishes—from Hitchcock's playful offering of corpse croquettes, to the cinematic horrors of fetus-filled dumplings or vomit, to the more commonplace news of the consumption of dogs or cats—is powerful evidence of the degree to which foodways that sharply depart from our cultural norms have the power to evoke fear and disgust. They shine a spotlight on the ways in which our food, from gastronomical delights to repugnant horrors, structures not only our patterns of consumption but also our individual and communal identities as eaters.

What's eating you?

The threat of being eaten faded, for humans, long ago. The deeply buried fear remains, however, surfacing periodically in tales of mutant piranhas, marauding sharks, and resurrected dinosaurs.[10] Tales of cannibalism tap into the same fear—the prospect of being transformed from predator to prey, and from person to meat—but they add an extra frisson of horror. Beasts, we tell ourselves, act on instinct. They are hungry and we look like food to them. When fellow humans regard us as food, however, they do so thoughtfully, rationally, and with specific intent: They do not simply want to eat another human being, they want to eat *us*.

The horrors of cannibalism, however, extend well beyond the prospect of being eaten. Human flesh is the ultimate culinary taboo, and cannibalism the ultimate act of transgression: an act unacceptable even in settings where extreme violence is countenanced,[11] one that can never be wholly expunged, just as those who commit it can never be wholly redeemed. We accept that castaways, lacking any other food, might hold off starvation by eating the flesh of their dead comrades, but this acceptance comes with a shudder and—for the survivors—with the weight of society's unvoiced judgment and revulsion.[12] To become a cannibal, even out of necessity, is to step across a line that (we tell ourselves) divides the brightly lit world of civilization from an outer darkness populated by madmen, criminals, and other social deviants.[13]

Even as cannibalism makes us shudder, however, it also exerts a dark fascination. Zombies occupied a comparatively minor place in the pantheon of twentieth-century monsters until, in 1968, George Romero reimagined them as cannibalistic ghouls driven by a mindless, insatiable hunger for human flesh.[14] Images of the undead sinking their teeth into the bodies of the living—and, by their bite, condemning their victims to the same hunger—are inextricably woven through modern zombie lore. Our fascination with them, then, rests on the fact that cannibalism is a central expression of their identity and thus "reveal[s] the ugliest human truth: we are piles of matter than consume and excrete other piles of matter."[15] Vampires—once-and-future kings among the monsters of our imagination—are likewise defined by their appetites. Whether delicately piercing victims' necks, or draining blood so ferociously that they leave behind not bodies but crumpled husks, their attacks are framed in culinary terms: "feeding" or even "feasting" on the blood of the living.

Undead beings that feast on the flesh and blood of the living fascinate and terrify because they are visibly, tangibly Others. Living, fully human cannibals add another dimension, concealing their Otherness behind a mask of utter normalcy.[16] The humans that once represented the face of cannibalism in popular culture were comfortably removed from our everyday lives: isolated on tropical islands, amid far-off jungles, or in the distant past where priests consumed the flesh of sacrificial victims on behalf of their bloodthirsty gods.[17] The fictional human cannibals of recent decades are closer to home and more subtle in their disguises. Dr. Hannibal Lecter and his cannibalistic ilk are unsettling precisely because we recognize them, or their terrible handiwork, at a glance. They are, their secret aside, us; and we are one ill-judged meal away from starting to become them.

Food and horror

Memories of bad-tasting food—along with the childhood admonition "don't put that in your mouth!"—linger at the edges of our thoughts whenever we confront an unfamiliar dish. We learn to suppress those memories, and try new things, but the chapters in the first of the four thematic sections of *What's Eating You* focus on the ghastly consequences of failing, at the wrong moment, to pay attention to those instincts. It begins with "Death at the Drive-Thru," Cynthia J. Miller's chapter on two cult films that mock our collective willingness to trade quality for convenience: Peter Jackson's satirical *Bad Taste*, and Troma Films's ultra-low-budget *Poultrygeist*. Both, Miller argues, satirize our willing sacrifice of taste, quality, and even health on the altar of convenience—*Poultrygeist* by imagining diners at an American Chicken Bunker franchise besieged by the undead carcasses of its signature product, and *Bad Taste* by confronting New Zealanders with alien invaders bent on turning *them* into ingredients for the intergalactic Crumb's Crunchy Delights chain.

Beginning with a chunk of raw steak that comes grotesquely alive on a kitchen counter in *Poltergeist*, Hans Staats considers the role of food in a cycle of films that reached its climax in the 1982 tale of suburban horror. His chapter, "Let Them Eat Steak: Food and the Family Horror Film Cycle," contends that *Poltergeist*, along with *Psycho* (1960) and *The Texas Chainsaw Massacre* (1974), represents a critique of the farm-to-table ethos, and dramatizes the failure of industrial food and animal production to maintain a standard of living that is commensurate with the cultural logic of late capitalism. Zombies, of course, eschew both farm *and* table. They are defined, in the post-Romero cinematic universe, by their urge to eat us, but as Sue Matheson contends in her chapter "Much Still Depends on Dinner," we are—even amid a zombie apocalypse—defined by what *we* choose to eat and how we choose to eat it. Focusing on *Shaun of the Dead* (2004) and *Zombieland* (2009), two of the definitive zombie films of the new millennium, her chapter argues that they both use carnivalesque comic inversions, centered on fast food and mindless earing, to signal the collapse of social order, while presenting family bonding over food as a sign of its rebirth.

Knowing where one's food comes from, and how it is produced, seems like a way of maintaining a wholesome diet in an age of industrialized edibles. As Alex Pinar and Salvador Jiminez Murguia's chapter on "the commodification of capitalism and the liminal condition of consumption" in *Dumplings* shows, however, intimacy between producer and consumer can be fraught with perils that extend far beyond the culinary. Set in present-day Hong Kong, the film explores the relationship between wealthy Mrs. Li and Auntie Mei, on whose "special dumplings" she depends to maintain her youthful beauty. Li's obsession with her appearance, and with remaining part of Mei's inner circle of customers, gives the doctor-turned-chef power over her, and makes her witness to (and thus complicit in) the dark secret of what makes the dumplings themselves so potent. The sinister food in the science-fiction/horror film *The Stuff* is far removed Mei's artisanal dumplings. It is a mass-produced, chemical-laden treat whose origin and composition are a mystery to the millions who eagerly consume it. A. Bowdoin Van Riper's chapter approaches *The Stuff* as a parable about the complex web of restraints that rein in the excesses of industrialized food production, and the horrors that could ensue if they break down. The nature of "The Stuff" itself—not just addictive and toxic, but seemingly alive—suggests that our most insidious enemy may not be ravenous predators, but food itself.

The second thematic section, "Sins of the Flesh," explores the troubled relationship between food and the dark side of human nature. In "Cannibalism as Cultural Critique: Peter Greenaway's *The Cook, The Thief, His Wife, and Her Lover* (1989) and Thatcherism," Thomas Prasch offers an examination of director Greenaway's unflinching tale of the ties between food and sadistic violence, a pairing that introduces consumption—or the threat of consumption—as torture. In Greenaway's films, dining spaces become sites of violence, rather than community, and death may be the least of the wages of sin, preferable to being forced into horrific consumption. The interconnections of food with sin also loom large in Bart Bishop's chapter " 'The red gums were their own" ': Food, Flesh, and the Female in *Beloved*." The title character, dead because of a terrible choice her mother was forced to make when she was a young child, returns as a revenant—a petulant, vengeful child whose demands for nourishment threaten to consume her mother and destroy the new life she built in the aftermath of the tragedy. Bishop's exploration of the film, based on Toni Morrison's haunting novel, considers how easily the bond of nourishment that links mother and child can be tainted, with the ghostly Beloved reveling in her draining of her mother's body and spirit.

The central bond in "Do I Look Tasty to You?," Tom Hertweck's exploration of Chul-soo Park's film *301/302*, is between two women, neighbors in an apartment building, who use food to ease their traumatic self-loathing—one through a refusal to eat, and the other through obsessive cooking. When they meet, and their paths intertwine, the sins of their individual pasts overtake them, and the pair literally and figuratively feed and nurture each other until their interdependence results in death and release. Cannibalism here becomes the cure, rather than the object, of monstrosity. The situation is quite the opposite, however, in Jennifer Holm's chapter "Flesh and Blood in Claude Chabrol's *Le Boucher*." A butcher by trade and heritage, the film's protagonist was also a soldier—"a butcher for the army"—and as the lines between the two continually blur for him, human and animal, body and carcass, occupation and murder all become one and the same. Flesh consumes him, and the sins of his past bleed, literally, into the sins of his present. As Holm illustrates, the butcher is so much defined by a sense of carnality that all flesh and blood becomes equal.

Concluding the section, and making manifest the relationship between sin and consumption is Ralph Beliveau's chapter "A Hunger for Dead Cakes: Visions of Abjection, Scapegoating, and the Sin-Eater." The Sin-Eater, a character with a long history in Welsh folklore, is engaged by the families of the newly dead to eat a symbolic meal in the presence of the corpse, taking in the sins of the deceased (adding them to their own) along with the food. Framing the Sin-Eater as a consumer of the abject—those substances or experiences that must be expelled or shunned in order to maintain social coherence—Beliveau shows how *Night Gallery*'s "Sins of the Fathers" finds horror in a young man's first performance of the role: a nightmarish experience made worse by patriarchal expectations, desperate hunger, and the exploitation of the poor.

The volume's third section, "The Extreme End of Consumption," takes our discussion of food and horror beyond the realm of polite conversation. The opening chapter, Mark Henderson's "Coprophagia as Class and Consumerism in the *Human Centipede* Films" focuses on one of the most controversial and reviled film series of recent years, looking beyond the visceral repulsion of the films' depictions of excrement-eating to uncover their commentary on the more figurative consumption of "waste." Henderson introduces notions of ideological domination, cultural coercion, and the role of self-reflexive metanarrative to examine the three films, as the trope of coprophagia is thus fully developed as a metaphor for consuming cultural waste—not only in the form of consumer products, but in the excesses of the upper classes as well.

In "Eat, Kill . . . Love? Courtship, Cannibalism, and Consumption in *Hannibal*," Michael Fuchs and Michael Phillips turn our attention from one of the most abhorrent horror narratives to one of the most popular. Fuchs and Phillips carefully examine the role of food in this most recent construction of Dr. Hannibal Lecter—"Hannibal the Cannibal"—discerning the ways in which his gourmet cannibalism redefines the character and creates an opportunity for savvy social commentary. Food, in the series, mediates Hannibal's relationships with other characters, as well as with the viewing audience, creating a complex web of identification, intrigue, and even compassion around the character. The cinematic cannibalism described in Rob Weiner and A. Bowdoin Van Riper's "Catering to the Cult of Ishtar: *Blood Feast*" is anything *but* elegant, with the low-budget tale considered by many to be the predecessor of the contemporary slasher film. Drawing on well-established exploitation strategies, the film blends gore, sexuality, and fictive Egyptian lore into a story of supernatural obsession, as a mad caterer attempts to stage a "blood feast" for the goddess Ishtar, created from the organs of desirable young women. The film operates in good exploitation tradition, the authors argue, promising lurid and horrifying sights but never (fully) delivering them.

INTRODUCTION

Despite its scantily clad *Playboy*-model cast, there is no nudity or sex, and for all the horrific preparations shown on screen, the Feast of Ishtar is never eaten.

Karen A. Ritzenhoff and Cynthia J. Miller's "From Gourmet to Gore: Jean-Pierre Jeunet's *Delicatessen*" weaves together themes already well-established in the volume—poverty, abjection, mistrust of individuals whose professions bring them into close contact with death and the dead, horrific acts of murder, and cannibalism—but views them through a new critical lens. Examining the complex relationship between those who commit atrocities and those who, clinging to their desire for normalcy, are silently complicit, Ritzenhoff and Miller draw parallels between the dystopian world of the film—where the tenants of an apartment building tacitly condone, and benefit from, the murderous acts of the butcher in the titular shop—and that of occupied France under the collaborationist Vichy regime. Erin Wiegand further probes the link between complicity and monstrosity in her chapter "Who Can Be Eaten? Consuming Animals and Humans in the Cannibal-Savage Horror Film." Focusing on the relationship between consuming animals and consuming humans in this cult genre, she argues that the films draw attention to Western cultural anxieties about what it means to be human, to the violence inherent in the acquisition of meat, and to the complex question of what species may be eaten. Wiegand's chapter appropriately ends the section with a critical look at the ways in which what we eat speaks to who and what we are.

The final section of the book, "You Are What You Eat," explores the surprisingly complicated interactions of food and identity in the horror film. LuAnne Roth's "'You are what others think you eat': Food, Identity, and Subjectivity in Zombie Protagonist Narratives," for example, shows that the grotesque eating habits of the walking dead have consistently served as more than just a sign of their "otherness." Her wide-ranging survey of zombie cinema explores the intertwining of food with zombie's sexuality, their attempts at socialization, and even their (seemingly paradoxical) attempts at forging a self-identity. Foodways have, she argues, played a central role in recent experiments with humanizing the zombie. The serial murderers profiled in Mark Bernard's chapter "From Sugar-Fueled Killer to Grotesque Gourmand" are likewise set apart from their victims (and from audiences) by their transgressive, often grotesque, violations of "normal" tastes and eating patterns. Examining serial-killer films from Fritz Lang's *M* (1931) to modern classics such as *Silence of the Lambs* (1992) and *American Psycho* (2000), Bernard demonstrates that the killers' inner demons manifest themselves at the table long before they erupt into violence. From Norman Bates's distracted nibbling of "wholesome" sandwiches and milk in *Psycho* to Jonathan Doe's coldly precise steeping of a tea bag in *Se7en* (1995), food reveals the characters' inner darkness.

The Mexico City family at the center of *Somos lo que hay* (2010) is defined by two elements: their desperate poverty and their embrace of cannibalism as a way of life. They transgress the most profound of all food taboos—the consumption of human flesh—with a bland matter-of-factness; as the English translation of the title declares: "We are what we are." As Stacy Rusnak's chapter "Consumption, Cannibalism, and Corruption in Jorge Michel Grau's *Somos lo que hay*" shows, however, Grau uses this intertwining of cannibalism and identity not to shock, but to comment on the grimness of life among Mexico's urban poor. The meaning of cannibalism in Grau's film, Rusnak argues, lies in its banality. "Sinister Pastry: British 'Meat' Pies in *Titus* and *Sweeney Todd*" continues the section's focus on quotidian cannibalism. Vivian Halloran considers a pair of grim, stylized fantasies in which the kitchen and the abattoir merge, and food intertwines with female sexuality and brutal revenge. Both films, Halloran contends, derive horror not just from the main characters' conversion of enemies into food, or from the unwitting cannibalism into which they lead (or force) their dinner guests, but from the sinister nature of the covered dish. The consumption of a meat pie, Halloran argues, demands an unspoken bond of trust between diner and cook: trust that the revenge-minded heroes of both films carefully create, and then horrifically betray.

The bond between undead vampires and the living victims on whose blood they feed is, traditionally, shaped not by trust but by power: classic vampires are portrayed as mesmerizing, seductive predators whose stunned victims barely resist as the blood is drained from their bodies. Recent vampire tales complicate that narrative, however, while using food choices as a means of defining their undead characters. Alexandra Frank's chapter "All-Consuming Passions: Vampire Foodways in Contemporary Film and Television" explores the diverse intersections of food and identity in these narratives: ethical vampires who haunt blood banks and feed on animals; the reshaping of vampire–human relations by the introduction of synthetic blood; and the complex bonds between vampires and humans who, for reasons of their own, willingly allow themselves to be "eaten."

Notes

1 Priscilla Walton, *Our Cannibals, Ourselves* (Champaign: University of Illinois Press, 2004), 4.
2 Ibid.
3 Mark Bousquet, "A Little Shakin', Little Tenderizin', and Down You Go," in *Food on Film: Bringing Something New to the Table*, ed. Thomas Hertweck (Lanham, MD: Scarecrow Press, 2014), 173.

4   Mary Douglas, *Purity and Danger* (London: Routledge, 1984), 12.
5   James R. Keller, "Introduction: The Cinematic Hunger Artists," in *Food, Film and Culture: A Genre Study* (Jefferson, NC: McFarland, 2006), 1.
6   Blair Davis, "Banquet and the Beast" in *Reel Food*, ed. Anne L. Bower (New York: Routledge, 2004), 281–96.
7   Donald Spoto, *The Art of Alfred Hitchcock: Fifty Years of His Motion Pictures* (Norwell, MA: Anchor Books, 1991), 378.
8   Claude Levi-Strauss, *The Raw and the Cooked* (New York: HarperCollins, 1969), 133.
9   Leon Rappoport, *How We Eat* (Toronto: ECW Press, 2003), 1.
10 David Quammen, *Monster of God: The Man-Eating Predator in the Jungles of History and the Mind* (New York: Norton, 2004), 3–15.
11 See, for example, Thomas S. Abler, "Scalping, Torture, Cannibalism and Rape: An Ethnohistorical Analysis of Conflicting Cultural Values in War," *Anthropologica* 34, no. 1 (1992): 3–20.
12 One prominent case is recounted in Nathaniel Philbrick, *In the Heart of the Sea: The Tragedy of the Whaleship Essex* (New York: Viking, 2000), 190–206.
13 Catálin Avarmescu, *Intellectual History of Cannibalism: The Intellectual History of Cannibalism* (Princeton, NJ: Princeton University Press, 2009), 95–8.
14 Kim Paffenroth, *Gospel of the Living Dead: George Romero's Visions of Hell on Earth* (Waco, TX: Baylor University Press, 2006), 1.
15 Angela Tenga and Elizabeth Zimmerman, "Vampire Gentlemen and Zombie Beasts: A Rendering of True Monstrosity," *Gothic Studies* 15, no. 1 (2013): 80.
16 Mark Twain's darkly humorous short story "Cannibalism in the Cars" turns on this idea.
17 On Western narratives of cannibalism as a form of "othering," see, for example, William Arens, *The Man-Eating Myth: Anthropology and Anthropophagy* (New York: Oxford University Press, 1980), 139–45; and Gananath Obeyeskere, "Cannibal Feasts in Nineteenth-Century Fiji: Seaman's Yarns and the Anthropological Imagination," in *Cannibalism and the Colonial World*, ed. Francis Barker, Peter Hulme, and Margaret Iversen (Cambridge: Cambridge University Press, 1998), 63–5.

Bibliography

Abler, Thomas S. "Scalping, Torture, Cannibalism and Rape: An Ethnohistorical Analysis of Conflicting Cultural Values in War." *Anthropologica* 34, no. 1 (1992): 3–20.
Arens, William. *The Man-Eating Myth: Anthropology and Anthropophagy*. New York: Oxford University Press, 1980.

Avarmescu, Catálin. *The Intellectual History of Cannibalism.* Princeton, NJ: Princeton University Press, 2009.

Bousquet, Mark. "A Little Shakin', Little Tenderizin', and Down You Go." In *Food on Film: Bringing Something New to the Table,* edited by Thomas Hertweck. 173–86. Lanham, MD: Scarecrow Press, 2014.

Davis, Blair. "Banquet and the Beast: The Civilizing Role of Food in 1930s Horror." In *Reel Food,* edited by Anne L. Bower, 281–96. New York: Routledge, 2004.

Douglas, Mary. *Purity and Danger: An Analysis of the Concepts of Pollution and Taboo.* London: Routledge, 1984.

Keller, James R. "Introduction: The Cinematic Hunger Artists." In *Food, Film and Culture: A Genre Study.* New York: McFarland Publishing, 2006.

Levi-Strauss, Claude. *The Raw and the Cooked.* New York: HarperCollins, 1969.

Obeyeskere, Gananath. "Cannibal Feasts in Nineteenth-Century Fiji: Seaman's Yarns and the Anthropological Imagination." In *Cannibalism and the Colonial World,* edited by Francis Barker, Peter Hulme, and Margaret Iversen, 63–85. Cambridge: Cambridge University Press, 1998.

Paffenroth, Kim. *Gospel of the Living Dead: George Romero's Visions of Hell on Earth.* Waco, TX: Baylor University Press, 2006.

Philbrick, Nathaniel. *In the Heart of the Sea: The Tragedy of the Whaleship Essex.* New York: Viking, 2000.

Quammen, David. *Monster of God: The Man-Eating Predator in the Jungles of History and the Mind.* New York: Norton, 2004.

Rappoport, *How We Eat: Appetite, Culture, and the Psychology of Food.* Toronto: ECW Press, 2003.

Spoto. Donald. *The Art of Alfred Hitchcock: Fifty Years of His Motion Pictures.* Norwell, MA: Anchor Books, 1991.

Tenga, Angela, and Elizabeth Zimmerman. "Vampire Gentlemen and Zombie Beasts: A Rendering of True Monstrosity." *Gothic Studies* 15, no. 1 (2013): 80 [full article 76–87].

Walton, Priscilla. *Our Cannibals, Ourselves.* Champaign: University of Illinois Press, 2004.

PART ONE

Let the Eater Beware

1

Death at the Drive-Thru: Fast Food Betrayal in *Bad Taste* and *Poultrygeist*

Cynthia J. Miller

[*Bad Taste*] does for brains what McDonald's did for hamburgers: spread 'em all over the place.[1]

In 1976, the first McDonald's arrived in New Zealand, beginning a gradual shift in the nation's food consumption emphasis from lamb to fast food. Just over a decade later, Kiwi filmmaker Peter Jackson released the now-cult film *Bad Taste* (1987)—a send-up of fast food chains and their wares. The connection, many have argued, is no accident.

Bad Taste pits a slapstick New Zealand paramilitary defense force against aliens who invade the nation in order to harvest humans for their intergalactic fast food chain. The invaders, in the employ of Crumb's Crunchy Delights and intent on factory-farming Earth for human ingredients, make the equation of Crumb's and the multinational burger giant fairly straightforward as a cautionary tale of the ills of fast food consumption, as well as the exploitive practices that bring it into being.

In a similar, splattery caution against the dangers of America's status as a "fast food nation," Troma Studios introduced *Poultrygeist: Night of the Chicken Dead* (2006), portraying the plight of everyday New Jersey consumers trapped in a fast food restaurant under attack by undead chickens. While animal rights activists protest outside the newly opened American Chicken Bunker, the chickens, destined for the fryolator, begin a grotesque rampage, killing employees and patrons alike. Viewers learn that, in addition to its gastronomic transgressions, the fast food chain had constructed its latest outlet atop an ancient Native American burial site. This willful desecration of sacred ground has angered the spirits of those buried there, along with those of the billions of slaughtered chickens sent to "concentration coops," all of whom now seek their revenge.

Both films, while brimming over with gratuitous mayhem and gore, raise significant issues about the nature, pervasiveness, and consequences of fast food enterprise. Betrayal is the hallmark of consumers' embrace of fast food culture, from a wholesale indictment of production—the harvesting of humans, the brutal butchering of chickens—to grotesque manifestations of the true nature of eagerly consumed "mystery meat" and the dangers it presents to those who ingest it. While exploring these "on the ground" issues, this chapter will also examine the larger, and even more monstrous, political-economic framework, as both films also speak to the multinational corporate betrayal of culture, as fast food, both literally and figuratively, walks on the graves of traditional lifeways.

Crunchy delights and zombie chicken

The young Peter Jackson shot *Bad Taste*—which pits an eager but incompetent team from the Astro Investigation and Defense Service against the invaders bent on marketing humans as the new intergalactic fast food taste sensation—on weekends, near his home Pukerua Bay, using friends and himself as the cast. As star Craig Smith (Giles) observes, "We were *all* oddball, nerdy fan-boys, hanging out together, going to movies and then trying to *make* a movie."[2] Filmed over the course of four years, *Bad Taste*—Jackson's first feature-length film—was produced on a notoriously low budget, yet achieved recognition almost immediately at Cannes and elsewhere for its innovative satire of genres, fast food, and Kiwi cultural identity.

The film opens with a pre-title prologue that sets the stage for the action that follows: A panicked emergency caller claims that the townsfolk of the small (fictional) village of Kaihoro, New Zealand, have been attacked by an unknown force whose arrival was accompanied by "a roaring noise and a big white light in the sky." The offbeat protagonists—Derek (Peter Jackson), Frank (Mike Minett), Ozzie (Terry Potter), and Barry (Pete O'Herne)—known collectively as "The Boys" and bearing a closer resemblance to Pythonesque jesters than saviors of a nation, are sent to investigate the possibility of an alien presence. Their mission to bring back proof, in the form of a live alien, goes comically sideways when Derek tortures a captured suspect (the alien Robert, also played by director Jackson) while waiting for his team's return, only to have the alien's screams draw his companions, leading to bloody mayhem, Derek's presumed death after a fall from the cliffs, and Robert's escape.

As the team pursues their quarry, Giles, a famine-relief charity collector, passes through the village, but all of its residents have vanished. He is attacked by a hungry Robert, but escapes, seeking refuge at a nearby house that turns out to be cover for the aliens' headquarters. Knocked unconscious and captured, Giles awakens to find himself bound, with an apple in his mouth, marinating in a tub of vegetables and broth ("Reg's eleven secret herbs and spices"). It is here that the interweaving of food, eating, and the grotesque takes center stage. The aliens hungrily eye their dinner-to-be, noting that they haven't had any meat since their arrival on the planet, and inform the panicked Giles that it is an "honor" to be consumed.

Giles escapes his privileged fate, however, when the team infiltrates the house. Disguised as one of the extraterrestrial minions, who are uniformly clad in blue work shirts and conveniently resemble dimwitted rural New Zealanders, Frank joins the aliens as they assemble for a triumphant speech by their leader, Lord Crumb (voiced by Peter Vere-Jones), an intergalactic fast food magnate whose empire is threatened by a fierce rivalry. He informs the workers that they will soon be shedding the reviled human form that they all have adopted, leaving Earth—taking with them the butchered and boxed remains of the residents of Kaihoro—and heading for home, to regain their place at the top of the fast food chain. "Isn't it amazing how you can fit a whole town of humans into a few cardboard boxes if you slice off the fat?" he muses. "All the livestock we need are right here—four billion of them!"

At Lord Crumb's signal, Robert is carried to a large bowl, held by the disguised Frank, into which he hurls a seemingly unending stream of green vomit, which still retains chunks of brain from his last meal. "Ahhh, I see the gruel is ready!" Lord Crumb pronounces. "Exquisite bouquet, Robert." The bowl is passed from one alien worker to the next in a sort of communal dinner, and Frank, unable to avoid slurping his share, finds it surprisingly appealing. Crumb promises them a dinner party the next evening, with "fresh local meat" (the marinating Giles) to show his appreciation for their loyal service.

The team, of course, rescues Giles before he meets his end as the main course. Their escape route cut off, they have no choice but to battle their way out. Midway through the mayhem, Derek—not dead, but deranged, his brains held in place by his belt—joins the battle. As the Boys make their escape and Lord Crumb flees in the house-turned-spaceship, Derek, armed with a chainsaw, dispatches the alien leader, dons his skin, and warns the homeworld "I'm comin' to get you bastards!" as the house careens into space.

Fueled by the supernatural, rather than the extraterrestrial, Troma Entertainment's *Poultrygeist* updates the horrors of fast food for the twenty-first century. This "musical comedy horror" codirected by Lloyd Kaufman and Gabriel Friedman, six years in the making, also begins with a troublesome, if not so mysterious, prologue. High school sweethearts Arbie (Jason Yachanin) and Wendy (Kate Graham)—about to graduate and go their separate ways—meet late at night in the ancient Tromahawk Indian burial ground to nervously consummate their relationship and promise their undying love. Their transgressions disturb the dead interred around them, and soon, zombie hands rise from beneath them and join in the couple's brief lovemaking, leaving the pair convinced that, for them, the earth really did "move."

Fast forward one college semester: Arbie returns to the memorable site, only to discover that the burial ground has been bulldozed, and in its place stands an American Chicken Bunker (ACB) franchise—a transparent stand-in for Kentucky Fried Chicken—founded and owned by General Lee Roy, a villainous corporate magnate with a diaper fetish, who bears an uncanny resemblance to Colonel Sanders. Outside the establishment, a protest has formed, made up of Native American rights activists, animal rights activists, environmental activists, angry lesbian activists (among them, his beloved Wendy—now a "leftist lipstick lesbo liberal"—and her lover Micki (Allyson Sereboff), and dozens of drunken hangers-on.

Disillusioned and seeking revenge, Arbie takes a tedious, minimum-wage job at American Chicken Bunker and is introduced to a range of oddball coworkers, who not only represent stereotypes of exploited fast food labor but whose names (like Arbie and Wendy) also evoke associations with fast food: Denny (Joshua Olatunde), an overbearing manager; Carl Jr. (Caleb Emerson), a perverse redneck; Paco Bell (Khalid Rivera), a gay Mexican; Humus (Rose Ghavami), a mysterious, burqa-clad, patriotic Muslim; and an unnamed middle-aged "lifer" in the chain's employ, who is later revealed to be Arbie's future self (Lloyd Kaufman), a harbinger of things to come. The monotony of their daily routine, however, is soon disrupted, as things spin horribly out of control, punctuated by full production musical numbers that add their own touch of irony to the film's commentary on the wages of fast food.

The spirits of the Tromahawk tribe—and of all the factory-farmed and inhumanely slaughtered chickens—have begun to seek revenge on American Chicken Bunker, its employees, and its customers. The gruesome mayhem that follows is the no-holds-barred gore for which Troma Entertainment has become (in)famous: An uncooked chicken pushes Paco into the meat grinder, turning him into a "Sloppy Jose"; Carl Jr. loses his penis while violating another of the reanimated fowl in the storage room; and after eating mysterious, veined, pulsing eggs, patrons experience explosive diarrhea that leaves the walls, floors, and their fellow customers covered in blood, offal, and excrement.

As Arbie and his coworkers attempt to battle the "chicken dead," Micki, Wendy's girlfriend and leader of the protest outside, switches sides—proclaiming that the chicken is delicious, and then revealing herself to be both an employee of American Chicken Bunker and the General's lover—resulting in throngs of protesters rushing to their doom in the restaurant and a disillusioned Wendy returning to Arbie. As the crowds consume the General's chicken, they are possessed by the spirits of the chicken dead—sprouting beaks and feathers, then attacking and consuming their still-human counterparts in scenes that rival a zombie apocalypse. The inside of the restaurant brims over with bloody chaos—screams of terror barely drowning out satisfied belches.

As patrons and employees (along with the zombie chicken General) battle for survival, Humus sheds her clothing and reveals that she has C-4 strapped to her body. She sacrifices herself so that Arbie, Wendy, and a small child whom they've rescued can escape the slaughter. The building explodes as the three make their way to safety. Once on the road, however, the thirsty child drinks a soda saved from the restaurant and, after complaining of stomach cramps, lays an egg in the back seat. The car crashes and explodes, killing everyone inside, leaving the zombie chickens dancing in triumph to the film's theme song as the credits fade.

The horrors of fast food

Neither of these films represents the horror genre in any traditional sense; they are lacking in suspense, jump-scares, and the means of conveying any particular sense of dread to their audiences. They are, however, playful examples of *cinéma vomitif*: the kind of cinema that, as Mikita Brottman observes "produces physical effects on the body of the spectator":

> At its most successful, it presents a frontal assault on the audience; it is total theater, in which all forces of expression and persuasion can be brought to bear . . . Its ultimate aim is the arousal of strong sensations in the lower body—nausea, repulsion, weakness, faintness, and a loosening of bowel or bladder control—normally by way of graphic scenes featuring the by-products of bodily detritus: vomit, excrement, viscera, brain tissue, and so on.[3]

Whatever else they lack, both films offer these in abundance: living bodies are dismembered, brains are spilled (and stuffed back into place), excrement paints walls and floors (and is, in one memorable scene, filmed by an in-toilet camera), and there is seemingly no end to the vomit. Together, they stand, along with films such as *Blood Feast* (1963) and *The Texas Chainsaw Massacre* (1974), as representatives of "the most bodily of filmic forms"—"a disreputable substream of the horror/exploitation genre."[4]

Jim Barratt agrees, pointing out that *Bad Taste* is a horror film "in gore only"—an observation that is equally true of *Poultrygeist*.[5] Jackson's film blends together postadolescent comedy, action, and science fiction, simply using horror effects as the icing between the layers, creating what is now known as "splatstick." This collision of comedy and horror synthesizes genres that, as Barry Keith Grant suggests, "are both rooted in the physical body"[6]; but even more deeply rooted in the body than the physical responses to humor and the grotesque to which Grant refers, however, are the acts of eating and becoming food. When consumption is implicated in those gore-laden scenes, the emotional and visceral effects suggested by Grant, Barratt, and others are heightened, in line with what Linda Williams has referred to as "low" forms of horror's ability to "sensationally display bodies on the screen and register effects in the bodies of spectators."[7]

From *Bad Taste*'s signature image of brains being scooped from an open skull (Figure 1.1) to the climactic scene featuring a bowl of vomit, shared

FIGURE 1.1 *The alien Robert dines on brains but is careful to use the proper utensil.*

communally among the aliens, revolting consumption (or the threat of it) drives the film. As the aliens eat the bowl of vomit, Lord Crumb shares his vision of fast food triumph with his employees: "We'll bring out the whole line of *Homo sapien* low-calorie delicacies. Juicy raw rump. Brains soaked in lemon juice. Spinal fluid sauce. Assorted organ stews. *Sapien* burgers. And chewy *Homo* nuggets!" His aspirations are, for many, as unnerving as the images themselves, drawing uncomfortable parallels to real-world rhetoric about "mystery meat" in a range of fast food, as well as claims of secretive "special sauce" by numerous chains in the industry. Here, however, little mystery is involved. Viewers have already watched in disgust as the alien Robert, on command, vomited a seemingly unending stream of green "chuck" into the waiting bowl.

Throughout Lord Crumb's speech, as Jackson's handheld camera—following the bowl of vomit—moves from one alien to the next, the sound of indulgent slurping is highlighted, pushed to the front of the sound mix in order to heighten the revulsion of the scene.[8] When the vomit bowl is passed to Frank, the camera initially cuts away, focusing on another member of the human defense team, Ozzie, who looks on with a perverse smile of anticipation. Will his friend do the unthinkable? Ozzie (and viewers) delights in his dilemma, giving in to what Steven Shaviro sees as films' seductive qualities, the temptation to "surrender and revel in cinematic fascination."[9] Once Frank overcomes his initial revulsion, so as not to give himself away, he finds the vomit delicious—a guilty, cannibalistic pleasure—and tries to sneak in a second gulp. He later feigns disgust at the act he was forced to perform, but his comrades, and the audience, know differently.

For the film's viewers, this grotesque appeal to both visual and auditory senses prompts a visceral reaction tied more closely to the notion of vomit-eating than cannibalism. While those watching the film will likely never experience the latter, the former violates a taboo against abject fluids that strikes much closer to the commonplace. That Robert's vomit is composed of partially digested human brains is of far less consequence here than the fact that regurgitation of any sort is being consumed.

Scenes such as this, as Barratt points out, tip the film into self-parody, reminding us that "the primary motive" for watching films such as *Bad Taste* is to delight in "yucky pleasure" as revulsion is transformed "into a sought-after goal."[10] Cult film director John Waters agrees, "To me, bad taste is what entertainment is all about. If someone vomits watching one of my films, it's like getting a standing ovation," but argues that "[i]t's easy to disgust someone; I could make a ninety-minute film of people getting their limbs hacked off, but this would only be bad bad taste, and not very stylish or original . . . Good bad taste can be creatively nauseating, but must, at the same time, appeal to the especially twisted sense of humor.[11]

Poultrygeist, even more actively than *Bad Taste*, plays with just such twisted humor, as one scene after another challenges viewers to continue watching the film's grotesque displays of the horrors of fast food, as it satirizes both them and the industry. While some, such as critic Kim Newman, appraise Troma films as "never serious, but they have no idea how to go about being funny,"[12] others, such as reviewer Phil Fasso, argue: "The fact that Kaufman's films involve torn limbs, head crushing, rape and scores of other in-your-face atrocities belies that they're also the most socially conscious horror movies this side of George Romero."[13] When the chickens exact their revenge on American Chicken Bunker's employees, their retaliation is well earned. Before meeting his bloody demise, we see Paco masturbating into a freshly ground batch of beaks and claws (making manifest the consumer's nightmare about "mystery meat," as well as about underpaid employees acting out on fast food as a form of rebellion), beneath signed instructions for how to prepare a "Sloppy Jose" the General's way. With Humus in the background, praying toward Mecca, he proceeds to add his own "secret zest sauce." He explains:

> You see, Humus, I'm doing this because I am a freedom fighter. I am Che Guevara, Martin Sheen, and Janeane Garofalo all rolled into one fabulous burrito of political activism. By masturbating in this food, I am waking up the world! *Viva la Revolución!!*

As he climaxes, the sound of agitated clucking is heard. The camera shifts to a phantom chicken's-eye-view as the meat grinder mysteriously switches on and an unseen force rushes the young worker and topples him into the grinder. Blood and guts spew from the machine—covering the kitchen, a horrified Humus, and in the final shot of the scene, the General's "how to" sign.

Carl Jr., Denny, the General, Micki, and scores of customers who storm the establishment to gorge on fast food fare also get their comeuppance at the hands of the chicken dead, meeting grisly ends or transforming into the vengeful fowl themselves (Figure 1.2); and when a morbidly obese customer named Jared (Joe Fleishaker) consumes a heaping order from American Chicken Bunker's menu and is sucked out his own anus by the chicken dead—emerging as a new, slim version of himself—echoes of advertising propaganda about miraculous fast food weight loss by a well-known sandwich chain are not far from the audience's mind. In each case, viewers find themselves rallying behind the zombie chickens, delighting in the downfall of corporate fast food and its archetypes.

FIGURE 1.2 *Denny (Joshua Olatunde) falls victim to the "chicken dead."*

The appeal—and effectiveness—of films such as *Bad Taste* and *Poultrygeist*, then, extends beyond mere gore and are firmly rooted in the parody and satire that are interwoven throughout. Gore, however, as Barratt observes, is what lingers in the mind longest after viewing, and so remains one of both films' defining characteristics, as well as the vehicle for delivering cutting social commentary about our relationship with the fast food industry.[14]

The political economy of betrayal

Filmed in the early years of commercial fast food's incursion into New Zealand culture,[15] *Bad Taste*'s comic send-up of the hazards of the burgeoning industry takes aim not only at corporatized cuisine as revolting-but-irresistible "mystery meat"—the culinary equivalent of Adorno and Horkheimer's seductively produced and thoughtlessly consumed mass culture[16]—but also as both culinary and ideological "invasion" of low-quality, unhealthy foodways from outside the nation's borders.

As Christian Long observes, it is difficult to not read the aliens in *Bad Taste* "as stand-ins for McDonald's and, in a large sense, American cultural imperialism" making "the equation of Crumb's Crunchy Delights—McDonald's fairly straightforward."[17] Lord Crumb, a caricature of the cutthroat corporate magnate, triumphantly assures his employees that

> I am certain that when the *Homo Sapien* taste takes the galaxy by storm as it will, Crumb's Crunchy Delights will be back at the top! Macloppollo's Fried Moon Rat won't know what hit them! All the livestock we need are right here. Four billion of them! Once the Fast Food Authority have checked the samples and issued the mass slaughter permit, this grotty little planet will tremble under the full might of the Lord Crumb restaurant chain! Within a year, the giant mincer will descend from the sky, the sun reflected from its silver bits and no army on Earth will be able to stop the Noddy Burger Machine!

As the aliens prey on local New Zealanders, harvesting their brains for Crumb's Crunchy Delights, they do so under a veil of secrecy—masking their presence, safeguarding the secret of their ingredients, and violently eliminating all those who oppose them. Forces that would defend the nation from these external enemies are small in number and met with skepticism, anarchic renegades who spend much of the film seeking proof of their allegations in order to gain support. The tension between these rebels and the Crumb Corporation, in fact, mirrors the nearly contemporaneous struggle between London Greenpeace and McDonald's that resulted in the infamous "McLibel" case, in which the corporate giants brought a defamation suit against five activists over their allegations of health, labor, economic, and advertising abuses.

Bad Taste suggests that the arrival of multinational fast food chains in New Zealand threatens to subjugate its citizens and their culture in a network of global commodification. Satirical but determined cultural freedom fighters, the n'er-do-well New Zealanders seek to repel the external corporate forces that are attempting to exploit their bodies for economic gain, a direct confrontation of the real-world globalized fast food system in which resources are drained out of diverse local economies into the hands of the multinational elite.[18] Should they fail, their countrymen, like the townspeople of Kaihoro, will fall victim to the spread of the homogenization and (literally) mindless consumption that corporate—and specifically American—fast food represents.

While the threat of fast food betrayal in the 1980s of *Bad Taste* was cast as a menace from outside the nation's borders, the gastronomic danger in

Poultrygeist is a product of the mindless devolution of the nation's culture itself. As the context shifts from remote New Zealand to the United States, nearly twenty years later, fast food has become a pervasive part of American culture. Troma's splatterfest joins the ranks of cinematic critiques of the industry, preceded by Morgan Spurlock's *Super Size Me* (2004) and released the same year as Richard Linklater's *Fast Food Nation* (2006).

Linklater's film is based on investigative journalist Eric Schlosser's 2001 exposé of "fast food, the values it embodies, and the world it has made."[19] Citing the industry's "extraordinary growth" between 1970 and 2000, Schlosser observes that "the whole experience of buying fast food has become so routine, so thoroughly unexceptional and mundane, that it is now taken for granted . . . It has become a social custom as American as a small, rectangular, hand-held, frozen, and reheated apple pie"[20]—unreflexive and ingrained, but exploitive, culturally corrosive, and unhealthy.

Speaking out in the early 1970s against what he termed "the McDonaldization of America," farmer-activist Jim Hightower warned of the social, cultural, and economic ills of the then-emerging fast food industry.[21] From low-paid, unskilled workers to childhood obesity, fast food chains are, for Hightower, either the cause or the symptom of numerous significant social problems, both local and global, external and internal to the consumer. Their products and service represent "a set of attitudes, systems, and beliefs" that characterize twentieth-century American values—of progress, technology, conformity, speed, and the willingness to exploit land, labor, and food sources—that quickly spread around the world.[22] In response, Hightower, Schlosser, and other detractors have been accused of acting as "food police" who recklessly disparage "an industry that has contributed tremendously to our nation."[23]

Fast food, as its critics suggest, "enters the body and becomes part of the consumer"[24]—and in this, Troma saw the ideal fodder for a tale of the horrors of mass consumption, as bodies convulse, morph, and explode through a horrific "return of the repressed." Much has been written regarding the relationship of this psychoanalytic theme to the horror genre. In particular, Robin Wood has argued that horror films present a symbolic return of the repressed social anxieties preoccupying society at a given moment, opening up a space for subversive thought, reactions, and responses. Repression, he contends (as do Freud and others), is universal and inescapable. In its most basic form, it makes possible our individual and social development; in a more complex and ideological form, "it makes us into monogamous, heterosexual, bourgeois, patriarchal capitalists."[25] Through both the narrative and its cast, Troma—and more specifically, Kaufman—mock multiple layers of that latter form of repression, not only force-feeding audiences with images that speak to anxieties about the nature, production, and consequences of fast food consumption, but also (and more importantly) our growing cultural anxieties about the ideologies, economies, and systems of labor in which it is implicated.

As patrons of American Chicken Bunker sprout feathers and beaks, those remaining unchanged become food for the "chicken dead," in a bizarre twist on cannibalism that turns consumers into the consumed, portraying them as graphically overtaken by the fast food industry as it spirals out of control toward its own (and society's) destruction. The resultant over-the-top gore reassures viewers that the film is all in good fun, but while played for laughs, American Chicken Bunker's zombified poultry makes manifest extreme critiques of the industry, its moguls, its practices, and its menu. As satire, however, it also mocks the authors of those very critiques, casting them as militant Others, whose mindless followers are carried along on waves of uninformed passion. In the end, their protests against the factory farming of the corporation's chickens, exploitation of its employees, the mysterious ingredients processed into its meals, and the local franchise's desecration of the local Native American burial ground prove to be as false as the corporation's wholesome, family-friendly image. Micki, the driving force behind the Others' protests, is "assimilated"—rendered safe as a supporter not only of capitalism but also of patriarchy and heterosexuality.[26] Both sides, it is revealed, are in it for the profits, and only the grossly naïve hold fast to their beliefs in the doctrines of either American entrepreneurship or social and environmental justice. The film closes, however, on a note of ambiguity about the status of both ideology and economy: American Chicken Bunker and all those associated with it are destroyed, but so are those who stood in opposition. Both Icon and Other are no more, the heroes and villains have all met their ends, and the zombified products of fast food culture are all that remain.

Conclusion

While, as Jackson and Kaufman remind us, both the bloody mayhem and the commentary are all in good fun, it is difficult to overlook the ways in which both films connect with the anxieties prevalent in their respective eras regarding the fast food industry. Many of these overlap, demonstrating consistency in the perceived horrors of fast food, from concerns over the means of production, to anxieties about exactly what it is that consumers are, ultimately, eating, to fears about local foodways being unable to compete with the lure of the global fast food industry. Attraction and resistance are, as popular culture narratives such as *Bad Taste, Poultrygeist, Fast Food Nation, Super Size Me*, and others illustrate, the hallmarks of fast food's history around the world.

However, the twenty-year interval between the two films and the significant cultural shifts between New Zealand and the United States in relation to multinational corporate pressures are telling. In both contexts, we see a small band of quirky comrades: The Boys of *Bad Taste*, who, were they not out thwarting alien invaders, might well be playing video games and strategizing about how to talk to women; and the workers of *Poultrygeist*, who, were they not out thwarting zombie chickens, would still be stuck in their minimum-wage rut. Arbie and his fellow American Chicken Bunker employees, in fact, bring to mind a classic exchange from George Romero's *Land of the Dead* (2005):

MIKE: It's like they're pretending to be alive.
RILEY: Isn't that what we're doing, pretending to be alive?

Unlikely heroes, all—representatives of "invisible" sectors of their respective societies—and like their real-world individual and cultural counterparts, not necessarily destined to survive their battles against fast food horrors.

That, however (along with the blood, guts, vomit, brains, and dark comedy), is where the similarities end. In the late 1980s, the Boys are summoned to thwart the incursion of an "alien" fast food industry—deliberately rejecting the introduction of its hazards and horrors—at a time when fast food was still a fairly recent enterprise in New Zealand, and not the oppressive, taken-for-granted cultural fixture that it is in the early years of the twentieth century, when Arbie, Wendy, Humus, and Arbie's future self take up the mantle. Here, there is no alien enemy, no colonizing, factory-farming oppressor. We find the exploitive horrors of fast food betrayal looming from within the culture itself, and collapsing under the weight of its crimes, even as the unreflective consumers of Tromaville continue to embrace it. Considering the two films together, we see that the struggle against the horrors of fast food may be as old as the industry itself, a struggle that is both local and global, of economic systems and classes: "an uninterrupted, now hidden, now open fight" that can only end in either "revolutionary reconstitution" of local foodways, as promised by the Boys' victory in *Bad Taste*, or in the "common ruin" suffered by the combatants in Tromaville's American Chicken Bunker.[27]

Notes

1. Mario Cortini and Philip Nutman, "Profile: Peter Jackson: Master of Bad Taste," *Gorezone* 5 (January 1989): 20.
2. Brian Sibley, *Peter Jackson, A Filmmaker's Journey* (London: HarperCollins Entertainment, 2006), 83; emphasis in the original.
3. Mikita Brottman, *Offensive Films: Toward an Anthropology of Cinéma Vomitif* (Westport, CT: Greenwood Press, 1997), 34, 11.
4. Ibid., 4, 11.
5. Jim Barratt, *Bad Taste* (London: Wallflower Press, 2008).
6. Barry Keith Grant, *A Cultural Assault: The New Zealand Films of Peter Jackson* (London: Kakapo Books, 1999), 4.
7. Linda Williams, "Film Bodies: Gender, Genre, and Excess," in *Film Theory and Criticism*, 6th edition, ed. Leo Braudy and Marshall Cohen (New York: Oxford University Press, 2004), 730.
8. Christian B. Long, "New Zealand Lamb Is People: Bad Taste, Black Sheep, and Farming," in *Food on Film: Bringing Something New to the Table*, ed. Tom Hertweck (Lanham, MD: Rowman & Littlefield Publishing Group, 2015), 204.
9. Steven Shaviro, *The Cinematic Body* (Minneapolis: University of Minnesota Press, 1993), 64.
10. Barratt, *Bad Taste*, 65.
11. John Waters, *Shock Value: A Tasteful Book about Bad Taste* (New York: Thunder's Mouth Press, 1981), 2.
12. Kim Newman, *Nightmare Movies: Horror on Screen since the 1960s* (1988. London: Bloomsbury, 2011), 262.
13. Phil Fasso, "*Poultrygeist: Night of the Chicken Dead*," Death Ensemble, January 8, 2012. http://deathensemble.com/blog/2012/01/08/poultrygeist-night-of-the-chicken-dead/ (accessed June 10, 2016).
14. Barratt, *Bad Taste*, 45.
15. While not the first American fast food chain to make its presence felt in New Zealand (that honor went to Kentucky Fried Chicken, in 1971), McDonald's holds a particular cultural and symbolic value that cannot be ignored.
16. Max Horkheimer and Theodore W. Adorno, "The Culture Industry: Enlightenment as Mass Deception," in *Dialectic of Enlightenment* (1947. Stanford, CA: Stanford University Press, 2007), 325–9.
17. Long, "New Zealand Lamb Is People," 203–204.
18. For more on this, see www.mcspotlight.org.
19. Eric Schlosser, *Fast Food Nation: What the All-American Meal Is Doing to the World* (New York: Penguin Books, 2002), 9.
20. Ibid.

21 Jim Hightower, *Eat Your Heart Out: How Food Profiteers Victimize the Consumer* (New York: Vintage/Random House, 1976).
22 Schlosser, *Fast Food Nation*, 101.
23 Ibid., 97
24 Ibid., 11.
25 Robin Wood, "American Nightmare, Horror in the '70s," in *Hollywood from Vietnam to Reagan and Beyond* (New York: Columbia University Press, 2003), 25.
26 See ibid., 27, for a detailed discussion of this process.
27 Karl Marx and Frederick Engels, *The Communist Manifesto* (New York: Verso, 1998), 35.

Bibliography

Barratt, Jim. *Bad Taste*. London: Wallflower Press, 2008.
Brottman, Mikita. *Offensive Films: Toward an Anthropology of Cinéma Vomitif*. Westport, CT: Greenwood Press, 1997.
Cortini, Mario, and Philip Nutman. "Profile: Peter Jackson: Master of Bad Taste." *Gorezone* 5 (January 1989).
Fasso, Phil. "*Poultrygeist: Night of the Chicken Dead*," *Death Ensemble*, January 8, 2012. http://deathensemble.com/blog/2012/01/08/poultrygeist-night-of-the-chicken-dead/ (accessed June 10, 2016).
Grant, Barry Keith. *A Cultural Assault: The New Zealand Films of Peter Jackson*. London: Kakapo Books, 1999.
Hightower, Jim. *Eat Your Heart Out: How Food Profiteers Victimize the Consumer*. New York: Vintage/Random House, 1976.
Horkheimer, Max, and Theodore W. Adorno. "The Culture Industry: Enlightenment as Mass Deception." In *Dialectic of Enlightenment*. 1947. Stanford, CA: Stanford University Press, 2007.
Long, Christian B. "New Zealand Lamb Is People: Bad Taste, Black Sheep, and Farming." In *Food on Film: Bringing Something New to the Table*, edited by Tom Hertweck, 201–18. Lanham, MD: Rowman & Littlefield Publishing Group, 2015.
Marx, Karl, and Frederick Engels. *The Communist Manifesto*. New York: Verso, 1998.
Newman, Kim. *Nightmare Movies: Horror on Screen since the 1960s*. 1988. London: Bloomsbury, 2011.
Schlosser, Eric. *Fast Food Nation: What the All-American Meal Is Doing to the World*. New York: Penguin Books, 2002.
Shaviro, Steven. *The Cinematic Body*. Minneapolis: University of Minnesota Press, 1993.
Sibley, Brian. *Peter Jackson, A Filmmaker's Journey*. London: HarperCollins Entertainment, 2006.
Waters, John. *Shock Value: A Tasteful Book about Bad Taste*. New York: Thunder's Mouth Press, 1981.

Williams, Linda. "Film Bodies: Gender, Genre, and Excess." In *Film Theory and Criticism*, 6th edn, edited by Leo Braudy and Marshall Cohen, 727–41. New York: Oxford University Press, 2004.

Wood, Robin. "American Nightmare, Horror in the '70s." In *Hollywood from Vietnam to Reagan and Beyond*, 23–44. New York: Columbia University Press, 2003.

2

Let Them Eat Steak: Food and the Family Horror Film Cycle

Hans Staats

In "Ten Horror Movie Food Scenes That Will Make You Shudder," Lisa Bramen celebrates the horrors of consumption in Tobe Hooper's *Poltergeist* (1982) in the company of classics such as *Nosferatu* (1922) and *Psycho* (1960), thanks to its use of food as a source of not only pleasure but disgust. The film's grotesque depiction of a piece of raw steak that crawls across a kitchen counter and vomits up its insides demonstrates, Bramen observes, that "movie directors know that the quickest way to the audience's gag reflex is through its stomach."[1] The steak scene from *Poltergeist* is, in her view, among "the most notable food scenes in the history of the horror genre," but it also highlights the joined concepts of food, eating, and nourishment as the pivot point between the normative and monstrous American family.[2]

Bramen's consideration of this diverse gathering of horror films—from German expressionist to Anglo-American gothic to Hollywood cult classic—supports, albeit inadvertently, a definition of the horror genre as that which "either exceeds everyday use of the term 'horror' or excludes films that are widely recognized as such."[3] The list's focus on food—and the intersection of the edible and the incredible—underscores this challenge to the conventions of genre studies and the limitations of "defining the appropriate intertexts" for films' interpretations.[4] Bramen suggests that the concept of food, rather than the subtleties of genre analysis, illuminates the sociopolitical and economic conditions of the modern family horror film cycle (1960–82), precisely because it is an *in*appropriate topic of discussion.[5] Following Bramen's lead, then, this chapter focuses on horror movies that abide by the everyday principle that you are what you eat.

More specifically, *Poltergeist*, *The Texas Chainsaw Massacre* (1974), and *Psycho* focus on the concept of food as a critique of the family and the dominant ideology of bourgeois patriarchal society. Not unlike the steak that terrorizes the Freeling family in *Poltergeist*, the monstrous families in *The Texas Chainsaw Massacre* and *Psycho* are theoretically defined by the failure of industrial food and animal production to maintain a standard of living that is commensurate with the values of consumer society and cultural commodification.[6] Ultimately, the concept of food as Other in the aforementioned films acts as a critical intervention that focuses on the monstrous family and their opposition to the terrorizing force of the status quo epitomized in the gated community of Cuesta Verde in *Poltergeist*.[7]

In addition, each of these films' representation of the connection between the killer and victim establishes food as a pictorial trope that underscores the crisis and disintegration of bourgeois consciousness and the nuclear family. Hence both Hooper's reactionary horror film and the more progressive *Texas Chainsaw Massacre* expand upon a concept that I refer to as the free-range stalk-and-slash narrative, popularized in *Psycho* and further discussed in this chapter. As a result, the distinction between the progressive and reactionary—as well as the classic and modern—horror film is complicated and improved upon by the shocking representation of food and the collapse of the farm-to-table ethos, which imagines a renewed embrace of the land as a source of nourishment and well-being that overlooks the problems of economic hardship and social inequality.

As Tony Williams has noted, the image of the American family as "a positive icon of 'normal' human society . . . underwent severe assault" in horror films in the 1970s.[8] The superstitions and mid-European folk memory of 1930s horror films (*Dracula* (1931), *Frankenstein* (1931)) were gone, replaced by the monstrous children depicted in *Night of the Living Dead* (1968), *Rosemary's Baby* (1968), and *The Exorcist* (1973), who represented the collapse of the nuclear family and the dominant values of bourgeois society (security, fidelity, prosperity, and sobriety). The monstrous child and childish monster, Williams argues, represent the encounter between the typical American family and its monstrous counterparts in films like *The Last House on the Left* (1972), *The Texas Chainsaw Massacre*, and *The Hills Have Eyes* (1977). The modern horror film's disruption of the ideological norms of the family thus introduced a new way of thinking about the postwar American Dream portrayed in television series such as *Father Knows Best* (1954–60) and *The Donna Reed Show* (1958–66).

In particular, Williams presents *Psycho* as a key text in the transition between the classic and modern phases of the horror film, and a cinematic gateway to the realm of family horror. According to Williams, the figures of the castrating mother and violent, castrated son in *Psycho* "enact the Oedipal trajectory's socially sanctioned psychic violence," paving the way for "later grotesque representations" and "spectacular bloodbaths" in films like *Halloween* (1978), *Friday the 13th* (1980), and *A Nightmare on Elm Street* (1984).[9] The connection between *Psycho* and the modern American horror film is thus rooted in the stalk-and-slash narrative, in which teenage protagonists are murdered, one after another, by a psychopathic killer whose point of view is represented as the dominant perspective of the camera and focal point for spectator identification.[10]

In this chapter, I complicate the origin story of the slasher movie by considering the family horror film in relation to the concept of food. Specifically, I argue that the reactionary politics or "Reaganite entertainment" associated with *Poltergeist* is prefigured by the morally ambiguous killer in *Psycho*, Norman Bates (Anthony Perkins), who is framed by a monstrous family history that is situated in precisely the same locale that the farm-to-table ethos associates with the nourishment and well-being of the body politic. The free-range stalk-and-slash narrative in *Psycho*, in other words, is characterized by a killer who hides away from the victims that he encounters. Rather than pursuing his quarry with unrelenting purpose, Norman, like Leatherface (Gunnar Hansen) in *The Texas Chainsaw Massacre*, is a reclusive figure who is intruded upon by the victim.

Furthermore, *The Texas Chainsaw Massacre* and *Psycho* represent the countryside of America—like the planned community of Cuesta Verde in *Poltergeist*—as imperiled by industrialization and the concomitant threats of economic hardship and social inequality. Indeed, all of the films in this chapter represent these factors as greater threats than the monsters plotting against the suburban and rural communities that function as sites of unfettered simplicity and ideological stability. Ultimately, the Freeling family in *Poltergeist* epitomizes the victim as a force of destruction that imperils the livelihood of the killer and the land they have claimed as their own.

Tastes like chicken: *Poltergeist* and the food politics of Reaganite entertainment

Midway through *Poltergeist*, Dr. Marty Casey (Martin Casella), a parapsychologist from the University of California–Irvine, enters the Freeling family's kitchen for a late-night snack. Unlike his associates Dr. Lesh (Beatrice Straight) and Ryan (Richard Lawson), Casey is essentially oblivious to the fantastic events that have transpired in the Freeling home and the planned community of Cuesta Verde. Hearing that the Freelings' youngest daughter Carol Ann (Heather O'Rourke) has been spirited away by a malevolent force, he is at first dubious and suspects an elaborate hoax. However, Casey's sense of disbelief changes to panic when goes in search of a bite to eat. He finds the refrigerator well-stocked with chicken, steak, and other fare. The Freelings may be terrorized by the spirit world, but their kitchen is brimming over with everything that a famished parapsychologist—or the dominant ideology of bourgeois patriarchal society—desires.

Unfortunately, for Casey, his banquet is interrupted by an unexpected development. Staring at the kitchen counter with a drumstick held between his teeth mid-bite, he is shocked and disgusted by the sight of a raw piece of steak crawling across the counter by itself and erupting into a grotesque and sickening lump. Dropping the drumstick from his mouth, Casey looks down at his once-mouthwatering snack and finds that it is covered in maggots. His panic is reinforced as he stumbles into the adjoining utility room and stares in horror at the mirror as the flesh melts from his face in blood-soaked chunks that resemble the insides of the steak on the nearby kitchen counter. Then, just as quickly as his world decomposed around him, a sudden flash of light reveals that it was merely a figment of his imagination.

Feelings of pleasure and disgust at the sight of food are conflated, in this scene, with the decomposition of the human body and, by extension, the subversion of the kitchen as a privileged location within the suburban American home. The intersection of the edible and the incredible underscores the opposition between the normative American family and its monstrous counterpart. Indeed, throughout the film, the Freeling kitchen is represented as the focal point of the nuclear family's activities, as well as a symbol of suburban prosperity and ideological certainty. Not surprisingly, it is in the kitchen that Diane Freeling (JoBeth Williams) first discovers the presence of paranormal activity. *Poltergeist* cuts directly from its most famous scene— five-year-old Carol Ann announcing the poltergeist or thing-without-a-name ("They're heeeere!")—to the Freelings enjoying a hearty American breakfast. This scene, especially, uses the concept of food as a critique of the family— danger may be lurking around every corner, but there is always time for a heaping portion of bacon and eggs. Even the family dog shares in the feast, being fed a waffle doused in syrup under the table while the children playfully fling bits of cereal at each other and Diane offers up second helpings.

More specifically, the juxtaposition of the two scenes frames the nuclear family as threatened by the poltergeist via the concept of food as Other.

The impending chaos that will envelop the Freelings is foreshadowed, at the conclusion of breakfast, when eight-year-old Robbie's (Oliver Robins) oversized cup of milk shatters over his older sister Dana's (Dominique Dunne) school books and clothes. Later, at the table by himself, Robbie is puzzled by his bent fork and equally damaged spoon. The idea of domestic instability, and the concomitant need to reassert the dominant ideology, is reinforced by the crisis of the nuclear family and the fact that the first sign of paranormal activity (a stack of chairs on the kitchen table) appears in the room where the Freelings, and the normative American family, feel most at home.

Furthermore, the representation of food in *Poltergeist* points to a certain naiveté—to the inability of reason to fully comprehend the supernatural. Compared to *The Texas Chainsaw Massacre* and *Psycho*, *Poltergeist* is figuratively built upon the refusal to consider a reality, or cultural context, that exists outside the dominant ideology of patriarchal capitalism. Cuesta Verde is built upon a tribal burial ground, and further evidence that the American Dream is rapacious and gluttonous abounds. The Freelings' porcine neighbor Ben Tuthill (Michael McManus), for example, epitomizes the narcoleptic suburban dweller, mindlessly gobbling a plate of baked beans as the Freelings appeal to him for assistance. Cuesta Verde may be teetering upon the brink of catastrophe, but those baked beans are yummy! In other words, the concept of food in *Poltergeist*, if only for a moment, underscores the fearful proposition that the pleasure of eating is a reversible dichotomy—the joy of consumption is not easily distinguished from the horror of being consumed.

Indeed, the most disturbing moments in *Poltergeist* arise when characters are consumed by the suburban home itself. Robbie, for example, is eaten by the tree outside his bedroom window, and Carol Ann is swallowed up by her closet, which functions as the portal into the spirit world. By the end of the film, however, the horrifying possibility that the Freelings will be eaten alive by their suburban home, not to mention the American Dream, is replaced by the rebirth and resurrection of the dominant patriarchal order. The concept of food in *Poltergeist* reinforces this ideological renewal, especially when Diane saves Carol Ann at the end of the film and is reborn from the depths of her unconscious fears of inadequacy as the All-American Mom. The film treats this "rebirth" as more than a metaphor. After Diane boldly ventures into Carol Ann's closet, mother and daughter emerge from the ceiling of the Freelings' living room, covered in a substance that resembles ectoplasm or amniotic fluid. Steven, cleansing his daughter in the bathtub, welcomes her (back) to the world. The return of Carol Ann, absent for the majority of film, is thus conflated with Diane's act of sacrifice and her return to the position of housewife under the watchful eye of the male order.[11]

The portrayal of the nuclear family in *Poltergeist*, to borrow from Andrew Britton, is ultimately complicit with "a general movement of reaction and conservative reassurance in the contemporary Hollywood cinema."[12] Compared to the characters in films like *The Texas Chainsaw Massacre* and *Psycho*, the Freelings are represented as a family unit that reinforces the dominant ideology of prosperity and the patriarchal order. Successful realtor Steven (Craig T. Nelson) and housewife Diane are happily married, and their children reflect stereotypical developmental stages of childhood and adolescence. Robbie is a fan of *Star Wars*, older sister Dana is preoccupied with talking on the phone late at night, and young Carol Ann is the embodiment of childlike innocence. The "structure, narrative movement, pattern of character relationships, and ideological tendency" of *Poltergeist* are, in short, concerned with "staging the purification and resurrection of capitalism" and the male order, rather than calling them into question.[13]

This point is vital to the distinction between the progressive and reactionary horror film during the 1960s and 1980s. As Robin Wood notes, the progressive horror film is imbued with a sense of social and political activism, specifically opposition to patriarchal capitalism. Wes Craven's *The Last House on the Left*, Hooper's *The Texas Chainsaw Massacre*, and George Romero's *Dawn of the Dead* (1978) are all, for Wood, examples of this trend. The reactionary horror films of the 1980s, however, reinforce the dominant ideology, representing monsters as simply evil and unsympathetic, depicting Christianity as a positive presence, and confusing the repression of sexuality with sexuality itself.[14] Examples cited by Wood include Craven's *Swamp Thing* (1982), Romero's *Creepshow* (1982), and—most importantly for this chapter—*Poltergeist*.[15]

The representation of the suburban home and nuclear family in *Poltergeist*, to borrow from Fredric Jameson, "seems by its structure the fittest to express the secret truths" of Reaganite entertainment and the cultural function of the concept of food.[16] Jameson's description of the modern, capitalist age as a period in which "the deep underlying materiality of all things has finally risen dripping and convulsive into the light of day" points to the scene in *Poltergeist* when the flooded cavity of the Freelings' unfinished pool opens up, not unlike the steak that crawls across the kitchen counter, to reveal an army of mud-encrusted skeletons. Rising from the earth to avenge themselves upon the residents of Cuesta Verde—whose homes are built atop their desecrated graves—the skeletons also lay siege to the suburbanites' disregard for the secret truths of the American Dream, particularly the problems of economic hardship and social inequality that it masks. Hence the concept of food as Other in *Poltergeist* acts as a critical intervention that focuses on the terrorizing force of the status quo epitomized in the gated community of Cuesta Verde.[17]

Ultimately, the cultural function of the concept of food in *Poltergeist* raises a deceptively unassuming question: what exactly does the normative American family hunger for? The nuclear family in *Poltergeist* is defined by the apparent success of industrial food production in maintaining a standard of living that is commensurate with the values of consumer society and cultural commodification. Yet the family is also banished from the planned community of Cuesta Verda as punishment for their complicity in the expansion of bourgeois capitalist society. Though horrified by the secret truths of Cuesta Verde, the closest that Steven comes to making a political statement is wagging his finger at his employer Mr. Teague (James Karen) before leaving town. That is to say, the representation of the bourgeois American Dream in *Poltergeist* rests on monstrous injustices. Those who partake of it choose to be oblivious to those injustices, and make no attempt to mitigate their effects. In that respect, the Freelings are as predatory as Leatherface or Norman Bates.

Farms, tables, and chainsaws: cannibalism and community-supported agriculture in *The Texas Chainsaw Massacre*

The opening narration of *The Texas Chainsaw Massacre* evokes, oddly, the spirit of Alexander Payne's comedy-drama film *Sideways* (2004), in which a group of middle-aged bohemians frolic through the wine country of California in search of friendship, good food, and the perfect bottle of Pinot noir. In both *The Texas Chainsaw Massacre* and *Sideways*, the American landscape is bathed in sunlight and the idealism of youth. That "idyllic summer afternoon," as narrator John Larroquette describes it, promises to disclose the American Dream of heteronormative bliss for Sally Hardesty (Marilyn Burns) and her boyfriend Jerry (Allen Danziger). Sally, however, ends up spending more time with her disabled brother Franklin (Paul Partain) than with Jerry. The trio's road trip with their friends Kirk (Will Vail) and Pam (Teri McMinn), moreover, takes them not through the Santa Barbara wine country but through the countryside of rural Texas, where a monstrous family is making a mad, macabre attempt to reclaim a fabled golden age of American agricultural and industrial prosperity.

The horrors of the American Dream in *The Texas Chainsaw Massacre*, like those in *Poltergeist*, are buried within a seemingly harmless and familiar locale that beckons to the unsuspecting victim. The opening image of *Texas Chainsaw*, however, is far more shocking than *Poltergeist*'s television that disrupts the boundaries between this world and the next. Working in a more progressive vein than he would in *Poltergeist*, Hooper begins *The Texas Chainsaw Massacre* with a sustained critique of the dominant ideology of bourgeois society. The opening moments of the film show the desecration of a burial ground, accompanied by the flash of a camera documenting the event. The camera belongs to Nubbins Sawyer (Edwin Neal), whose proclivity for documenting this graveyard desecration—along with the ghoulish barbecue recipe of his older brother Drayton Sawyer (Jim Siedow)—points to the moral ambiguity of the monstrous family. Unlike Marty's melted face in *Poltergeist*, the newly unearthed, decomposed body in *Texas Chainsaw* is very much a diegetic reality that "feeds" into the horrors of consumption via the practice of cannibalism and the secret truths of the farm-to-table ethos.

The scene particularly illuminates the concept of food and the transition from reactionary to progressive horror film. In his portrayal of the nuclear family in *Poltergeist*, especially, it is clear that Hooper has backed away from the progressive outlook of *The Texas Chainsaw Massacre*. Compared to the images of the football game and *Mister Rogers' Neighborhood* that flicker across the Freelings' television, the camera flash in the opening moments of *Texas Chainsaw Massacre*—along with radio broadcasts that describe acts of murder and body-snatching—underscores the connection between the decomposition of the human body and the disintegration of bourgeois consciousness and the nuclear family.

Even before introducing the five protagonists, Hooper communicates his morbidly delightful sense of humor by juxtaposing Nubbins's graveyard desecration with an image of a dead armadillo, creating an allusion to the concept of road kill that foreshadows the film's themes of cannibalism and food which is not fit for consumption. The point is reinforced when Sally and the others, after visiting the defiled cemetery, drive past a slaughterhouse and are disgusted by the smell in the air. Cutting between the cemetery and the abattoir, Hooper establishes that, in *The Texas Chainsaw Massacre*, the concepts of food and nourishment exist within a landscape where only death and decomposition are available for consumption. Images of cattle waiting to be slaughtered similarly highlight a disturbing renunciation of the sanctity of life and the significance of beef in American foodways—a point that is also made in *Poltergeist* through Casey's grotesque steak.

Contrary to *Poltergeist*, however, the more progressive *Texas Chainsaw Massacre* uses the concept of food as a critical intervention that ultimately focuses on the terrorizing force of the status quo embodied by the teenagers who intrude upon the monstrous family and Leatherface in particular. For example, Hooper first films the slaughterhouse from the point-of-view of the teenagers as they drive by in their green Ford Club Wagon, then reverses the camera's position, so that the teenagers and the car are framed from the point of view of the slaughterhouse. He thus alludes to the imminent death of the teenagers in a fashion resembling the fate of the cattle and associated with the stench of death that the teens cannot tolerate. More specifically, the slaughter of the teenagers in *Texas Chainsaw* represents the connection between the free-range stalk-and-slash narrative and the horrors of the farm-to-table ethos.

Hooper's politically progressive interrogation first of the slaughterhouse and then of the monstrous family's abandoned farm in *The Texas Chainsaw Massacre* prefigures his critique of the homogeneity of Cuesta Verde in *Poltergeist*. His interrogation of the normative American family is more pronounced in *The Texas Chainsaw Massacre*, however, focusing on the childish monster Leatherface and framing him as an inversion of Diane Freeling and the figure of the All-American Mom. As the film progresses it becomes abundantly clear that Leatherface is a homemaker, as well as a homicidal maniac. Leatherface's role in the kitchen, especially, represents a monstrous inversion of the cultural role of the kitchen in *Poltergeist*, a point made particularly clear by Leatherface's decision to dress up for dinner later that evening, complete with makeup and wig.

The home economics of the monstrous family in *The Texas Chainsaw Massacre* points to the question of adaptation to economic hardship and social inequality. Over the course of the film Hooper reveals that the monstrous family were once employed at the slaughterhouse, but lost their jobs due to modernization and the replacement of the sledgehammer with the captive bolt pistol as a means of killing cattle. As a result, they have resorted to extreme measures, including murder and cannibalism, to provide for themselves. This is a dilemma that is reflected in their living quarters—a remote farmhouse decorated with the remains of animals and humans that have no doubt been served up as barbeque at Drayton's nearby gas station.

Taking the same line of argument further, the representation of the monster as Other in *Texas Chainsaw* is more complex than that in *Poltergeist*, particularly with respect to Leatherface as a sympathetic figure. Clearly it is not heroic for Leatherface—in an act suffused with the concept of slaughter and food manufacture—to murder Kirk with a sledgehammer and dismember him with a chainsaw. Nevertheless, after Leatherface captures Pam and places her on a meathook he begins to pace throughout the house, looking nervously through the window and sitting down with his head in his hands (Figure 2.1). Leatherface, in other words, is a sympathetic character inasmuch as he finds himself in the midst of a home invasion, becoming—in his paranoia about the outside world and its bewildering contingencies—a horrifying inversion of the All-American Mom and beleaguered housewife. Trying to put food on the table, Leatherface looks out through his parlor

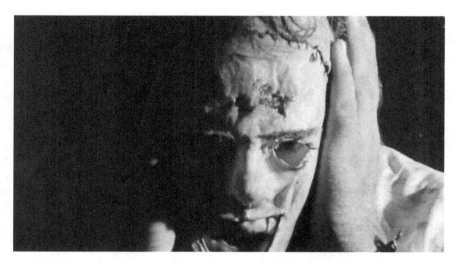

FIGURE 2.1 *Leatherface: homicidal maniac or beleaguered housewife?*

window, festooned with animal and human remains, and wonders what to do next in the face of this onslaught of teenagers who are curious about his piece of the American Dream.

In the case of Leatherface and *The Texas Chainsaw Massacre*, the turn to cannibalism is a countercultural rejection of the status quo and the dominant ideology of bourgeois patriarchal society. The farm-to-table ethos, as practiced by the film's monstrous family, embodies a notion of cooperation and effective social organization that harkens to the community building potential of the human body and the interdependence of the stages and specializations of food manufacture. The loss of community resulting from the modernization of the slaughterhouse forces Leatherface and his kin to attempt, albeit haphazardly, to replicate the social organization they once knew by preying upon the random travelers that cross their path.

The Texas Chainsaw Massacre is also indebted, however, to the free-range stalk-and-slash narrative in *Psycho* and to the figure of the killer who hides away from the victims that he encounters. Rather than pursuing his quarry with unrelenting purpose, Leatherface is a reclusive figure who is, himself, intruded upon by the figure of the victim. The promised land of rural Texas—a site of unfettered simplicity and ideological stability not unlike the planned community of Cuesta Verde in *Poltergeist*—is imperiled by "progress" and the concomitant threats of economic hardship and social inequality, rather than by a supernatural embodiment of the return of the repressed. Hence the distinction between the progressive and reactionary—as well as the classic and modern—horror film is complicated and improved upon by the shocking representation of food and the collapse of the farm-to-table ethos.

You never did eat lunch, did you? or, Marion Crane's untimely death row meal

In *Psycho*, Marion Crane (Janet Leigh) is sentenced to death long before the viewer is properly introduced to her. Not unlike the female victim-heroes in *Poltergeist* (Carol Ann Freeling) and *The Texas Chainsaw Massacre* (Sally Hardesty), Marion's fate is sealed by the joined concepts of food, eating, and nourishment as the pivot point between the normal and pathological American family. At the start of *Psycho* in particular, director Alfred Hitchcock uses the concept of food to objectify Marion as oversexed and emotionally unsatisfied within the dominant patriarchal order. The first line of the film ("You never did eat your lunch, did you?"), spoken by Marion's working-class lover Sam Loomis (John Gavin), does not refer only to Marion and Sam's "extended lunch" or romantic rendezvous (Figure 2.2). It is also a signifier of their failed pursuit of middle-class respectability—particularly Sam's financial hardship and their postponement of marriage. Long before she is stabbed to death by Norman Bates, midway through *Psycho*, Marion is sentenced to death by a sandwich—and matrimonial bond—that she is unable to consum(mat)e.

FIGURE 2.2 *Eating the Other: Marion Crane as the object of desire.*

The opening of *Psycho* indicates, in hindsight, that the deferral of Marion's lunchtime is a sign of moral ambiguity and imminent death. Marion's extended lunch hour and afternoon tryst with Sam is represented by Hitchcock as a balancing act between respectability and infamy that underscores the collapse of the nuclear family and the dominant values of bourgeois society. Her failed pursuit of middle-class respectability is conflated with her failure to eat her lunch and thus claim the happiness and sense of well-being that others flaunt—notably oil-lease man Tom Cassidy (Frank Albertson), who is buying a house for his daughter with the help of Marion's employer. Later, as she drives away with Cassidy's $40,000 that her boss has entrusted to her, it comes as no surprise that Marion's flagging moral fiber is indicated by her failed vision and growing hunger late at night on the road. Next stop: Bates Motel. Indeed, more so than any of the other characters in this chapter, it is Norman who is most adept at using food as a signifier of death and destruction. As a diversion and lure for his unsuspecting victims, food in *Psycho* is as effective, and perhaps more frightening, a killing machine as the ubiquitous kitchen knife.

Further emphasizing the importance of the concept of food as a signifier of moral ambiguity, untimely death, and the place of the female victim within the dominant ideology of bourgeois patriarchal society, Norman gamely offers to whip up a plate of sandwiches and a glass of milk. Moreover, food is both a contributing factor in Marion's decision to stop at the Bates Motel and a trigger for Norman's repressed memories, sexuality, and murderous instincts. It is the topic of discussion that opens *Psycho*, and the means of introducing the viewer to Norman's mother Norma, who refuses to allow her son to have supper with Marion "by candlelight . . . in the cheap erotic fashion of young men with cheap erotic minds."

Norma's scolding of Norman contributes to Marion's already noticeable feelings of guilt and shame by characterizing food, and by extension Marion, as morally reprehensible. "She'll not be appeasing her ugly appetite with my food, or my son!" Norma(n) shouts. At every turn, Marion's pursuit of happiness and satisfaction is thwarted. By extension, food represents the most basic conceptualization of Marion's frustrated desires and precarious standing in relation to the monstrous Bates family.

Nowhere is this dramatic tension more evident than in the conversation between Norman and Marion in the parlor of the Bates Motel. Norman uses food to manipulate Marion, steering her away from her room to the motel office before "changing his mind" and deciding to eat in the parlor. Slowly but surely, Marion is lured into the hunting grounds that Norman prefers, as evidenced by the birds mounted throughout the parlor.

Inevitably, the topic of conversation turns to the expression "eats like a bird." Norman's observation that the expression is a falsity is complemented by shots of Marion looking suspiciously at Norman's handiwork, almost aware of the fact that she is being fattened up for the kill. More specifically, Norman explains that he prefers to stuff birds because they are passive to begin with, a notion that Hitchcock would thoroughly disprove with his film *The Birds* in 1963. Hence birds and Marion are compared to one another in terms of Marion's appetite and her passivity or, to borrow from Laura Mulvey, the process by which figure of the woman is represented as the object of desire and the male gaze.[18]

Ultimately, Marion's last meal in Norman's parlor underscores how the consumption of food is a distraction from the inevitability of death, as well as a false promise of shelter from the patriarchal symbolic order. It is only a matter of time before Marion begins to sense that the food she has been offered is the bait, after listening to Norman declare that "we're all in our private traps. Clamped in them. And none of us can ever get out. We scratch and claw, but only at the air, only at each other. And for all of it, we never budge an inch." To emphasize this point, Marion stares down at her sandwich and comments, "[S]ometimes we deliberately step into those traps." Not unlike the unconsumed sandwich at the beginning of *Psycho*, Marion is objectified and prosecuted by the Law of the Father during her conversation with Norman. Conversely, Norman, not unlike Sam Loomis, uses the concept of food as a reason to pass over details that would obviously alarm Marion and himself, for example, his decision to murder his mother and her boyfriend. "I guess it's nothing to talk about while you're eating," Norman says with a smile.

More specifically, food plays an active role in coding the monstrous family and the relationship between Norman and his mother, both in life and in death. Ultimately, Norma is hidden in the fruit cellar by Norman. Norma accuses Norman of thinking that she's "fruity," underscoring the ambiguous relationship between mother and son and Norman's sexuality and manhood in particular. Norman's masculinity is regularly questioned by Norma. Thus Norman's decision to hide his crime and his mother's body in the fruit cellar is a plea to "cure" the act that he has committed. That is to say, as his mother's corpse ripens into a repressed memory, Norman becomes his mother, especially in moments of duress and sexual excitement. In the end, criminality, masculinity, and the figure of the mother are entwined with the concept of food. This is especially germane to the free-range stalk-and-slash narrative that is introduced in *Psycho* and later extrapolated upon in *The Texas Chainsaw Massacre*. Ultimately, Norman, like Leatherface, attempts to maintain the creature comforts of home by complicating the difference between the concept of food and the human body.

Conclusion

As Lisa Bramen points out, food has a way of capturing the imagination. By extension, one thing that the male characters in *Poltergeist*, *The Texas Chainsaw Massacre*, and *Psycho* share in common is the figure of the radical environmentalist. If there is a tension between the production of food and environmental conservation in the films that I write about in this chapter, then the figures of Steven Freeling, Leatherface, and Norman Bates work to police the boundaries between industrialization and the heartland of America. Freeling's disgust with the planned community of Cuesta Verde at the end of *Poltergeist* is matched by the intensity with which Leatherface responds to intruders and trespassers on his plot of Texas countryside. The same can be said for Norman Bates, who lives quite peacefully in his gothic home on a road forgotten by the California freeway system. Those who intrude upon his quaint motel are executed with extreme prejudice. In short, the concept of food in each of the three films is entwined with a sense of frontier justice directed toward the preservation of the American countryside and a way of life that is coded as imperiled by the encroachment of industrial development, housing, and the freeway system. Contrary to the phrase "let them eat cake," the figure of the radical environmentalist illuminates the cultural function of the concept of food, the struggle for social equality, and the sociopolitical and economic conditions of the modern family horror film cycle.[19]

Notes

1 Lisa Bramen, "Ten Horror Movie Food Scenes That Will Make You Shudder," Smithsonian.com (October 28, 2011), http://www.smithsonianmag.com/arts-culture/ten-horror-movie-food-scenes-that-will-make-you-shudder-122983794 (accessed March 7, 2016).

2 Ibid.

3 According to Richard Nowell, scholars like Robin Wood ("Introduction to the American Horror Film," in *The American Nightmare: Essays on the Horror Film*, edited by Robin Wood and Richard Lippe, 7–28 (Toronto: Festival of Festivals, 1979)) and Noël Carroll (*The Philosophy of Horror, or Paradoxes of the Heart* (London: Routledge, 1990)) attempt "to pin down the horror film's unique formal, structural, or thematic characteristics," a pursuit that

is flawed due to the imposition of "a trans-cultural, trans-historical ideal on to a discursive phenomenon that is subject to levels of contestation and flux that make this endeavor unviable or impossible: horror, like other genres, simply means too many things to be distilled into a universal essence." See Richard Nowell, "There's Gold in Them There Chills," in *Merchants of Menace: The Business of Horror Cinema* (New York: Bloomsbury, 2014), 2.

4 Mark Jancovich, "General Introduction," in *Horror: The Film Reader* (London: Routledge, 2001), 14.

5 Examples of the modern family horror film during the 1960s and 1970s include: *Rosemary's Baby* (1968), *Night of the Living Dead* (1968), *The Exorcist* (1973), *It's Alive* (1974), and *The Omen* (1976).

6 According to bell hooks, the commodification of Otherness, or "eating the other," is partially defined by the repression of social change via "those 'nasty' unconscious fantasies and longings about contact with the Other embedded in the secret (not so secret) deep structure of white supremacy." See bell hooks, "'Eating the Other,' 'Eating the Other: Desire and Resistance,'" in *Black Looks: Race and Representation* (Boston: South End Press, 1992), 21–2.

7 Ibid., 22.

8 Tony Williams, *Hearths of Darkness: The Family in the American Horror Film* (1996. Madison, NJ: Fairleigh Dickinson University Press, 2014), 11.

9 Ibid., 72.

10 A noteworthy rebuttal to the hypothesis that *Psycho* is a proto-slasher film is proposed by Richard Nowell, who argues that commerce, rather than artistic vision, prompted the emergence of the slasher film with *Black Christmas* (1974). See *Blood Money: A History of the First Teen Slasher Film Cycle* (New York: Continuum, 2011), 8, 58–62.

11 In a moment of anticlimax, ideologically speaking, Diane's final challenge in *Poltergeist*, after saving Carol Ann and being "reborn" as the figure of the All-American Mom, is to once again protect Robbie and Carol Ann from the gaping maw of the closet which ceaselessly hungers for the life force of the Freeling children. From the excremental cavity of the unfinished swimming pool—itself a symbol of the unfinished project of the nuclear family—to the pustular esophagus of her children's closet, Diane battles against the Beast of Cuesta Verde. Marking the return of the repressed, the Freeling home figuratively regurgitates the outraged corpses of the Native American burial ground upon which the dominant ideology of patriarchal capitalism is erected.

12 Andrew Britton, "Blissing Out: The Politics of Reaganite Entertainment," in *Britton on Film: The Complete Criticism of Andrew Britton*, ed. Barry Keith Grant (1986. Detroit: Wayne State University Press, 2009), 97.

13 Ibid., 99.

14 While the representation of monstrosity and sexuality is nonexistent in *Poltergeist*, and of minor importance in *The Texas Chainsaw Massacre*, it is a crucial detail in *Psycho* regarding the connection between Norman and his mother.

15 Wood, "Introduction," 23–4.
16 Fredric Jameson, *Postmodernism, or, the Cultural Logic of Late Capitalism* (Durham, NC: Duke University Press, 1991), 67.
17 The crisis and disintegration of bourgeois consciousness and the nuclear family that takes place in *Poltergeist* is foreshadowed, in the film's opening moments, by the Freelings' subordination to the "master medium" represented by their television set. Indeed, the beginning of *Poltergeist* portrays the normative American family as asleep to the realities of the Reagan era: fear of evil-non-Americans, the liberated woman, and the fear that democratic capitalism may not be cleanly separable from Fascism. The film opens with a black screen, accompanied by the sound of "The Star-Spangled Banner," played at midnight as the station to which the set is tuned prepares to cease broadcasting for the day. Images of national monuments in extreme close-up flicker on the screen. The television signal stops and the camera is placed behind Steven Freeling as he slumbers in his La-Z-Boy recliner. The family dog sneaks up and eats from Steven's plate: a further use of the concept of food to critique the dominant ideology of bourgeois society and its expression in the patriarchal family. See Robin Wood, *Hollywood from Vietnam to Reagan* (1986. New York: Columbia University Press, 2003), 150.
18 See Laura Mulvey, "Visual Pleasure and Narrative Cinema," *Screen* 16, no. 3 (Autumn 1975): 6–18.
19 The French phrase *"Qu'ils mangent de la brioche,"* commonly misattributed to Marie Antoinette (1755–93), appears in Jean-Jacques Rousseau's *Confessions* (1782).

Bibliography

Bramen, Lisa. "Ten Horror Movie Food Scenes That Will Make You Shudder." Smithsonian.com, October 28, 2011. http://www.smithsonianmag.com/arts-culture/ten-horror-movie-food-scenes-that-will-make-you-shudder-122983794 (accessed March 7, 2016).
Britton, Andrew. "Blissing Out: The Politics of Reaganite Entertainment." In *Britton on Film: The Complete Criticism of Andrew Britton*, edited by Barry Keith Grant, 97–154. 1986. Detroit: Wayne State University Press, 2009.
Carroll, Noël. *The Philosophy of Horror, or Paradoxes of the Heart*. London: Routledge, 1990.
hooks, bell. "Eating the Other: Desire and Resistance." In *Black Looks: Race and Representation*, 21–39. Boston: South End Press, 1992.
Jameson, Fredric. *Postmodernism, or, the Cultural Logic of Late Capitalism*. Durham, NC: Duke University Press, 1991.
Jancovich, Mark. "General Introduction." In *Horror, The Film Reader*, 1–20. London: Routledge, 2001.

Mulvey, Laura. "Visual Pleasure and Narrative Cinema." *Screen* 16, no. 3 (Autumn 1975): 6–18.
Nowell, Richard. *Blood Money: A History of the First Teen Slasher Film Cycle*. New York: Continuum, 2011.
Nowell, Richard. "There's Gold in Them There Chills." In *Merchants of Menace: The Business of Horror Cinema*, edited by Richard Nowell, 1–10. New York: Bloomsbury, 2014.
Williams, Tony. *Hearths of Darkness: The Family in the American Horror Film*. 1996. Madison, NJ: Fairleigh Dickinson University Press, 2014.
Wood, Robin. "An Introduction to the American Horror Film." In *The American Nightmare: Essays on the Horror Film*, edited by Robin Wood and Richard Lippe, 7–28. Toronto: Festival of Festivals, 1979.
Wood, Robin. *Hollywood from Vietnam To Reagan*. 1986. New York: Columbia University Press, 2003.

3

Much Still Depends on Dinner: Cannibalism and Culinary Carnival in *Shaun of the Dead* and *Zombieland*

Sue Matheson

As Margaret Visser remarks in *Much Depends on Dinner*, "[W]e echo the preferences and the principles of our culture in the way we treat our food ... food shapes us and expresses us even more definitively than our furniture and houses."[1] "Food is 'everyday,'" she says, but it is "never just something to eat," because "[c]ivilization entails shaping, regulating, constraining, and dramatizing ourselves; we echo the preferences and the principles of our culture in the way we treat our food."[2] At the dinner table, Visser points out, the correct use of fork, knife, and spoon is "a valuable opportunity for a demonstration" of middle-class values—"that we have been Well Brought Up, and are therefore the kind of people who will unquestionably Do."[3] A meal is therefore "an artistic social construct, ordering the foodstuffs which comprise it into a complex dramatic whole, as a play organizes actions and words into component parts such as acts, scenes, speeches, dialogues, entrances, and exits, all in the sequences designed for them."[4] Dinner, above all, is a socially prescribed, communal event for the family: "those eating it will refrain from other pursuits while it is in progress. No one will knit, watch television, or read a newspaper. The possibility of physical violence of any sort will not even cross anyone's mind; and neither will such rudeness as leaving the table . . . absolutely everyone will adhere to a complex code of behavioral ethics called 'table manners'—a set of rules far too complex to discuss in detail here."[5]

In literature and film, food and meals also serve as compelling signifiers of cultural norms and values, agents by which complex relationships between the self/Other and life/death are negotiated. In zombie movies, food is a particularly important trope demarcating the boundaries of self and Other. As John Russo, cowriter of *Night of the Living Dead*, points out in *Scare Tactics*, he and George Romero presented zombies as "cannibals—eaters of human flesh"—to horrify their audiences.[6] Romero's shock schlock uses food to reveal the darker side of the American character. Overturning humanist assumptions about human nature, grotesque depictions of cannibalism in *Night of the Living Dead* (1968)—also known as *Night of the Flesh Eaters*— examine our anxieties of alienation and predation, while acts of cannibalism in *Dawn of the Dead* (1978) graphically demonstrate the social pollution that attends our participation in capitalism and rampant consumerism. Almost forty years later, consumerism remains a seminal concern of the zombie movie: zombies continue to prey on twentieth-century Americans who, in turn, are also insatiable consumers.

In the critical arena, foodways have always been recognized as an important motif in zombie movies. As Michael Newbury remarks:

[N]o genre is more routinely, even structurally, and disturbingly obsessed with food supply, food chains, and the question of who eats what or whom than the apocalyptic zombie movie. The dislodging of humans from their comfortable place atop the industrial food chain is, in the end, one of the central, even defining features of recent zombie films. In them, models of Western modernity necessarily become scavengers, hunters and gatherers, locavores on the landscape of a devastated consumerism emblematized crucially by the flotsam and jetsam of corporate junk and fast food. At the same time as humans who once had mass-produced food funneled toward them become scavengers, they also become food themselves.[7]

The relationship between food and family in the modern zombie comedy, however, has not been closely examined. This chapter remedies that—breaking new critical ground by investigating eating behaviors in Edgar Wright's *Shaun of the Dead* (2004), a critical and commercial success in the United Kingdom, and Ruben Fleischer's *Zombieland* (2009), the top grossing zombie film in the United States.[8] Both films celebrate and critique consumerism via comic inversions that signal the collapse of social order. They identify fast food and mindless eating as manifestations of that collapse, and subsequently present family bonding over food as a sign of order's restoration.

Culinary carnival

A British horror comedy written by Edgar Wright and Simon Pegg, *Shaun of the Dead* is the story of a middle-aged loser whose dull life is restricted to working at an electronics store, drinking at the local pub, and playing video games with his roommate (Nick Frost). Shaun's (Simon Pegg) life falls apart when his girlfriend Liz (Kate Ashfield) leaves him, but surviving a zombie apocalypse turns his geeky life around. Leading a small band of Survivors, Shaun regains Liz's respect despite numerous mishaps, and, after they are rescued by the British Army, the two resume their relationship. An American zombie comedy written by Rhett Reese and Paul Wernick, *Zombieland* follows the adventures of a college nerd, Columbus (Jesse Eisenberg), during a zombie apocalypse. Attempting to find a zombie-free sanctuary, Columbus teams up with three other survivors, Tallahassee (Woody Harrelson), Witchita (Emma Stone), and Little Rock (Abigail Breslin), on a road trip to California. Both Kyle Bishop and Nicholas Kelly attribute the success of these two films to the addition of humor to traditional zombie horror, or "splatstick" as Bishop calls it. Kelly points out that "the walking dead have changed from being used as foci for cultural contemplation to being used as figures for bloody fun and aggression."[9] Celebrating the grotesque and gory nature of human corporeality, "bloody fun" in both these films is Rabelaisian in its highly exaggerated, horrific, and comic portrayals of the human body and its attention to the body's primary need to ingest and digest food.

As Robert Stam remarks in *Subversive Pleasures: Bakhtin, Cultural Criticism, and Film*, Rabelaisian imagery is "intimately linked to the topos of the banquet, of the feast: virtually every page [in Rabelais's work] alludes to food and drink."[10] Rabelais's banquets playfully "undermine the norms of good sense and etiquette."[11] In *The Dialogic Imagination: Four Essays*, Mikhail Bakhtin points out that Rabelais's grotesque exaggerations of eating and drinking are designed to create awareness of social imbalance: Gargantua's and Pantagruel's gross gluttonies are graphically depicted in *Gargantua and Pantagruel*'s eating and drinking series that "at its positive pole . . . ends in nothing less than ideological enlightenment, the culture of eating and drinking, which is an essential feature of the new human image, a man who is harmonious and whole."[12] In *Shaun of the Dead* and *Zombieland*, "splatstick's" similarly gross depictions of zombies feasting on human flesh also are carnivalesque, expressing what Stam would recognize as "a positively corrosive force" that disrupts social norms and forms hierarchical distinctions and barriers, generates festive laughter, and ends up offering a new image of humanity.

Wright's zombie apocalypse graphically depicts the grotesquely material nature of the undead's insatiable, gargantuan appetites. In *Shaun of the Dead*, the zombies that trespass into the yards and gardens of their prey appear, at first, merely to be disorderly objects of fun.[13] "Look at her," Shaun sniggers to Ed while watching Mary (Nicola Cunningham), a grocery clerk who has become one of the undead, attempt to turn around in his backyard: "She is *so* drunk." Mary, however, is not a member of the "working dead," mindlessly and listlessly scanning purchases as a grocery store cashier; she is a dangerous predator with an insatiable, disordered craving for human flesh. Fast food junkies Shaun and Ed soon realize this to their dismay, once they themselves have become potential sources of food. Wright, however, inverts the horror of their discovery by informing the viewer through a presentation of Shaun's face framed in the circular opening where Mary's stomach should be. After Mary attacks them, Shaun and Ed begin to take the zombies much more seriously, even though the viewer cannot. The presence of the undead prompts Shaun to do what their fastidious roommate Pete (Peter Serafinowicz) has been asking them to for months—shut the front door.

Both *Shaun of the Dead* and *Zombieland* mark the passing of the cozy, if somewhat restrictive, lifestyle of the middle class, but they do not mourn it. Wright and Fleischer instead use gastric gaiety to transpose the social inversion of man's descent down the food chain (Figure 3.1). Their dystopias celebrate what Stam recognizes as "an alternative cosmovision characterized by the ludic undermining of all norms" in which "the carnivalesque principle abolishes hierarchies, levels of social classes, and creates another life free from conventional rules and restrictions."[14] In *Shaun of the Dead*, the sociocultural "low" hilariously becomes the "high" as civilization crumbles—Shaun becomes the head of his family when his stepfather Philip (Bill Nighy) turns into a zombie; Ed (the slacker) becomes a hero, offering to hold off the zombies in the cellar of the local pub so that his friend can escape being eaten. Wright uses humor to celebrate these and other social overturnings and reversals in the movie. Because "[f]ood shapes us even more definitively than our furniture or houses or utensils do,"[15] he comically anarchizes English foodways through Shaun's restive plan to drink tea or have a "nice cool pint" until the apocalypse "blows over"; attacks patriarchal authority when Shaun airs his problems with his father; privileging the lower bodily functions in a running joke about farting

FIGURE 3.1 *Shaun and Ed stop to have a snack after their encounter with Mary, the checkout clerk.*

as Ed breaks wind at inopportune and comically inappropriate moments (after his touching speech to Shaun in the cellar, for example).

In *Zombieland*, too, the low becomes the high. A hapless social recluse, Columbus finds himself elevated socially when he acquires not only the girlfriend he has always wanted but also a family to which to belong. As in *Shaun of the Dead*, *Zombieland* also privileges another important principle of human corporeality, the lower bodily stratum, emphasizing the act of elimination as well as ingestion. Columbus is always looking for a bathroom "to go number 2," and zombies, the new street people, root around in trashcans and dumpsters. Pacific Playland, the shuttered California amusement park that becomes the shared destination of Columbus and his companions and is the backdrop for the climax of the movie, is a sanctioned site for social inversion echoing that of the old-time carnival itself.

"Splatstick" humor also overturns and carnivalizes the body. As Bishop notes, it is used to exploit the human body and explore the body's abjection "through extreme violence, its physical pratfalls, and lots and lots of blood and gore."[16] In *Shaun of the Dead* and *Zombieland*, "splatstick" overturns horror tropes, making acts of cannibalism in these movies both appalling *and* humorous. In *Shaun of the Dead*, for example, Wright balances horror with humor by highlighting the absurdity of situations while leaving nothing to the imagination about the ghastly nature of what is going on. For example, while Shaun's friend David (Dylan Moran) is being eviscerated and dismembered by zombies outside The Winchester, his sausage-like intestines gobbled up and his head ripped off, Shaun and the others who attempt to save him by dragging him back into the pub succeed only in pulling his legs off. Jumping up, David's girlfriend Diane (Lucy Davis) rushes irrationally to the front door, still intent on rescuing him. Opening the door to disaster, she beats the undead with one of his severed limbs (a weapon more likely to attract than repel zombies) until she herself is devoured.

Ruben Fleischer favors extreme close-ups to record zombies devouring their victims and, in so doing, overturns the horrific. Exaggerating the act of eating human flesh, Fleischer's close-ups not only underscore the unbridled nature of the eating (a visual metaphor for America's societal problem with overconsumption), but also burlesques its gruesomeness on screen. At the beginning of *Zombieland*, Fleischer sets the tone of the film in a defining moment of grotesque social farce: violating cultural taboos and good manners, a Secret-Service-agent-turned-zombie tears a hunk of flesh from the buttocks of a news cameraman, but does not swallow his dripping mouthful. Noticing the camera, the zombie moves toward it, creating an extreme close-up, and lets the bloody hunk of meat drop from his mouth. Improbably using the camera as a mirror, he picks the shreds of flesh from between his teeth with his gore-stained fingers before giving an overamplified belch into the lens.

At first, Wright's and Fleischer's excessive use of blood and gore appears to be parodic—an attempt to top the zombie movie's gross-out tropes of carnivorous predator and human-as-foodstuff and to equate consumption with social dysfunction. As in *Dawn of the Dead*, the undead in *Zombieland* feast on the living, and the living render the undead unable to eat them by severing their heads from their bodies. As in *Dawn of the Dead*, the undead do not consume to sustain themselves: without need, they eat like gluttons. As such, the insatiable zombie is horrifyingly Other: an eating machine bereft of the sexual fascination of the Byronic vampire, the scientific curiosity that attends the werewolf, and the moral sensibility of the living hero or heroine. Eating mindlessly, zombies participate in one of the most fundamental forms of carnival culture, the *festa stultorum* or feast of fools.[17]

"Splatstick's" over-the-top treatments of the zombie movie's feast of fools grounds the consumption of human flesh and blood in the secular. As Robert Stam points out, cannibalism, as a metaphor, has often been the " 'name of the other,' the ultimate marker of difference in a coded opposition of light/dark, rational/irrational, civilized/savage."[18] Human beings have always tended to be "touchy about cannibalism," Visser says. "[T]hey are nauseated by the thought of eating (or, of course, being eaten by) anyone they know."[19] Indeed, the very idea of cannibalism—the notion that human beings might become food, and eaters of each other—is Other, one of the oldest and most frightening of taboos, "carefully walled off from ordinary consideration and discourse."[20] Wright and Fleischer, however, comically invert the horror of situations in which human beings either become food or attempt to escape becoming dinner by exaggerating further the unrestrained eating habits of the undead. In *Zombieland*, Columbus reels from the grotesque spectacle of a zombie gorging itself on a corpse that is lying on the highway. As the gore-smeared woman first lifts and then sucks a handful of a bloody colon out of the man's body, he remarks to Tallahassee: "Oh my God, it makes you sick." At a loss for words to describe the grotesque spectacle taking place in front of him, Columbus continues: "It makes you think if you can go back to the way things were right now you know you'd be in the back yard, you know, trying to catch fireflies but instead *this*."[21] As the zombie continues her feast, loudly slurping marrow out of what appears to be part of a femur, what should be horrifying becomes humorous. The exaggerated sounds of the woman munching and crunching make what should be a dehumanizing and unappetizing activity into something that makes Tallahassee simultaneously angry and hungry—in short, like a zombie. Braining the zombie by opening his truck door as he drives by her, the "hongry" Tallahassee tells Columbus that he is craving fast food, "Look, whatever you have waiting for you . . . I promise you it ain't any prettier than our friend here enjoying her *Manwich*."[22]

Fast food/mindless eating

References to fast food abound in *Shaun of the Dead* and *Zombieland* and explain the apocalypse as, in Columbus's words, it goes from "bad to total shitstorm." The least polite and decorous form of dining in the twenty-first century, fast food is identified, in *Zombieland*, as having signaled the beginning of the end of human civilization. The virus that created the running dead was first detected in an individual who ate a contaminated burger at a fast food franchise, the Gas 'n' Gulp. As the name of this gas station convenience store suggests, the comestibles found in it occupy the lowest rung of the fast food ladder. They are eatables whose salt and sugar ratios are designed to stimulate rather than suppress the appetite. Their lack of fiber further encourages gluttony, for only one of these items cannot satisfy hunger. In

Zombieland, it is not surprising that unrestrained and unsatisfied appetite caused society to collapse. As Columbus walks down an abandoned highway strewn with wrecked vehicles, he outlines the trajectory of the plague of the twenty-first century as being anything but civilized: "mad cow became mad person became mad zombie," he says. "It's a fast acting virus that left you with a swollen brain, a raging fever, and made you hateful, violent, and gave you a really, really bad case of the munchies." As his story continues, it becomes apparent that people have become prey, zombies having supplanted them in the food chain. As zombies became alpha predators, the pace of life accelerated. The first victims of the apocalypse were the "Fatties"—the weak, the slow, and the vulnerable. After the slowest are eaten, food for zombies becomes speedier—consumers on the run, zombies in search of a meal are depicted not running but "sprinting" after their dinners. His strategies for survival, which include "cardio" and always knowing where to exit, are those of prey animals. America, Columbus says, is no longer America—"there are no people here. This is the United States of Zombieland." Ravenous blood-smeared zombies roam city streets like savage beasts: even before the opening credits have rolled, they chase and attack the living, snapping and snarling like lions (and other carnivores)—one zombie gallops down a football field after an overweight man, downing his prey at the thirty-three yard line; a second predator, just returned from the dead, gnaws at a woman's ankle; a third wriggles under the door of a bathroom stall to eviscerate the occupant. Those unlucky enough to be caught and eaten by zombies, Columbus says, become a "Human Happy Meal."

Notably, the intersection of fast food and social collapse in *Zombieland* is carefully identified before the contaminated burger at the Gas 'n' Gulp was devoured and zombies appeared on the streets of America. Before the zombie apocalypse, fast food was a normal, everyday part of the single lifestyle. A flashback shows Columbus at his computer on a Friday night during a "third straight week indoors," playing World of Warcraft amid a leaning tower of pizza boxes and drinking Code Red Mountain Dew. In *Shaun of the Dead*, Shaun and Ed are also bachelors who live like shut-ins, playing video games and glutting themselves on delivery pizzas and pub snacks. Distinguishing between Columbus, Shaun, and Ed's eating behaviors and those of the zombies who pursue them is therefore a matter of degree, not kind. It was simply a matter of luck that Columbus, living on fast food, did not happen to eat the Gas 'n' Gulp's contaminated burger himself. Alone in his apartment, Columbus does not perform the social niceties of dining, eating without cutlery and slopping Mountain Dew on his clothing as he attempts to drink from a paper cup while playing a video game. Ironically, it is Columbus's irritable bowel syndrome that saves him from the corpulence that such a lifestyle generates. Aptly, when Tallahassee views the bodies of the "fat" zombies scattered on the floor in the aisles at Blaine's Grocery, he comments: "Wow, these fellas really let themselves go." Fast food gluttons, the zombies have been feasting at the grocery store. Although they have gorged themselves on Human Happy Meals, they are unable to resist the demands of their alimentary canals when Tallahassee appears and immediately attack him. Grossly overweight, these zombies are outstanding corporeal symbols of consumer culture, markers of the orality and cornucopian gluttony that Stam notes attends the carnivalesque.[23]

Situated opposite polite prohibitions, Columbus's and Tallahassee's digestive needs and appetites shape, regulate, constrain, and dramatize their actions. A slave to his colon, Columbus is inordinately interested in bathrooms. Tallahassee is also driven by his "gut feelings": as he travels the only thing that interests him "more than killing Zombies [is] finding a Twinkie." Tallahassee's need to devour the last Twinkie in America is much more than a simple craving to satisfy a sweet tooth. As Columbus points out, there is something about a Twinkie that reminds Tallahassee of "a time not so long ago when times were simple . . . it was like if he had a taste of that comforting childhood treat, the world would become innocent again, and everything would return to normal." Ironically, Tallahassee's search for normality focuses upon one of the most highly processed and unnatural foodstuffs to be found on the shelves of grocery stores. Full of refined sugar, refined flour, additives and fixers, the Twinkie is a nutritionist's nightmare, a food so filled with monoglycerides, diglycerides, emulsifiers, and sodium stearoyl lactylate and so dissociated from the stuff of which it is made that it has lost its way from farm to fork.

When carnival removes the barrier between the farm and the fork, dining becomes a savage affair—a terrifying violation of social norms. As Visser points out, one of the greatest ironies of our processing and refining of foodstuffs is our need to dissociate ourselves from the animals that we want to eat: "many of us prefer not to be acquainted with them beforehand," Visser says. "We generally avoid actually killing what we eat ourselves, and do everything we can to prevent ourselves from realizing that a death has occurred at all."[24] For the living, preparing food to be eaten is an aggressive, messy activity. "Violence after all is necessary if any organism is to ingest another," Visser says. "Animals are murdered to produce meat; vegetables are torn up, peeled and chopped; most of what we eat is treated with fire; and chewing is designed remorselessly to finish what killing and cooking began. People naturally prefer that none of this should happen to them."[25] The zombies, however, have no need to be dissociated from their food. Killing what they eat and even eating their victims before they are dead, they erase the distance between diner and dinner, the cooked and the raw. As Simon Pegg (who plays Shaun) points out, "[T]he zombie represents a number of our deeper insecurities. The fear that deep down, we may be little more than animals, concerned only with appetite."[26]

In *Zombieland*, ingesting a Twinkie incongruously becomes the measure of normative behavior, a means by which one may confirm one's humanity. Consisting mostly of flour and sugar, Twinkies are completely divorced from the violence of preparing a meal—so highly processed that they melt in one's mouth. Dressed in cowboy boots, a snakeskin jacket, and a leather cowboy hat, Tallahassee may situate himself at the top of the food chain—modeling himself after NASCAR champion Dale "The Intimidator" Earnhardt by painting a large number three on the doors of his truck—but the viewer knows that, like a Twinkie, he really has a soft center. At heart a gentle soul, Tallahassee, who loves puppies and children, is even unable to eat Sno Balls because of the chewy consistency of their coconut coating. Ironically, Tallahassee's comic opposite, Columbus, a mild-mannered misandrist more afraid of clowns than zombies, enjoys eating Sno Balls because of their texture. Supersensitive, Columbus has always been aware of the violence underpinning life. He avoided people "like they were zombies before they were zombies." Knowing that "zombies aren't the most loveable creatures," he therefore bears no ill will toward his former neighbor (Amber Heard) who, after a frightening encounter with a zombie on the opening night of the apocalypse, first turns to him for comfort and then (having become zombified herself) tries to kill him. After braining her with the lid of his toilet tank, he merely remarks, "See? You can't trust anyone. The first girl I let into my life, and she tries to eat me."

In *Shaun of the Dead* and *Zombieland*, how one eats is as important as what one eats. Because the act of dining signifies social norms and forms, the prohibitions of the polite table distinguish the living from the ravenous hordes of the undead that mindlessly consume whomever they encounter and overwhelm. After all, table manners or the lack thereof are social agents by which complex relationships between self/Other are negotiated via social barriers and prohibitions. As Stam points out, in carnival good manners "are never simply good manners; the social control of bodily functions such as eating, yawning, spitting, and touching serves to repress "socially undesirable impulses or inclinations."[27] Having discarded whatever table manners they had when living, the undead are instantly recognizable as social undesirables. In *Night of the Living Dead*, they eat without restraint. Lacking even the most basic of social graces, they rip apart their middle-class victims as one would a lobster. In the scene in which they picnic on Tom's and Judy's body parts after their truck explodes, the zombies pick up dismembered human limbs and eat them like fried chicken legs. In *Shaun of the Dead*, they continue to feast on the living without the social mechanisms of polite conversation, table napkins, and knives and forks. What should be meals are instead, mayhem, as they dismember their meals with their hands and teeth.

As Visser remarks, human society cannot exist without table manners, which "are as old as human society itself."[28] It is the "active sharing of food—not consuming all of the food we find on the spot, but carrying some back home and then doling it systematically out—that is the root of what makes us different from animals."[29] Zombies, of course, do not share food with one another. Thus, the presence of fast food, meant to be eaten with one's hands thereby diminishing the need for table manners, becomes another signifier of social collapse in zombie movies. In *Shaun of the Dead* and *Zombieland*, however, it seems that only zombies, who also eat with their mouths open, drop food out of their mouths, eat with their hands, do not wait to be served, and never sit at a table, have time to stop and dine. The living, always on the move, usually have to eat while walking. Their comestibles are necessarily—pardon the pun—finger foods, like Tallahassee's, designed to be eaten on the run. At The Winchester, David complains that Shaun expects them to be saved "by nibbles": by "our Mini-Cheddars, our Twiglets . . . Hog Lumps," encased in cellophane wrappers. All Shaun can offer as his friends shelter at a table in The Winchester to wait out the apocalypse is "a peanut." During their adventures, kitchens are not used to cook meals. But even before the apocalypse truly begins, society is seen to be on the downturn. The only person to eat in a kitchen before going to work, Shaun devours only a piece of toast while standing up. Even Barbara (Penelope Wilton), Shaun's mother, who always seems to be busy in her kitchen when she is seen at home and attempts to bond with her son by feeding him, serves her son fast food when he comes to visit—she offers him sandwiches.

Meals and family bonding

The importance of dinner, home-cooked or otherwise, being presented as a sit-down meal, to which guests are invited, lies in its imposition of harmony, order, and decorum. Meals separate the low from the high by distinguishing between those who dine at the table from those who do not, and by grounding individuals in their social and cultural traditions. As Visser points out, food is a form of ritual relaxation (a "break" in the working day), our chance to choose companions and talk to them, the excuse to recreate our humanity as well as our strength, and to renew our relationships.[30] Thus Liz, who wants to renew her rapport with Shaun, attempts to do this by asking him to eat a meal with her. In the movie's opening scene, she "wants to live a little and do interesting stuff," like dining at a fine restaurant. Shaun, however, is unable to conceive of eating anywhere but at The Winchester. Because he is unable to "set aside quality time" to eat with Liz or take her to a formal meal at his parents' home, their relationship crumbles.

Visser remarks that "[f]amilies meet for meals . . . It is often part of a society's code of manners never to eat between meals, so that not only meals, but also the spaces between them, are controlled. This turns every shared family dinner into a mini-feast or festival, so that it can, like a feast, celebrate both the interconnectedness and the self-control of the group's members."[31] At the conclusion of *Shaun of the Dead*, the interconnectedness and self-control associated with the family dinner has been firmly established. When Shaun visits the garden shed to see Ed before leaving for the pub, Ed, who has become a zombie, exercises self-restraint and refrains from biting him. By not eating between meals, the two friends are able to carry on in their new relationship as they did before the apocalypse, amicably playing video games. Moreover, a new family unit that returns Shaun and Liz to their traditional roots has also been created. Together at last, the lovers plan an evening around their dinner—a roast waiting for them at their table on their return from The Winchester. Dinner, featuring a roast as the principal meal of the day, has "a broadly British structure," emblematic of cozy domesticity.[32]

The importance of meals as signifiers of companionship and family is even more apparent in *Zombieland*. Columbus, who has always wanted to be part of a "cool functional family," is shown in flashbacks eating alone, secluded in his apartment. Later, as he travels with Tallahassee, Wichita, and Little Rock to Pacific Playland, they do not stop to share a meal—or even collect food from Blaine's Grocery, where one would expect them at the very least to stock up on canned goods. Until they reach the amusement park, theirs are utility friendships, made out of expediency and easily ended. Unable to satisfy his appetites, Tallahassee simply refuses to eat any substitutes until he finds that last Twinkie (Figure 3.2). Little Rock is only interested in finding "sugarless gum," and Columbus and Wichita do not express the desire to eat at all. In Hollywood, when Bill Murray offers his guests some West Coast hospitality, they do not sit down to dinner but to a hookah pipe. Columbus, Tallahassee, Wichita, and Little Rock do not share meals with one another because they do not trust each other. Columbus shares a bottle of wine with

FIGURE 3.2 *Columbus and Tallahassee go shopping for Twinkies at Blaine's Grocery.*

Wichita and a bowl of popcorn with Little Rock after Murray dies, but they do not bond. Instead, the girls drive off (as they have before) with Tallahassee's truck and weapons. It is only when Little Rock finally shares food with Tallahassee, throwing him the last Twinkie in America, that Columbus realizes that he and all his traveling companions have become what he has always dreamt of being a part of—a family—even though that family subsists entirely on fast food.

With this in mind, it seems that consumer relations have changed considerably from those found in horror films of the 1970s when cannibalism emblematized "the logical end of human relations under capitalism."[33] Unlike Romero's movies, which break food taboos in order to locate and critique social imbalance, *Shaun of the Dead* and *Zombieland* overturn the ghastly gastronomy of their genre and celebrate the vagaries of consumerism, overindulgence, and social ennui of middle-class life to advance their critiques of gross consumerism. While carnival ends in *Shaun of the Dead* and *Zombieland*, laughter affirms human beings and reinstates them at the top of the food chain. As Stam points out, laughter, being the goal as well as the means of knowledge, has cognitive value: "[l]aughter demolishes fear and piety before an object, before a world, making of it an object of familiar contact and thus clearing the ground for an absolutely free investigation of it."[34] In both movies, the interplay between the body and world in the ingestion and expulsion of food celebrates and critiques consumer lifestyles by linking consumerism with the grotesque. In the twenty-first century, fast food may have become a social custom—as American as apple pie and as British as fish and chips—but in *Shaun of the Dead* and *Zombieland*, much still depends upon dinner.

Notes

1. Margaret Visser, *Much Depends on Dinner: The Extraordinary History and Mythology, Allure and Obsessions, Perils and Taboos, of an Ordinary Meal* (Toronto: McClelland & Stewart, 1986), 12.
2. Ibid.
3. Ibid., 20.
4. Ibid., 14.
5. Ibid., 15.
6. John Russo, *Scare Tactics: The Art, Craft, and Trade Secrets of Writing, Producing, and Directing Chillers and Thrillers* (New York: Dell, 1992), 11.
7. Michael Newbury, "Fast Zombie/Slow Zombie: Food Writing, Horror Movies, and Agribusiness Apocalypse." *American Literary History* 24, no. 1 (Spring 2012): 87.
8. According to Box Office Mojo, *Shaun of the Dead* has grossed $16.5 million worldwide since its opening weekend, and *Zombieland*'s lifetime gross currently stands at $102 million. See http://www.boxofficemojo.com/movies/?id=shaunofthedead.htm (accessed June 9, 2016) and http://www.boxofficemojo.com/movies/?id=zombieland.htm (accessed June 9, 2016).
9. Kyle Bishop, "Vacationing in *Zombieland*: The Classical Functions of the Modern Zombie Comedy," *Journal of the Fantastic in the Arts* 22, no. 1 (2011): 30; Nicolas M. Kelly, "Zombies Go to the Amusement Park: Entertainment, Violence and the Twenty First Century Zombie in *Zombieland* and Left 4 Dead 2." *Iowa Journal of Culture Studies* 14 (Spring 2013): 84.
10. Robert Stam, *Subversive Pleasures: Bakhtin, Cultural Criticism, and Film* (Baltimore, MD: Johns Hopkins University Press, 1989), 87.
11. Ibid.
12. Mikhail Bakhtin, *The Dialogic Imagination: Four Essays*, ed. Michael Holquist, trans. Caryl Emerson and Michael Holquist (Austin: University of Texas Press, 1981), 186–7.
13. Kelly, "Zombies Go to the Amusement Park," 84.
14. Stam, *Subversive Pleasures*, 86.
15. Visser, *Much Depends on Dinner*," 12.
16. Bishop, "Vacationing in *Zombieland*," 31.
17. The Feast of Fools, held annually on January 1, was a popular festival during the Middle Ages, which burlesqued Christian morality and worship.
18. Stam, *Subversive Pleasures*, 125.
19. Visser, *Much Depends on Dinner*, 144.
20. Margaret Visser, *The Rituals of Dinner: The Origins, Evolution, Eccentricities, and Meaning of Table Manners* (New York: HarperCollins, 2008), 8.
21. *Zombieland*; italics added.

22 Ibid.; italics added.
23 Stam, *Subversive Pleasures*, 97.
24 Visser, *Much Depends on Dinner*, 144.
25 Visser, *Rituals of Dinner*, 8.
26 Quoted in Kyle Bishop, "Raising the Dead: Unearthing the Literary Origins of Zombie Cinema." *Journal of Popular Film and Television* 33, no. 4 (Winter 2006): 204.
27 Stam, *Subversive Pleasures*, 114.
28 Visser, *Much Depends on Dinner*, 6.
29 Ibid.
30 Ibid., 30.
31 Ibid., 29
32 Ibid., 15.
33 Robin Wood, "An Introduction to the American Horror Film," in *Planks of Reason: Essays on the Horror Film*, ed. Barry Keith Grant, 107–41 (Metuchen, NJ: Scarecrow Press, 1984), 189.
34 See Stam, *Subversive Pleasures*, 120; and Bakhtin, *The Dialogic Imagination*, 23.

Bibliography

Bakhtin, Mikhail. *The Dialogic Imagination: Four Essays*. Edited by Michael Holquist. Translated by Caryl Emerson and Michael Holquist. Austin: University of Texas Press, 1981.
Bishop, Kyle. "Raising the Dead: Unearthing the Literary Origins of Zombie Cinema." *Journal of Popular Film and Television* 33, no. 4 (Winter 2006): 196–205.
Bishop, Kyle. "Vacationing in *Zombieland*: The Classical Functions of the Modern Zombie Comedy." *Journal of the Fantastic in the Arts* 22, no. 1 (2011): 24–38.
Kelly, Nicolas M. "Zombies Go to the Amusement Park: Entertainment, Violence and the Twenty First Century Zombie in *Zombieland* and Left 4 Dead 2." *Iowa Journal of Culture Studies* 14 (Spring 2013): 83–105.
Newbury, Michael. "Fast Zombie/Slow Zombie: Food Writing, Horror Movies, and Agribusiness Apocalypse." *American Literary History* 24, no. 1 (Spring 2012): 87–114.
Russo, John. *Scare Tactics: The Art, Craft, and Trade Secrets of Writing, Producing, and Directing Chillers and Thrillers*. New York: Dell, 1992.
Shaun of the Dead. Directed by Edgar Wright. 2004. DVD. Universal City, CA: Focus Features, 2013.
Stam, Robert. *Subversive Pleasures: Bakhtin, Cultural Criticism, and Film*. Baltimore, MD: Johns Hopkins University Press, 1989.
Visser, Margaret. *Much Depends on Dinner: The Extraordinary History and Mythology, Allure and Obsessions, Perils and Taboos, of an Ordinary Meal*. Toronto: McClelland & Stewart, 1986.

Visser, Margaret. *The Rituals of Dinner: The Origins, Evolution, Eccentricities, and Meaning of Table Manners*. New York: HarperCollins, 2008.
Wood, Robin. "An Introduction to the American Horror Film." In *Planks of Reason: Essays on the Horror Film*, edited by Barry Keith Grant, 107–41. Metuchen, NJ: Scarecrow Press, 1984.
Zombieland. Directed by Ruben Fleischer. 2009. DVD. Culver City, CA: Sony Home Pictures Entertainment, 2010.

4

Dumplings: The Commodification of Cannibalism and the Liminal Condition of Consumption

Alex Pinar and Salvador Jiminez Murguia

While international cinema is riddled with horror films exploring issues of food consumption and the taboos associated with what can and cannot be eaten—all in the service of implicitly advancing political and social commentary about a world saturated with the ironies of capitalism—no other film out of Asia has accomplished as much within the genre as *Dumplings*, a 2004 Hong Kong horror movie directed by Fruit Chan.

Originally one of three short segments in an anthology-style film titled *Three . . . Extremes* (2004), *Dumplings* tells the story of a woman intent on regaining her youth by consuming an illicit Chinese dumpling stuffed with unborn fetuses.[1] Like the other two filmmakers involved in the *Three . . . Extremes* project, Chan is known for incorporating critical interpretations of social issues in his films—often alluding to political anxieties and identity crises occasioned by the British transfer of Hong Kong's sovereignty to China in 1997.[2] Even in comparison to Chan's prior works, however, *Dumplings* is an unusual, perhaps atypical, horror movie: it does not adhere to the conventions of films typically considered to be "Asian Horror" or "Asian Extreme,"[3] wherein storylines are filled with hauntings, illicit schoolgirl romances, and folkloric monsters run amok.[4] Instead of supernatural creatures, Chan offers an aesthetically striking cinematography, a colorfully innovative mise-en-scène, and a realistic, but ultimately horrific, plot couched within the cultural underpinnings of Chinese society. In an interview with Boris Trbic in 2005, Chan suggests that *Dumplings*' plot introduces social criticism by playing on the ironies of traditional Chinese medicine, especially beliefs that consuming certain animal organs—the liver, the brain, or the blood, for example—can be particularly beneficial to the equivalent parts of the human body. A narrow gulf separates such belief in the healing power of "unusual" foods from belief in socially accepted forms of cannibalism, and *Dumplings* steps across it.

The film

The film's storyline follows three main characters and their complex interrelationships: "Aunt Mei" (Bai Ling), her client Mrs. Li (Miriam Yeung), and Mr. Li (Tony Leung Ka-Fai). Aunt Mei is a retired medical doctor in her sixties with a checkered past. As a former gynecologist and member of the Red Army Guard of the Communist Party, Mei's job was to conduct abortions in mainland China. Her past behind her, Mei is now a migrant living in one of Hong Kong's more dilapidated public housing projects. Crossing the border from Hong Kong to China regularly, she makes her living by illegally acquiring human fetuses from her former clinic and preparing them as filling for her "special" dumplings (Figure 4.1).

FIGURE 4.1 *Aunt Mei acquires fetuses for her dumplings at a clinic where she used to work.*

Mrs. Li, a former famous TV soap opera actress struggling to come to terms with getting older, is desperate to regain her youth. After fifteen years of marriage, she anguishes over the fact that her husband is no longer interested in her, as he philanders about with younger women. A successful and wealthy businessman, Mr. Li is a quintessential representative of Hong Kong's economic power, placating his wife's yearning for attention by writing her checks for large sums of money. In an attempt to win back her husband, Mrs. Li approaches Mei for help and indulges in the dumplings. Soon, she is returning more and more frequently for additional servings—not unlike a drug addict—as her patience runs thin and her suspicions increase about what she believes to be her husband's multiple affairs. Seeing no immediate results, Mrs. Li's frustration mounts, driving her to seek more drastic measures. Mei, who is all too willing to accommodate her, explains that faster results can be achieved by consuming fetuses in more advanced stages of development, and promises to find one for her.

Shortly afterward, Mei receives a visit from a mother (Mi Mi Lee) and her daughter "Kate" (Miki Yeung), a fifteen-year-old who has been raped by her father and is five months pregnant. Kate and her mother beg Mei for an abortion, and although she initially declines their request, Mei realizes the potential profit she may receive from Mrs. Li if she acquires a five-month-old fetus, and subsequently agrees to perform the operation. Once the abortion is complete and the dumplings prepared, Mrs. Li, although initially repulsed, consumes them, and receives nearly instant results. Wasting no time, she seeks out Mr. Li, and the change in her appearance brought about by the consumption of the potent dumplings has an immediate effect. Their relationship rekindled, they engage in open displays of affection and have passionate sex.

Startled (though pleased) by the changes in his wife and curious about how they came about, Mr. Li secretly investigates her actions. Learning the secrets of the dumplings, he then solicits Mei's assistance in helping him to regain his own youth. Agreeing to help Mr. Li, Mei sees an opportunity for greater fortune, and during their consultation, she seduces him, commencing what becomes a new sexual affair. No longer beholden to Mrs. Li's requests, Mei refuses her any further assistance.

Soon Mrs. Li learns that Mr. Li's girlfriend is pregnant with his child and intends to carry the pregnancy to term. Without Mei and her dumplings, Mrs. Li panics, imagining her husband with a young wife and newborn child. Knowing she will receive no further help from Mei and desperate to continue recapturing her youth, she meets with Mr. Li's girlfriend, offering up an enormous sum of money in exchange for aborting the baby. After some negotiation, the young woman agrees and arranges to have the abortion performed. Taking custody of the unborn fetus, Mrs. Li proceeds to cook the dumplings herself. In the final scenes, she is depicted in her lavish kitchen, preparing to slice the meat, eagerly anticipating her newfound youth.[5]

Reception and interpretation

Dumplings was generally well received, even earning Bai Ling an award for Best Supporting Actress at the 2005 Hong Kong Film Awards. Film industry critics and scholars were particularly taken with the film, penning numerous critical reviews and articulating a host of interpretations about its significance. The vast majority of these interpretations can be situated between two analytical camps: analyses of postfeminist themes on one hand, and of allegorical representations of the transformative relationship between China and Hong Kong on the other.

The postfeminist depictions of Aunt Mei and Mrs. Li invoked by the former focus on symbolic references to the transition from the principles of the Cultural Revolution to those of a mixed economy—a transition filled with the materialist contradictions of the feminism of yesteryear. Indicative of this is the way in which Aunt Mei takes advantage of Mrs. Li's desperation, capitalizing on her vulnerabilities and solidifying a revenue stream that operates on an insatiable desire to meet unachievable standards of beauty. Mei recognizes that Mrs. Li's insecurities are generated by a false consciousness and a patriarchal hegemony that equates a woman's worth with her youthfulness and beauty. Rather than form a sisterly bond with her, however, she chooses to exploit Mrs. Li for personal gain instead. As Johnston suggests, "[T]here is a female perspective in that situation, post-feministic rather than feminist, as there is definitely no female solidarity on display."[6]

The two female protagonists are, to be sure, squarely individualistic, but the extent to which their individual ambitions override their shared identity as women is only part of the postfeminist analysis of the film. *Dumplings* pays equal attention to the rise of new, market-driven economy, and is rife with examples of the pursuit of wealth and affluence. Stemming the aging process is not, for Mrs. Li, only an issue of vanity or pride; it is also a way of protecting her financial well-being.[7] Her now-fading relationship with her wealthy husband represents security to her, in the wake of her already faded career as an actress, and she is determined to preserve it at any cost.

More than *just* economic security is at stake, however: Mrs. Li is highly materialistic, seeking all of the superficial amenities associated with the illusions of consumer culture. The other principal characters echo this focus on the superficiality and materialism created by the new economy. Mr. Li, it is implied, sees his wife more as a possession than a person: having married her when she was young, beautiful, and famous, he discards her both romantically and socially as she ages. Upon discovering Aunt Mei's secret, his immediate thought is of how (through her dumplings) to buy back his own fading youth and sexual potency. Aunt Mei, a successful neoliberal predator who has forgotten the socialist ideology and adapted to the capitalist ethos of competition, is more than willing to exploit her fellow citizens. Even she, however, is not immune to the allure of her product, noting enigmatically that she is older than she looks.

Analyses concerned with national identity and cultural transformation, however, focus on the allegorical significance of Chan's work in the wake of the 1997 transfer of Hong Kong's sovereignty from the United Kingdom to China.[8] This transfer had a substantial impact on all forms of cultural expression, and among Chan's productions, the use of fatalistic themes is said to "signify the need to turn over a new leaf when Hong Kong re-entered China's political and cultural realities."[9] The incorporation of cannibalism has also been read as a metaphor for designating China as an antiquated and primitive homeland of folk beliefs and passé ideologies, vis-à-vis Hong Kong's more modern market-oriented society. Focusing on Chan's multiple uses of scenes depicting Aunt Mei's border crossings from China to Hong Kong, Lu notes:

> This repeated scene has no other function but to emphasize the northern origin of her cannibalistic practice. Cannibalism has originated from the north, is carried by a northerner, and is expressed in the exemplary northern culinary fashion, dumplings, as the title indicates. Furthermore, Mei's past career as an abortionist closely associates her current dumpling making to China's politics through its well-known one-child policy.[10]

Chan himself emphasizes the lore surrounding the medicinal benefits of various cannibalistic acts in China. As he explains in an interview with *Bright Lights Film Journal*,

> The film is related to popular beliefs in South China. There, some people still believe that if you eat liver, your liver function will improve, if you drink blood—animal, of course—your blood will improve. Gall bladder is good against cough, monkey brain is good for brain, and a fetus can, some believe, give permanent youth to those who eat them.[11]

Chan's comments eerily add to the historical accounts of cannibalism in China recorded among the well-known scholarship of Donald Sutton and Yi Zheng, who argue that the large-scale acts of cannibalism that occurred near the end of the Cultural Revolution followed a custom with its own "political and cultural logic" as a systematized, politicized "ritual of struggle" carried out by individuals from all walks of life.[12]

It is little wonder, then, that cannibalism is a frequent trope in literature, cinema, and other cultural expressions across all modern regions of China, Hong Kong, and Taiwan. According to Rojas, for example, cannibalism is a feature "grounded on a complex hermeneutics of identity," frequently used as a metaphor for the self-destructive tendencies of contemporary Chinese society.[13] Hong Kong cinema, in particular, is rife with cannibalistic references, as Lu explains: "Whether crude or elegant, mad or calculating, Hong Kong horror seems obsessed with cannibalism. The highly competitive capitalism in Hong Kong has become a man-eating monster, if we borrow a Marxist metaphor."[14]

This social-symbolic significance aside, cannibalism is nothing if not monstrous, and so inextricably linked to the horror genre—evoking anxiety and revulsion at its violation of moral constructs against humans consuming other humans. In *Dumplings*, Chan uses this sense of horror to challenge viewers' everyday assumptions about moral, and perhaps ethical, behaviors of consumption. Diet, though nominally an individual decision, is in fact subject to ongoing social scrutiny and judgment. The foods that an individual chooses to consume in order to enhance their quality of life, the quantities in which they are consumed, and the motives for their consumption are—particularly if they depart from cultural norms—subject to public disapproval or outright censure. Cannibalism illustrates this process at its most extreme: The mere mention of the act, let alone serious discussion or actual practice of it, is sufficient to provoke expressions of horror and revulsion. The consumption of human flesh is a taboo so strong that Western societies countenance its violation only under extreme circumstances—as an alternative to death by starvation, when no other option exists—and then only reluctantly and with distaste. The consumption of human fetuses for the sake of maintaining youth troubles these sharply drawn distinctions on two fronts. It raises questions about whether an unborn fetus is human (making its consumption cannibalistic) or less-than-human (placing it in the same category as "unusual" animal parts), and whether—if it *can* be consumed—doing so in order to preserve youth is as legitimate as doing so in order to preserve health. Chan threads such questions throughout *Dumplings*, but does not answer them, instead leaving them, with all of their uncertainties, for his audience to interpret.

The consumption of human fetuses is, by its nature, calculated to provoke horror in the film's viewers. Chan, however, accentuates that sense of horror—and the effectiveness of *Dumplings* as a horror film—through his handling of two key elements of the plot. The first is the anxiety associated with cannibalism itself—anxiety intensified by the audience's growing familiarity with the source of the "special" ingredients that fill Mrs. Li's dumplings. As fetuses from an anonymous mainland clinic give way to the fetuses of identifiable characters, and fetuses terminated for unknown reasons give way (in the final instance) to fetuses terminated in exchange for cash, the audience becomes more and more deeply immersed in the horrific act. The second is the audacity with which the film normalizes this horror, reducing it (on screen) to banal scenes of preparing, filling, cooking, and eating dumplings, and (in the characters' world) to a series of commercial transactions remarkable only for the amount of money that changes hands. Each of the principal characters—first Aunt Mei, then Mrs. Li, and finally Mr. Li and his pregnant mistress—is drawn, some willingly and others after initial resistance, into a system where treating unborn fetuses as a commercially marketable ingredient is considered normal.

These two themes are mediated by notions of both fear and morbid curiosity—two seemingly opposite ends of an emotional experience bound to horror. The audience, even if, like Mrs. Li, initially repulsed by the sight and the thought of the reality behind the "special" dumplings, is drawn inexorably back to Aunt Mei's kitchen (Figure 4.2). Youth is the root of the appeal for them, as it is for Mrs. Li. Their own may not be at stake (as hers is), but Mrs. Li's seemingly magical transformation, and the contrast between Aunt Mei's age and her vigorous, conspicuously sexual appearance, exert their

FIGURE 4.2 *Mrs. Li eagerly consumes the special dumplings in order to regain her youth.*

own fascination. The temptation to look and keep looking exists, however, in tension with fear of what might be revealed if we do, and fascination coexists with loathing that we *are* fascinated, creating a precarious tone that lingers throughout the film.

This tension between fear and fascination also operates on another, deeper level in Chan's film. Viewers experiencing its portrayals of cannibalism may be repulsed by images of the characters consuming unborn fetuses, but are presumably not unaware of, or even averse to, thoughts of recapturing the vitality of their youth or the lore related to means of doing so. As Lu notes, "Chan's usual documentary style reinforces the realism and normalcy of cannibalism as if all of us could at any moment have participated in it if the opportunity were presented."[15]

Commodification of cannibalism and the liminal condition of consumption

Cannibalism, as it is central to this film, is no simple or inconsequential phenomenon; complex and multifaceted, intraspecies consumption is manifested in a variety of different ways. Lindenbaum's survey of anthropological typologies of cannibalism compiles extensive and diverse examples of the practice that extend well beyond the mere popular image of humans feasting on other humans out of either necessity or even aggression.[16] According to Lindenbaum, contemporary anthropological typologies organize cannibalism into two broad categories: "endocannibalism" and "exocannibalism."[17] In the former, cannibalism occurs within a group of individuals that share common cultural attributes; typically the consumption of a group member's body parts during funerary rituals as an act of respect, appreciation, or affection. In the latter, cannibalism occurs outside of such a grouping as an act of belligerence, commonly executed during, or after, battle. Although there are certainly acts of cannibalism that test the boundaries of these categories, the vast majority can be situated within one or the other. The form of cannibalism Chan features in *Dumplings*, however, is a rather peculiar exception to this classificatory framework, as it fails to fit neatly into either of them.

The dumplings stuffed with unborn fetuses in Chan's storyline certainly qualify as human consumables, yet the motive for which they are consumed lies beyond the boundaries of endocannibalism and exocannibalism. Consuming unborn fetuses for the purpose of regaining one's youth, beauty, or even virility is an act that straddles both categories, while also introducing elements that conform to neither. The consumption of dumplings in Chan's film introduces conditions that the traditional framework can, by definition, not accommodate. All the characters (even, implicitly, the patients at the mainland clinic) share a common cultural identity—one that the fetuses, if carried to term and born into that world, would likewise have shared. The fetuses' inability to actually commence their lives, however, leaves the eaten not simply outside of the cultural grouping shared by the eaters, but (at least nominally) outside of the bonds of shared humanity. Indeed, as suggested earlier, the fetuses' arguably not-human status may be the only reason why their consumption is acceptable at all.

In this way, Chan's depictions of cannibalism reflect the fetuses' liminal position: between conventional anthropological categories—ambiguously alive, ambiguously human—and within the gray area of the arbitrary. The very existence of this liminal condition weakens the relevance of classifications as such, and by extension, it undermines the mode of categorical reasoning on which moral constructs about those categories traditionally rest. Morality is, after all, as much a social construction as the categories used to organize the anthropological interpretations of a given action. Neither morality nor categories are perfect universal and constant truths.

A similar construction of categories is central to Mary Douglas's *Purity and Danger*, an anthropological treatise on such concepts as defilement and abomination. Douglas intended the book to challenge stereotypes about the irrationality of so-called primitive mentalities by showing that ideas about ritual purity and pollution possessed internal consistency and close links to local social and cultural structures. One latent result of her work, however, was to begin to establish the groundwork for a cultural theory of risk as it relates to individual notions of good versus evil. Douglas argued that such notions are informed by one's perception of phenomena that he or she views as threating. In this way, everything from filthy toothbrushes and body odor to epidemic scares and natural disasters are often associated with social transgressions in a system of informal classification. That which is out of place, and thus unclassifiable, creates an impression of danger. According to Douglas:

> Shoes are not dirty in themselves, but it is dirty to place them on the dining-table; food is not dirty in itself, but it is dirty to leave cooking utensils in the bedroom, or food bespattered on clothing; similarly, bathroom equipment in the drawing room; clothing lying on chairs; outdoor things indoors; upstairs things downstairs; under-clothing where over-clothing should be and so on. In short, our pollution behavior is the reaction which condemns any object or idea likely to confuse or contradict cherished classifications.[18]

Social order thus rests on a system of classifications that straightforwardly defines the Other, and clearly distinguishes the pure from the impure, the legitimate from the horrific, and—particularly relevant here—that which can be eaten from that which cannot be. The behavioral pressures created by such classifications serve to reinforce hierarchies and other forms of organization and differentiation.[19]

The idea that even cannibalism can potentially fall into the realm of the unclassifiable substantiates the arbitrariness of categorical distinctions such as "right and wrong" or "thinkable and unthinkable." Cannibalism, perhaps only second to incest, is the very definition of an unconscionable act—the ultimate taboo, seemingly immune to all but the most narrowly defined, and grudgingly admitted justifications. And that second-tier status may be, as René Girard provocatively notes, what it is "only because cannibalism has not yet found its Freud and been promoted to the status of a major contemporary myth."[20] It seems more likely, however, that cannibalism's taboo status depends upon further taboos designed to prevent discussion that might render it otherwise. Chan's film breaches those secondary taboos, opens that discussion, and in the process raises the possibility that cannibalism, far from being absolute, may be one more arbitrary limit imposed by cultural groups on their members in the service of the group's interests.

If cannibalism is to be classified and reacted to as if it exists on a spectrum with all other forms of consumption, then understanding how Chan's film elicits horror means understanding the mechanism that generates emotional responses to *what* one consumes, rather than *how* it is consumed. That is, there is nothing inherently evil or frightening about consuming dumplings, processed meats, or even the meats derived from unborn animals, per se; yet the idea that humans, who are socialized to be repulsed by the consumption of their own species might act against common conventions and test the boundaries between foods deemed edible versus those proscriptively classified as inedible, provokes uneasiness, disgust, anxiety, or even fear. This, however, is only the rudimentary foundation of the horror that Chan introduces. It is the social criticism of the characters' personal motivations, tied to the conventions of capitalism, that mediates throughout the plot, bringing to bear the more evocative relationship between cannibalism and consumption.[21]

Having revealed cannibalism's taboo status as arbitrary and socially determined, and thus framed the act as one form of consumption among many—albeit an extreme and, to some, distasteful one—Chan renders it (and the feelings that might otherwise be associated with it: shame, horror, revulsion) subject to the forces of the marketplace. Cannibalism, in *Dumplings*, becomes one more anomalous social phenomenon that emerges in capitalist societies—an unintended result of their abundant rewards for, and relentless promotion of, financial success. The social consciousness, or even sense of guilt, in marketing or consuming fetuses that might be present under different productive conditions is absent. Lu characterizes this quite succinctly:

> All three protagonists appear flawlessly cold. They think about only their own interests, without the least concern for the lives and deaths of others. Instead of being victimized, like Chan's usual characters, they elegantly and cruelly dominate their environments.[22]

Mei procures, markets, and sells the contents of her expensive dumplings as if the process were simply part of a transaction of any other consumer product, while Mrs. Li reciprocates through purchasing power and consumption with a similar indifference to any underlying principles of morality. Mei, aware that she will be judged according to the arbitrary moral precepts of others, even if she does not herself share them, mounts a preemptive defense of her practice, unleashing a diatribe in which she lists justification after justification for the consumption of humans, ranging from honorable leaders and their pursuit of exotic delicacies, to vague atrocities executed by the Japanese and the necessity to find food during times of famine in China.

Mei is not burdened by moral dilemmas, but is instead self-assured, convinced, and confident that cannibalism is no different than any other animal instinct afforded by one's privileged status as a human, situated on the highest rung of the food chain and presiding over all other forms of intelligence. Whether understood through theories of false consciousness or the notions of pathology derived from modern psychology, these beliefs are nonetheless anomalies engendered by capitalist production.

Such anomalies are direct products of the profit motive in all of its manifestations, inclusive of everything from the amassing of private property and the advancement of competition to the cultivation of individualist values and even the transformation of one's appearance for the sole purpose of further personal gain. The form of cannibalism Chan features in his film is a viable capitalist enterprise because the "product" being sold is not the dumplings themselves, but the promise of youth that they represent to those who buy them. The drive to regain one's lost youth is a particularly pure (albeit symbolic) manifestation of the capitalist drive to amass profit. It involves the search—at great cost in time, effort, and inconvenience—for a rare and elusive commodity that, if only it can somehow be acquired, promises to confer opportunities and degrees of happiness accessible no other way. The search for profit is, in a capitalist system, capable of producing anomalous behaviors that dissolve the traditional norms governing human activity. It is certainly no coincidence, then, that cannibalism—once commodified and deployed in the service of regaining lost youth—accelerates that dissolution.

Conclusion

In *Dumplings*, cannibalism becomes a critical metaphor for contemporary capitalist culture and the effects perceived to accompany it: consumerism, class inequality, alienation, and, more specifically within this this context, obsession with youth and affluence. In this sense, and in direct relation to the major analyses of *Dumplings* discussed earlier, cannibalism nuances the social criticism of postfeminist theories, while introducing an allegory of consumerist society and the social pressure to retain beauty and power by pursuing one's youth. Chan presents audiences with a provocative look at worldly desires, the means to acquire them, and the moral quandaries that bemuse, distract, engage, and even encourage individuals in determining their social action. The cast and their performances are awash with what most viewers would find unconscionable, perhaps even reprehensible, acts. Yet, if they all appear myopic with regard to their own transgressions of conventional moral aptitude, this need not necessarily—and certainly not holistically—be viewed as merely an affront to such moralistic values, but rather as a subtle challenge to the parameters of what humans often assume are universal beliefs about what is right and what is wrong. The moral principles assumed to be ubiquitous pillars of society or common ideals are, in actuality, propped up by notions of evolution, thinly veiled by communal socialization and mediated by a host of different cultural, political, economic, and social vulnerabilities. To see cannibalism in any other light is reductionist—precisely, however, what classificatory systems of science, both natural and social, implicitly seek to achieve.

As Chan presents it, cannibalism is commodified. Situated beyond the two categories of endocannibalism and exocannibalism, it is instead a liminal condition corrupted by broadly defined profit motives, resulting in a very different form of intraspecies consumption. It is contingent upon the pursuit of superficial and materialist perceptions of what one will gain by consuming the flesh of fellow humans. This commodification complicates perceptions of cannibalism within societies beholden to capitalist production. To pursue the recapturing of one's youth for the sake of appeasing another is a delusional endeavor, exceeded only by violating the personhood of others by literally consuming the young—even unborn—in order to become younger. Youth is equated to wealth, affluence, and prosperity. To be young is to be many things that one will never be so perfectly, nor so categorically, again: sexy and powerful; beautiful and interesting; wanted and needed; or even human and simultaneously inhumane. Therein lies an irony: this method of becoming young requires that one literally consume the young, which only serves to assure that the youth die young, never experiencing life themselves, but ultimately embodying the antidote for aging. All of this, in the context of the film, creates the potential for audiences to rethink their perceptions of morality vis-à-vis the adage "eat or be eaten."

Notes

1   *Three . . . Extremes* is an East Asian horror film collaboration that includes *Dumplings*, directed by Fruit Chan (Hong Kong); *Cut*, directed by Park Chan-Wook (Korea); and *Box*, directed by Takashi Miike (Japan).
2   Emilie Yueh-yu Yeh and Neda Hei-tung Ng, "Magic, Medicine, and Cannibalism: The China Demon in Hong Kong Horror," in *Horror to the Extreme: Changing Boundaries in Asian Cinema*, ed. Choi Jinhee and Mitsuyo Wada-Marciano (Hong Kong: Hong Kong University Press, 2009), 145–60; Tonglin Lu, "Fruit Chan's *Dumplings*: New 'Diary of Madman' in Post-Mao Global Capitalism," *The China Review* 10, no. 2 (Fall 2010): 177–200; Zhang Yingjin, "The Dynamics of Off Centeredness in Hong Kong Cinema," in *A Companion to Hong Kong Cinema*, ed. Esther Cheung and Gina Marchetti; Cheung, *A Companion to Hong Kong Cinema* (Malden, MA: Wiley-Blackwell, 2015), 489–98.
3   Lim, "Pan-Asian Cinema of Allusion," 410–39.
4   Yeh and Ng, "Magic, Medicine, and Cannibalism."
5   This ending differs from the short-segments of the *Three . . .Extremes*. In that feature, it is Mrs. Li who is pregnant and the story ends with her devouring her own fetus in the bathtub.
6   Ian Johnston, "Compliments to the Chef: *Three . . . Extremes' Dumplings* Expertly Mixes Social Critique and Questionable Cuisine," *Bright Lights Film Journal* 48 (May 2005). http://brightlightsfilm.com/compliments-to-the-chef-three-extremes-dumplings-expertly- mixes-social-critique-and-questionable-cuisine/#.VwIQUxjVI_K (accessed June 8, 2016).
7   Keinhans, Chuck. "Serving the People-*Dumplings*." *Jump Cut: A Review of Contemporary Media* 49, no. 5 (2007). http://www.ejumpcut.org/archive/jc49.2007/Dumplings /index.html (accessed June 8, 2016).
8   Cheung, *Fruit Chan's Made in Hong Kong*, general point made throughout the volume; Lu, "Fruit Chan's *Dumplings*;" Yingjin, "Dynamics of Off Centeredness in Hong Kong Cinema."

9. Chueng, *Fruit Chan's Made in Hong Kong*, 2.
10. Lu, "Fruit Chan's *Dumplings*," 191.
11. Boris Trbic, "The Immortality Blues: Talking with Fruit Chang about *Dumplings*." *Bright Lights Film Journal*, 50 (2005). http://brightlightsfilm.com/immortality-blues-talking-fruit-chan-dumplings/#.VvHENBjVI_I (accessed June 8, 2016).
12. Donald S. Sutton, "Consuming Counterrevolution: The Ritual and Culture of Cannibalism in Wuxuan, Guangxi, May to July 1968," *Comparative Studies in Society and History* 37, no. 1 (January 1995): 136–72; Yi Zheng, *Scarlett Memorial: Tales of Cannibalism in Modern China* (Boulder, CO: Westview Press, 1998).
13. Carlos Rojas, "Cannibalism and the Chinese Body Politic: Hermeneutics and Violence in Cross-Cultural Perception," *Postmodern Culture* 12, no. 3 (May 2002): 10. http://muse.jhu.edu/journals/postmodern_culture/toc/pmc12.3.html (accessed June 8, 2016).
14. Lu, "Fruit Chan's *Dumplings*," 188.
15. Ibid., 13.
16. Shirley Lindenbaum, "Thinking about Cannibalism," *Annual Review of Anthropology* (2004): 475–98.
17. Ibid., 478.
18. Mary Douglas, *Purity and Danger: An Analysis of the Concepts of Pollution and Taboo* (London: Routledge & Kegan Paul, 1966), 44–5.
19. Basil Bernstein, *Class, Codes and Control* (London: Routledge, 1977), 49–53.
20. René Girard, *Violence and the Sacred* (Baltimore: Johns Hopkins University Press, 1979), 276–7.
21. Social criticism and the exploration of ethical issues of capitalism, class inequalities, and the tenuous position of migrants in Hong Kong also appear in previous films directed by Chan including *The Prostitute Trilogy*: *Durian, Durian* (2000), *Hollywood Hong Kong* (2001), and *Public Toilet* (2002).
22. Lu, "Fruit Chan's *Dumplings*," 187.

Bibliography

Bernstein, Basil. *Class, Codes and Control*. London: Routledge, 1977.
Cheung, Esther. *Fruit Chan's Made in Hong Kong*. Hong Kong: Hong Kong University Press, 2009.
Cheung, Esther, and Gina Marchetti. *A Companion to Hong Kong Cinema*. Malden, MA: Wiley-Blackwell, 2015.
Douglas, Mary. *Purity and Danger: An Analysis of the Concepts of Pollution and Taboo*. London: Routledge & Kegan Paul, 1966.

Girard, René. *Violence and the Sacred*. Baltimore: Johns Hopkins University Press, 1979.
Johnston, Ian. "Compliments to the Chef: *Three . . . Extremes'* Dumplings Expertly Mixes Social Critique and Questionable Cuisine." *Bright Lights Film Journal* 48 (May 2005). http://brightlightsfilm.com/compliments-to-the-chef-three-extremes-dumplings-expertly-mixes-social-critique-and-questionable-cuisine/#.VwIQUxjVI_k.
Keinhans, Chuck. "Serving the People-*Dumplings*." *Jump Cut: A Review of Contemporary Media* 49, no. 5 (2007). http://www.ejumpcut.org/archive/jc49.2007/Dumplings /index.html (accessed June 8, 2016).
Lim, Bliss Cua. "A Pan-Asian Cinema of Allusion. *Going Home* and *Dumplings*." In *A Companion to Hong Kong Cinema*, Esther Cheung and Gina Marchetti, 410–39. Malden, MA: Wiley-Blackwell, 2015.
Lindenbaum, Shirley. "Thinking about Cannibalism." *Annual Review of Anthropology* (2004): 475–98.
Lu, Tonglin. "Fruit Chan's *Dumplings*: New 'Diary of Madman' in Post-Mao Global Capitalism." *The China Review* 10, no. 2 (Fall 2010): 177–200.
Rojas, Carlos. "Cannibalism and the Chinese Body Politic: Hermeneutics and Violence in Cross-Cultural Perception." *Postmodern Culture* 12, no. 3 (May 2002). http://muse.jhu.edu /journals/postmodern_culture/toc/pmc12.3.html (accessed June 8, 2016).
Sutton, Donald S. "Consuming Counterrevolution: The Ritual and Culture of Cannibalism in Wuxuan, Guangxi, May to July 1968." *Comparative Studies in Society and History* 37, no. 1 (January 1995): 136–72.
Trbic, Boris. "The Immortality Blues: Talking with Fruit Chang about *Dumplings*." *Bright Lights Film Journal* 50 (2005). http://brightlightsfilm.com/immortality-blues-talking-fruit-chan-dumplings/#.VvHENBjVI_I (accessed June 8, 2016).
Yeh, Emilie Yueh-yu, and Neda Hei-tung Ng. "Magic, Medicine, and Cannibalism: The China Demon in Hong Kong Horror." In *Horror to the Extreme: Changing Boundaries in Asian Cinema*, edited by Choi Jinhee and Mitsuyo Wada-Marciano, 145–60. Hong Kong: Hong Kong University Press, 2009.
Yingjin, Zhang. "The Dynamics of Off Centeredness in Hong Kong Cinema." In *A Companion to Hong Kong Cinema*, Esther Cheung and Gina Marchetti, 489–98. Malden, MA: Wiley-Blackwell, 2015.
Zheng, Yi. *Scarlett Memorial: Tales of Cannibalism in Modern China*. Boulder, CO: Westview Press, 1998.

5

The Goo in You: Food as Invader in *The Stuff*

A. Bowdoin Van Riper

The industrialization of food production and distribution gave citizens of nineteenth-century United States access to a more expansive, more varied, and more reliable food supply. New technologies like the refrigerated railroad car, along with business models designed to exploit economies of scale, enabled the nation's steadily depopulating rural areas to feed its ever-growing cities. As railroads, trucks, and eventually airplanes stretched the distance from farm to table by orders of magnitude, fresh fish became available inland and tropical produce flowed northward. The consumption of food grown somewhere else, once limited to wealthy elites, became a fact of everyday life for the middle and working classes as well. The processing of crops into food was similarly centralized: moved out of the home kitchen, the neighborhood butcher shop, and the local mill and into distant factories capable of producing a seemingly endless, and ever-expanding, array of edible delights.[1]

Americans remain, to this day, ambivalent about the social costs of the transformation: the decline of family farms, the loss of diversity among food crops, and the displacement of whole foods by heavily processed ones. We no longer worry, however, about an issue that—well into the twentieth century—loomed larger than any of them: the lack of transparency in what might be called the food–industrial complex.[2] We do not know the ingredients that go into the food we consume, or the steps that are taken to produce it, and we are—most of us, for the most part—comfortable in our ignorance. The possibility that the food on grocery-store shelves could be adulterated, spoiled, or toxic seems remote: a relic, like polio epidemics or boiler explosions, of another age. Processed foods may not be as *good* for us as whole foods, we reason, but a web of checks and balances—regulations imposed by government agencies, monitoring by doctors and nutritionists, and the self-preservation instinct of corporations—keeps it from being actively harmful.[3]

The Stuff, a 1985 horror-comedy film written and directed by Larry Cohen, invites audiences to imagine that such trust may be fatally misplaced. It revolves around a food product—the appealing, yet lethal, white fluff of the title—that oozes onto the market through gaps in the network of regulations that supposedly keep the food supply safe.[4] Too appealing for individuals to set aside, too reliably addictive for manufacturers to walk away from, and too (seemingly) innocuous for government regulators to ban, it spreads like wildfire and—once safely ensconced in the nation's refrigerators—begins to transform the population. Regular consumers of The Stuff are "hollowed out" from the inside, in one character's apt description, they become empty husks that ripple and distort grotesquely as the goo moves inside them, more Stuff than human.[5]

Loss of control—powerlessness to prevent imminent harm—is among the most elemental of all human fears. The consumption-from-within depicted in *The Stuff* is a particularly grotesque example, but these instances of body horror—though emphasized in the poster image and trailer—are secondary to the film's larger message. Modeled on alien-invasion tales such as *Invaders from Mars* (1953), *Invasion of the Body Snatchers* (1956), and *The Brain Eaters* (1958), *The Stuff* is primarily interested in a deeper, more profound loss of control. Victims of The Stuff lose control over their personalities and thoughts, as well as their bodies, and as their numbers multiply the fabric of society begins to fray and disintegrate. The film hints, in fact, that the fraying is not an accident but a deliberately sought goal: that the Stuff is a living, sentient organism, using humans as a tool for pursuing its own evolutionary success. What if, *The Stuff* suggests, the food we ingest so blithely and casually was not simply "bad for us," but actively out to displace us from our accustomed role as masters of the food chain?

The story of *The Stuff*

The Stuff, like many horror films of its era, involves a seemingly safe environment rendered suddenly, terrifyingly unsafe.[6] The threat comes, however, in a distinctly *un*threatening form: not a knife-wielding maniac (as in *Halloween*) or evil spirits from a desecrated burial ground (as in *Poltergeist*), but a white plastic tub with a swirling pink-and-orange logo. Restless and unable to sleep in the summer heat, twelve-year-old Jason (Scott Bloom) pads downstairs to plunder the refrigerator for a midnight snack. Opening the door, he is startled twice in rapid succession: first by the sight of The Stuff, oozing and twisting across the shelf beside its opened, toppled container, and then by his father (Robert Frank Telfer), who grabs his arm and angrily demands to know what he's doing in the kitchen. The father's simmering anger—seemingly out of all proportion to his son's transgression—contrasts with the coolness with which he dismisses Jason's claim that The Stuff is alive, and, after opening the refrigerator to find the container upright, picks up a spoon and digs in. Jason scuttles back to bed, but the strange behavior of both his food and his father leave him awake and disturbed.

Strange behavior also preoccupies the characters in the next scene: a gathering of senior executives from ice-cream-manufacturing conglomerate Amalgamated Dairies alarmed by the meteoric rise of The Stuff, its manufacturer's plan to roll it out nationwide, and their complete inability to discover what the secret of the product is. Desperate, they hire disgraced FBI agent turned industrial spy David "Mo" Rutherford (Michael Moriarty) to penetrate the rival company and bring back the secret of The Stuff so that they can copy it. A shrewd investigator who uses a goofy, distracted good-old-boy persona as a disguise, Rutherford—after revealing that he bugged the suit of the CEO of Amalgamated Dairies and knows their reservations about him—agrees to take on the job in exchange for a hefty fee. "I don't think you're as dumb as you appear to be," remarks the CEO, Evans, looking at him with new respect. "*Nobody*'s as dumb as I appear to be," Mo responds, and departs in search of the truth.

The two storylines unfold in parallel throughout the long first act of the film. Jason—the personification of suburban childhood innocence—becomes increasingly alarmed as his mother and older brother begin to exhibit the same mix of eerie calm and angry obsession that his father displayed in the kitchen. All three become increasingly fixated on consuming The Stuff, placidly dismissing Jason's claims that something is terribly wrong with it. Mo, meanwhile, finds that the company behind The Stuff is an exception to his motto that "every stone wall has a chink in it"; even Fletcher (Patrick O'Neal), the head of the company, claims not to know what's in his flagship product. Frustrated, both characters take more extreme steps. Jason goes berserk in a supermarket, smashing displays of The Stuff while shouting to all who will listen that the popular product is dangerous. Mo, visiting the Virginia town where The Stuff was test-marketed, is attacked by its zombie-like residents, whose bodies split open when struck and disgorge bubbling flows of The Stuff. He fights his way to freedom, now convinced—like Jason—that the product is a mortal threat.

The two plot threads merge as Mo, who has driven to Long Island to interview Jason about the supermarket incident, drives up just as the boy flees from his home to avoid being force-fed The Stuff by his family. "I saw it move too," Mo tells Jason, establishing his bona fides in a sentence, and the unlikely pair drive away into the night. Joined by Nicole (Andrea Marcovicci)—a director of television commercials for The Stuff, who is simultaneously charmed by Mo and appalled by her unwitting complicity in selling a dangerous product—the pair head for rural Georgia, where Mo and Nicole hope to dupe their way into the plant from which The Stuff emerges. Suspicious of the plant manager's evasiveness, Mo and Nicole soon discover the true secret behind the product: it is not made, but harvested—collected from a seething, bubbling pool surrounded by a heavily guarded installation. Behind the walls and fences of this industrial fortress, The Stuff is being pumped into gleaming tanker trucks by workers already addicted to it—preparation for nationwide distribution.

Extricating himself, Nicole, and Jason from a series of increasingly close calls, Mo goes on the offensive. He uses explosives to cause a landslide that buries the bubbling pool from which The Stuff emerges, and enlists the aid of retired US Army colonel Malcolm Spears (Paul Sorvino)—now an ultra-right-wing activist who controls a radio network and a private militia. Spears's men storm the distribution center, disrupting production and thwarting the planned roll-out of the product, and the colonel delivers a nationwide radio broadcast denouncing The Stuff as an alien invader and urging patriotic citizens to take action: "do not eat it . . . do not sell it . . . if you have a distributorship, close your doors and make no more sales." Mo chimes in, urging listeners to seek medical attention for Stuff-addicted loved ones, and destroy their stocks of The Stuff by cooking it. An orgy of destruction follows—tubs of the once-beloved product thrown into giant bonfires, drive-through restaurants blown up—orchestrated and observed by determined crowds.

The immediate threat over, Mo returns to corporate headquarters to confront Fletcher, only to find him plotting a new joint venture with Evans, the Amalgamated Dairies CEO who hired Mo in the first place. The destruction of the Stuff "mine" in Georgia, Fletcher explains, was only a temporary setback. The mysterious goo is once again bubbling to the surface, and will soon be on the market as part of a new product called "The Taste"—12 percent Stuff and 88 percent ice cream—which will, Fletcher and Evans assure Mo, offer consumers the irresistible taste of the original without its zombifying side effects. Unimpressed, Mo carries out his planned act of revenge: forcing Fletcher and Evans, at gunpoint, to gorge themselves on tubs of The Stuff. "Are you eating it, or is it eating you?" he asks rhetorically as the sound of police sirens draws closer, then slips away into the night.

Losing our minds

The possibility that our loved ones might be monsters is uniquely horrifying, and—for precisely that reason—an evergreen horror film trope. Alfred Hitchcock's psychological thrillers such as *Suspicion* (1941) and *Shadow of a Doubt* (1943) ring genteel changes on it, while *Dracula* (1931) and *The Wolf Man* (1941) use scenes of characters brutally dispatching monstrous loved ones to generate both visceral horror and pathos. Scenes where survivors are attacked by, and forced to destroy, undead loved ones—lovers, parents, siblings, and even children—have become a staples of modern zombie movies, along with dialogue where the living warn their friends to show them no mercy if they join the ranks of the undead. Fear that friends and neighbors have been replaced by alien Others drives many of the great science-fiction horror films, from *Invasion of the Body Snatchers* to *The Thing* (1982) and *Terminator 2* (1991).

The Stuff explores the "monstrous loved one" trope primarily through Jason, cataloging, in meticulous detail, his parents' and brother's increasingly bizarre behavior. Jason's deepening suspicions about whether something has gone terribly wrong with the other members of his family defines his character and drives his actions in the first half of the film. Even his rampage through the supermarket—a mindless spasm of destruction that plays more as a frustrated tantrum than an act of protest—can be read as a response to their bland, smothering dismissal of his fears. Once Mo rescues him, and confirms his suspicions, he fades into the background of the story, and—except for one or two scenes—remains there.

The evidence that Jason's loved ones are being altered, and that his once-safe suburban home has become a den of monsters, is rooted in the complex food-related rituals of middle-class American families. Like the death of a caged canary in a mine, small changes in those rituals are early warning signs of larger and more terrible changes not yet visible to casual observers. Jason's midnight raid on the fridge is a case in point. Such late-night snacks are, at most, misdemeanors: a small step—but *only* that—beyond sneaking a predinner cookie from the jar. Jason's father's intense, sustained anger surprises and alarms the audience, as well as Jason, because it is so utterly

FIGURE 5.1 *Jason's parents' ever-growing obsession with The Stuff, and with encouraging him to eat it, convinces him that they have lost their humanity and been transformed into monsters.*

unexpected—punishment far out of proportion to the offense. A later scene, when Jason angrily throws a heaping bowl of The Stuff against the wall of the family's kitchen during a meal, reverses the mismatch. Jason's actions—those of a twelve-year-old behaving like a two-year-old—violate a clutch of middle-class social taboos, from wasting food and deliberately damaging property to violating the quiet calm of the family table. Rather than respond sternly, however, Jason's mother (Colette Blonigan) placidly wipes down the wall, declaring—like a preternaturally joyful housewife from a television commercial—that The Stuff is "not only tasty and low in calories . . . it doesn't even stain! (Figure 5.1)."

The reversals and inversions that signal the slipping away of the parents' humanity become more acute, and more visible, when they involve not just the act of eating but the food being eaten. A varied, healthful diet is—like a single-family house and store-bought clothes—a key marker of middle-class identity, and the production of home-cooked, rather than store-bought meals a key measure of maternal success. Failure to meet either standard is grounds for social disdain, or even—if extreme or prolonged—of government intervention on behalf of the children thus victimized. A glimpse of a refrigerator filled entirely with containers of manufactured food is routinely used, even for characters without children, as cinematic shorthand for failure to master the challenge of living a well-balanced adult life.

Jason's parents, in their enthusiastic and unwavering embrace of The Stuff, do not simply depart from those standards, but ostentatiously trample on them. The product's soft, white, fluffy appearance—as well as the way it mounds in bowls and clings to spoons—evokes products like sour cream, marshmallow fluff, whipped dessert topping, and soft-serve ice cream: pleasurable to eat, but hardly nutritious. The wide-mouthed plastic containers it comes in, and the garish, cartoonlike logo displayed on them, reinforce The Stuff's association with fun, snacking, and sensual pleasure rather than the serious business of nutrition. The family's arguments over Jason's eating habits seem, therefore, to take place in topsy-turvy world presided over by some unseen Lord of Misrule: The parents repeatedly extoll the sensual pleasures of The Stuff by declaring that "it's good!" and "we all love it," while Jason stoutly counters with sober, worried proclamations that it's "not good for you" and "there's something wrong with it." A scene where Jason pulls open the door of the family fridge to find it stuffed with nothing *but* containers of The Stuff evokes the pleasure-saturated fantasy worlds of songs like "The Big Rock Candy Mountain" or "Pleasure Island" in Disney Studios' *Pinocchio* (1940)—the vital difference being that the one in Jason's kitchen was conceived not by the will of naughty children, or indolent hoboes, but of (supposedly) responsible suburban parents.

Jason's efforts to avoid ingesting The Stuff, which grow more desperate as his family's devotion to it grows more obsessive and cult-like, culminates in a final, gag-inducing ruse in which—handed a container of The Stuff and told to finish it in one sitting—he surreptitiously flushes the contents down the toilet and refills the tub with shaving cream, which he eats instead in order to deceive his parents. That he subjects *himself* to the type of food-based prank that young children typically play on older family members—swapping the tasty for the inedible—suggests the fear induced in him by the transformation of his family into monstrous, menacing Others. The final confirmation of his desperation comes as the ruse fails and he flees into the night. Mo drives by and, on the strength of a single sentence of reassurance, Jason dives in and is driven away. The darkest, media-fueled fear of countless 1980s parents—a child voluntarily entering the car of a male stranger—thus becomes, in the topsy-turvy world of *The Stuff*, a moment of relief and triumphant liberation.[7]

Unraveling the social fabric

When Jason flees into the night, he is running not just from once-familiar individuals who have turned monstrous and alien, but from the ruins of a family that is no longer a family. Obsessed with The Stuff, Jason's parents and brother abrogate their tradition-sanctioned social roles: his father issues angry demands instead of dispensing stern wisdom; his mother offers an addictive, mind-altering goo instead of nourishment; and his older brother (pursuing the fleeing Jason in response to their father's shouted command of "Get him!") morphs from irritation to actual threat. Jason scrambles into Mo's car, sight unseen, because the monster that Mo *might* be is unlikely to be any worse than the self-absorbed, Stuff-obsessed monsters he is leaving behind.

The dissolution of Jason's family is, however, only the tip of the iceberg. Scenes throughout *The Stuff* suggest that the unraveling of the social fabric brought about by the titular treat is pervasive, and insidious. The film, structured as a paranoid thriller rather than a science-fiction dystopia (and constrained by a modest budget), hints at this unraveling rather than depicting its full effect. Hints of it, however, are a constant presence—creating an impression of a society that, like Jason's family, is slowly and steadily coming apart at the seams under the pernicious influence of mysterious white goo.

One scene, for example, shows Mo passing a small drive-up stand that serves nothing but The Stuff. It is 2:30 a.m.—an hour when food service is limited to sparsely populated all-night diners, and hamburger kiosks dispensing bags of sliders to bleary-eyed bar patrons after Last Call—but the drive-up is brightly lit and thronged with excited customers. Desire for another serving of their new favorite food has, for them, trumped every other need: a good night's sleep, a clear head for the morning commute, and a focused mind for whatever awaits them at work. Mo shakes his head in disbelief as he passes, more baffled than ever at the effect of The Stuff. Jason's supermarket rampage is triggered by a similar scene: shoppers clutching containers of The Stuff as they stroll through the aisles of the store, casually eating from them as they add other, less favored food items to their carts. Driving downtown for a snack when you "should be" home asleep, or snacking on not-yet-purchased food in the grocery store aisle are individual transgressions of social norms, but they are transgressions committed in public and thus subject, under normal circumstances, to looks of silent disapproval and other forms of informal social control. Censure is wholly absent, however, in both scenes: nobody notices, and nobody cares.

Probing for answers to how The Stuff got past regulators, Mo finds evidence of a second level at which the social fabric is fraying. Every member of the FDA panel that approved it is, he quickly discovers, unavailable—out of the country, on vacation, or incommunicado—except for a former administrator named Vickers (Danny Aiello), recently retired after nineteen years with the agency and living with his dog Ben. "You've got to understand," he explains to Mo, "this is a dessert, not a prescription medicine. If there's no reason to forbid the use of a product, we have to okay it. And in this instance it was a pleasure—an absolute pleasure." Suspicious, perhaps, of the relish with which Vickers pronounces the word "pleasure," Mo investigates and soon finds that the house is packed with containers of The Stuff. Vickers's statement that "we all agreed it was a good product" suddenly takes on new, sinister overtones, suggesting that bribery and collusion, rather than an open-minded commitment to the public good, motivated them.

Vickers, tellingly, spoons out Stuff for both himself and Ben after Mo leaves, saying: "I have a treat for both of us. We *deserve* it, don't we?" A similar blend of personal entitlement and pleasure-seeking pervades the *faux* commercials for The Stuff that are sprinkled through the film. One shows an elegantly attired older woman (Clara Peller) slamming knife and fork onto her half-empty plate at "Andre's exclusive Continental restaurant, which caters to only the most exclusive clientele," and demanding: "*Where's* The Stuff?"[8] Another features a fur-clad model breathily declaring that as a little girl she thought there was nothing better than ice cream, but that "now that I'm a big girl, I've found something better . . . *much* better." This barely concealed conflation of sex and dessert continues with her delivery of the product's four-word slogan, which echoes through the film (Figure 5.2). "When it comes to The Stuff," she intones, "believe me, enough is *never* enough."

FIGURE 5.2 *Appealing to consumers' willingness to "reward" themselves by choosing self-gratification over health, commercials for The Stuff openly associate the creamy white dessert with sexual pleasure.*

The ads' relentless emphasis on The Stuff's irresistibility suggests that the company is not only well aware of its addictive, mind-altering nature, but sees the property as an aid to sales rather than a nascent public-health crisis. The conversation between Fletcher and Evans that Mo interrupts in the climax underscores the point, focusing as it does on a product whose virtue is that it tempers The Stuff's zombifying (and thus customer-killing) side-effects while leaving its market-expanding nature intact. As a tobacco-industry official noted in an internal 1963 memo discussing the Surgeon General's soon-to-be released report on smoking: "Nicotine is addictive. We are, therefore, in the business of selling . . . an addictive drug."[9]

The tobacco-industry memo was not yet public knowledge in the early 1980s, but the attitude it embodied—the pursuit of corporate profits at the expense of public safety—appeared routinely in news headlines. The federally ordered cleanup of toxic waste dumped, decades earlier, at Love Canal in western New York was well under way.[10] The first lawsuits claiming that tobacco companies had failed to warn smokers of the hazards posed by their product were being filed. *Mother Jones* had, in 1982, published Ford Motor Company memos documenting the company's deliberate choice to settle the anticipated lawsuits resulting from the Ford Pinto's tendency to catch fire in rear-end crashes.[11] The idea that a corporation would enrich itself by deliberately, knowingly addicting its customers to a poisonous dessert was, in such a world, horrifying but hardly implausible.

The ideology of the cancer cell

Images of insatiable desire, and characters consumed by a relentless search for More, fill *The Stuff*. When Jason first opens his family's fridge, it contains a single container of The Stuff; by the time he flees the house a few days later, it contains nothing *but* row upon row of neatly stacked containers. Vickers, the Stuff-addicted former FDA administrator, maintains what looks like a miniature warehouse of it in his dining room. "You eat it," Jason's father tells him, "that's what you're supposed to do . . . you eat as much of it as you can and you *keep* eating it." The faux ads for The Stuff are subtly devoid of the pro forma nods to moderation familiar from real-world ads for alcoholic beverages ("drink responsibly") and sugar-laden cereals ("part of this balanced breakfast"); instead, they enthusiastically seek to normalize mindless consumption—chanting, purring, and whispering to the audience that "enough is never enough."

The corporations in *The Stuff* exhibit the same mindless, obsessive hunger, but theirs is directed toward market share (and, by extension, profits) rather than a specific product. They have no compunction about selling an addictive substance, or about tweaking its composition to find the perfect middle ground between maintaining their customers' insatiable desire and prolonging their lives (and thus their ability to consume). When Mo explains his nickname to the food-industry tycoons—"No matter how much money they give me, I always want mo' "—they look at him like something scraped off the bottom of their shoes, but they exhibit precisely the same attitude.[12] Their desire to regain, then expand, their market share is, in fact, the reason why they are hiring him in the first place.

The Stuff satirizes both levels of this quest for More, depicting a world in which both consumers and consumption become literally "mindless," and producers' only real concern with the death-by-evisceration-from-within of their customers is its impact on their sales figures. Doing so, the film implicitly aligns itself with Edward Abbey's famous declaration that "growth for the sake of growth is the ideology of the cancer cell."[13] It also hints, however, that a third form of obsessive consumption—deeper-buried than the other two, and more horrific in its implications—may be under way, and that Abbey's famous comparison may, in the case of The Stuff, be more than just a vivid metaphor.

The Stuff, though it does not dwell on the point, establishes that The Stuff is not only alive, but sentient.[14] The speech in which Jason's father defines what the family is "supposed to do," and his subsequent use of the phrase "now that we've started eating properly," both imply that the white goo is capable of planting thoughts in the minds of those who ingest enough of it—he is clearly parroting someone else's ideology, and there is no apparent source for it other than The Stuff itself.[15] A similar quality is apparent in the announcement that plays over the public address system of the Stuff-mining complex as Mo lays his explosive charges. The Stuff, a human voice reassures the workers, is coming forth from the Earth "in great and plentiful supplies for the good work you're doing. Soon hunger in the world will be a thing of the past. Earth is giving off the food that will nourish all, and guide us all to a new order of life." The transcendental—even messianic—elements of this exhortation have no counterpart in the company's rhetoric, either public or private. It is, rather, the thoughts of The Stuff itself, voiced by a human who—like Jason's father—believes them to be his own.

The relationship between The Stuff and the humans it takes control of is, therefore, more sophisticated than it appears at first glance. Consumers of The Stuff do not simply become dehumanized vessels for an alien consciousness, like the citizens of Santa Mira in *Invasion of the Body Snatchers*; nor do they merely serve as pre-portioned meals, as implied in the *Twilight Zone* episode "To Serve Man" (1962). Humans possessed by The Stuff lose their "normal" personality, but not their humanity, and while their bodies are consumed from within the consumption is slow enough to suggest that it is a side effect rather than a primary goal. Often described as a parasite, The Stuff—particularly to the extent to which it functions as one enormous organism with a shared consciousness—is closer to a symbiote: it benefits its human hosts by providing them with the intensely pleasurable experience of consuming small portions of itself, and derives benefit *from* them by molding their thoughts and "encouraging" them to take actions that will allow it to further its own ends. "A human being," biologist Richard Dawkins observed, "is a gene's way of making more genes." In the world of *The Stuff* humans have also, without ever realizing it, become a sentient white goo's way of quickly, efficiently spreading itself across the face of the Earth. That the Stuff seems as committed to the pursuit of More—to the doctrine of growth-for-the-sake-of-growth—as the humans it co-opts is the film's final, cosmic-level irony.

Conclusion: the enemy within

It is not the monsters that attack us directly—descending from the skies, rising from the depths, or emerging from the unexplored corners of the Earth—that frighten us most. No matter how large and powerful they may *seem*, we tell ourselves, they have weaknesses; given time, we will find those weaknesses, devise ingenious weapons and innovative tactics to exploit them, and defeat the monster. Even if our battle plan ultimately consists of faith and sheer bravado, we tell ourselves that—like David facing Goliath—we will, somehow, prevail. The monsters that truly unsettle us are those that attack us from within: insidiously scraping away at our *own* weaknesses until we crumble or, worse yet, do their work for them by turning against one another.

The Stuff is the latter kind of monster. It not only attacks from us within, but does so at multiple levels. The fact that it scrapes and nibbles away at the bodies of its hosts—grotesque as the final stage of the process is to watch—may actually be the *least* disturbing thing about it. Its dissolution of its victims' personalities, transforming them into brainwashed minions who address their unsuspecting fellow humans with *its* thoughts expressed in their own voices, adds another layer of disquiet. So, too, does the realization that humans—the supposed lords and masters of the Earth—have been co-opted into the service of a sentient organism that they had, in their arrogance, mistaken for a tasty, low-calorie dessert.

The Stuff unsettles, even as it amuses, because the human weaknesses that its gooey white monster exploits are utterly familiar, and alarmingly relatable. We know ourselves well enough to see ourselves doing what the characters in the film do: seizing on the promise of a dessert that offers taste without guilt, succumbing to the siren song of advertisements that equate food and sex, and telling ourselves that after *this* carton we'll stop (then picking up *just one more*, because we "deserve it"). We suspect that—in similar circumstances—we, too, would be tempted not to look too deeply or question too closely, trusting the social responsibility of food companies and the vigilance of government regulators to keep any *truly* dangerous product from reaching grocery-store shelves. We are accustomed to looking outward, into the darkness and the unknown, for our monsters. Even as we do, however, *The Stuff* whispers to us that it is already too late: that the monster is inside us, that *we* allowed it in, and that—having done so—we grinned and asked for seconds.

Notes

1 On the history of these changes, see Susan Williams, *Food in the United States, 1820s–1890* (Westport, CT: Greenwood Press, 2006); and Megan J. Elias, *Food in the United States, 1890–1945* (Westport, CT: Greenwood Press, 2009).

2 Loraine Swainston Goodwin, *The Pure Food, Drink, and Drug Crusaders, 1870–1914* (Jefferson, NC: McFarland, 2011).

3 The depth of Americans' comfort with, and disinterest in the inner workings of, the food–industrial complex may be gauged, albeit roughly, by the vast literature devoted to dispelling it, of which bestsellers like Eric Schlosser's *Fast Food Nation* (2001) and Michael Pollan's *The Omnivore's Dilemma* (2006) are only the most visible portion.

4 For a fuller exploration of *The Stuff* as a critique of ineffectual food-safety regulation, and a sociopolitical satire of America in the Reagan Era, see Tony Williams, *Larry Cohen: The Radical Allegories of an Independent Filmmaker*, rev. ed. (Jefferson, NC: McFarland, 2015), 134–8.

5 *The Stuff* is, therefore, also part of the ongoing cinematic association of zombies and "mindless" consumerism, discussed in (for example): A. Loudermilk, "Eating *Dawn* in the Dark: Zombie Desire and Commodified identity in George A. Romero's *Dawn of the Dead*," *Journal of Consumer Culture* 3, no. 1 (2003): 83–108; Michael Newbury, "Fast Zombie/Slow Zombie: Food Writing, Horror Movies, and Agribusiness Apocalypse," *American Literary History* 24, no. 1 (2012): 87–114; and the essays by Roth and Matheson in this volume.

6 Jason Zinoman, *Shock Value: How a Few Eccentric Outsiders Gave Us Nightmares, Conquered Hollywood, and Created Modern Horror* (New York: Penguin Press, 2011); Richard Nowell, *Blood Money: A History of the First Teen Slasher Film Cycle* (London: Bloomsbury, 2010).

7 Leigh Moscowitz and Spring-Serenity Duvall. " 'Every Parent's Worst Nightmare': Myths of Child Abductions in US News," *Journal of Children and Media* 5, no. 2 (2011): 147–63; Joel Best, *Threatened Children: Rhetoric and Concern about Child-Victims* (Chicago: University of Chicago Press, 1993), 151–3; Brian Palmer, "Why Did Missing Children Start Showing Up on Milk Cartons?" Slate.com, April 20, 2012.

8 The scene is a play on Peller's then-famous role in a series of Wendy's ads: peering under the bun of a fast-food hamburger and demanding, "*Where's* the beef?"

9 "Addison Yeaman Memo," *Frontline: Inside the Tobacco Deal.* http://www.pbs.org /wgbh/pages/frontline/shows/settlement/case/yeaman.html (accessed June 9, 2016).

10 Richard S. Newman, *Love Canal: A Toxic History from Colonial Times to the Present* (New York: Oxford University Press, 2016).

11 Mark Dowie, "Pinto Madness," *Mother Jones*, September/October 1977. http://www.motherjones.com/politics/1977/09/pinto-madness (accessed June 9, 2016).

12 Whether Mo is being serious or whether the self-description is part of his put-on persona is never made clear.

13 Edward Abbey, "The Second Rape of the West," in *The Journey Home* (1977. New York: Plume, 1991), 183.

14 Both Jason and Mo see it move, and both are later the victims of Stuff attacks that involve advance planning and the ability to penetrate enclosed structures. The attack on Mo, in which The Stuff erupts from the center of the motel bed he is sharing with Nicole, could legitimately be called an ambush.

15 On the cultural broader context for this nightmare, see David Seed, *Brainwashing: Fictions of Mind Control* (Kent, OH: Kent State University Press, 2011).

Bibliography

Abbey, Edward. "The Second Rape of the West." In *The Journey Home*, 158–88. 1977. New York: Plume, 1991.

"Addison Yeaman Memo," *Frontline: Inside the Tobacco Deal.* http://www.pbs.org/wgbh/pages/frontline/shows/settlement/case/yeaman.html (accessed June 9, 2016).

Best, Joel. *Threatened Children: Rhetoric and Concern about Child-Victims*. Chicago: University of Chicago Press, 1993.

Dowie, Mark. "Pinto Madness," *Mother Jones*, September/October 1977. http://www.motherjones.com/politics/1977/09/pinto-madness (accessed June 9, 2016).

Elias, Megan J. *Food in the United States, 1890–1945*. Westport, CT: Greenwood Press, 2009.

Goodwin, Loraine Swainston. *The Pure Food, Drink, and Drug Crusaders, 1870–1914*. Jefferson, NC: McFarland, 2011.

Loudermilk, A. "Eating *Dawn* in the Dark: Zombie Desire and Commodified Identity in George A. Romero's *Dawn of the Dead*." *Journal of Consumer Culture* 3, no. 1 (2003): 83–108.

Moscowitz, Leigh, and Spring-Serenity Duvall. "'Every Parent's Worst Nightmare:' Myths of Child Abductions in US News." *Journal of Children and Media* 5, no. 2 (2011): 147–63.

Newbury, Michael. "Fast Zombie/Slow Zombie: Food Writing, Horror Movies, and Agribusiness Apocalypse." *American Literary History* 24, no. 1 (2012): 87–114.

Newman, Richard S. *Love Canal: A Toxic History from Colonial Times to the Present*. New York: Oxford University Press, 2016.

Nowell, Richard. *Blood Money: A History of the First Teen Slasher Film Cycle*. London: Bloomsbury, 2010.

Palmer, Brian. "Why Did Missing Children Start Showing Up on Milk Cartons?" Slate.com, April 20, 2012. http://www.slate.com/articles/news_and_politics/explainer/2012/04 /etan_patz_case_why_did_dairies_put_missing_children_on_their_milk_cartons_.html (accessed June 9, 2016).

Seed, David. *Brainwashing: Fictions of Mind Control*. Kent, OH: Kent State University Press, 2011.

Williams, Susan. *Food in the United States, 1820s–1890*. Westport, CT: Greenwood Press, 2006.

Williams, Tony. *Larry Cohen: The Radical Allegories of an Independent Filmmaker*, rev. ed. Jefferson, NC: McFarland, 2015.

Zinoman, Jason. *Shock Value: How a Few Eccentric Outsiders Gave Us Nightmares, Conquered Hollywood, and Created Modern Horror*. New York: Penguin Press, 2011.

PART TWO

Sins of the Flesh

6

Cannibalism as Cultural Critique: Peter Greenaway's *The Cook, The Thief, His Wife, and Her Lover* and Thatcherism

Thomas Prasch

Rampaging through the kitchen—terrorizing staff as he tosses about pots, pans, and whatever else comes in his way as he searches for the trysting spot of his wife Georgina (Helen Mirren) and her bookish lover Michael (Alan Howard)—Albert Spica (Michael Gambon), the thief of the title, rages: "I'll bloody find him, and I'll bloody kill him, and I'll bloody eat him." He will find him, torturing an angelic kitchen boy, Pup (Paul Russell), to get information about his whereabouts, leaving Pup so mauled he ends up hospitalized. He will kill him (rather bloodily), stuffing the lover with pages of his own books. And he will eat him, although not as he intended: prepared by Richard (Richard Bohringer), the cook, in an exquisite lampoon of French haute cuisine (glazed and sauced and steaming, circlets of fruit clinging to shoulder and thigh with a vegetable surround), served up by his wife as the legion of victims of Albert's violence and excess watch silently. "Try the cock," she tells him, "It's a delicacy. And you know where it's been." When he finally—after vomiting a bit at his first attempt—chokes down a bite, she kills him with a single bullet, denouncing him as a "cannibal."

That final meal is one for which we have been well prepared. Albert's indelicate remarks and brutal acts feed toward the human feast at the end. He interrogates one of his companions about whether he "ever tasted human milk? I mean recently, not all those years ago . . . I've heard human milk is quite a delicacy in some countries. It ought to be here." When the moll of another gangster alludes to his wife's having an affair, Albert stabs her in the cheek with a fork. Torturing the kitchen boy, he feeds him buttons torn from his shirt, and when he runs out, adds: "Well, there's one more button, your belly button." At Michael's murder scene, alluding to a previous dinner conversation about "prairie oysters," Albert tells an associate: "Now you're gonna have your chance, you're gonna chew his bollock," before reconsidering: "I didn't mean you had to literally eat his bollocks off, I meant it metaphorically. I don't want this to look like a sex murder." He may be willing to murder, but he does not want people to get the wrong idea.

Meanwhile, at another level, Albert's increasingly abusive and ever more public actions—escalating in abuse of Georgina from public slaps with a menu to blows that leave visible bruises, building in the restaurant from mere loudness and crudeness to rearranging tables to provide space for cabaret girls, attacks on other diners, and upending the kitchen in search of his adulterous wife—track a pattern toward the ultimate violation. Michael Walsh notes that Albert is "a triumph of Greenaway's impulse to catalog: he is sadistic, bullying, nagging, crude, loud, callous, self-important, sanctimonious, anti-Semitic, racist, misogynist, homophobic, drunken, unlettered, and possessed of a poor French accent."[1] And those traits amplify over the film's course. Taking Albert as exemplifying consumerist excesses of the era, Greenaway told one interviewer: "What I wanted to do was take cannibalism out of the margins and put it right in the center of the table and garnish it with the most expensive French sauces and surround it with beautiful sautéed vegetables and see what would happen—to try and understand the implications of that. Cannibalism can be easily used as a metaphor for the end of consumer society. After we've eaten everything else, we shall eat up one another. Two hundred years ago, Jonathan Swift encouraged us to take that step, albeit very satirically. In *CTW&L*, I was only being ironic."[2] The film's ending thus follows the arc of the story.

That arc tracks ever downward, toward chaos and ruination, toward the final cannibal feast. And yet it is all presented in a highly aestheticized manner, from the level of film style, production design, and music (Michael Nyman's exquisite meshing of baroque and minimalist styles) down to prop and costume details. Nigel Wheale notes: "The opulent restaurant itself is redolent of consumer excess of the 1980s. Two of the decade's style gurus were on hand to advise: Jean Paul Gaultier designed costumes for the waiters and waitresses, and Giorgio Locatelli of the Savoy Hotel, London, created fantasy food for display."[3] The aestheticized vileness and violence established distance.

The resulting disjunction between the assaultive and the aestheticized has deeply divided critics. Caryn James, in the *New York Times*, concluded of Greenaway's "elegant, stylized, and brutal new film" that it was "a work so intelligent and powerful that it evokes our best emotions and least civil impulses, so esthetically brilliant that it expands the boundaries of film itself."[4] Bert Cardullo, speaking of the "sheer vulgarity" of the film, dismisses it as "a mindless orgy of unspeakable brutality" that "has no idea at its heart, no premise that would justify its visual and corporeal excess . . . Greenaway's film is simply black, towards nothing in particular, despite the director's claim that its target is the savage gluttony of Thatcherite England."[5] Roger Ebert wonders, at the start of his review: "So, which is it? Pornographic, a savage attack on Thatcher, or both? Or is it simply about a cook, a thief, his wife and her lover?"[6] (Ebert concludes Thatcher is the main target). The film was, whatever the critical qualms, the nearest Greenaway has come to a box-office hit.[7]

As Cardullo's remarks suggest, at least part of the difficulty is in understanding the film's politics. Greenaway has repeatedly insisted that the film attacks Thatcherism: "*CTW&L* is a passionate and angry dissertation for me on the rich, vulgarian, Philistine, anti-intellectual stance of the present cultural situation in Great Britain, supported by that wretched woman who is raping the country, destroying the welfare state, the health system, mucking up the educational system, and creating havoc everywhere."[8] But the form of attack here—essentially, a cultural critique, coinciding only in some respects to the more familiar criticisms of the Left—confused many critics. To appreciate the character of this cultural critique, it is first necessary to evaluate Greenaway's method: to explore what he does with eating, to outline his layered formalism, and to unpack his range of allusions.

Eating emblematically: the form of the feast

The arc, from the outset—when, as blue curtains are drawn aside, feral dogs chew on chunks of discarded meat, and Albert and his associates arrive to abuse an unlucky competitor, stuffing his mouth with dog excrement ("learn to appreciate your food," Albert yells), before stripping him, kicking him, and urinating on him—had been about degradation, with a distinctly alimentary component. Greenaway's *Cook* followed a cornucopia of food films—including *Babette's Feast* (1987), *Long Live the Lady* (1987), and *Tampopo* (1985)[9]—in which corrupted feasts played out metaphors of social decay. Greenaway's own previous film, *Drowning by Numbers* (1988), featured lots of eating and decaying food, but he seemed less interested in dining than with the paradoxes of lushness and decay, themes he earlier played with in *Belly of the Architect* (1987) and *A Zed and Two Noughts* (1988). Here, he places the feast at the center. Albert embodies the impulse, in his implacable hunger, the shaping form for his greed, his selfishness, and his will to possess. Even his violence against others is shaped by his hunger: both Michael and the kitchen boy are assaulted by being force-fed. He is hungry, he says, "always"; because his desires can never be fulfilled, he always craves more. And he craves it to the exclusion of all others. As he tells Richard, "I am the only diner who matters here." Albert, insofar as he develops at all, becomes merely more all-consuming

Even here, Greenaway seems less interested in dining than in digestion. Vernon Gras observes: "Spica denies all transubstantiation or spiritualization of matter. Indeed, his greed turns haute cuisine, art, manners, style, even love into secondary effects of the alimentary canal."[10] Greenaway notes:

> Most of the food in the film is wasted, thrown away, destroyed, abandoned. You don't have to see the starving Ethiopians in this movie. They're there simply by the excess that's going in the other direction. "What do I care what the bookseller ate?" Albert says. "Everything ends up as shit in the end." So the film is about the alimentary canal, mouth to anus, mouth to anus. This idea very vigorously starts the film, with the awful scene where the man is forced to eat not human excrement, but dog excrement.[11]

The most visible example of such wanton waste is the two truckloads of meat Albert brings to the restaurant near the film's opening. Like everything else Albert contributes to the restaurant—the neon lights that splutter and spark and plunge the neighborhood into darkness (Richard wryly notes, "Thanks to Mr. Spica's *générosité*, the lights are out everywhere"), or the gold cutlery that, Richard demonstrates, can be easily bent—the dubious quality of Albert's offering makes it useless. So it is left in the carpark, the meat rotting until, days later, one truck provides the naked lovers a noxious escape from Albert's jealous rampage.

Albert shares Greenaway's orientation toward the endpoint of the alimentary canal, an obsession evident from the opening scene and reiterated in his constant reminders to people to "Wash your hands." After noting that the triumph of the good chef is that he "puts together unexpected things," Albert observes of his own passions: "You know, I'm an artist in the way I combine my business and my pleasure. Money's my business, eating's my pleasure. And Georgie's my pleasure too, but in a more private kind of way than

FIGURE 6.1 *Albert (right), in his element, shows off two manifestations of his compulsion to consume: his wife Georgina (center), and the extravagant table set for him by the Cook.*

stuffing the mouth and feeding the sewer." His eating is thus a component of his broader compulsion to consume and to possess (Figure 6.1).

The concluding cannibal feast is thus a culmination, a completion, of a pattern established earlier. As Greenaway told the New York Times: "I think we would all accept to some degree that consumerism is running wild and could very well destroy us all . . . The use of cannibalism in this film is to somehow imply that, having eaten and raped the rest of the world, the next step is to eat one another."[12] Albert's cannibalism is there all along, only literalized in his final bite.

Curtains, color coding, menus, and dichotomies: Greenaway's formalist layering

"I've always had a desire to organize things," Greenaway has said.[13] His forms of organization create an aesthetic distance between film spectacle and spectator. No less than four sets of formal codes govern the organization of *The Cook*: the deliberately theatrical setting, the ritual of daily menus, color-coded rooms, and thematic dichotomies.

The simplest of these devices is the deliberate invocation of the stage, beginning with curtains. Greenaway has noted:

> My cinema is deliberately artificial, and it's always self-reflexive . . . *The Cook, the Thief* opens with curtains opening and closes with curtains

closing . . . It refers very much towards the proscenium arch. When the camera moves, it moves in a very, very subjective, inorganic way.[14]

The controlled camera most overtly separates Greenaway's practice from typical portrayals of violence in mainstream cinema, where tracking shots pull the viewer into the action and point-of-view camera angles draw the audience into identification. Greenaway's tactics block identification and enforce a more neutral spectatorship. Also part of the movie's organizing conceit is that the restaurant functions as a stage: overtly artificial, deliberately un-naturalistic. As stage, it also functions as microcosm. The restaurant provides the stage not just for feasts but for all else in life: love, business, violence.

The daily menus (a week's sequence) frame and divide the film's time and space. The action of the film, up to the time of the lovers' flight, is limited to the restaurant and organized around the ritual of the evening meal. The menu cards thus nod to Aristotelian rules of unity of time and space. When the final menu card declares the restaurant closed for a private function, we know the film's conclusion is near. But the menus mark as well the absences, the unseen. Albert's daily business, a protection racket preying primarily on the small-fry of ethnic restaurants and street sellers, is spoken of but unrevealed. His brutality to Georgina is mostly unseen, visible only in the next evening's bruises. His brute sexuality is also heard, not seen, in his own bragging asides and in Georgina's anguished confession to her dead lover. The menu cards thus mark time but simultaneously evoke the absent social realities that alone give meaning to the nightly feast.

The color coding reinforces the inclusiveness of the setting by establishing specific zones for different activities. The outside world, the restaurant's desolate loading zone, is lit a deep blue; the kitchen green; the dining room red (and more luridly so as the film progresses); the bathrooms white. Lighting is not all that the color code covers: Georgina's dress, as she crosses from loading dock through the kitchen to her table, changes color to match, and her cigarette papers always correspond to the decor. The lovers, save in their first encounter in a toilet stall, are bathed in yellow light. Michael always dresses in brown. Only their love nest, the book repository, the one important location outside the restaurant, changes in hue: orange when the lovers arrive, night blue after Michael's death, yellow in the morning when Georgina confesses her past to her lover's corpse.

Greenaway has supplied meanings for his color choices:

> I wanted to work out a system that would allow color to come back dominantly and somehow organize the material . . . [W]e have certain,

fairly fixed ideas about color symbolism. Blue obviously means cold; green, in the West, means safety . . . There are obvious reasons why the cold exterior car par is blue-coded—it's the nether region, furthest away from the center of the whirlpool of action. The greens of the kitchen, apart from indicating safety, suggest the color of nature—therefore it's healing and embracing, the color of chlorophyll. Green represents the mythological jungle where all food comes from. Red means violence, carnivorousness, blood—the dining room where the center of violence happens. The uses of white in the toilet are a bit different. It's the place where the lovers fuck for the first time—it's heaven. Also, all colors combine to make white, so it's the focal point.[15]

These meanings can easily be multiplied: red suggests luxury as well as blood; all the off-site locations share a yellow-tinged hue.[16] But, whatever the thematic uses of these devices, one of their principal functions for Greenaway is as a tactic of distancing.

More central to the content of the film is Greenaway's use of fundamental dichotomies as organizing elements—birth/death, eating/defecating, eating/sex, eating/death, sex/death. What makes these oppositions sources of tension is the slippage between the terms, the undercurrents of relation that underpin the antitheses. "The pleasures are related," Albert expatiates at the table, "the naughty bits and the dirty bits are so close together." Georgina leaves this discourse to rendezvous with Michael in a stall in the woman's room, as if to prove his point. Albert, as noted, cannot separate eating and defecating. Richard, late in the movie, explains his culinary secrets to Georgina: "I charge a lot for anything black . . . Eating black food is like consuming death." Caviar, he suggests, is the most expensive because it is linked to both birth and death. The confession sets up the finale's cannibal feast. Georgina's obsessions are more orally fixated, as we know from her cigarettes and her first encounter with Michael. Sex and eating come together in the end, when she suggests Albert "Try the cock." The oppositions thus serve to characterize as well as to suggest broad themes.

These oppositions play off a more central one, of degradation and transcendence, evident in the film's repeated motif of cleansing. The film features three episodes of washing after degradation: the man smeared with feces at the opening, hosed clean by the kitchen staff; the kitchen boy bathed after being defiled by witnessing Albert's brutality to Georgina; and Georgina and Michael hosed down after their trip with the decaying meat. The kitchen boy's haunting recurrent choir song reiterates the theme, ever pleading, in the words of Psalm 51, "Wash me thoroughly from my inequities, and cleanse me." The motif's meaning is complex, multivalent.

At a literal level, the boy sings while cleaning plates (making the wasted food "iniquities," alluding to the excesses of a culture of consumption even at this level). But beyond that, when debtors are smeared in feces, when women like Georgina must submit to the brutalities of men like Albert, when his associates belch and drool vomit in the dining room, degradation defines the times; cleansing functions as a solution, a restoration of civility. When, finally, Albert himself is degraded, forced to eat his victim, the reversal provides expurgation.

Greenaway's formalist devices ensure the allegiance of the filmmaker to the ordering forces of civilization. Good manners are, after all, no more than a formal code. Critics have tended to lump Greenaway's formalism—which so strongly insists that we understand we are watching a movie rather than having an experience, and so deeply resists naturalism and the mechanics of identification that goes with it—with Brechtian alienation effect (*Verfremdungseffect*).[17] There are reasons for such conflation; Greenaway's practice of stripping away the illusionistic apparatus of cinema (letting us see, for example, that we are on a soundstage) derive from the precedents, especially, of Jean-Luc Godard, who, both formally and ideologically, draws directly from Bertolt Brecht's model.[18] But Greenaway is up to something somewhat different.

Brecht's alienation effect aimed to serve the dialectic (by creating space instead of losing it to audience identification) and to encourage didactic exposition, both to promote an explicitly Marxist aim. As Brecht wrote in "Theatre for Pleasure or Theatre for Instruction" (c. 1957): "Choruses enlightened the spectator about facts unknown to him. Films showed a montage of events from all over the world. Projections added statistical material. And as the 'background' came to the front of the stage so people's activity was subjected to criticism."[19] Distancing thus serves the didactic and dialectic interests of Brecht's "epic theatre."

But Greenaway, even if he starts at a similar point and employs some of the same devices, ends up somewhere else. Developing on the idea that actors "are ciphers . . . coat-hangers on which to hang ideas," he asserts: "It's part Brechtian alienation, it's part distance; but I want to make cinema a total form."[20] The aestheticizing impulse, rooted in Greenaway's painterly background, moves us some distance from Brechtian aims. As Paula Willoquet-Maricondi and Mary Alemany-Galway argue: "While Greenaway continues to use many of the self-reflexive and politically critical modes of the Brechtian cinema, his self-reflexivity is taken up in the service of a more radical form of free play of meaning that does not lead to closure."[21] We can read "closure" as "revolution" here, and Greenaway's distance from Brechtian distantiation first as a departure from ideological certainties, and second as an aesthetic assertion of "total cinema" (a recurrent phrase in his vocabulary[22]). As Greenaway has noted:

> All these minute references rely on the great cultures—Western civilization, the Greco-Roman, and the Judeo-Christian, which has tried to order and explain the world to its inhabitants for over 2,000 years. These devices should emphasize to viewers that they're watching artifice, a construction overlaid on the world. It is not natural, not slices of life . . . The very effort of placing cultural artifacts into a filmic frame is an attempt to order them.[23]

While this is every bit as distancing and alienating as Brechtian formulations, it is far from his "theatre of instruction." It presumes an audience that can do the uncoding.

Dutch painting, Jacobean tragedy, the French Revolution, and religious iconography: Greenaway's allusive layering

Reviewing *The Cook* for the *Washington Post*, Desson Howe alludes to Greenaway's "grand, multi-themed design" that "touches upon, among other Greenaway obsessions, religious themes, the French Revolution, Thatcherian England, Jacobean drama, [and] Dutch paintings."[24] But these are not just recurrent personal obsessions. Rather, they constitute a layered historical framework, drawn again from that template of "2,000 years" of Western civilization, deployed to guide our understanding. Thatcher's England is illuminated through analogies (to the Dutch "Golden Age," the Jacobean stage, France's revolutionary decades), while religious iconography hints at deeper meanings.

Greenaway secures the connection with Golden Age Dutch painting with the large-scale reproduction of Frans Hals's *The Banquet of the Officers of the St. George Civic Company* (1616), which dominates the rear wall of the dining room, the identification reinforced by the fact that Spica's gang wears costumes derived from the painting.[25] Dutch painting is also alluded to in the ways arrangements of food (especially in the pantries where the lovers tryst) recall the era's still lifes. Critics divide over the interpretation of the Hals backdrop, split over whether to see it as critical commentary on the present scene (as Vernon Gras argues, "He [Albert] and his cohorts dress like the Dutch merchants in the Franz [sic] Hals group portrait but the happy coexistence between commerce and culture found there has undergone an extreme perversion"[26]) or whether the Dutch burghers and Spica's gang amount to two versions of the same thing (as Ruth Johnston suggests, "[T]he feasting Haarlem corps is a representation of conspicuous consumption duplicated by Spica and his gang. At the same time, Spica's vulgarity and ruthlessness expose aspects of the emergent bourgeoisie that the group portrait of the militia fails to represent"[27]). Greenaway's own description of Hals's painting at a talk at the Courtauld Institute align him more with the latter camp:

> [A] dozen gentlemen with military pretentions, in fancy costume, vain, patriotic with their flag, celebrating their maleness and togetherness, a club keen to pay special prices for their separateness, roistering, throwing their money about, no doubt chauvinists, drinking heavily, snobbish, belching, farting, telling dirty sexist jokes, perhaps peeing behind the curtain . . . This gang of mediocre rogues, so brilliantly painted that you feel they might offer you a drink, or alternatively, smash your face, are always with us, 1616, 1990. No change.[28]

It is less a matter of critical commentary or historical development for Greenaway than simply the way triumphant commercial elites always behave.

The Jacobean stage, which inflects the core style of *The Cook*, above all in its depiction of violence, has a parallel place in Greenaway's imagination: "The golden age of Dutch painting is contemporary with Jacobean revenge tragedy and is also distinguished by the same mixture of the received and the real worlds."[29] While the cannibal feast the film envisions has deep roots in European culture, going back to the Greeks—the myth of Atreus serving Thyestes a stew of his slaughtered sons, the root cause of the curse on the House of Atreus[30]—the Greek theatrical convention of off-stage violence suits Greenaway less than the far bloodier Roman variation, in Seneca's *Thyestes*, which, he has argued, just getting translated in the Jacobean era, influenced the staged bloodiness of their revenge tragedies:

> At the time, roughly between 1590 and 1630, the Roman poet and dramatist Seneca was just being translated all over northern Europe. The plays of Seneca took things to extreme limits. The cutting off of limbs before the public—quite sensational stuff. I think there was also a sort of *fin de siècle* sensibility in Jacobean theatre. For me, these plays contain this peculiar mixture of violence and melancholia . . . [In *CTW&L*], those bodies bleed, copulate, fart, shit, pee—the bodily functions are very much emphasized, which relates back to Jacobean drama.[31]

As with the Dutch references, the Jacobean citations establish parallels between historical eras, as Greenaway has noted:

> The Jacobeans were looking over their shoulder at the [Elizabethan] Great Empire; Britain still looks over its shoulder at the Great Empire. In Jacobean times, syphilis was the new sexual scourge; we now have AIDS. There's a certain comparison in that sexuality became complicated, so there's a similar spirit of melancholy. The same sensation of fatalism exists vis-à-vis the sort of cruelty we see every day, especially cruelty in the home, the abuse of children, and so on.[32]

Beyond the specific historical referencing, a more general coincidence of aims is evident in the centrality of excess. As Carol Mejia LaPerle has argued about cannibalism in both Seneca and Shakespeare's *Titus Andronicus*, "[F]rom the perspective of a general economy, the revenger is a means to manage surplus, a side effect of pressures that emerge from excess."[33] Both the Dutch and Jacobean allusions thus refer to cultural manifestations of excess, to glut.

The French Revolution is the lover's obsession, the subject of his reading at the table where he dines alone, and the subject he is cataloging in the piles of old volumes at the book depository. It is a book titled *The French Revolution* with which Michael is killed, its torn pages stuffed down his throat. Albert later, feasting at the restaurant, mockingly recalls: "What did he say? The French Revolution was easier to swallow than Napoleon?" But the French Revolution has particular resonance in this context because of the deeply entrenched image of its own cannibalism. As Jacques Mallet du Pan put it in 1793, in his often quoted formulation: "Like to Saturn, the Revolution devours its own children."[34] Certainly by the time British cartoonists James Gillray and George Cruikshank were waging their war of images against the French Revolution in 1794–95, that image of the cannibalism of the revolution had become common currency, represented in, for example, images of the guillotine's consuming maw.[35]

Atop these specific historical reference points, Greenaway layers a range of religious iconography.[36] He has pointed out that

> the kitchen can also be seen as a cathedral. The cook sits at a kind of altar in a rounded apse area. The kitchen boy has a nimbus around his head and sings the 51st Psalm, which is about being an unworthy sinner—which the thief certainly is . . . The lovers who make love naked amid the food and foliage of the kitchen recall Adam and Eve. When they leave, they go to the book depository, the Tree of Knowledge.[37]

FIGURE 6.2 *Albert, in a grotesquely literal inversion of the cannibalism implicit in "The Last Supper," prepares to consume (under duress) the exquisitely glazed and sauced body of his wife's murdered lover.*

The repeated ritual cleansings also draw on religious iconography; the seating around the central table, with Albert always at the center, recalls the Last Supper (Figure 6.2); and the film's cannibal last supper perversely inverts the sacramental feast.[38] All of this additional resonance contributes to the layered meaning in the film, while also insisting on deeper meanings.

The enemies and allies of culture: the cultural critique of Thatcherism

No aspect of Greenaway's film more confounds critics than its politics, the form of its assault on Thatcherism. Greenaway has insisted on the point: "[T]he situation in England during the last years did anger me a great deal—this vulgar, unimaginative, anti-intellectual Thatcher government and its social pendant, the new Yuppie middle-class [*sic*] that decorates itself with art works and cultural achievements—so that some of my fury did surface again in the film."[39] Most reviewers have followed Greenaway's lead and read this film as explicitly political in ways his earlier work was not. But the form of the politics, and the success of it, has been a more difficult point.

Roger Ebert, asking "What is his motivation here?," answers himself: "[I]t is anger—the same anger that has inspired large and sometimes violent British crowds to demonstrating against Margaret Thatcher's poll tax that whips the poor and coddles the rich." But it is not particularly the disenfranchised on whose behalf Greenaway rails. Ebert adds:

> Some British critics are reading the movie this way: Cook = Civil servants, dutiful citizens. Thief = Thatcher's arrogance and support of the greedy. Wife = Britannia. Lover = Ineffectual opposition by leftists and intellectuals . . . But I am not sure Greenaway is simply making an Identikit protest movie, leaving us to put the labels on the proper donkeys. I think *The Cook, the Thief, His Wife, and Her Lover* is more of a meditation on modern times in general. It is about the greed of an entrepreneurial class that takes over perfectly efficient companies and steals their assets, that marches roughshod over timid laws in pursuit of its own aggrandizement, that rapes the environment, that enforces its tyranny on the timid majority.[40]

But this account overemphasizes the political dimensions of Thatcherism.

Others take the Left political critique of Thatcherism as a standard against which to measure Greenaway's failure. Hal Hinson complains of Albert: "In Greenaway's scheme of things, he is the incarnation of pure capitalist evil. But, watching the film, you get the impression that . . . his greatest crime is that he has appalling table manners and mispronounces the names of the French dishes."[41] Leonard Quart argues:

> In political terms, Albert is supposed to embody one of Thatcher's more terrifying success stories. He's an arriviste and philistine who mispronounces the entrees on the menu and is relentlessly and amorally attuned to the world of avarice and crass materialism . . . All of this is much too literal and facile. Viewing gross, working class Albert as a representative of the Thatcher ethos lets the audience off the hook.[42]

Nigel Wheale suggests that "there are also questions about the nature of his critique of Reagano-Thatcherite politics. If *The Cook* is a metaphorical film, as the director claims, what exactly could the figure of Spica stand for, in terms of an attack on the consequences of Thatcherism? Spica as a graceless monster, 'unleashed' from the working class by the new economic regime, is as much a victim of the new values as anyone else."[43] But this interpretation reads Thatcherism as privatization of formerly state-owned industries, utilities and assets to enforce competitive efficiency; reshaping of labour markets and trade-union law, again in the interests of a freer market; promotion of the entrepreneur economy in order to break the supposed "dependency culture," and finally, an assault on the privileges and protective practices of the established, professional classes and their institutions—legal, medical and scholastic.[44]

This is rather more of a range of targets, and more politically focused an understanding of the Thatcher regime, than what Greenaway proposes.

Michael Walsh takes the argument even further, making Greenaway's film as guilty as the Thatcherism it condemns: "[T]he film is symptomatic as much as analytical of Thatcherism . . . [T]he proletarian monster central to *The Cook* suggests that this film has joined in Thatcher's vengeance on the imagined values of the lower class orders."[45] This corresponds to Nita Rollins's analysis of the film's fashion sense: "[T]he fashions cannot be sustained as a class critique and completely serve the allegory of late capitalism's evils; they equivocate between enhancement and indictment."[46] Those whose understanding of the era is rooted in New Left critique find Greenaway on the wrong side of the revolutionary hopes of Thatcher's opposition.

But such readings misinterpret Greenaway's position in two ways: first, by positing revolutionary hope in his vision, when Greenaway's own position is, like that of the Jacobeans he echoes, more despairing; second, more critically, by missing the essentially cultural thrust of Greenaway's critique, which overlaps but does not coincide with the Left's position. Gavin Smith catches some of this:

> An unrepentant formalist, Greenway understands why the Eighties was the decade of Form; what he's after is an investigation of what happens when Style falls into the hands of a powerful philistine. British and European Style Culture, which emerged in the early Eighties as a youth-oriented, subversive, postmodern response to the banalities of consumerism, was eventually co-opted by precisely the market-led, conservative, elitist establishment it was designed to resist. This was partly because there was nothing egalitarian about it—it was an elitist proposition in the first place.[47]

Or, as Peter Wollen points out, "Greenaway's antipathy toward Thatcherism stems from an ethical and aesthetic dislike for the philistinism and vulgarity of her regime."⁴⁸ A defense of high culture, not the working class, underpins Greenaway's argument.

Those wanting a political critique of Thatcherism would be better served by looking elsewhere: to Stuart Hall, for example.⁴⁹ As cultural critique, Greenaway's film shares common ground with several other contemporaneous projects, Derek Jarman's *Last of England* (1987),⁵⁰ Mike Leigh's *Naked* (1993), and especially Martin Amis's *London Fields* (1989),⁵¹ which share Greenaway's essentially cultural ground of critique.⁵² But, as cultural critique, the focus shifts away from the political interests of the Left's attack on Thatcherism in significant respects. The point is to defend (essentially elite) cultural norms, specifically against the classless, tasteless, untrained newcomers who undermined it with their nouveau-riche excesses. This has more in common with snarky comments about Margaret Thatcher's being the daughter of a grocer (as often muttered by her Conservative critics as by her opponents on the left) than with political interpretations rooted in Marxist critiques of the capitalist order.

Albert embodies the assault on culture. His protection racket is sleazy, his dealings with underlings and foes brutal, his sexual tastes brutish. He is uncouth and ill-mannered at table, mispronounces French, does not read books. Within the framework of the film, these two lists are equated; his violence and his indelicacy are all one. Civilization equals civility, barbarism shades into barbarity.

Central to his character is misogyny. Late in the film, Georgina confesses: "I don't think he was interested in sex, at least not with me, not with women." What she hints at is not latent homosexuality but a more asexual self-absorption, with sexuality only as instrumentality, as power. "I do what I want with a woman," he declares at one point. In his relations with Georgina, this power is exercised through acts of force and degrading submission and through declarations of possession. His claims of possession are absolute. When he suspects her of masturbating in the bathroom, he yells: "You playing with yourself? That's not allowed, that's my property." But ownership is for Albert an end in itself; his sexuality is sterile, and possibly sterilizing. "The three miscarriages I've had so far," Georgina tells Michael, "have messed up my insides." The consolation she derives—that this "makes me a good lay"—applies only to sexuality completely divorced from reproduction, a dead-end vision of human society. Albert's sexuality is of a piece with his appetite: voracious in a purely destructive, consuming way.

Albert is oblivious to his own status as destroyer of culture. He believes his money has bought him class, even made him an arbiter of class. This most boorish of diners delivers lectures on table manners to his associates. He even envisions ways to improve Richard's restaurant: "If Richard were more interested in slogans, he'd do more business . . . Gold, it needs more gold . . . I like a lot of glasses, it highers the tone." But the consequences of Albert's gaudy tastes have already been made clear, in the blackout that results from his new neon sign.

Against Albert's darkness, his cultural black hole, Greenaway arrays the allies of culture, principally Georgina, Michael, and Richard, and brings them into a coalition through Georgina and Michael's affair, arranged through the contrivance and cooperation of Richard and the kitchen staff. As defenders of culture, however, they make a rather dismal, unhopeful set. For one, both Georgina and Richard are compromised already. They have made their pacts with Albert. Georgina has traded her body, an emblem of class, to Albert in exchange for a nice house, a clothing budget of 400 pounds a week, and a petrol allowance. For such material goods she endures Albert's abuse, offering only the token resistance of smoking against his wishes. Even such resistance, however, is merely self-destructive, harming him not at all. For his part, Richard has offered a regular table and an interest in the restaurant in exchange for what Albert calls "protection from the rash tempers of my men." Albert's own rash tempers Richard endures. Michael, while not so overtly compromised, lacks any leverage against Albert. He is a man of books in an unlettered age. The only time he tries to spread learning, by loaning books to the kitchen boy who brings meals to the couple in hiding, his actions put Albert on their trail. His commitment to culture—to fine meals and books—betrays Michael and results in his death.

And if Michael and Georgina's affair constitutes a form of resistance, an alliance of the cultured against culture's enemy, it is also, at best, an inside joke, a tweaking of the giant's nose. The affair also puts the couple in a compromised position. They can only undermine the enemy of culture by becoming uncultured themselves, by liaisons in toilets and pantries. When Georgina abandons underwear in the interest of speed, she assures Michael: "I'm learning fast how to cut corners, save time." As a method for facilitating sex, such sentiments are not far removed from Albert's. And, finally, their affair is as sterile as Georgina's marriage, as much a product of a civilization's dead end. Their first real conversation is, in this light, revealing. Michael asks her: "Why?" She answers: "Why what? Why am I married to him? Well, why aren't you married?" Michael has no answer for her. She has no answer for him. Confronting their own failure to perpetuate civilization, they both come up empty-handed.

The compromises and limitations of Albert's foes correspond to a broader problem as well: high culture itself is similarly compromised. Recall Hals's portrait: a product of the patronage of the triumphant capitalist class, however ill-mannered and boorish, upon whom painters have depended ever since private markets supplanted state-church commissions as artists' principal path of success. Greenaway points out: "Dutch painting is very bourgeois. It celebrates domesticity, rich accouterments, and all that."[53] Consider the restaurant: however much a bastion of manners and taste, still utterly in the sway of commercial imperatives.

Final feast

If the cannibalistic conclusion consists of a victory over Albert, it comes too late for Michael, and too late for at least a few of his favorite books. It does not save Georgina, for whom at best it simply offers revenge. It does not restore her lover, her innocence, her fertility. No clear direction is offered for any cultural restoration. At worst, the final episode can be read as Albert's triumph: at the moment the others recognize his cannibalism, they stoop to his methods. Albert's cannibalism, as noted, extends to his whole consuming agenda as much as to the final feast, but it becomes literal only because Georgina forces him to take a bite. Nor does the final murder restore a social order; the film makes clear that other gangsters wait in the wings to take Albert's place.

The hopelessness of the ending reflects the form of Greenaway's cultural critique. There is no aesthetic position outside of the entanglement of art and politics, any more than there is a humanity that can escape the alimentary imperatives or the inevitability of death and decay. Thus, even while confessing the roots of *The Cook* in fury against Thatcherism, Greenaway also insists: "I view the whole matter from a cosmic perspective. I don't take a position. I believe there are no more positions to take, no certainties, no facts."[54] In this, again, the Jacobean tenor of Greenaway's perspective is made clear; he shares their fatalism as well as their bloody stages.

Notes

1 Michael Walsh, "Allegories of Thatcherism: The Films of Peter Greenaway," in *Fires Were Started: British Cinema and Thatcherism*, ed. Lester Friedman (Minneapolis: University of Minnesota Press, 1992), 272–3.

2 Joel Siegel, "Greenaway by the Numbers," in *Peter Greenaway: Interviews*, ed. Vernon Gras and Marguerite Gras (Jackson: University Press of Mississippi, 2000), 86; see also 85.

3 Nigel Wheale, "*The Cook, the Thief, His Wife, and Her Lover*," in *Fifty Key British Films*, ed. Sarah Barrow and John White (London: Routledge, 2008), 183. Gaultier also designed costumes for Georgina.

4 Caryn James, "Review/Film; Peter Greenaway's Elegant and Brutal 'Cook.'" *New York Times* (April 6, 1990), http://www.nytimes.com/movie/review?res=9C0CE4DE1F3DF935A357 57C0A966958260 (accessed June 8, 2016).

5 Bert Cardullo, "Lovers and Other Strangers," *Hudson Review* 43, no. 4 (Winter 1991): 647.

6 Roger Ebert, "*The Cook, the Thief, His Wife, and Her Lover* (1999)" (January 1, 1999), http://www.rogerebert.com/reviews/the-cook-the-thief-his-wife-and-her-lover-1999 (accessed June 8, 2016).

7 Amy Lawrence, *The Films of Peter Greenaway* (Cambridge: Cambridge University Press, 1997), 165. These things are all relative; the Internet Movie Database lists the film's box office receipts as $7,724,701 in the United States and £640,213 in the United Kingdom. See http://www.imdb.com/title/tt0097108/business (accessed June 8, 2016).

8 Siegel, "Greenaway by the Numbers," 81.

9 Greenaway also mentions, aside from these, two earlier films: *Eating Raoul* (1982) and *La Grande Bouffe* (1977). Ibid., 85.

10 Vernon Gras, "Dramatizing the Failure to Jump the Culture/Nature Gap: The Films of Peter Greenaway," *New Literary History* 26, no. 1 (Winter 1995): 157.

11 Siegel, "Greenaway by the Numbers," 85.

12 Terry Trucco, "Film: The Man Will Eat Literally Anything," *New York Times* (April 1, 1990), http://www.nytimes.com/1990/04/01/movies/film-the-man-will-eat-literally-anything.html?pagewanted=all (accessed June 8, 2016).

13 Marcia Pally, "Cinema as the Total Art Form: An Interview with Peter Greenaway," in *Peter Greenaway: Interviews*, ed. Vernon Gras and Marguerite Gras (Jackson: University Press of Mississippi, 2000), 107.

14 Gavin Smith, "Food for Thought: An Interview with Peter Greenaway," in *Peter Greenaway: Interviews*, ed. Vernon Gras and Marguerite Gras (Jackson: University Press of Mississippi, 2000), 98.

15 Siegel, "Greenaway by the Numbers," 76–7; see also Palley, "Cinema as the Total Art Form," 109.

16 On color coding, see also William F. Van Wert, "Reviews: *The Cook, the Thief, His Wife and Her Lover*," *Film Quarterly* 44, no. 2 (1990–91): 48–9; Douglas Keesey, *The Films of Peter Greenaway: Sex, Death, and Provocation* (Jefferson, NC: McFarland, 2006), 86–7.

17 See, for example, Nicholas O. Pagan, "*The Cook, the Thief, His Wife, & Her Lover*: Making Sense of Postmodernism." *South Atlantic Review* 60, no. 1 (January 1995): 43; Wheale, "*The Cook, the Thief, His Wife, and Her Lover*," 184–5; Keesey, *The Films of Peter Greenaway*, 42–3, 96–7; Bridget Elliot and Anthony Purdy, *Peter Greenaway: Architecture and Allegory* (Arden, NC: Academy Press, 1979), 70–9.

18 Greenaway regularly references Godard in interviews. See Michel Ciment, "Interview with Peter Greenaway: *Zed and Two Noughts (Z.O.O)*," in

Peter Greenaway: Interviews, ed. Vernon Gras and Marguerite Gras (Jackson: University Press of Mississippi, 2000), 319; Alan Woods, "Arts of Painting: An Interview with Peter Greenaway," in *Peter Greenaway: Artworks 63–98*, ed. Peter Greenaway, Paul Melia, and Alan Woods (Manchester: Manchester University Press, 1999), 132; Peter Greenaway, "Body and Text & Eight and a Half Women: A Laconic Black Comedy," in *Peter Greenaway's Postmodern/Poststructuralist Cinema*, ed. Paula Willoquet-Maricondi and Mary Alemany-Galway (Lanham, MD: Scarecrow Press, 2001), 295–6. Critics reference his referencing of Godard. See, for example, Lawrence, *Films of Peter Greenaway*, 8, 79, 102, 204 n. 34; Alan Woods, *Being Naked—Playing Dead: The Art of Peter Greenaway* (Manchester: Manchester University Press, 1996), 16–17; Pagan, "*The Cook, the Thief, His Wife, and Her Lover*: Making Sense of Postmodernism," 44–5; Ruth D. Johnston, "The Staging of the Bourgeois Imaginary in *The Cook, the Thief, His Wife, and Her Lover*," *Cinema Journal* 4, no. 2 (Winter 2002): 22; Randy Laist, *Cinema of Simulation: Hyperreal Hollywood in the Long 1990s* (London: Bloomsbury, 2015), 190.

19 Bertolt Brecht, "Theatre for Pleasure or Theatre for Instruction," in *Brecht on Theatre: The Development of an Aesthetic*, ed. John Willett (New York: Farrar, Strauss, and Giroux, 1964), 71–2. Brecht asserts that the theatre could be both, but instruction, clearly, matters more. For fuller explanation, see (aside from the rest of Willett's collection of Brecht's theatre writings) Peter Brooker, "Key Words in Brecht's Theory and Practice," in *The Cambridge Companion to Brecht*, ed. Peter Thomson and Glendyr Sacks (Cambridge: Cambridge University Press, 1994), 185–200.

20 Paula Willoquet-Maricondi, "Two Interviews with Peter Greenaway," in *Peter Greenaway's Postmodern/Poststructuralist Cinema*, ed. Paula Willoquet-Maricondi and Mary Alemany-Galway (Lanham, MD: Scarecrow Press, 2001), 305.

21 Paula Willoquet-Maricondi and Mary Alemany-Galway, "Introduction: A Postmodern/Poststructuralist Cinema," in *Peter Greenaway's Postmodern/Poststructuralist Cinema*, ed. Paula Willoquet-Maricondi and Mary Alemany-Galway (Lanham, MD: Scarecrow Press, 2001), xvi, xvii.

22 See especially Pally, "Cinema as the Total Art Form: An Interview with Peter Greenaway," 106–19; Lawrence Chua, "Peter Greenaway," *BOMB* 60 (1997): 26–9. On the costuming, see Nita Rollins, "Greenaway-Gaultier: Old Masters, Fashion Slaves," *Cinema Journal* 35, no. 1 (Autumn 1995): 65–80.

23 Pally, "Cinema as the Total Art Form," 110.

24 Desson Howe, "*The Cook, the Thief, His Wife & Her Lover* (NC-17)," *Washington Post* (April 7, 1990), http://www.washingtonpost.com/wp-srv/style/longterm/movies/videos /thecookthethiefhiswifeherlovernc17hinson_a0a91c.htm (accessed June 8, 2016).

25 The uniforms also hint more subtly at the common-costumed hooligans of Stanley Kubrick's *A Clockwork Orange* (1971). The dominating place of the Hals reproduction in the restaurant means it has received

significant critical commentary. See Gras, "Dramatizing the Failure," 135–7; Johnston, "Staging the Bourgeois Imaginary," 20–1, 25–7, and 35–6 n. 8; Lawrence, *The Films of Peter Greenaway*, 169–70; Rollins, "Greenaway-Gaultier," 72–6; Keesey, *Films of Peter Greenaway*, 88–9; Woods, *Being Naked*, 72–3; Ingeborg Hoestery, *Pastiche: Cultural Memory in Art, Film, and Literature* (Bloomington: Indiana University Press, 2001), 73–4; David Paseos, *Peter Greenaway: Museums and Moving Images* (London: Reaktion Books, 1997), 173–80; Dayana Stetco, "The Crisis of Commentary: Tilting at Windmills in Peter Greenaway's *The Cook, the Thief, His Wife and Her Lover*," in *Peter Greenaway's Postmodern/Poststructuralist Cinema*, ed. Paula Willoquet-Maricondi and Mary Alemany-Galway (Lanham, MD: Scarecrow Press, 2001), 210, 218–20. See also Greenaway's comments on Dutch painting in Siegel, "Greenaway by the Numbers," 79–80.

26 Gras, "Dramatizing the Failure," 137; see also Rollins, "Greenaway-Gaultier," 75.
27 Johnston, "Staging the Bourgeois Imaginary," 20–1.
28 Quoted in Willoquet-Maricondi and Alemany-Galway, "Introduction," xxviii n. 1.
29 Siegel, "Greenaway by the Numbers," 79.
30 See Robert Graves, *Greek Myths*. 2 vols (Harmondsworth: Penguin, 1955), 2: 43–51, for the full story.
31 Siegel, "Greenaway by the Numbers," 68–9, 83. See also Pascale Aebischer, *Screening Early Modern Drama: Beyond Shakespeare* (Cambridge: Cambridge University Press, 2013), 66–75.
32 Quoted in Peter Wollen, "The Last New Wave: Modernism in the British Films of the Thatcher Era," in *Fires Were Started: British Cinema and Thatcherism*, ed. Lester Friedman (Minneapolis: University of Minnesota Press, 1992), 48.
33 Carol Mejia LaPerle, "The Crime Scene of Revenge Tragedy: Sacrificial Cannibalism in Seneca's *Thyestes* and Shakespeare's *Titus Andronicus*," *Concentric: Literary and Cultural Studies* 38, no. 1 (March 2012): 11. Usefully, LaPerle anchors her reading in the theories of Georges Bataille, whom Greenaway identifies among the inheritors of the Jacobean tradition.
34 Jacques Mallet du Pan, *Considerations on the Nature of the French Revolution and on the Causes That Prolong Its Duration* (London: J. Owen, 1793), 90; in the French text, published that same year, *Considérations sur la Nature de la Révolution de France*, 80. For critical analysis of the French Revolutionary theme in the film, see Keesey, *The Films of Peter Greenaway*, 94–5; Stetco, "The Crisis of Commentary," 219–20.
35 See John Richard Moores, *Representations of France in English Satirical Prints, 1742–1832* (London: Palgrave, 2015), chapter 5; see also Ronald Paulson, *Representations of Revolution, 1789–1820* (New Haven: Yale University Press, 1983).

36 Indeed, he challenged Joel Siegel to find the patterns: "Greenaway asks me if I had spotted any of the religious allusions he had included in *CTW&L*." Siegel, "Greenaway by the Numbers," 87. Siegel does not follow up on the prompt.

37 Pally, "Cinema as the Total Art Form," 110. Keesey also notes the Edenic motif of the lovers' locale and the expulsion motif when they are driven out of the kitchen; see *Films of Peter Greenaway*, 88.

38 Keesey, *Films of Peter Greenaway*, 91; Siegel, "Greenaway by the Numbers," 71.

39 Andreas Kilb, "I Am the Cook: An Interview with Peter Greenaway," in *Peter Greenaway: Interviews*, ed. Vernon Gras and Marguerite Gras (Jackson: University Press of Mississippi, 2000), 64; see also Siegel, "Greenaway by the Numbers," 81; Smith, "Food for Thought," 93.

40 Ebert, "*The Cook, the Thief, His Wife, and Her Lover*," http://www.rogerebert.com/reviews/the-cook-the-thief-his-wife-and-her-lover-1999.

41 Hinson, "*The Cook, the Thief, His Wife, and Her Lover*," 1990.

42 Leonard Quart, "*The Cook, the Thief, His Wife and Her Lover*," *Cineaste* 18, no. 1 (1990): 46.

43 Wheale, "*The Cook*," 185.

44 Ibid., 181.

45 Walsh, "Allegories of Thatcherism," 181.

46 Rollins, "Greenaway-Gaultier," 76.

47 Smith, "Food for Thought," 92.

48 Wollen, "Last New Wave," 47.

49 See especially Hall, *Hard Road to Renewal*.

50 Peter Wollen notes that both Jarman and Greenaway were absent from the more rigorously political discussions of film theory spearheaded by Peter Sainsbury at BFI in the 1970s. See "Last New Wave," 48.

51 Amis and Greenaway share a range of common tropes, including the fascination with the alimentary (see Keith Talent's love of fiery curries), attention to the deeply rooted racism of Britain's lower classes (Keith again), and an insistent interest in unproductive sexuality (Nicola Six's preference for anal sex), as well as a looming apocalyptic sensibility. See Martin Amis, *London Fields* (London: Jonathan Cape, 1989).

52 For a somewhat parallel argument, with a longer list of similar works, see Stephen Brooke, and Louise Cameron. "Anarchy in the UK?: Ideas of the City and the 'Fin de Siècle' in Contemporary English Film and Literature," *Albion* 28, no. 4 (Winter 1996): 635–6. Amy Lawrence's argument that *The Cook* is essentially a gangster genre picture (see *The Films of Peter Greenaway*, chapter 7) opens up other parallels, notably including *The Long Good Friday* (1980), *Mona Lisa* (1986), and *The Krays* (1990). I remain less than fully convinced by her argument.

53 Siegel, "Greenaway by the Numbers," 79.

54 Kilb, "I Am the Cook," 64.

Bibliography

Aebischer, Pascale. *Screening Early Modern Drama: Beyond Shakespeare.* Cambridge: Cambridge University Press, 2013.

Amis, Martin. *London Fields.* London: Jonathan Cape, 1989.

Brecht, Bertolt. "Theatre for Pleasure or Theatre for Instruction" (c. 1957). In *Brecht on Theatre: The Development of an Aesthetic*, edited by John Willett, 69–77. New York: Farrar, Strauss, and Giroux, 1964.

Brooke, Stephen, and Louise Cameron. "Anarchy in the UK?: Ideas of the City and the 'Fin de Siècle' in Contemporary English Film and Literature." *Albion* 28, no. 4 (Winter 1996): 635–56.

Brooker, Peter. "Key Words in Brecht's Theory and Practice." In *The Cambridge Companion to Brecht*, edited by Peter Thomson and Glendyr Sacks, 185–200. Cambridge: Cambridge University Press, 1994.

Cardullo, Bert. "Lovers and Other Strangers." *Hudson Review* 43, no. 4 (Winter 1991): 645–53.

Chua, Lawrence. "Peter Greenaway." *BOMB* 60 (1997): 26–9.

Ciment, Michel. "Interview with Peter Greenaway: *Zed and Two Noughts (Z.O.O)*." In *Peter Greenaway: Interviews*, edited by Vernon Gras and Marguerite Gras, 28–41. Jackson: University Press of Mississippi, 2000.

Du Pan, Jacques Mallet. *Considerations on the Nature of the French Revolution and on the Causes that Prolong Its Duration.* London: J. Owen, 1793.

Du Pan, Jacques Mallet. *Considérations sur la Nature de la Révolution de France, et Sur les Causes qui prolongent la Durée.* London/Bruxelles: Chez Emm. Flon, 1793.

Ebert, Roger. "*The Cook, the Thief, His Wife, and Her Lover*," http://www.rogerebert.com/reviews/the-cook-the-thief-his-wife-and-her-lover-1999

Elliot, Bridget, and Anthony Purdy. *Peter Greenaway: Architecture and Allegory.* Arden, NC: Academy Press, 1979.

Friedman, Lester, ed. *Fires Were Started: British Cinema and Thatcherism.* Minneapolis: University of Minnesota Press, 1992.

Gras, Vernon. "Dramatizing the Failure to Jump the Culture/Nature Gap: The Films of Peter Greenaway." *New Literary History* 26, no. 1 (Winter 1995): 123–43.

Gras, Vernon, and Marguerite Gras, eds. *Peter Greenaway: Interviews.* Jackson: University Press of Mississippi, 2000.

Graves, Robert. *Greek Myths.* 2 vols. Harmondsworth: Penguin, 1955.

Greenaway, Peter. "Body and Text & Eight and a Half Women: A Laconic Black Comedy." In *Peter Greenaway's Postmodern/Poststructuralist Cinema*, edited by Paula Willoquet-Maricondi and Mary Alemany-Galway, 289–300. Lanham, MD: Scarecrow Press, 2001.

Hall, Stuart. *The Hard Road to Renewal: Thatcherism and the Crisis of the Left.* London: Verso, 1988.

Hoestery, Ingeborg. *Pastiche: Cultural Memory in Art, Film, and Literature.* Bloomington: Indiana University Press, 2001.

Howe, Desson. "*The Cook, the Thief, His Wife & Her Lover* (NC-17)." *Washington Post*, April 7, 1990. http://www.washingtonpost.com/wp-srv/style/longterm/movies/videos/ thecookthethiefhiswifeherlovernc17hinson_a0a91c.htm (accessed June 8, 2016).

James, Caryn. "Review/Film; Peter Greenaway's Elegant and Brutal 'Cook.'" *New York Times*, April 6, 1990. http://www.nytimes.com/movie/review?res=9C0CE4DE1F3DF935A357 57C0A966958260 (accessed June 8, 2016).

Johnston, Ruth D. "The Staging of the Bourgeois Imaginary in *The Cook, the Thief, His Wife and Her Lover*." *Cinema Journal* 4, no. 2 (Winter 2002): 19–40.

Keesey, Douglas. *The Films of Peter Greenaway: Sex, Death, and Provocation*. Jefferson, NC: McFarland, 2006.

Kilb, Andreas. "I Am the Cook: An Interview with Peter Greenaway." In *Peter Greenaway: Interviews*, edited by Vernon Gras and Marguerite Gras, 60–5. 1989. Jackson: University Press of Mississippi, 2000.

Laist, Randy. *Cinema of Simulation: Hyperreal Hollywood in the Long 1990s*. London: Bloomsbury, 2015.

LaPerle, Carol Mejia. "The Crime Scene of Revenge Tragedy: Sacrificial Cannibalism in Seneca's *Thyestes* and Shakespeare's *Titus Andronicus*." *Concentric: Literary and Cultural Studies* 38, no. 1 (March 2012): 9–28.

Lawrence, Amy. *The Films of Peter Greenaway*. Cambridge: Cambridge University Press, 1997.

Moores, John Richard. *Representations of France in English Satirical Prints, 1742–1832*. London: Palgrave, 2015.

Pagan, Nicholas O. "*The Cook, the Thief, His Wife, & Her Lover*: Making Sense of Postmodernism." *South Atlantic Review* 60, no. 1 (January 1995): 43–55.

Pally, Marcia. "Cinema as the Total Art Form: An Interview with Peter Greenaway." In *Peter Greenaway: Interviews*, edited by Vernon Gras and Marguerite Gras, 106–19. Jackson: University Press of Mississippi, 2000.

Paseos, David. *Peter Greenaway: Museums and Moving Images*. London: Reaktion Books, 1997.

Paulson, Ronald. *Representations of Revolution, 1789–1820*. New Haven: Yale University Press, 1983.

Quart, Leonard. "*The Cook, the Thief, His Wife and Her Lover*." *Cineaste* 18, no. 1 (1990): 45–7.

Rollins, Nita. "Greenaway-Gaultier: Old Masters, Fashion Slaves." *Cinema Journal* 35, no. 1 (Autumn 1995): 65–80.

Siegel, Joel. "Greenaway by the Numbers." In *Peter Greenaway: Interviews*, edited by Vernon Gras and Marguerite Gras, 66–90. 1990. Jackson: University Press of Mississippi, 2000.

Smith, Gavin. "Food for Thought: An Interview with Peter Greenaway." In *Peter Greenaway: Interviews*, edited by Vernon Gras and Marguerite Gras, 91–105. 1990. Jackson: University Press of Mississippi, 2000.

Stetco, Dayana. "The Crisis of Commentary: Tilting at Windmills in Peter Greenaway's *The Cook, the Thief, His Wife and Her Lover*." In *Peter Greenaway's Postmodern/Poststructuralist Cinema*, edited by Paula Willoquet-Maricondi and Mary Alemany-Galway, 203–22. Lanham, MD: Scarecrow Press, 2001.

Trucco, Terry. "Film: The Man Will Eat Literally Anything." *New York Times*, April 1, 1990. http://www.nytimes.com/1990/04/01/movies/film-the-man-will-eat-literally-anything.html?pagewanted=all (accessed June 8, 2016).
Van Wert, William F. "Reviews: *The Cook, the Thief, His Wife and Her Lover*." *Film Quarterly* 44, no. 2 (1990–91): 42–50.
Walsh, Michael. "Allegories of Thatcherism: The Films of Peter Greenaway." In *Fires Were Started: British Cinema and Thatcherism*, edited by Lester Friedman, 255–77. Minneapolis: University of Minnesota Press, 1992.
Wheale, Nigel. "*The Cook, the Thief, His Wife, and Her Lover.*" In *Fifty Key British Films*, edited by Sarah Barrow and John White, 181–6. London: Routledge, 2008.
Willoquet-Maricondi, Paula. "Two Interviews with Peter Greenaway." In *Peter Greenaway's Postmodern/Poststructuralist Cinema*, edited by Paula Willoquet-Maricondi and Mary Alemany-Galway, 301–20. Lanham, MD: Scarecrow Press, 2001.
Willoquet-Maricondi, Paula, and Mary Alemany-Galway, eds. *Peter Greenaway's Postmodern/Poststructuralist Cinema*. Lanham, MD: Scarecrow Press, 2001.
Willoquet-Maricondi, Paula, and Mary Alemany-Galway. "Introduction: A Postmodern/Poststructuralist Cinema." In *Peter Greenaway's Postmodern/Poststructuralist Cinema*, xi–xxviii. Lanham, MD: Scarecrow Press, 2001.
Wollen, Peter. "The Last New Wave: Modernism in the British Films of the Thatcher Era." In *Fires Were Started: British Cinema and Thatcherism*, edited by Lester Friedman, 35–51. Minneapolis: University of Minnesota Press, 1992.
Woods, Alan. *Being Naked—Playing Dead: The Art of Peter Greenaway*. Manchester: Manchester University Press, 1996.
Woods, Alan. "Arts of Painting: An Interview with Peter Greenaway." In *Peter Greenaway: Artworks 63–98*, edited by Peter Greenaway, Paul Melia, and Alan Woods, 129–41. Manchester: Manchester University Press, 1999.

7

"The red gums were their own": Food, Flesh, and the Female in *Beloved*

Bart Bishop

It took more than a decade for *Beloved*, Toni Morrison's 1987 novel of a former slave haunted by the child she killed, to be adapted for the screen. Thematically rich, the film explores complex issues of race, gender, sex, and motherhood. This is done through the lens of familiar horror movie tropes, with all of these elements converging around the central, unifying concept of sustenance, whether literal food—especially that which a mother passes to her child—or figurative essence.

The literary and screen versions of *Beloved* share almost identical plots, based upon the true story of Margaret Garner, a slave who killed her own daughter to prevent her enslavement. Garner and her family escaped from Maplewood farm in Boone County, Kentucky, in January 1856, crossing the frozen Ohio River to Cincinnati. They took shelter in the home of one of Garner's relatives while awaiting passage to Canada but were discovered by slave-catchers, accompanied by US Marshals acting under the Fugitive Slave Law of 1850. Garner had killed her two-year-old daughter with a butcher knife and was preparing to kill her other children and herself when the Marshals took her into custody. Garner's defense attorney pressed to have her declared a person and tried for murder under Ohio state law (in order to keep her in the state), but after an unprecedented two-week trial the presiding judge ruled that the federal Fugitive Slave Law took precedence and declared her to be property. She was duly returned to her master, who sent her first to Kentucky, then south to Arkansas, and finally to New Orleans, where she died in a typhoid epidemic in 1858. Garner's story went on to inspire Frances Harper's 1859 poem "Slave Mother: A Tale of Ohio," the 1867 painting *The Modern Medea* by Thomas Satterwhite Noble, the 2005 opera *Margaret Garner*, and of course *Beloved*.

In *Beloved*, Sethe (Oprah Winfrey), the character based on Garner, is a former slave living in Cincinnati with her teenage daughter Denver (Kimberly Elise) in 1873. Eighteen years earlier, while pregnant with Denver, Sethe escaped from slavery on the Sweet Home plantation, but was pursued to Cincinnati by her former owner, known only as School Teacher. Rather than allow her children to be returned to slavery, Sethe killed her baby, Beloved, and attempted to do the same to Denver, who had already been born, and two sons. Told through flashbacks and oral storytelling, the film uses stylistic touches such as quick-cut editing and Dutch angles to evoke the off-kilter world of the house at 124 Bluestone Road, tainted by the vengeful energy of the martyred baby.

The plot is set in motion by the arrival of Paul D. (Danny Glover), a former resident of Sweet Home himself, who exorcises the ghost of Beloved through sheer force of will. The plan backfires, however, and Beloved manifests in the flesh as the young woman (Thandie Newton) she might have become had she lived. Jealous of the burgeoning love between Sethe and Paul D., Beloved bewitches him and forces herself on him sexually, feeding on his life energy and eventually driving him away. Sethe, guilt-ridden, tries to appease the increasingly jealous and possessive Beloved with sweets and food, neglecting Denver and eventually impoverishing and starving herself in the process. Denver leaves home—allowing Beloved to achieve her goal of having Sethe to herself—but eventually gathers the other women of their African American neighborhood and returns with them to 124 Bluestone. The women confront Sethe, along with a swollen and perhaps pregnant Beloved, on the steps of the house and achieve closure at last. Beloved disappears and Sethe, with Paul D.'s encouragement, is finally able to forgive herself.

Beloved won a Pulitzer Prize in 1988, and Winfrey acquired the rights shortly afterward, intending to bring the story to the big screen with herself in the role of Sethe. Adapted by Adam Books, Akosua Busia, and Richard LaGravenese, the film was directed by Jonathan Demme, whose two previous films—*The Silence of the Lambs* (1991) and *Philadelphia* (1993)—had enjoyed both box-office success and critical acclaim. Despite the prestige brought to the project by Morrison, Winfrey, and Demme, however, *Beloved* was a disappointment both commercially (grossing only $22,852,487 domestically compared to an $80 million budget) and on the awards circuit, where it was nominated for, but did not win, a single Academy Award (for Best Costume Design). Fifteen years later, when asked about *Beloved*, Winfrey defended the project:

> Was it a mistake to not try and make that a more commercial film? To take some things out and tell the story differently so that it would be more palatable to an audience? Well, if you wanted to make a film that everybody would see, then that would be a mistake. But at the time, I was pleased with the film that we did because it represented to me the essence of the *Beloved* book..[1]

Food and the fantastic

One reason the public may not have responded to the movie is because of its genre-bending subject matter. At its heart, *Beloved* is a historical drama about the toll taken by slavery—even years after the fact—on the lives of those enslaved. Winfrey's desire to honor the "essence" of the novel, however, led the filmmakers to weave in other elements that may have startled audiences expecting a straightforward "prestige" adaptation of a Pulitzer Prize–winning piece of literary fiction.

These elements include horror-movie conceits ranging from poltergeists to zombies to vampires; a magical-realist tone reflecting a naturalistic handling of fantastical elements; and the recurring use of animals, liquids, the kitchen and the color red as motifs. They are utilized to portray three primal archetypes with obsessive needs to consume that will be examined in this argument: the *vagina dentata*, the trickster, and the devouring mother. Beloved is a succubus, representing both a *vagina dentata* that preys upon Paul D.'s manhood and a vampire that feeds on Sethe's motherly love. Paul D. is a trickster, crashing into Sethe's life and feeding off of her both financially and emotionally. And Sethe is a devouring mother that sees her own worth in how she can feed her children—first with breast milk and later with candy and sweets—but in doing so keeps herself and them from ever gaining individual identities. The result is a story of self-destructive relationships that pervert nourishment, resulting in the crumbling of family bonds.

Beloved appropriates familiar horror-movie-monster concepts and imagery to explore existential questions of guilt and how the past defines the present. Nöel Carroll focuses on this theme as formative in horror genre narratives, what he calls the theme of discovery: "In the overreacher plot, the overreacher discovers some secret of the universe, often to the dismay of the rest of humanity. And, in most of the plot structures derived from the complex discovery plot, the discovery of that which heretofore was denied existence is foregrounded."[2] In *Beloved*, the three leads, Sethe, Denver, and Paul D., overreach through need, want, and arrogance in their behavior toward the titular character by welcoming her in after provoking her supernatural threat in the first place.

This overreaching is part of the allegorical nature of the story that is complemented by the tone of magical realism carried over from the novel. Magical realism, "what happens when a highly detailed, realistic setting is invaded by something too strange to believe,"[3] can also be found in many films with fantasy elements. These characteristics tend to be presented matter-of-factly and occur without explanation, such as in this case, where the presence of the paranormal, ghosts and the return of the dead, although acknowledged with trepidation, are accepted as not only possible but probable. One of the very first things Denver says to Paul D. upon his arrival at 124 Bluestone is, "We have a ghost here, you know?" Paul D.—who, it is clear, sees the ghost as a threat—accepts this immediately, and without doubt.

This may not be as far from "reality" as it seems. Ghosts were an ever-present aspect of plantation life; some were merely pranksters stealing umbrellas and hiding tools, but most were sinister. As Zora Neale Hurston wrote in her 1935 compilation of African American folktales *Mules and Men*: "All over the South and in the Bahamas the spirits of the dead have great power which is used chiefly to harm."[4] Hurston describes some ghosts as growing "very fat if they get plenty to eat," and being "very fond of honey," reminiscent of Beloved's tastes for sweets suggesting Morrison's familiarity with *Mules and Men* or the folklore itself.[5] This voraciousness forebodes a desperate clinging to the physical world and a bottomless need that drives the unsettled spirits. These spirits not only function in a literal sense but speak volumes about ex-slaves haunted by their pasts. Sethe is a kind of face of the trauma of America's sins, eaten away by factors outside of her control and carrying the guilt of an entire country and pain of an entire race.

The magical realist tone lends the story an allegorical quality that allows for the prominence of motifs that express the theme of consumption: animals, liquids, the kitchen, and the color red. The first motif draws parallels between the characters and animals. Paul D. is shackled like a beast in his youth and as an older man works in the meatpacking district of Cincinnati—known as "Porkopolis" at the time because its proximity to the Ohio River made transportation easy—herding the swine to their deaths. Beloved's reintroduction to the living world sees her covered in beetles and butterflies.

Most importantly, however, in a flashback to her attempted escape from Sweet Home, Sethe's milk is suckled directly from her breasts against her will by teenage boys. Shot in a startling first-person perspective, the scene shows School Teacher presiding over his nephews and instructing them to "Milk it like a cow. That's what we mean by animal characteristics."

Stephanie Demetrakopoulos views this act as "motherhood in its most denied form, the mother enslaved, reduced to a brood mare."[6] Sethe has been separated from her three children, including the still-breastfeeding Beloved, while carrying a fourth; the most primordial connection between mother and child is tainted and psychologically tied to her life as a slave. For Sethe her only sense of freedom comes from agency over her own motherhood. Robbed of those bonds, she later reverts to an animalistic, instinctual state of mind when School Teacher arrives at 124 Bluestone, where Sethe has been hiding with her children. Sethe's subsequent slitting of Beloved's throat is, appropriately enough, not unlike the slaughtering of a cow. It's no coincidence that later in the movie when Paul D. is told this story he admonishes Sethe that she has two feet, not four.

The second motif, the omnipresence of liquids, recurs throughout the movie. Sethe's breast milk is stolen from her, which causes a rift between her and Denver because feeding the new baby and the toddler Beloved becomes an obsession—to the point that it is one of the few ways she knows how to express love. When Sethe is discovered with the dead Beloved in her arms, covered in blood, Demme frames the shot as if the baby is breastfeeding, tainting the imagery. Upon seeing the grown Beloved for the first time in her yard, Sethe runs away with the uncontrollable urge to urinate, not unlike her water breaking before labor. Beloved's stealing of Paul D.'s semen, examined later, robs him not just of his life force but also of his masculinity and brings him in line with the thematic association of females with liquid.

The third motif, the kitchen setting, plays an important role in major turning points of the story as the house functions as a personification of Sethe's womanly body and the kitchen is her womb, under her control. The very first scene has the family dog attacked by the poltergeist in the kitchen and knocked against a wall hard enough to cause one eye to pop out. Sethe calmly places the eye back in the socket, imposing some bit of order on the situation. One of her sons, meanwhile, is ransacking the place in his bid to escape, but when he tries to steal a piece of cake already marked by two child-sized hands, it pulls away from him, establishing Beloved's voracious hunger from the start.

Later, when Paul D. first arrives, he struggles to make his way to the kitchen, asking Sethe, "Good God, girl. What kind of evil you got in there?" to which Sethe replies with remarkable dignity, "It ain't evil. Just sad." What results

FIGURE 7.1 *Tensions rise at the dinner table for Denver (Kimberly Elise), Paul D. (Danny Glover), and Beloved (Thandie Newton).*

is a kind of simultaneous rape and forced abortion, as Paul D. tussles with Beloved in her place of power and primary residence. Once Paul D. strong-arms his way into the kitchen he rages against the terrorizing revenant to drive it out, not unlike a male lion eating the cubs of a lioness he has claimed.

Afterward, the kitchen and adjoining dining area are a communal zone and the heart of the house, symbolic of the promise of a new life together. This is upset, of course, by Beloved's arrival and new place at the dinner table, which creates a palpable tension between her and Paul D. (Figure 7.1). The fragile family unit is ultimately broken when Paul D. confronts Sethe there and she reveals her story about how Beloved died. Finally, the kitchen is where, near the climax of the narrative after Paul D. has abandoned the farm and the women have devolved into a frenzied state, Sethe, Denver, and Beloved gorge themselves on cakes and pie in a state of animalistic indulgence and where—when her food supply is nearly exhausted—Sethe prepares the last egg for Beloved, relinquishing her final bit of control in what was once her center of power.

Temptress and trickster

The fourth motif is the color red and captures this battle of phallic and vaginal archetypes conveyed strongly through the cinematography as Demme brings Morrison's themes to life through visual storytelling. From the moment that

Paul D. is invited into 124 Bluestone by Sethe, he is confronted by the female energy of Beloved, and their relationship serves as a powerful platform for exploring gender expectations and the mythical history of women as eaters of life force and manhood. Demme bathes the scene in red light, and intercuts images of a younger Sethe after her murder of Beloved, covered in the blood of her own child.

Red is not only connected to blood, both from the brutal slaying of Sethe's baby and the female menstrual cycle, but has been historically associated with women. Because of its close connection with emotion, red has represented sexuality, specifically women's sexuality, especially sin and prostitution. Prostitutes in many cities were required to wear red to announce their profession. Nils Johan Ringdal explains, "By the late Middle Ages, dress codes were being enforced" that included half red, half black hats in Denmark and Norway, red toques in Berne and Zurich, and (across much of Europe) the wearing of a scarlet cord that "symbolized the rope that the Bible's Rahab had used to help Joshua and his men."[7] This parallel between female sexuality and sin in the Western world has long taken inspiration from the Bible, going all the way back to the story of Eve and her (presumably red) apple in the Book of Genesis. This theme's connection to red runs in Christian theology all the way to the Book of Revelation, which describes the "scarlet whore of Babylon" riding the Antichrist, a creature that is also red. The fear of female sexuality and the female body predates even biblical times, however, with ancient cultures vilifying the *vagina dentata*.

Paul D. first encounters this concept during his walk to the kitchen down a tight, threatening hallway. The *vagina dentata* is crucial, in both novel and film, to Beloved's emasculation of Paul D., as she functions as a kind of personified *vagina dentata* for the house and Sethe that Paul D. is attempting to penetrate. "The female body, as it has been written in the oral tradition and in sexist literature," according to Trudier Harris, "is in part a source of fear, both an attraction and a repulsion, something that can please, but something that can destroy."[8] As Camille Paglia notes in *Sexual Personae*, her 1991 work on sexual decadence in Western literature and the visual arts: "The toothed vagina is no sexist hallucination: every penis is made less in every vagina, just as mankind, male and female, is devoured by mother nature."[9] Patriarchal societies thus evolved tales of trickster gods taming unruly women, giving the diminishing phallus an altruistic spin.

These tricksters are neither good nor evil, but get into adventures while causing chaos along the way, with their most notable trait being their insatiable appetites. "Food is the basic building block of life itself and is a focus of the traditional Trickster tales as well as those found in postmodernity," according to Ricki Stefanie Tannen.[10] This selfish hunger makes them inadvertent agents of change, such as their sexual need leading to a taming of the woman. As Harris points out: "The tricksters of tradition find one of their chores the task of bravely entering the vagina to break those teeth that tradition has long identified with it. Such actions are considered heroic—and at times helpful even to the woman herself, for the poor dear never realizes what difficulty she is in until some man tells her and proceeds to rescue her."[11] Thus, becoming a man by taking a girl's virginity, even if by rape, is legitimized by coloring the whole experience as a kind of dragon-slaying. A systematic manipulation by men of women to attain sexual pleasure is thus perpetuated by women who believe themselves at fault, and the cycle continues.

Paul D. is the trickster figure in *Beloved*. He has been a rambling man for years, imbued with a palpable world-weariness compounded by a fragile optimism, and forces his way into Sethe's life with an ache for food, sex, and stability. His arrival alone is enough to induce change, but Sethe's world is resistant to bending. Upon his entrance, the house becomes "the enveloping enclosure of the vagina . . .[he] feels the physical threat of the house. The red light of the baby's spirit drains him, makes him feel overwhelming grief, feminizes him."[12] As Paul D. is the audience surrogate at this point, Demme frames this sequence through Paul D.'s gaze that is quickly distorted as the world is made askew. When Paul D. arrives in the kitchen, he asserts his own masculine energy—acting as "a demon-slaying hero returned to claim his prize"—raging through the place and tearing it apart. Pinned against the wall by a table, he shoves it violently away, pushing it across the room.[13] This show of strength continues as Paul D. forcibly casts out Beloved. Immediately afterward, he takes Sethe upstairs and they make love, further underscoring his manhood.

Essentially, having forced out another man's offspring, Paul D. is seeking to stake his claim on Sethe and her life. He even later proposes having more children with Sethe, in an attempt at establishing himself as a respectable father and *paterfamilias*. As the movie continues, however, Paul D.'s manly dominance proves short-lived as Beloved attempts to metaphysically castrate him, feeding on his life force like a succubus. Nancy Kang argues that

> Beloved strips Paul both of his emotional and physical life force (that is, his sperm) in characteristic succubus fashion. In Spanish idom, the metaphor "mala leche" ("bad milk") denotes the recipient of milk from a mother who has questionable health, morals, or lifestyle. It also tropes upon a man's semen, but negatively embellishes it with connotations of illness, bad humor, and general moral and physical lethargy. Thus, the signifier slides on a referential continuum from being undoubtedly female to undeniably male.[14]

Beloved first drains Paul D. by entrancing him into a kind of narcoleptic state, as he keeps waking up around the house in fugues, feeling not a bit refreshed. Beloved "moves him out of Sethe's room and places him in the emasculating maternal space of the rocking chair" and in the bed of Sethe's former mother-in-law, Baby Suggs.[15] He retreats to a shed in front of the house, but she enters there one night, undressing in a startling moment of full-frontal nudity. Although he tries to resist, she forces herself on him, demanding that he cry out her name, as if the name itself would codify her existence. He also cries out "red heart" over and over during their tryst, a reference to a scene in the novel (but omitted from the film) where a rusted tin can lid that has come loose symbolizes his hardened heart bursting with emotion. The movie leaves his cries ambiguous, but the scene is once again bathed in red light, connecting it not only to his entry into the house but also to his symbolic castration by Beloved. "The seduction by Beloved in the cold-house," explains Steven V. Daniels, "culminates her effort to rid the household of Paul D and to assure the needy child's dominance in Sethe's life. From another perspective, its goal is to restore the past's control over any possible future."[16] Paul D.'s guilt over this experience leads to his abandoning 124 Bluestone and the possibility of a future with Sethe and striking out on his own.

The devouring mother

Sethe's relationship with her daughters is very different than with Paul D., and is defined by Erich Neumann's concept of the "devouring mother," an extension of the *vagina dentata*. Demetrakopoulos uses this idea of the devouring mother to explain Sethe's actions at the pivotal moment when she believes her children will be damned to a life of slavery: "Sethe attempts to return the babies to perhaps a collective mother body, to devour them back into the security of womb/tomb death much as a mother cat will eat her babies as the ultimate act of protection."[17] Even years later, Sethe is unable to free herself from this compulsion, and keeps her only living daughter, Denver, isolated and naïve about the world. Although this is mostly a reaction to the death of Beloved, it starts even earlier, with the theft of Sethe's breast milk, sucked directly from her breasts as if she were an animal—a piece of property, less than human. The "mossy mouths of the white boys," as Reginald Watson explains, "have indeed soured much more than Sethe's milk because they have also sucked away all hope for bonding between mother and child, husband and wife."[18]

This experience creates a psychic rift that keeps Sethe from forming a bond with her daughter, as she only knows how to provide, not how to teach Denver how to live. Her entire escape from Sweet Home in 1855 is based around getting the milk to her babies, the toddler Beloved and Denver still in her belly, with milk being the linchpin of the liquid motif. "Milk and water imagery is prevalent," Watson argues, "representing not only the death that occurred during the Middle Passage, but also the loss of black motherhood," and Sethe's obsession with possessing her own body informs her behavior.[19] She works hard to make money to put food on the table, but in the process holds Denver too tight. As Paul D. puts it, her love is "too thick."

Sethe's relationship with the returned and grown Beloved is a fascinating extension of her relationship with Denver in how both mother and daughters feed off each other's emotions. Beloved was the eldest daughter—the "crawlin' already" baby, as Baby Suggs refers to her—when the family, newly escaped, arrived at 124 Bluestone. "That the child first killed is a girl is important," says Demetrakopoulos of Beloved's premature death, as for Sethe "to kill her daughter is to kill her own best self, to kill her best and self-gendered fantasy of the future. The act is like killing time itself, especially its redemptive gifts, which the daughter, as a potential mother, symbolizes."[20] Sethe, who has only survived and continued on by ignoring the past, is thus initially in denial about the woman that appears on her doorstep being her dead daughter. Beloved, however, is so traumatized by her experience that "[i]t is no wonder that she comes back with a hunger and greed for mother's milk."[21] Sethe tolerates Beloved ambivalently at first, but that changes after Paul D. finds out the truth and abandons the precarious home he has made with them.

Beloved is simpleminded and acts as if her body is a machine that she doesn't understand how to operate, as she is both like a child and has not recovered from her neck wound. An angry scar adorns her neck, the vital passage for sustenance, air, and food, rendered irrelevant by a drastic act. It's clear, however, that she wants Sethe to herself and is quite vocal to Denver about her jealousy and need. Once Paul D. is gone, Sethe comes to the realization that Beloved is apparently the physical embodiment of her murdered child, and that—whoever she is—Sethe needs her. As a mother she responds in the only way she knows: lavishing Beloved (and, consequently, Denver) with food. Rather than satisfy the woman-child, however, her indulgence leads Beloved to repeated and increasingly petulant declarations that "I want a sweet!" Sethe spends the last of her life's savings on this, deeming it acceptable because she herself earned the money.

As Dean Franco explains, the "experience of the black characters is decidedly the experience of property—stealing or being stolen, freeing or being freed, repossessing, and hauntingly, claiming," as what can be consumed can be possessed.[22] Sethe becomes so absorbed in Beloved, and the process of reclaiming her with food bought with her own money, that she loses her job. She grows more and more absorbed in her isolation, and physically withers away. When the last bit of food left in the household is a single egg, she gratefully prepares it for Beloved, not realizing or caring she has forsaken herself and Denver.

It's at this point that Denver realizes she has to break away and branch out into the community to achieve self-actualization and save her mother. Portrayed as a stubborn and resentful child at first, she blossoms into a powerful woman, embodying what Demetrakopoulos calls "the history that Sethe so resists entering."[23] When Denver eventually returns to 124 Bluestone she is followed by the women of the local African-American community. They find Sethe dazed and distant from the world, and Beloved grotesquely swollen, like a leech, having drained the life force from Sethe, much as she did from Paul D. (Figure 7.2). She also may or may not be pregnant with Paul D.'s child, a question that is left a dreadful mystery.

FIGURE 7.2 *Sethe (Oprah Winfrey) confronts the mob surrounding her house with a swollen Beloved (Thandie Newton) by her side.*

Conclusion

In the end, the three main characters—Sethe, Denver and Paul D.—attain closure and fulfillment by exorcising Beloved from their lives. More than an actual person, the strange being is the personification of their guilt, an anthropomorphic thing that drains their bodies and souls of life. Meanwhile Sethe, the center of the story's unifying themes, reduces the complexities of motherhood to a single, all-consuming obsession: providing life-sustaining sustenance, first through the milk from her body and later through food she can buy with the money she earned. It is only after this nearly brings about her destruction that she realizes that reducing her own needs and the needs of her children to a single, primary urge—to feed—is preventing her, and them, from ever finding closure. Beloved must accept her own death, Denver must grow up and provide for herself, and Sethe must learn to love herself. Paul D. himself gains a bit of closure and permanence in the film's closing moments, turning away from his trickster ways and instead creating order by telling Sethe that she, and no one else, is "her best thing."

This is a story told by transplanting antediluvian abstractions, the *vagina dentata*, the trickster, and the devouring mother, into a timely American tale. The result is a horror movie with much on its mind, including slavery's stain on history and the complex navigation of a woman's life as both mother and individual. But at its core it has a simple message: hunger must be satiated.

Notes

1 Alex Suskind, "Oprah Winfrey on 'Lee Daniels' 'The Butler,' Returning to the Big Screen, and the Commercial Failure of 'Beloved.'" *Moviefone* (August 8, 2013), http://news.moviefone.com/2013/08/08/oprah-winfrey-lee-daniels-the-butler-interview/ (accessed June 29, 2015).

2 Nöel Carroll, *The Philosophy of Horror, or, Paradoxes of the Heart* (New York: Routledge, 1990), 125.

3 Matthew C. Strecher, "Magical Realism and the Search for Identity in the Fiction of Murakami Haruki," *Journal of Japanese Studies* 25, no. 2 (1999): 263.

4 Zora Neale Hurston, *Mules and Men* (New York: Perennial Library, 1990), 227.

5 Ibid., 228.

6 Stephanie Demetrakopoulos, "Maternal Bonds as Devourers of Women's Individuation in Toni Morrison's *Beloved*," *African American Review* 26, no. 1 (1992): 52.

7 Nils Johan Ringdal, *Love for Sale: A World History of Prostitution* (New York: Grove, 2004), 147.
8 Trudier Harris, "Woman, Thy Name Is Demon," in *Toni Morrison's Beloved: A Casebook*, ed. William L. Andrews (New York: Oxford University Press, 1999), 129.
9 Camille Paglia, *Sexual Personae* (New Haven, CT: Yale University Press, 1990), 47.
10 Ricki Stefanie Tannen, *The Female Trickster: The Mask That Reveals, Post-Jungian and Postmodern Psychological Perspectives on Women in Contemporary Culture* (London: Routledge, 2007), 128.
11 Harris, "Woman, Thy Name Is Demon," 129.
12 Ibid., 130.
13 Deborah Ayer-Sitter, "The Making of a Man: Dialogic Meaning in *Beloved*," in *Critical Essays on Toni Morrison's Beloved*, ed. Barbara H. Solomon (New York: G.K. Hall, 1998), 193.
14 Nancy Kang, "To Love and Be Loved: Considering Black Masculinity and the Misandric Impulse in Tony Morrison's *Beloved*," in *Toni Morrison's Beloved*, ed. Harold Bloom (New York: Bloom's Literary Criticism, 1990), 36.
15 Ibid., 32.
16 Steven V. Daniels, "His Story Next to Hers: Choice, Agency and the Structure of *Beloved*," in *Toni Morrison's Beloved*, ed. Harold Bloom (New York: Bloom's Literary Criticism, 1990), 9.
17 Demetrakopoulos, "Maternal Bonds," 53.
18 Reginald Watson, "Derogatory Images of Sex: The Black Woman and Her Plight in Tony Morrison's *Beloved*," in *Toni Morrison's Beloved*, ed. Harold Bloom (New York: Bloom's Literary Criticism, 1990), 100.
19 Ibid., 94.
20 Demetrakopoulos, "Maternal Bonds," 53.
21 Watson, "Derogatory Images," 100.
22 Dean Franco, "What We Talk About When We Talk about *Beloved*," in *Toni Morrison's Beloved*, ed. Harold Bloom (New York: Bloom's Literary Criticism, 1990), 119.
23 Demetrakopoulos, "Maternal Bonds," 55.

Bibliography

Ayer-Sitter, Deborah. "The Making of a Man: Dialogic Meaning in *Beloved*." In *Critical Essays on Toni Morrison's Beloved*, edited by Barbara H. Solomon, 189–204. New York: G.K. Hall, 1998.

Carroll, Nöel. *The Philosophy of Horror, or, Paradoxes of the Heart*. New York: Routledge, 1990.

Daniels, Steven V. "His Story Next to Hers: Choice, Agency and the Structure of *Beloved.*" In *Toni Morrison's Beloved*, edited by Harold Bloom, 5–23. New York: Bloom's Literary Criticism, 1990.

Demetrakopoulos, Stephanie. "Maternal Bonds as Devourers of Women's Individuation in Toni Morrison's *Beloved.*" *African American Review* 26, no. 1 (1992): 51–60.

Franco, Dean. "What We Talk About When We Talk about *Beloved.*" In *Toni Morrison's Beloved*, edited by Harold Bloom, 109–31. New York: Bloom's Literary Criticism, 1990.

Harris, Trudier. "Woman, Thy Name Is Demon." In *Toni Morrison's Beloved: A Casebook*, edited by William L. Andrews, 127–57. New York: Oxford University Press, 1999.

Hurston, Zora Neale. *Mules and Men*. New York: Perennial Library, 1990.

Kang, Nancy. "To Love and Be Loved: Considering Black Masculinity and the Misandric Impulse in Tony Morrison's *Beloved.*" In *Toni Morrison's Beloved*, edited by Harold Bloom, 25–47. New York: Bloom's Literary Criticism, 1990.

Paglia, Camille. *Sexual Personae*. New Haven, CT: Yale University Press, 1990.

Ringdal, Nils Johan. *Love for Sale: A World History of Prostitution*. New York: Grove, 2004.

Strecher, Matthew C. "Magical Realism and the Search for Identity in the Fiction of Murakami Haruki." *Journal of Japanese Studies* 25, no. 2 (1999): 263–98.

Suskind, Alex. "Oprah Winfrey on 'Lee Daniels'The Butler,' Returning to the Big Screen, and the Commercial Failure of 'Beloved.' " *Moviefone*, August 8, 2013. http://news.moviefone.com/2013/08/08/oprah-winfrey-lee-daniels-the-butler-interview/ (accessed June 29, 2015).

Tannen, Ricki Stefanie. *The Female Trickster: The Mask That Reveals, Post-Jungian and Postmodern Psychological Perspectives on Women in Contemporary Culture*. London: Routledge, 2007.

Watson, Reginald. "Derogatory Images of Sex: The Black Woman and Her Plight in Tony Morrison's *Beloved.*" In *Toni Morrison's Beloved*, edited by Harold Bloom, 99–100. New York: Bloom's Literary Criticism, 1990.

8

"Do I Look Tasty to You?": Cannibalism beyond Speech and the Limits of Food Capitalism in Park's *301/302*

Tom Hertweck

Something is amiss on the third floor of the New Hope Bio Apartments. A young professional woman (Sin-Hye Hwang)—named Yun, but referred to throughout the film by her apartment number, 302—has gone missing without a trace, and a detective (Chu-Ryun Kim) is calling on her cross-hall neighbor, Song (Eun-Jin Pang), in apartment 301 as he investigates her disappearance. In the film's present, the story of 301 and 302's meeting is recounted (and presented on-screen in flashback) while the detective listens for clues; more deeply, the women's shared history of trauma is presented within this story as a second layer of flashback. These tales of personal woe and of 301 and 302's friendship are only ever partially revealed to the detective; the more private, more horrifying parts of the friends' secret history remain known only to themselves and to the viewer. Among these secrets is the truth behind the mystery. As the viewer learns in the double-embedded flashback, 301 has killed her neighbor in an act of mercy and then—with 302's full prior knowledge—cooked and eaten her.

While *301/302* is clearly a horror movie, its feminist message is evident enough that even casual viewers are unlikely to view it *only* as a horror movie. Some critics have offered a deeper and more nuanced reading of the relationship of the film's two women by examining it within a specifically Korean cultural context.[1] Feminist readings of the film emphasize that, trapped as they both are within their social circumstances, the skilled cook 301 relieves the traumatized and anorexic 302 of her suffering while getting to experience the most exotic and unspeakable meal one could imagine. Because the detective never discovers the killing and cannibalism, one could argue that they have perpetrated some sort of pact of mutual empowerment, and are able finally to act outside the masculine social order that otherwise constrains them.

Critics go to considerable lengths in order to rehabilitate the final morally charged act in the film—302's gift of her body to 301 as food—as liberatory. Joan Kee, for example, reads the space between the horror movie and the thriller as symptomatic of the antagonism over Korean women's empowerment during a time of emerging cultural modernization. She writes: "[T]he use of the horror-cum-thriller format argues for this patriarchal continuum to the extent that it couches the independent woman as a singularly frightening spectacle. The jarring series of cuts that reveal the discovery of 302 suggests the implied dismemberment of 302's body and has the effect of a horror story."[2] This effect serves as a lesson, it would seem, to those who would seek to oppress women. Gretchen Papazian, who explores the film's representation of 302's anorexia, suggests the film claims that "as one woman ingests the other . . . social norms inhibit the possibility of a self-assured, independent woman. Only by breaking those norms, by breaking taboos, can a woman come into her own."[3] Most strongly, Diane Carson's exploration of the "unaccommodating female subject" in Korean films of this era more broadly acknowledges the difficulty of condoning violence while nonetheless celebrating the breaking of an oppressive national narrative convention, and ends by calling the film "a treasure" because of the act of violent communion that serves as the fissure.[4] Because of Korea's strict codes of gender conduct, only something as shocking as murder-cannibalism can unmoor seemingly immovable social roles.

This state of affairs is troubling because the film, though a visually engaging and at times beautiful and moving picture of women trying to overcome abuse, is far more ambivalent about the end results than its critics suggest. It is, after all, a film that plays with time, image, and our sense of right and wrong. *301/302* is suggestive, and asks us to take much from the brief glimpses it affords into these women's intertwined lives. The symbolic economy, while difficult to explain given how little we know about the characters, carries immense affective power. Director Chul-Soo Park has put together a film that asks us to extrapolate, diagnose, and marvel at the traumas these women have endured in the briefest moments of scenes, but also to wonder at the strength of will that allows them to be powerful enough to strike out on their own and make the morally horrifying choices that they make for one another. Surprisingly little scholarship has attended to the rich and grotesque depictions of food in the film except to mention them in passing.[5] When a film leads to the presentation of a taboo act of eating such as this, reading for the way food appears in the film seems essential.

This chapter focuses on the extended filmic depictions of food and eating in *301/302*. Specifically, it explores the relationship between capitalism and eating: a visual feast, as it were, that unites the subject matter of oppression by pushing women and food together into frame. Each act of eating is supplemented by the social order that capitalism authorizes, from moments of grocery shopping to the merger of domestic spaces with butcher shops. Park's use of these narrative and visual techniques encourages the audience to take seriously the perils that women face in a modernizing Korea, and brings into question the possibility of new gender roles in social modernity itself. This move to food as a means of exploring how women go about doing certain kinds of work, especially along gendered lines, expands our understanding of the film's figuration of female empowerment. Rather than the positive image many critics find, however, I argue that the film's expression of self-determination, as much as the moral choices at its center, is rather terrifying. Though they act in concert to achieve something that looks like liberation from, or rebellion against, the patriarchal order, the film's insistent ambivalence about food finds these women firmly enmeshed within capitalism's social order, because the escape suggested by taboo eating merely reinscribes their oppression.

Consuming meat, consuming women: 302 and traumatic markets

For both of the women in the film—as for those in so many tales about struggling with patriarchy—capitalism, in the guise of the marketplace, is a vexed space of social engagement. Within this framework, the food market is cast as an acutely important site in their respective primal scenes of trauma.

For 302, an actual food market operates as a dangerous space that the film uses to dramatize the beginnings of her anorexic psychopathology, and to show the viewer, in concrete terms, why she is unable to eat. In flashback, we see that 302 was raised by her mother and stepfather in an apartment in back of their family-run butcher shop.[6] The flashbacks reveal a home life that is anything but nurturing: her mother is distant and distracted by the apparently good income the shop makes, and is seen counting stacks of money and berating 302 for interrupting her. This distraction provides ample opportunity for her stepfather—the butcher-proprietor of the shop—to sneak into 302's bedroom, remove his clothes, and molest her. He exploits his wife's avariciousness by encouraging her to spend time at the bank and take long walks so that he can corner the girl and abuse her. At night, 302 lies in bed with her eyes closed, expecting the intruder; during the day she fights back, but is able to escape only temporarily. These scenes frame the home and butcher shop as spatially conjoined places that merge into a singular horrible environment: one of obvious sexual, physical, and psychic violence.

This repeated abuse becomes the basis for a more specific trauma, revealed to the audience in further flashback detail. One afternoon, having thrown off her stepfather's advances, 302 hides in the shop's walk-in meat locker. A precocious younger neighbor girl sees her exit the locker, and—believing that they are playing hide and seek, a game they frequently play together—sneaks in herself. Later that night, after the girl's frantic mother has called on the shop to see if anyone has any clue where her daughter could be, 302 intuits what has happened. She opens the meat locker to find her playmate dead, having succumbed to the low temperatures.

The entire series of flashbacks to the butcher shop shows 302 in vignettes and rapid-fire images bathed in bloody-red light (unlike 301's later, more linear flashback) in order to establish the way that her stepfather's abuse had become normalized, as well as to prefigure what Kee describes as the dismemberment of her body through film cuts.[7] At the same time, Park goes to lengths to firmly connect food to abuse in ways that go well beyond the fact the sexual predation takes place in a butcher shop, underscoring food capitalism's role in consuming women. Interspersed with the flashback are cuts to snippets showing thick bones being sawn for marrow and broth, hands doing the work of butchery, and filets being cut—all in close-up. These glimpses of commercial meat preparation hint at the usual dangers lurking in a butcher shop: fingers clad only in flimsy gloves move anxiously close to saw and knife blades. However, given their proximity to 302's abuse, the overall effects of these flashes merge both for the viewer and the young 302, as we begin to see how the customers' consumption of meat and meat products mirrors the stepfather's sexual appetite and consumption of 302. In short order, 302 becomes a commodity—just, as the feminist complaint about objectification goes, some piece of meat.[8]

This image-stream of cuts away from the narrative action of the flashback hits a fever pitch when they show up again after the neighbor's accidental death. Identical cuts from earlier in the flashback are revealed to show 302 hacking at something—the dead neighbor girl's body, Park encourages the viewer to believe—with her stepfather's hands clasping her from behind and guiding her movements. Real or not (did 302's stepfather force her to chop the dead girl's body into salable pieces while he groped her, or does she project herself into this macabre scenario out of guilt?), it is clear that 302 locates this as the source of her inability to eat and reports it as such to 301. Triangulating food, sex, and trauma, she explains, "My body is filled with dirtiness—how am I supposed to have a man in me, or food in my body?" Though the sympathetic viewer wants for her to see how wrong she is to blame herself for her abuse, it remains nonetheless clear that 302 has concretized a symbolic affective linkage between food and trauma. She, like the viewer, has come to believe that the space where one buys food is also a place where young girls are consumed, some figuratively through abuse, and others perhaps quite literally.

Similarly, 302's place in the capitalist system is increasingly precarious at the moment she and 301 meet. We discover that her career as a professional writer is in danger. During a moment of reflection, 302 considers the rejection notice she has received from *Monthly Literature*, narrated by its editor in voiceover. As the man explains, "We don't print personal experiences in our serious literature" because the readership cannot "relate" to it. While the viewer does not know exactly what material she was trying to sell, one imagines, given the bits of 302's personal history revealed elsewhere in the film, that it is harrowing. Her traumatic past therefore appears to make her impotent within the writing marketplace, a doubly painful situation because she does not make money from it and because the so-called unrelatability of her experience serves to reaffirm her outsider social status. In response to this lack of power, we witness her plugging away at another manuscript: advice on "Terms for an Ideal Sex Life." Her suggestions—"drink a lot of water, eat apples, enjoy one hour of exercise . . . only after exercising, you can eat 100 g[rams] of chicken breast"—are carefully tailored for the women's magazines for which she is evidently writing. The viewer knows enough, however, to realize that such advice rings false: that 302 is incapable of eating, and is painfully thin not from exercise but from self-imposed starvation. The audience also sees that, given her lack of a sex life, the advice comes off as much like a personal manifesto—or even a to-do list—as it does a salable column. Whatever the intention, 302 knows that her work will not sell if she remains true to witnessing her own lived experiences—yet one more troubling effect of her place under the capitalist system. As she confesses to 301 without being specific, "I can't really write about what I want," we know she cannot even offer her own trauma as a literary commodity in the writer's marketplace. Instead, she has to force herself into platitudes and banalities to sell to mass cultural outlets. Rather than speaking her truth and perhaps holding out hope of shaking up the social order, 302 supports the cultural hegemony by writing for women's magazines that seem to place the responsibility of a couple's sex life squarely on the woman's shoulders.

Marriage roles and appetites: 301 and a desire to be sated

If 302 is (however, ironically) a producer of popular literature on weight loss and sex advice, 301 is its consumer. Seemingly obsessed with body image and what weight loss can do for her, we see 301 eating apples, exercising, and cooking and weighing lean chicken as she tries to rebound after her divorce. The advice she assiduously follows is gleaned, it would seem, from popular publications that peddle cheerfully illustrated, faddish programs such as "The Mind Control Diet." Consumption, then, is 301's métier, at least inasmuch as she sees food preparation and consumption as positive aspects of culture. Like 302, 301 links food and sex, but in an eager way, at one point telling her neighbor: "Sex is just like cooking—I can't control my desire for them. Although there was no love, I still enjoyed sex with my ex-husband." While 302's experience of food-market trauma is acute and accessible, the trauma created by the collapse of 301's marriage is more diffuse. In fact, 301's experience in the food marketplace is diametrically opposed to 302's: rather than see spaces of consumption as a source of tragedy, she embraces them as a central part of her identity (Figure 8.1). For 301, the markets for food and domestic goods serve as an essential component of her self-construction as an excellent Korean wife.[9]

The film dramatizes 301's primal traumatic scene, as it does 302's, but this time as part of an extended narrative flashback. She is a newlywed making a cautiously flirtatious call to her husband, telling him about the meal she is preparing for his return home that evening. Both are excited about the food as much as the palpable (yet wholly implied) sexual tension, the husband complaining that the call was making his work "seem boring." The scene cuts to that evening, and 301 has changed into a classic "little black dress" and sets the table, awaiting her husband's arrival. The meal itself is proper, rife with traditional Korean deferral of the wife's desire as she nervously watches her husband eat noodles, cabbage, and the complex squid-based stew that we saw her labor over earlier. 301 has no food for herself, though she plainly receives a kind of nourishment watching her husband take appreciative and excited mouthfuls. He eats somewhat indelicately, plainly enjoying himself

FIGURE 8.1 *Unlike her neighbor 302, 301 is completely comfortable in food markets: in this moment grocery shopping, she casually walks past a commercial meat slicer to a butcher's counter eerily reminiscent of where 302's traumatic primal scene took place.*

as he flits from dish to dish, sampling everything. Having demonstrated her culinary skills, to her husband's extreme pleasure, she moves the conversation to her own hunger, suggesting (without saying so explicitly) that she would like for them to have sex. "I've been thinking about it all day," she coos, not meeting his gaze, and never specifying what "it" is. The husband admits that he has been thinking the same, a notion that surprises 301. The shared moment of implicit confession heightens their arousal, and leads into an extended sex scene that begins right there at the table. In this way, both husband and wife are sated by the dinner, each in their own way.

The consensual nature of this sex scene stands in stark contrast to 302's abuse in the preceding flashback. At the same time, however, the extent to which none of it can be claimed or discussed explicitly by either party, and that 301 mentions it with something like a sense of shame, reveals much about the state of traditional relationships in Korea. In this order, silence attends traditional roles, and sex is to be performed for the husband as a duty.[10] 301's real desire for sex cannot be stated, as it would appear anomalous. Food's function here is therefore plainly that of lubricant, dinner making an occasion where married couples can discuss (cautiously and indirectly) their marital relations. The food is more than just a catalyst, however, as the meal serves as a necessary prerequisite to sex. Should 301 have failed at her wifely duty as a cook, one imagines it would have been impossible to broach the subject of sex. Well-prepared food, therefore, serves as a gateway to sex.

Food plays a central role in the mechanics of their relationship, then, as it becomes deeply imbricated with sexual relations. Specifically, 301's appetite for one or the other, as she tells 302, is interchangeable. During the honeymoon period of their marriage, 301 never eats; all eating that takes place early in the flashback is done by her husband. Only when he finally tires of all her cooking and refuses her sex does she begin to eat as a substitute. In the penultimate attempt to get him to enjoy her lavish cooking, 301 prepares another grand meal. He rejects it—limply suggesting that he could try lunch with McDonald's, street vendors, or "instant meals" which she scoffs at as "not real food"—and storms off to work alone in his office without finishing his dinner. Thinking that this is somehow a fault with the food and not with their relationship, she prepares an entire second meal of dumplings and soup from scratch, only to have abuse hurled at her for not understanding. Finally on the next night, in a last ditch effort to interest her husband, she produces something like an ultimatum: a simple meal she thinks he would like, proffered to him while wearing nothing beneath the silk robe that covers her when she enters the office to seduce and feed him. In a fitful nap—he appears to be avoiding her by sleeping in his office—he pushes her off of him and rolls away, leaving both her and the meal untouched. After each of these rejections, 301 takes the uneaten meal and gorges herself on it. Perhaps she is seeking the source of her rejection, or perhaps she simply wants to fill the void that her marriage has put in her. In either case, the film's presentation of the effort she expends trying to make a meal her husband would like comes off as heartbreaking since the viewer knows more is wrong than can be fixed with food.

301 plainly experiences the same sense of conflation of food with sex as 302, though for her the feeling seems naturalized rather than implanted by trauma.[11] It is naturalized, of course, because the dominant cultural order would make such a connection appear normal. It is an overabundance of this good food—an overqualification in one domestic skill—that is out of sorts, and serves as the metonymy that begins to tear the marriage apart.[12] As the flashback progresses, 301 cooks up prodigious quantities of delicious food, and in so doing, outpaces her husband's desire for it. This, in turn, obligates him to praise her virtuosity to excess and exhaustion, so much so that he eventually turns to another (presumably less culinarily skilled) woman. During their eventual

divorce proceedings, the only specific complaint that he can register is that he had to eat all of this food that was prepared for him *and* praise it.

Oppressive as this obligation may have been, the judge nonetheless returns the discussion to how this domestic skill as a food preparer is itself a kind of work, stating that it must be acknowledged through alimony compensation. The divorce hearing therefore retroactively transforms the expected work of traditional Korean marriage into a market transaction. Both as a legal arrangement as well as a spiritual or romantic one, 301 and her husband have certain obligations to the marriage: she met hers in the eyes of the court while he did not. As a result, the severance package (as it were) that she receives becomes the investment capital in her own independent life, a case she makes clear moments before when she, having found out about her husband's affair, declares she wants a divorce in order "to live her own way" and that she "needs money" to do so. While it may appear somewhat degrading for her to have to subject her identity as a woman and wife to the market, 301's canny business sense dictates that the only way for her to get out is to sue for breach of (marriage) contract. In her new life, rather than consume food (she subjects herself to a diet to "look hot") or sex (she wants to be attractive but says nothing of any desire for a relationship), she attempts to consume the fruits of her own labor. 301 takes the opportunity, then, to slough off the domestic entirely: when she moves in and renovates her new apartment, the effect is entirely commercial. When the detective first visits her, he comments that the space "looks like a restaurant," which she takes as a compliment.

Men and women, speaking and silence, eating and hunger

Eating, as many scholars rightly point out, is a place where connection can happen, and certainly *301/302* bears this out. While their relationship is at first adversarial—301 at one point force-feeds 302 the uneaten meals she finds in her garbage—revelations of one another's pasts joins the women together into a micro-community, one in which 301 attempts to prepare meals for 302 in order to coax her body back into accepting food. Through acts of storytelling, two women manage to find a space within Korea's masculine-dominated society (Figure 8.2). Much recommends this, then, to a feminist-positive reading of the film.

Even in this arrangement of sharing and caring, however, the forces of capitalism appear to affect 301's abilities. Previously resistant, 302 gamely chokes down the carefully prepared comfort foods, each time running to the

FIGURE 8.2 *302 (left) and 301 stare out at the viewer in the moment their storytelling congeals into a feminist micro-community. By interrupting the film's narrative flow and breaking the fourth wall, the characters signal their unity against Korean society as well as the audience.*

toilet to throw them up. 302 is apologetic, suggesting that the issue may be less about 301's skill than about the fact that the vegetables she gets from the local market "aren't the freshest," suggesting how capitalist provisioning interferes with her craft. At the same time, 301 seems anxious as 302's bodily rejection of the food reminds her of her husband's eventual fatigue with her cooking and marital rejection of her as wife. The idea that her great skill as a cook could be failing requires the externalization of the cause onto the food marketplace, and so we see her trying to get one of the vegetable sellers to reveal where the better produce is. Of course, the food itself is not the problem, but rather a psychological attempt at bodily control. So long as she remains traumatized, 302 remains unable to consume anything of substance.[13]

Such is the context as the film turns to the murder-cannibalism that precipitates 302's disappearance and the time-present mystery: two women at an impasse, merged by circumstance, each unable to help the other resolve her personal crisis. On the one hand, in order to regain her sense of self, 301 requires an appreciative audience for her cooking. She journals extensively about the meals she prepares, and combs cookbooks as if searching for an arcane secret that will unlock her neighbor's despair. On the other hand, 302 seeks a way out of her sadness through the writing marketplace, but is incapable of expressing the thing that is central to her identity. While her confession to 301 serves to give her a tiny, apartment-sized sanctuary, it does nothing for her anorexia or workplace predicament. Though they have become friends, both require the other to consume something that she is incapable of properly consuming, and so prepare us for the horror to come. Each woman finds capitalism insufficient in providing meaningful resolution, and uncovers, through their friendship, the limits of food, which unite them. 301 is forced to see herself as something other than a wife, and so is forced out of the domestic kitchen into a commercial one that is not, in the end, a real restaurant. One suspects at some point her alimony will cease to be sufficient, at which point the façade of her restaurant-home will as well, since it does not provide her with income. For 302, the linkage of food and danger means she has to look elsewhere for nourishment, but cannot even consume her own stories in order to make a living. This arrangement prefigures the cannibalism at the end of the film because, in essence, the women are trying (and failing) to symbolically consume themselves—turning their hearts and souls into salable commodities, food and writing, for which they cannot find customers. In the end, they turn deeper into their reliance on each other and consume something essential and human: for 301, it is the sole friendship she has; for 302, it is her own body.

In this way, the banality of the eventual death and dismemberment of 302 comes as a surprise. 302 strips off her clothes and says merely, "Do I look tasty to you?"[14] The seeds of such transgression had seemingly been planted earlier when 301 told the story of cooking her husband's beloved dog—as much as part of her quest for ever more "exotic" ingredients as in retaliation for his bad treatment of her. In the same way one might seek out increasingly transgressive sexual encounters, 301 is seen in the grocery at the moment when her thoughts turn to cannibalism as she scans the cuts of meat. In a highly suggestive moment, she seems to look through the shelves of food commodities into something unavailable in the stores, dropping her shopping basket and walking distractedly home. She laments directly at the camera: "There is absolutely no dish for Yun-Hee to eat. Not even something new." This is the only time in the film 301 uses her neighbor's actual name, and as she does, 302 walks up behind her consolingly. If newness—as signaled by capital's market provisioning—is no solution, then the only thing left is transgression of humanity's oldest taboo. When 302 offers her body as food, therefore, it is as if both women were thinking the same thing. Rather than exploit the moment for its lurid detail, Park allows it to unfold with little graphic violence. Without speaking, 302 drops to her knees so 301 can silently approach her from behind and smother her, out of frame or in such extreme close-up that it would be impossible to know what is happening. The butchering that follows, implied by bloodstains, is never explicitly shown. There are, in this scene, the briefest moments where 301 hesitates, as if realizing what she has done, but by the end of the process, she has quietly prepared a stew, placed it neatly on the table and commenced eating, imagining a happy 302 eating along with her—the only time we see 302 eat without being ill. The scene concludes, however, with the moral hammer dropping, as 301, in mid-bite, turns her head to think of what is in the refrigerator: her friend's decapitated head. She drops her fork and stares slack-jawed as the scene fades.

The interruption of her daydreaming about wish-fulfillment (i.e., of 302 eating and enjoying it) suggests the degree to which the film itself is ambivalent about 301's ability to overcome the frustrations she has been facing. Though she has perhaps saved her neighbor from spending the rest of her life suffering, she has nonetheless killed her only friend. More to the point, however, the film's pacing and complicated structure of embedded flashbacks requires the viewer to return to the opening scene, which is where the story of 301 and 302 actually ends. If 301's consumption of 302 is the narrative climax, by the end of the film the viewer knows that the movie began with the narrative's denouement. 301's ambivalent reaction of envisioning 302's smiling beatifically from across the table while also witnessing the material horror of her friend's lifeless head presents not a resolution to patriarchy's psychological and social oppression, but a continuation of the same unresolved tensions that now make her subject to very real systems of disciplinary action if her seeming act of mercy is discovered. And yet, there is no real tension in 301's interaction with the detective, no threat of discovery. Only 301, not the detective, ever hints at it, and when she does he summarily dismisses it. Instead, the detective's inquiry simply provides the narrative frame for the movie. The only action of any meaningful importance is that the detective interrupts 301's preparation of Korean-style fried chicken, and so is hospitably invited to try some for himself. As with everything she makes, it is delicious—so much so that on his first bite the detective declares: "This is by far the best chicken I have ever tasted."

301's preparation of fried chicken signals something far more horrifying that is not clear until the film is over and one has gathered all the facts: She has become more mainstream, more socially acceptable. Korean fried chicken is an ubiquitous cultural phenomenon, so much so that thousands of locations—from hole-in-the-wall outlets to major chains like Pelicana Chicken and Mexican Chicken (which has no connection to Mexico)—appear on nearly every block. Unlike its thickly coated American counterpart, the Korean version is dredged lightly in flour and fried twice (like Belgian *frites* to American fries). It is a relatively recent addition to the Korean cultural landscape, having evolved slowly from its introduction in the early 1960s to being a naturalized part of the culinary landscape by the 1980s.[15] Like American fried chicken, though, it has important connections to capitalism, as this and a beer (known by the portmanteau *chimaek*) is often considered a respite from or reward for the working day. As one worker put it in Violet Kim's report on the food, "Chimaek is like a sigh of relief . . . after work [it] lets me know I've survived another day." In throwing off her more complicated and avant-garde recipes, the viewer understands that 301 has embraced a kind of simplicity in her life. And, while her choice of meal represents a mainstreaming of her formerly more inspired cooking choices, the more distressing part of its cultural affect is the extent to which it represents a deferral of her supposed feminist identity. She seems genuinely delighted to have this man's approval of her cooking. In a response eerily reminiscent of how she acted when she seduced her husband with the grand meal after they were first married, she breathlessly demurs at the detective's compliment, "Really?" As this interaction takes place, too, 301's secondary importance is undergirded by the way the camera often treats her like an obstruction, frequently filming her from the back and having to pan left or right around her to better frame the detective.

The detective himself pushes at this distinction between the labor of handcrafted food and its alternatives. When he receives a call from one of his junior colleagues, he chastises the man for eating a foil-wrapped hamburger (held haphazardly in the takeout bag it was served in) during the call. He asks plainly "What are you eating?" only to tell the man that "that's not real food." One wonders whether the detective, with the delicious fried chicken still on his mind, 301's words of traditional deference to her husband fresh in his memory, and still in the impressive restaurant-like space of 301's apartment, has found just enough plausible deniability (or distraction) to discount any involvement by her in 302's disappearance. After all, having taken in 301's unassuming, passive, and wan features, who would suspect her? Because 301 has proven herself a master of culinary arts—an appropriate vocation for a woman in the traditional Korean order—she appears as merely a slight curiosity, a divorced woman who happened to live next door to a missing person. She fits into the picture of domesticity she has built for herself, rather than questioning—let alone challenging—it. The chicken is thus both an alibi and a sign of authorized conformity under the same systems of oppression that she and 302 were trying to escape. Chicken, the most popular global meat, is a far cry from the quest for "more exciting ingredients"—301 has become like her food: subdued, innocuous, and acceptable for mainstream consumption. What could be more horrifying than this? That in her search for self-determination, 301's story ends with her settling into mundane daily life, her act of will never to be told.

Conclusion: consuming Korean women's oppression

The film's narrative wrap-around asks the viewer to reevaluate the totality of the image economy contained within the film. As the viewer knows by the end, the frame of the investigation is the linear endpoint of the time-present action, but Park uses it creatively to instantiate the hermeneutic code. By the end of the film, the "will she or won't she be caught" question has fizzled. Instead, the viewer is left with an explanation for the two abhorrent acts that 301 has perpetrated. Now understood as the film's denouement, it becomes even more difficult to pinpoint precisely how the ending poses a kind of escape from oppression. Even at the most basic level, it is difficult to see how killing and eating one's friend is ever a moral victory, especially if, in the process, 301 becomes a woman haunted by the friend who is now (through the mechanism of digestion) literally part of her.

302's final act of giving herself over into the food system is one not of sharing, but of capitulation to an order in which she realizes she can play no part. While this can—and has—been seen as a moment of female empowerment, it is more plausibly read as a sign of 302's absolute powerlessness in the face of capitalism. Unable to work, enter into heteronormative relationships, and keep down the edible gifts of friendship, she offers herself as the object of 301's cannibalism, not as an act of female community, but as an act of resignation to the systems of oppression that have rendered her culturally and economically powerless. 301's participation in the cannibalism—an undisclosed act of vengeance on the men who seek to solve the mystery of 302's disappearance—completes 302's capitulation. In her death, which is itself never recognized as an act of killing in need of solving in the first place, 302 is rendered permanently silent as she is literally consumed and then passed over by the masculine forces of policing. Though the film may seek to suggest that secrets and silence function as the basis for communities of women's empowerment, the film's structural logic reveals something quite to the contrary.

As others who have looked deeply into the film have shown, the various systems of oppression, from cruel social norming to psychological and physical abuse, are pervasive. In adding the complex web of stressors attendant to capitalism and food to this mix, I have done little to alleviate the struggle, but rather expanded it. It seems now, more than ever, the social totality of life as dramatized by Park's film—even at the very level of preparing and eating daily meals—disregards both women's roles in creating and living their own desires by imposing these problems without ever letting them speak. This returns us, therefore, to the picture of their lives after the turmoil has been solved. For both the solution is silence: murder's ultimate silence for one, and solitary reflection for the other. 301 tells their tale—or at least as much of it as she is able to tell without imperiling her new life—but the tale does little to change even one mind about how women are to make their way in the world. If anything, her silence and her turn to delicious, but nonetheless plain, meals suggests the way that her hysteria has been attenuated by pushing her beyond the moral pale. She has gone so far outside the social order that it is as if she has transcended it. Far from being unaccommodating, as Carson would have it, 301 seems defanged and rendered a threat no longer.[16] And while she remains free to live as she chooses—that is, undiscovered and unpunished by the disciplinary structures present in the film—there is no tearful confession, no explanation of how and why she has lived the way she has. This haunted woman leads a life where the personal truth of her experiences must remain internal and unspoken, marking yet one more way that she and 302 have become one in a micro-community of women whose lives have been stunted by the ever-present cultures of oppression at work in a world not yet open enough to accept them. The film, therefore, is a shout into the void, a message to others of their despair, a horrific reminder of all that goes on untold around us, and a warning about the stories—and meals—that feed our souls.

Notes

1   Carson attributes Korean's women's subjugation to the traditionalism of Confucianism, which organizes much of domestic and public life around the idea of filial piety, which with certain nuanced differences still remains legible to Western forms of patriarchy. Conversely, Joan Kee, by describing the narrative as one of Korea's modernization rejects the national focus as this modernity is one where the women "operate in an environment that cannot be read as strictly 'Korean.'" Joan Kee, "Claiming Sites of Independence: Articulating Hysteria in Pak Ch'ul-su's *301/302*," *positions: east asia cultures critique* 9, no. 2 (2001): 451.
2   Kee, "Claiming Sites of Independence," 454.
3   Gretchen Papazian, "Anorexia Envisioned: Mike Leigh's *Life is Sweet*, Chul-Soo Park's *301/302*, and Todd Haynes's *Superstar*," in *Reel Food: Essays on Food and Film*, ed. Anne L. Bower (London: Routledge, 2004), 155.

4 Diane Carson, "Transgressing Boundaries: From Sexual Abuse to Eating Disorders," in *Seoul Searching: Culture and Identity in Contemporary Korean Cinema*, ed. Frances Gateward (Albany: SUNY Press, 2007), 278, 279.

5 Dotty Hamilton's essay is an excellent notable exception, though her work focuses on the viewer's phenomenological relationship between sight and taste/smell, and a conversation it has with another Korean film, *The Recipe*, directed by Seo-Goon Lee, *301/302*'s writer.

6 The film's English subtitles lose some of the nuance that a native speaker would perhaps be able to grasp. So, when the woman who is raising her chastises her by saying, "Quit acting like a stepchild!" it is unclear whether she means this literally (that her mother remarried) or metaphorically (that she could have been taken in by, say, an aunt and uncle). For the purposes of this chapter, I have followed the lead of most other critics and refer to the male antagonist here as her stepfather.

7 Kee, "Claiming Sites of Independence," 454.

8 See Carol J. Adams's exemplary study *The Sexual Politics of Meat: A Feminist-Vegetarian Critical Theory* (revised edn (London: Bloomsbury, 2010)) for more on the consumption of women through the symbolic economy of meat.

9 In this way, the depictions of Korean domestic spaces being gendered feminine connects with Western viewers who identify such structures as familiar in the notion of "separate spheres": 301 seems happy to stay at home and cook, while her husband ventures out to a corporate job.

10 Women's duty-bound role as sexual partner has been well documented. For a treatment relevant to the question of identity modernization in the 1990s, see So-Hee Lee, "The Concept of Female Sexuality in Korean Popular Culture," in *Under Construction: The Gendering of Modernity, Class, and Consumption in the Republic of Korea*, ed. Laurel Kendall (Honolulu: University of Hawaii Press, 2002).

11 Both appetites, however, are shown to be out of proportion for a proper Korean wife, a dysfunction she accesses when 301 repeatedly assumes that 302 thinks 301 is a "whore" because she is overweight. The assumption is itself a part of how she naturalizes the connection between food and sex: it is always one or the other with 301.

12 Dotty Hamilton sees 301's cooking as out of sorts when seen in relation to their traditional marriage. 301's creativity marks her fusion cuisine as modern and not traditional, and "which winds up giving no comfort and sustenance to any of the film's characters" ("Appetite and Aroma: Visual Imagery and the Perception of Taste and Smell in Contemporary Korean Film," in *Food on Film: Bringing Something New to the Table*, edited by Tom Hertweck (Lanham, MD: Rowman & Littlefield, 2014), 134). As such, despite its avowed deliciousness, 301's dishes could signal trouble from the very beginning.

13 To be sure, there is some difficulty in understanding the idea of "anorexia" as presented in the film. As Papazian explains, the film spends considerable

energy representing and dramatizing the affective experience of anorexia rather than sticking to the frequent (and mistaken) vernacular perception of the disease as being solely related to a desire for thinness ("Anorexia Envisioned," 154–8). The characters themselves frequently conflate both reasons.

14 In other versions of the subtitles, the line uses "appetizing" instead of "tasty."
15 Chong-Il Park, "The State of Fried Chicken," *Koreana* (Winter 2014), http://www.koreana.or.kr/months/news_view.asp?b_idx=3870&lang=en&page_type=list (accessed February 12, 2016); Julia Moskin, "Koreans Share Their Secret for Chicken with a Crunch," *New York Times* (February 7, 2007), http://www.nytimes.com/2007/02/07/dining /07fried.html (accessed February 12, 2016).
16 Carson, "Transgressing Boundaries."

Bibliography

301/302. Directed by Chul-Soo Park. 1995. Koch Lorber, 2004. DVD.

Adams, Carol J. *The Sexual Politics of Meat: A Feminist-Vegetarian Critical Theory*, revised edn. London: Bloomsbury, 2010.

Carson, Diane. "Transgressing Boundaries: From Sexual Abuse to Eating Disorders." In *Seoul Searching: Culture and Identity in Contemporary Korean Cinema*, edited by Frances Gateward, 265–82. Albany, NY: SUNY Press, 2007.

Hamilton, Dotty. "Appetite and Aroma: Visual Imagery and the Perception of Taste and Smell in Contemporary Korean Film." In *Food on Film: Bringing Something New to the Table*, edited by Tom Hertweck, 125–37. Lanham, MD: Rowman & Littlefield, 2014.

Kee, Joan. "Claiming Sites of Independence: Articulating Hysteria in Pak Ch'ul-su's *301/302*." *positions: east asia cultures critique* 9, no. 2 (2001): 449–66.

Lee, So-Hee. "The Concept of Female Sexuality in Korean Popular Culture." In *Under Construction: The Gendering of Modernity, Class, and Consumption in the Republic of Korea*, edited by Laurel Kendall, 141–64. Honolulu: University of Hawaii Press, 2002.

Moskin, Julia. "Koreans Share Their Secret for Chicken with a Crunch." *New York Times*, February 7, 2007. http://www.nytimes.com/2007/02/07/dining/07fried.html (accessed February 12, 2016).

Papazian, Gretchen. "Anorexia Envisioned: Mike Leigh's *Life is Sweet*, Chul-Soo Park's *301/302*, and Todd Haynes's *Superstar*." *Reel Food: Essays on Food and Film*, edited by Anne L. Bower, 147–66. London: Routledge, 2004.

Park, Chong-Il. "The State of Fried Chicken." *Koreana* (Winter 2014). http://www.koreana.or.kr /months/news_view.asp?b_idx=3870&lang=en&page_type=list (accessed February 12, 2016)

9

Flesh and Blood in Claude Chabrol's *Le Boucher*

Jennifer L. Holm

French filmmaker Claude Chabrol was a known gourmand. He peppered his films with food and meals that enlivened his plots and nourished the sense of realism for which he is celebrated. More than just a gourmand, however, Chabrol had a "carnal gaze,"[1] and in no other film is this more evident than in his 1969 film *Le Boucher* (*The Butcher*), in which the butcher's travail and product drive the plot and fuel the audience's anxiety.[2] Unlike other films about butchers, such as Jean-Pierre Jeunet's postapocalyptic *Delicatessen* (1991) and Anders Thomas Jensen's dark comedy *The Green Butchers* (2003), Chabrol eschews the fantastic. In *Le Boucher*, as in many of Chabrol's films, fear and anxiety arise out of a very real context in which uncertainty lies both in the characters on the screen and the viewers themselves. Through his titular figure, Chabrol manipulates the latent fears and abjection that lie beneath the forgotten, yet quotidian, violence that meat-eating necessitates.

The film's plot is relatively simple: in the small village of Trémolat in the Dordogne region of France, a series of murders occurs, and it slowly becomes evident that the town butcher is to blame. Chabrol structures his film around two characters: Paul, the quiet, brutish butcher who has recently returned home after serving in the colonial wars with the French army, and Hélène, the cultured, yoga-practicing teacher who moved to the town during Paul's absence to escape a disastrous love affair in Paris. Paul falls in love with Hélène, but she continually rebukes his advances, all the while harboring a growing suspicion that he may be guilty of murdering the town's young women.

A psychological thriller, *Le Boucher* is one of Chabrol's most successful and popular films and thus, has received much critical attention.[3] Dorian Bell, noting the atavistic images in the film, argues that Paul embodies "modern concerns about man's progressive and regressive natures,"[4] while Jonathan David York examines Paul as a product of the civilizing mission who forces viewers in the metropole to confront the aftermath and pathologies of the colonial wars.[5] Nevertheless, we have yet to understand how Chabrol engages with the more sinister aspects of food and why Paul's profession as a butcher is critical to constructing a thriller. Moreover, French critic and film historian Joël Mangy suggests that, more than any of Chabrol's other films, *Le Boucher* highlights the professional life of the two protagonists so much so that viewers identify the two characters through their occupations.[6] If this is the case, then it is necessary to elucidate the significance of Chabrol's job choice for Paul.

Claude Chabrol is one of the great masters of twentieth-century cinema, and many of his best-received and most remarkable films are thrillers, but thrillers of an atypical sort. As critic Terrence Rafferty notes in the *New York Times*, Chabrol is a master of films that thrill "calmly, deliberately and with exquisite perversity."[7] Chabrol's thrillers are reminiscent of the work of Fritz Lang and Alfred Hitchcock, two of his inspirations.[8] Rather than shock, Chabrol prefers "on the whole to unsettle, to disorient, to unnerve and to create the sort of apprehension that cannot finally be resolved. [. . .] He's more like a master of free-floating anxiety."[9] His films are brooding, slow-paced, and anxiety-producing. They are grounded in contemporary bourgeois realities and never veer into the fantastic, amplifying the notion that what happens on screen could play out in real life. In particular, Chabrol uses his films as a medium to explore the ambiguities of human character, noting "there are no entirely black souls, nor entirely white souls"[10] and that "the notion of good and evil is always relative to something."[11] Chabrol's pursuit of moral ambiguity is so successful in *Le Boucher* that Isabelle Vanderschelden deems the film an "archetype" of Chabrol's thrillers.[12]

In *Le Boucher*, Paul is the source of all ambiguities. At the outset, his presence is seemingly normal, but as the film progresses, viewers become unsure of how they are supposed to feel about him. He appears to be friendly, relatively handsome, and shy, if also sexually repressed and somewhat awkward. He is generous and caring towards Hélène as he tries to win her love: he helps her in her classroom, joins in on school activities, walks her home, and offers her gifts. Is it possible for this kind man to commit such horrors? If so, how? What drives him to murder?

To magnify the ambiguity surrounding Paul, as well as to evoke a mounting sense of anxiety, Chabrol mobilizes the latent fears that underlie the occupation of butchery. Butchers are figures of fascination and fear. Daily, they come face to face with blood, organs, and death. The job of a butcher is to transform live animals into consumable meat through slaughter. This job necessitates a physical strength as well as agility and skill in handling knives and in breaking down large carcasses. Typically, butchers are men with the strength necessary to lift entire animal bodies and to cut through flesh, muscle, and bone. Moreover, butcher shops tend to be masculine spaces in which sexual banter is thrown around and fleshy euphemisms are worked into metaphors of violent conquest.[13] The vocabulary of body parts and the handling of meat and organs supplants that of the female human body and, all by itself, this use of language may make customers uneasy as they attempt to buy dinner.[14] Much to the chagrin of these specialists of the flesh, popular culture has appropriated the title of *butcher* and applied it to abhorrent figures such as brutal murderers and torturers because of the similar violence and bloodiness that accompany the butcher's job (Figure 9.1).[15]

Butchers need to be not only strong, but smart. Knowing the intricacies of animal anatomy requires knowledge and training that elevate the status of the butcher.[16] Knowledge is especially important to Paul, who places a premium on being a good butcher and knowing how to cut meat with skill. Chatting with Hélène as they walk home from a wedding in the opening sequence, Paul gives a brief autobiography in an attempt to get to know

FIGURE 9.1 *Paul in his butcher's shop.*

Hélène. Discussing his childhood, Paul attempts to distinguish himself from his father, a man he hates, through his skill level. He says that his father was also a butcher, but that he was not "a good butcher" because he would cut meat "*n'importe comment*," or any which way. Later, he boasts about his own mastery by explaining that upon entering the army he was put in charge of butchery. Hélène is impressed and appears to be fascinated with Paul's know-how, asking him questions. She compliments Paul on his "exactitude," which she says is characteristic of butchers. It is just this precision, however, that causes concern about Paul. The detective in charge of investigating the murders notes that the victims were all killed with a knife and in the same manner. Hélène and the audience are left with the anxiety that Paul is seemingly the only person with the skill allowing him to stab someone with ease and precision.

Drawing on the varied significance of knives, Chabrol repeatedly focuses the camera's eye on Paul's handling of a knife in a clear attempt to raise suspicion and elicit tension, both nervous and sexual. Knives convey power, both in and out of the kitchen. This is particularly true for the butcher, for whom the knife is the principal tool. The knife is an object of violence, capable of slicing through flesh and bone in one swift movement, but it is also necessary for consumption, and so societies have developed strict codes to regulate its use at the table.[17] Consequently, the story of the knife is not only about cutting, but also "about how we manage the alarming violence" coupled with it.[18] Knives are often sexual representations as well. Indeed, there is hardly any symbol of penetration more exact or profound than the sliding of a knife into flesh, and the knife is thus a common metaphor for the phallus. Chabrol visually realizes this metaphor in the film's first sequence to establish the butcher as both sexual and potentially violent. When a waiter brings out the pièce de résistance, the wedding roast, the room erupts into applause as he presents it to the bride and groom, holding it out between them. Paul then demands that the waiter bring him the roast so that he may cut it. Giving in to his demand, the waiter understands that Paul, the butcher, is the most able man for the job of carving. As Paul grabs a carving fork in one hand and a large, shimmering knife in the other, the camera closes in on the roast. The entire frame is occupied by his knife slicing effortlessly through the meat. The positioning of the knife in front of him creates an image where the knife occupies the same space as his phallus, the former supplanting the latter. He then serves Hélène, as the camera frames them as a couple in a shot that replicates the earlier framing of the bride and groom united around the wedding roast. This parallel framing foreshadows that both couples' relationships will turn around Paul and his knife. Paul uses his trade to forge bonds with Hélène, and the young bride is one of his future victims.

Later, when Hélène visits the butcher shop in search of an escalope for dinner, Chabrol again emphasizes Paul's knife while also referencing the sexual relationship that he seeks to establish with Hélène. Inside Paul's shop, meat and knives are everywhere—terrines, salamis, and smoked meats decorate the front counter; sausages and saws intermingle as they hang on and along the side and back walls of the shop—a juxtaposition that serves as a reminder of the violence that quite literally surrounds Paul. Within the tight framing of the shot, Paul and his knife become one. The camera zooms in on Paul's profile with his shoulder looming in the foreground and then slowly follows the length of his arm down to his hands, one of which is gripping the meat from which he is cutting pieces. Chabrol again chooses a close-up shot as Paul makes quick, short cuts into the escalope to tenderize it.

Paul's knife skills and the confusion of knife and phallus explain the central oddity of the murders. The detective notes that the victims are stabbed, but not raped, which is "bizarre" in murders of beautiful young women. However, for Paul, the thrusting forth of his knife into flesh becomes a sexual substitute. In his death confession to Hélène at the end of the film, he admits: "I could not breath until I did it, until I thrust my knife." His recounting of the murders recalls the moment of sexual climax. The spilling of blood provides Paul sexual release from mounting tension. Blood is, of course, a symbol of the passions. To be hot-blooded is to be angry. Red meat in particular is also perceived as a sexual stimulant and meat-eating as a sign of virility.[19] For Paul, this is particularly true. Consequently, in the moments in which he prepares meat for Hélène, once pushing his shop assistant to the side in order to fulfill her order, Paul seeks to establish a sexual connection between them. Unable to develop that connection, however, Paul must satisfy himself with his acts of butchery—both professional and murderous.

Even butchers who do not turn their knives on fellow humans straddle the divide between life and death, rendering them liminal figures intimately involved in the sourcing of one of the most anxiety-ridden foods. It is this quotidian crossing of the boundary between living and dead that render both the butcher and meat as conflicted symbols and highly ambivalent. On one hand, meat is one of the most prestigious and sought-after foods because meat-eating symbolizes man's power over nature.[20] On the other, this same quality makes meat a potentially immoral substance because it necessitates killing of animals.[21] To process meat, butchers exercise power in making distinctions between life and death, body and carcass, human and animal. They slaughter, skin, slice, cut, and debone. They transform the animal body into loins, breasts, ribs, filets, and rounds. And while Chabrol's Paul proudly announces that he has mastered all of these tasks, he suggests that he often occupies himself with the more gruesome and violent responsibilities of the trade, telling Hélène that he slaughters the animals.

In almost any circumstance other than butchery, such carving of flesh, be it animal or human, would be murderous or cause for marginalization, because, "despite the material, conceptual and ethical differences between cutting into human flesh or an animal carcass, [. . .] both occupy a similar position in Western thought."[22] Yet, the butcher lives alongside these judgments; he exists in a gray area that society tacitly accepts but which is simultaneously the object of grotesque fascination. The profound and elemental horror that we feel in the face of the butcher and his profession arises out of his position as an intermediary between society and the abject. The butcher comes face to face with death. He earns a living on the margin of life and death so that we, the general consuming public, do not have to make such decisions and can avoid confrontation with, and even ignore, the abject.

In her foundational work on abjection, Julia Kristeva defines the "abject" as that which is ambiguous because it transgresses the imaginary boundaries we have constructed between self and other, human and animal, life and death.[23] Kristeva associates the most fundamental form of abjection with food and the human disgust response and moves directly from food loathing to the cadaver in her argument, suggesting that the two are related.[24] Departing from Kristeva's transition from the edible to the dead, I would suggest that meat is perhaps the ultimate abject object as it necessitates the death of a body to feed another body, bringing together life and death in the most direct of manners. Eating meat demands, at some point, the presence of a carcass or cadaver. The carcass, according to Kristeva, is a powerful source of abjection because it signifies death and causes us to confront that which we attempt to "thrust aside in order to live."[25] We consequently rely on butchers to confront the abject so that we can ignore the subjective horrors inherent in the source of our meat. There is an optimal distance necessary between human and animal that allows the former to consume the latter, and when the two become too close, consumption is impossible.[26] Today, consumers prefer their meat broken down and packaged neatly in foam trays and plastic wrap so that the pork loin or chicken breast in no way resembles its original source, creating as much distance as possible between man and animal. For some, though, there is no optimal distance; the inherent violence and consequent horror that arise from meat and its purveyor are, for them, motivating factors behind the turn to vegetarianism.[27]

Behind the butcher's inherent violence, there is a necessary tacit belief that he will remain conscious of the line between the killing of humans and animals. This, Paul cannot do.[28] At the end of the film, as he lies dying in Hélène's car, he says, "Once, when I was young . . . I noticed the smell of blood. All blood has the same odor. The blood of animals and the blood of men. Some blood is redder than others, but they all have exactly the same smell." Since childhood he seems to have had a fascination or obsession with blood, observing it, examining it, and taking it in. For Paul, blood is blood. Bodies are bodies. If blood is the bearer of life, Paul's mind and senses cannot distinguish the life of an animal from that of a human. This candidness sheds light on an earlier scene in which Paul also conflates human and animal. While visiting Paul's shop, Hélène laments a victim's death. Paul replies to her sadness saying, "You know, Mademoiselle Hélène, I have seen cadavers—with their heads in the wind, cut in half, mouths open. I have seen three or four, piled on top of one another." Rather than acknowledge the sadness of the murders, Paul speaks in ambiguous terms of death and violence that confound human and animal bodies and minimize death. He chooses the word *cadaver*, a term that is clinical and detached and that denies the presence of both biological life and personality. Moreover, when Paul explains what he has seen, the referent of cadaver is unclear. Because Paul is a butcher and a soldier, he could be speaking of either people or animals. This is especially true when he notes that they were cut in two. Butchers often bisect large animals before carving them down into smaller cuts. It is only after a pause when Paul says that he has seen "children with their eyes gouged out" that the referent becomes clear. He is speaking of the bodies that he witnessed as a soldier.

Paul's marginality and the sense of ambiguity that surrounds him are compounded by his dual occupations, as a butcher and a former soldier. The butcher occupies a liminal position because he is linked to killing. Likewise, the soldier is allowed to transgress the boundaries between life and death. Often the taking of a life is a military obligation and soldiers are trained to kill, albeit as a form of defense. Thus, Paul's professional relationship to death becomes twofold, and his job of soldier is an indication to both Hélène and the viewers that he has taken a human life and could do it again,.

Paul's violent nature comes to the fore when he tells Hélène about his work for the army. Paul explains to Hélène: "I have always been a butcher, a butcher for the army. In Algeria, in Indochina. It's a love, my work. Being a butcher." His repetition of the word "butcher" emphasizes the link between his profession and his identity as he conceives of it and as he wants Hélène to see him. He knows no other occupation. He is, and always has been, above all else, a butcher. This statement, of course, has a dual meaning. Figuratively, Paul makes reference to the fact that soldiers kill people and cause death. This phrase also has a literal meaning in that one of Paul's jobs in the army was to be a butcher and prepare meat in the army mess. Later, discussing this job, he says that it wasn't often that they would have meat at their meals, and when they did, it was of very poor quality. This contrasts with his later observation, "*il y avait du boulot, là,*" meaning that there was a lot of work to do while he was in Algeria and Indochina. These conflicting statements suggest that Paul himself confuses his two métiers and is, in fact, unable to separate the slaughter of animals and people.

Some scholars and critics offer the notorious colonial wars in which Paul served as the source of his murderous violence. For example, critic André Cornand suggests that before the wars, Paul was a good man, but that "war made him a monster."[29] However, while Paul's references to the war make it clear that the experience has marked him and that he carries with him experiences of death and violence, there is little to suggest that the war is entirely responsible for his downfall. Quite the contrary, it is more likely that the war awoke the murderous, villainous inclinations that had always been inside of him. Paul seems to have been destined to become a butcher, both literal and figurative. Butchery is a part of his heritage and upbringing; it is in his blood.

Indeed, blood is a powerful symbolic object in Paul's relationship with Hélène, which he attempts to establish through gifting. Paul uses food gifts to demonstrate his feelings for Hélène and to place her in a position in which she feels obliged to invite him to share his offerings. Marcel Mauss has argued that gift giving creates systems of exchange,[30] and the gifting of food is often a means of establishing or maintaining emotional bonds between the giver and the receiver.[31] According to sociologist Deborah Lupton, food is the "ultimate gift because it nourishes body and soul and is the object of psychological and symbolic consumption."[32] Food gifts unite the giver and receiver in more than a system of material exchange; they create a system of emotional exchange, based on love and caring. Preparing food for others is a sign of affection, and food gifts are sometimes a way of saying "I love you" when the words do not come easily.[33] Such is the case for Paul. When he gifts Hélène with *eau-de-vie* soaked cherries, the scene in which they share them is one of intense intimacy; together, they slip plump, blood-red cherries into their mouths as tears fall down Hélène's face. Paul tries to comfort her with the cherries, to give her strength through the *eau-de-vie*. Here, having assumed the color of the cherries floating within it, the liquor is a deep red color signifying life and passion as well as violence. It is blood-like, exaggerating the perceived life-giving qualities of the aptly named liquor whose name means "water of life." Even as Paul takes the life of other women, he gifts Hélène with objects that symbolize life and strength, but which are, at the same time, reminiscent of blood and violence.

The most significant gift that Paul offers Hélène to win her affection is a fresh, raw leg of lamb wrapped in butcher's paper that he brings to her at school one day. In front of her classroom full of students, Paul hands her the gift, whose shape resembles a bouquet of flowers—a traditional romantic offering. The way in which Paul and Hélène treat the leg of lamb accentuates this likeness. They both hold the gift at the bone, or where one would imagine the stems of the bouquet coming together. Hélène lifts the wrapped lamb to her face to smell it as if it actually were a bunch of flowers giving off a pleasant smell. This gift of lamb is laden with meaning and problematizes Paul's relationship to Hélène and to flesh. Given that gifts represent the giver, Paul's identifies him as virile, passionate, and powerful—all attributes Western culture ascribes to red meat.[34] Likewise, because cooks choose recipes and ingredients based on the likes and dislikes of the recipient, food gifts can carry with them the identity of the receiver, as well.[35] As such, by giving Hélène the leg of lamb, Paul attempts to establish a relationship of the flesh between them. Paul conceives of Hélène very similarly to how he conceives of the carcasses he butchers in his shop—as flesh. His gift is a carnal one, especially if we consider the dual meaning of this word. The adjective *carnal* signifies that which pertains to the flesh and also, by extension, the sexual. Consequently, this gift demonstrates how Paul conceives of Hélène and other women—as objects of the flesh, meant to be devoured.

Chabrol accentuates Hélène's position in Paul's mind in the final sequence of the film, in which she is dressed in a red-orange dress. The dress, tied around the waist like a package, visually transforms Hélène, via color and parallelism, into meat. As Hélène stands in the front of her classroom, in the spot where Paul originally handed her the leg of lamb, she now appears as the red meat-object about to be slaughtered, as Paul walks towards her with his knife extended (Figure 9.2). The pristine butcher's uniform Paul wears in this scene reinforces her position as the meat-object. Indeed, this metaphor is in play from the beginning of the film. On their walk home from the wedding, Paul offers to bring Hélène choice cuts of meat from his shop. She smiles and responds: "It's a dream. It's a dream to have a butcher choose your meat." Here, *your meat* is both literal and figurative. It is a culinary dream to have a butcher save you the best cuts, but it can also be a dream to have a specialist of the flesh choose your meat, your body, as the object of affection. Hélène is a pragmatist, however, and lives outside of the dream she references. For her, though not for Paul, the selection of meat only occurs at the butcher's counter.

Aware he will never win Hélène's love, as the film comes to a close, Paul turns the knife on himself as the screen cuts to black momentarily leaving the viewer in suspense as to who has been stabbed. His self-inflicted wound and his confession bring Paul's own abjection into the open. He is a seemingly kind and normal man, an integral part of the community, who seeks love with the local schoolteacher. Yet he is also marginalized and ambiguous. His

FIGURE 9.2 *Paul's confession.*

professions make him unknown and mysterious, unpredictable and violent. He is so bound to his identity as a butcher that he is unable to distinguish between life and death, and in fact, builds his own professional and personal lives through death. Paul is the face of abjection in its most sinister form—"a hatred that smiles, a passion that uses the body for barter instead of inflaming it."[36] He is a murderous butcher who deals in both human and animal flesh and finds pleasure in doing so. Paul reminds us of our own fragility and that of the faint lines that we draw between right and wrong and how easy those boundaries are to cross. He reminds us that while we may try to hide from or ignore the abject, it is not extinguishable and it resides quietly underneath our most quotidian experiences.

Notes

1. Joël Magny, *Claude Chabrol* (Paris: Seuil, Cahiers du Cinéma, 1987), 8. All translations in this chapter are my own.
2. *Le Boucher*, directed by Claude Chabrol. Paris: Parafrance Films, 1969.
3. Guy Austin, *Claude Chabrol* (Manchester: Manchester University Press, 1999), 62. Austin relates the popularity of *Le Boucher* to Chabrol's other films from this period in terms of audience size in France.
4. Dorian Bell, "Cavemen among Us: Genealogies of Atavism from Zola's *La Bête humaine* to Chabrol's *Le Boucher*," *French Studies* 62, no. 1 (2008): 41.

5. Jonathan David York, "Awaiting Oblivion: Decolonization and Deterritorialization in Chabrol's *Le Boucher*," *Quarterly Review of Film and Video* 31 (2014): 554.
6. Magny, *Claude Chabrol*, 138.
7. Terrence Rafferty, "A Master of the Thriller (Hold the Thrills)," *The New York Times*, July 20, 2006, 9.
8. Austin, *Chabrol*, 9. Chabrol comments on his inspiration from Lang and Hitchcock in Marie-Anne Guérin and Thierry Jousse, "Entretien avec Claude Chabrol," *Cahiers du cinema* 494 (September 1995): 30.
9. Rafferty, "A Master," 9.
10. Claude Chabrol, *Et pourtant je tourne . . .* (Paris: Robert Laffont, 1976), 53.
11. Dan Yakir, "The Magical Mystery World of Claude Chabrol: An Interview," *Film Quarterly* 32, no. 3 (1979): 6.
12. Isabelle Vanderschelden, *Studying French Cinema* (New York: Auteur Columbia University Press, 2013), 77.
13. Rosemary Pringle and Susan Collings, "Women and Butchery: Some Cultural Taboos," *Australian Feminist Studies* 8, no. 17 (1993): 36.
14. For a feminist reading of vegetarianism, see Carol Adams's foundational work, *The Sexual Politics of Meat: A Feminist Vegetarian Critical Theory* (New York: Continuum, 2010). See also Nick Fiddes, "The Joy of Sex," in *Meat: A Natural Symbol* (London: Routledge, 1991).
15. Vèziane de Vezins, "Ils n'ont jamais tué personne; Exaspérés, les bouchers se rebiffent," *Le Figaro*, November 26, 1997.
16. Fiddes, *Meat*, 74.
17. For an explanation of different rules regulating the use of knives at the dinner table, see Margaret Visser, *The Rituals of Dinner: The Origins, Evolution, Eccentricities and Meaning of Table Manners* (New York: Grove Weidenfeld. 1991), 181–8.
18. Bee Wilson, *Consider the Fork: A History of How We Cook and Eat* (Philadelphia: Basic Books, 2013), 44.
19. Julia Twigg, "Vegetarianism and the Meanings of Meat," in *The Sociology of Food and Eating*, ed. Anne Murcott (Croft, England: Gower, 1983), 23–4.
20. Fiddes, *Meat*, 2.
21. Claude Fischler, *L'Homnivore* (Paris: Odile Jacob, 2001), 122–4.
22. Pringle and Collings, "Women and Butchery," 39.
23. Julia Kristeva, *Powers of Horror: An Essay on Abjection*, trans. Leon S. Roudiez (New York: Columbia University Press, 1982), 4.
24. Ibid., 2–3.
25. Ibid., 3.
26. Fischler, *L'Homnivore*, 125.

27 Henry S. Salt, "The Humanities of Diet," in *Ethical Vegetarianism: From Pythagorus to Peter Singer*, ed. Kerry S. Walters and Lisa Portmess (Albany: State University of New York Press, 1999), 117.

28 The food system exacerbates the relationship between human and animal and eating brings these distinctions to the fore. Our sumptuary practices, in fact, arise out of the desire to distinguish ourselves from our animal ancestors and constitute what Norbert Elias has described as the "civilizing process" in *The Civilizing Process: The History of Manners*, trans. Edmund Jephcott (New York: Urizen Books, 1978).

29 André Cornand, "Le Boucher," *Image et Son: La revue du cinéma* 238 (1970): 38.

30 Marcel Mauss, *The Gift: The Form and Reason for Exchange in Archaic Societies*, trans. W. D. Halls (New York: Norton, 1990).

31 Carole M. Counihan, "Female Identity, Food, and Power in Contemporary Florence," *Anthropological Quarterly* 61, no. 2 (April 1988): 54.

32 Deborah Lupton, *Food, the Body and the Self* (London: Sage, 1996), 47.

33 Roland Barthes explains that food is a sign and, consequently, there exists a "veritable grammar of foods" and that food constitutes a form of communication in "Toward a Psychosociology of Contemporary Food Consumption," trans. Elborg Forster, in *Food and Drink in History: Selections from the Annales: Economies, Sociétés, Civilisations*, ed. Robert Forster and Orest Ranum (Baltimore: Johns Hopkins University Press, 1979).

34 Lupton, *Food*, 28. See also Twigg, *Vegetarianism*, 22.

35 Lupton, *Food*, 48.

36 Ibid.

Bibliography

Adams, Carol. *The Sexual Politics of Meat: A Feminist Vegetarian Critical Theory*. New York: Continuum, 2010.

Austin, Guy. *Claude Chabrol*. Manchester: Manchester University Press, 1999.

Barthes, Roland. "Toward a Psychosociology of Contemporary Food Consumption." Translated by Elborg Forster. In *Food and Drink in History: Selections from the Annales: Economies, Sociétés, Civilisations*, edited by Robert Forster and Orest Ranum, 166–73. Baltimore: Johns Hopkins University Press, 1979.

Bell, Dorian. "Cavemen among Us: Genealogies of Atavism from Zola's *La Bête humaine* to Chabrol's *Le Boucher*." *French Studies* 62, no. 1 (2008): 39–52.

Le Boucher. Directed by Claude Chabrol. Paris: Parafrance Films, 1969.

Chabrol, Claude. *Et pourtant je tourne . . .* Paris: Robert Laffont, 1976.

Cornand, André. "Le Boucher." *Image et Son: La revue du cinéma* 238 (1970): 105–108.

Counihan, Carole M. "Female Identity, Food, and Power in Contemporary Florence." *Anthropological Quarterly* 61, no. 2 (April 1988): 51–62.
Delicatessen. Directed by Jean-Pierre Jeunet. Santa Monica, CA: Miramax Films, 1991.
Elias, Norbert. *The Civilizing Process: The History of Manners*. Translated by Edmund Jephcott. New York: Urizen Books, 1978.
Fiddes, Nick. *Meat: A Natural Symbol*. London: Routledge, 1991.
Fischler, Claude. *L'Homnivore*. Paris: Odile Jacob, 2001.
The Green Butchers. Directed by Anders Thomas Jensen. Aalborg, Denmark: Sandrew Metronome, 2004.
Guérin, Marie-Anne, and Thierry Jousse. "Entretien avec Claude Chabrol." *Cahiers du cinéma* 494 (September 1995): 27–32.
Kristeva, Julia. *Powers of Horror: An Essay on Abjection*. Translated by Leon S. Roudiez. New York: Columbia University Press, 1982.
Lupton, Deborah. *Food, the Body and the Self*. London: Sage, 1996.
Magny, Joël. *Claude Chabrol*. Paris: Seuil, Cahiers du Cinéma, 1987.
Mauss, Marcel. *The Gift: The Form and Reason for Exchange in Archaic Societies*. Translated by W. D. Halls. New York: Norton, 1990.
Pringle, Rosemary, and Susan Collings. "Women and Butchery: Some Cultural Taboos." *Australian Feminist Studies* 8, no. 17 (1993): 29–45.
Rafferty, Terrence. "A Master of the Thriller (Hold the Thrills)." *The New York Times*, July 20, 2006.
Salt, Henry S. "The Humanities of Diet." In *Ethical Vegetarianism: From Pythagorus to Peter Singer*, edited by Kerry S. Walters and Lisa Portmess, 115–26. Albany: State University of New York Press, 1999. Originally published in Henry S. Salt. *The Humanities of Diet*. Manchester: The Vegetarian Society, 1914.
Twigg, Julia. "Vegetarianism and the Meanings of Meat." In *The Sociology of Food and Eating*, edited by Anne Murcott, 18–30. Croft, England: Gower, 1983.
Vanderschelden, Isabelle. *Studying French Cinema*. New York: Auteur Columbia University Press, 2013.
Vezins, Vèziane de. "Ils n'ont jamais tué personne; Exaspérés, les bouchers se rebiffent." *Le Figaro*, November 26, 1997.
Visser, Margaret. *The Rituals of Dinner: The Origins, Evolution, Eccentricities and Meaning of Table Manners*. New York: Grove Weidenfeld, 1991.
Wilson, Bee. *Consider the Fork: A History of How We Cook and Eat*. Philadelphia: Basic Books, 2013.
Yakir, Dan. "The Magical Mystery World of Claude Chabrol: An Interview." *Film Quarterly* 32, no. 3 (1979): 2–14.
York, Jonathan David. "Awaiting Oblivion: Decolonization and Deterritorialization in Chabrol's *Le Boucher*." *Quarterly Review of Film and Video* 31 (2014): 553–60.

10

A Hunger for Dead Cakes: Visions of Abjection, Scapegoating, and the Sin-Eater

Ralph Beliveau

Kinds of horror come and go, something like cuisines. These changes present an opportunity to ask questions about the cultural condition of a moment. Why, for example, would a particular culture seem fascinated by vampires in one moment and zombies in another? Why would Italian food become a site of interest and innovation, only later to be supplanted by Cajun tastes and styles? While asking such questions might not reveal a clear cause-and-effect relationship, considering possible answers can shed light on the workings of a particular cultural moment. The current popularity of *The Walking Dead*, along with a great number of recent zombie films from *World War Z* (2013) to *Cockneys vs. Zombies* (2012), includes the idea of horror generated by the thought of being consumed, of being eaten by other deceased people, and of the inevitability of ourselves becoming the walking dead. In fact, George Romero suggested, in an interview for the documentary *The American Nightmare* (2000), that since we know we are going to die, we are indeed the walking dead already.

This contemporary notion of horror appears far removed from the world of gothic sources of fear—but that appearance is deceptive. The transgressions and excesses that mark the gothic are still present, merely hidden by a mask of naturalism and realism, and the reasonableness of community. As Fred Botting argues,

> The Gothic strain existed in excess of, and often within, realist forms, both inhabiting and excluded from its homogenizing representations of the world. Psychological rather than supernatural forces became the prime movers in worlds where individuals could be sure neither of others nor themselves. As bourgeois modes of social organization and economic and aesthetic production demanded increasing realism, self-discipline and regulation of its individuals, with techniques being developed by social and scientific practices, those persons that deviated from its norms became fascinating objects of scrutiny.[1]

The current fashion in horror is comfortable with evil, but less so with the notion of sin—of a soul contaminated by a history of transgressions. An examination of the notion of the Sin-Eater brings to focus why this might be the case, and how our culture would use such a story to engage with what it means to consume, to eat, and alternately to starve in deprivation. Closely tied to this are notions of what it means to purge, of what it means to be clean or unclean, and of how power and politics interact with the need for purification. A community may use processes of abjection and scapegoating to cleanse its soul, but perhaps not be as successful in clearing its conscience.

Sin-Eaters: an unnatural mythology

Eating with or around the dead is a practice that has been traced back at least to Roman times.[2] The great significance of these feasts had to do with developing the relationship between the living and the dead. Regina Gee writes:

> On specific festival days of the Roman calendar, cities of the dead swelled with the living as Romans traveled out to necropolis and held funerary banquets in or near monuments to their beloved dead. These semi-annual banquets were the key ritual action for the transformation of the dead from polluted body to sanctified ancestor, and suggest this change in status was not fixed after burial rites and interment, but had to be perpetually renewed and renegotiated post-mortem.[3]

This tradition of sanctifying the dead was transformed in two ways in the Christian era. First, the communion ritual, which in the Catholic tradition was and remains a ceremony of transubstantiation (the symbol changes into the actual body and blood of Christ), instead in Anglican theology became symbolic. The Elizabethan Religious Settlement declared that the idea of transubstantiation was "repugnant to the plain words of Scripture, overthroweth the nature of a Sacrament, and hath given occasion to many superstitions."[4] Second, focus on the polluted body was replaced by a focus on the condition of the immortal soul, which needed to be free from sin in order to enter into eternal salvation. This was done through Church ritual absolution, but there were cases where absolution under the Church's eye did not or could not take place. Although the origins of sin-eating are not specifically known, the traces of its existence suggest it was a practice never sanctioned by the Church, and was perhaps an alternative that developed in culture as a way of cleansing sin from the recently deceased.

The practice has been noted in the history, literature, and lore of Wales,[5] as well as that of the Fens (a drained marshland in eastern England), and other areas. Tales circulate of the practice being brought to the United States through Appalachian communities, usually by people of Irish decent. One blog entry from 2013 reports stories of the practice in North Carolina, Virginia, and West Virginia, passed down to the author by his grandmother. The account suggests that the practice took place until 1915 or so in communities near where she lived. The account is worth noting because it includes the alleged words of the Sin-Eater's prayer: "I pledge my soul for your sins and ask that God Almighty remove those sins from you and place them up on me and I eat this food and drink from this cup to show that I have taken your sins upon me. If I lie may God strike me dead before I eat from this plate or drink from this cup." The same author claims to have spoken to a man from West Virginia who reported the practice occurring in the late 1950s.[6]

Much of the discussion in a contemporary, digital culture is preoccupied with the validity and legitimacy of the tales: "Did they really happen? Are they true?" Critical to this is the question of who is talking about whom. In other words, the discussion of the folk tale is a discussion about something outside, defining what counts as "what we do" against "what they do"— or in the case of the Sin-Eater stories, "what we *did*." Mikel J. Koven uses this point to discuss the incident in the film *The Wicker Man* (2006) where a human is sacrificed in a giant burning colossus, but it applies to the Sin-Eater idea as well. To discuss the Sin-Eater "as legend is to engage in a debate about whether people really did such a thing, but by a culture other than the one portrayed in the episode. That is, legends are, in addition to negotiations about the possible, negotiations about the other."[7] This idea of the outsider is as critical to the telling of the story as it is to the story itself, since the idea of the Sin-Eater as outsider becomes the Sin-Eater as outcast, and even the Sin-Eater as scapegoat.

As an unofficial practice, folk knowledge includes a variety of variations. Common to most of these retellings, the basic essence of the Sin-Eater story was that a person—usually unknown to the deceased (and usually in a position of being shunned by the community)—was hired to eat a ritual meal, on, over, or in the presence of the corpse. Ritual words were uttered by the Sin-Eater, which prayed for the transfer of the sins of the deceased into the food and into the Sin-Eater as he ate the meal.[8] Through the food, the sins were transferred to the Sin-Eater, who was then paid and sent away, taking with him the sins of the deceased.

Since this practice was conducted outside the sanction of the Church, it was discouraged and began to die out in the latter half of the nineteenth century. In the 1926 work *Funeral Customs: Their Origin and Development*, Bertram S. Puckle writes:

> A less known but even more remarkable functionary, whose professional services were once considered necessary to the dead, is the Sin-Eater. Savage tribes have been known to slaughter an animal on the grave, in the belief that it would take upon itself the sins of the dead. In the same manner, it was the province of the human scapegoat to take upon himself the moral trespasses of his client—and whatever the consequences might be in the after life—in return for a miserable fee and a scanty meal. That such a creature should be unearthed from a remote period of pagan history would be surprising enough, but to find reliable evidence of his existence in the British Isles a hundred years ago is surely very much more remarkable.[9]

In addition to noting the likely pagan origins of the practice, records indicate that the Sin-Eaters were always men, usually of little means. In 2010, however, a BBC story discussed the restoration of the grave of "the last Sin-Eater," Richard Munslow, who was buried in Ratlinghope, England, in 1906.[10]

So we are left with evidence that suggests that sin-eating was an actual historical practice, though the power of the idea is sustained by its indetermination. Particularly as a horror tale, the power rests in the idea that it *might* have taken place and that it required a demonstration of faith rather than a material manifestation of something supernatural.

All in the sin-eater family

While the origins of the Sin-Eater as either folklore or legend remain somewhat obscure, the resurgence of interest in contemporary media can be traced back to an episode of *Night Gallery* that was first broadcast on February 23, 1972. The teleplay was written by Halstead Welles, who adapted it from the short story by Christianna Brand, "Sins of the Fathers . . ."[11] The adaptation remains quite faithful to the original story, taking some of Brand's dialogue almost word-for-word. Brand's story starts with a note to the reader: "Sin-Eaters flourished in Wales, especially along the English border, up to the end of the seventeenth century; but, though less common, they continued long after that, possibly up to as little as a hundred years ago."[12]

Set in a rural part of Wales plagued by both famine and pestilence, Brand's story opens with an unnamed servant arriving, after traveling a great distance, at the desolate, rundown cottage of a Sin-Eater. He does not want to get too close to the cottage, and the woman within calls out to him. He explains that he has come some distance to find a Sin-Eater, since the ones near his master's house are either busy serving other dead or dead themselves. The woman claims her husband cannot come as he is quite ill as well, but the servant is insistent, promising a good meal and the traditional payment. The woman turns to her son, almost a man, but suffering from the famine. With the servant still outside, she tells the son that he can go in place of his father. But rather than eating the meal she says that he should claim to need to do the sin-eating alone with the body. She tells him to go through a charade of pretending to say the Sin-Eater's words, pretending to eat the food, wailing and crying out as if the sins were entering him. She tells him to smuggle the food in his cloak and then race away from the scene. She tells him not to eat a crumb of the food till he gets home. He goes to the Master's house and goes through the charade, racing away with the food before even receiving the payment. When he arrives home, his mother takes the food inside, and then invites him in to feast . . . over the body of his deceased Sin-Eater father.

The story is short—less than 3,500 words—but packs a powerful effect. After first appearing in *Rogue* (a men's magazine competing with *Playboy*) in February 1963, it found a wider audience when it was republished in *The Fifth Pan Book of Horror Stories* in 1964. But the widest audience for the story arrived when the story was adapted for *Night Gallery*. Frequently considered by fans and critics as one of the series' best episodes, it offered an unusual kind of horror. Rather than offering either a gothic presentation that included a depiction of the supernatural, or a representation of horror driven through bodily violation in a more contemporary mode, this version of the story builds its effect through a different approach that emphasizes a tragedy of human proportion that touches on gender roles, deception, questions of belief, and a society that uses material deprivation as a way to rid itself of its contagion. To discuss how meanings are constructed in these two versions of "The Sins of the Fathers . . ." we need to consider the idea of the abject between food and sin, the relation of sin-eating to scapegoating, and the way gender and family subvert meaning in a manner that is deeply uncanny as well as deeply disturbing.

Food, abjection, and the breakdown of meaning

In the *Night Gallery* episode there are two moments where the trauma of the moment of sin-eating is emphasized. In the first, Mrs. Evans (played by Geraldine Page) has sent her son Ian (played by Richard Thomas) to stand in for his father as the Sin-Eater, since the elder is too ill to go. As in the story, Mrs. Evans tells her son to deceive the family of the deceased, the Craghills. He is told to steal the food and bring it home. But in order for the deception to work, he must convince the people in the next room that the rite is taking place by crying and wailing (Figure 10.1). Ian's performance is quite convincing, but pales in comparison to what awaits him at home. When his mother has him act as the Sin-Eater for his Sin-Eater father, the levels of horror and disgust are terrifying, as he gulps down the food and screams horrifically. (Much of the horror is communicated through the performance by Richard Thomas, and his interpretation of the character's limited understanding combined with desperate starvation.)

The meaning of these moments of horror are well informed by the notion of abjection, as described by Julia Kristeva in her book *The Powers of Horror: An Essay On Abjection* (1982). Using a psychoanalytic frame to probe how we experience horror, Kristeva frames abjection as the human reaction to things that are disgusting: vomit, shit, rotting animal meat, and especially a rotting human corpse. These are sensory experiences that cause an immediate reaction of disgust, and a desire to get these things away from us, to escape. She writes:

> A wound with blood and pus, or the sickly, acrid smell of sweat, of decay, does not *signify* death. In the presence of signified death—a flat encephalograph, for instance—I would understand, react, or accept. No, as in true theater, without makeup or masks, refuse and corpses *show me*

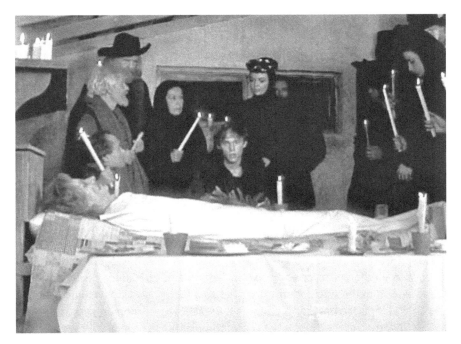

FIGURE 10.1 *A dinner scene like no other, the ritual of the Sin-Eater from "Sins of the Fathers." Ian (center, Richard Thomas) prepares to eat the wealthy man's sins, under the watchful eye of the man's Widow (Barbara Steele), who stands just behind him.*

what I permanently thrust aside in order to live. These body fluids, this defilement, this shit are what life withstands, hardly and with difficulty, on the part of death. There, I am at the border of my condition as a living being.[13]

Kristeva argues that these substances remind us of our mortality, of the potential and inevitable corruption of our own material form, which threatens our conceptual and spiritual senses of our selves. The ways we create the meaning of who and what we are demand the suspension of our awareness of our mortality and our future demise. This is a powerful notion that runs through much of our fictional, visual, and sensory horror experiences.

On the material level, the Sin-Eater is put in the position of contradicting meaning, breaking down the connection between food, life, and bodily materiality. Food—sustenance—sustains our life, yet at the place where the corpse is visible, the meaning of survival is in question, and the meaning that comes from the separation of food and corruption is exploded. All the cultural effort that goes into the disguise of food is stripped away. The meaning of being alive, and the end of life that is brought about in order for things that were alive to become *food* is stripped away, the closer the substance of food is to our experience as humans, especially in an urban setting.

From this perspective, both versions of this story derive much of their power from the way food is positioned. It lies in the vicinity of the corpse, proximal to the abject thing for which meaning has completely broken down, just as life has come to an end. Yet at the same time, the surrounding food offers the promise of sensory satisfaction, of easing the pain of hunger, and of ending the threat posed by starvation. The moment is tantalizing in the literal sense when it comes to meaning. The food offers a continuation of the meaning of life, even though it contains the impossible promise of suppressing the abject.

Brand, in the short story, must put the reader in the position of a poor person suffering from extreme food deprivation, like the poverty-stricken characters in the story who are trapped between famine and pestilence. They are, to a great extent, in the position of the abject as a group, serving as a reminder of the socioeconomic breakdown that is a breakdown of meaning as well. How do we relate to these people who are so pitiable? An ethics of care tries to bridge this dissonance, so that we feel as if we share substance with these desperate folks, we sense our connection to them because the meaning of their lives is such a shattered state that the meaning of our own lives as viewers is called into question. Brand does this through the description of the banquet that is seen by the son (named Ianto in the story) when he arrives in the room of the deceased: "The corpse was laid out in the little parlour where candlelight glowed from the tall dresser with its rows of gold lustre jugs. A white sheet was pulled up to the chin, a china dish balanced upon the dead breast."[14] With the scene set, in full knowledge of the abject, Brand switches to the object of desire:

> [A]nd heaped on the dish was food, thick slices of bacon, pink and glistening white, cut from the home-cured joints that hung from the beams in the kitchen ceiling; brown faggots, home-made also, aromatic with herbs; eggs boiled and shelled, raw onions sliced across, fresh-baked bread, spread thinly with the butter that the farmhouse wives so salted that the hired servants would not take too much of it: great wedges of cake, dark and sticky; slabs of crumbling white cheese . . . The boy stood looking at it and slavered at the jaws.[15]

The transition is complex. As we read through the passage, we are in the point of view of the young novice Sin-Eater, who we know is starving. Like him, we are suspended between the death of meaning in the corpse and the meaning of life in the food.

The television episode redoubles the effort to explore this contradictory moment. The Servant (played by Michael Dunn) arrives at the Sin-Eater's cottage, desperate to find a man to complete the ritual. He attempts to persuade the Sin-Eater's wife to send him through a detailed description of the feast that awaits the starving person: "There's roast lamb, and boiled eggs, and raw onions sliced across, and thick slices of bacon, fresh baked bread heavy with butter, all there waiting for him. Great wedges of cake and whole slabs of white cheese."[16]

While this speech does end up successfully talking Mrs. Evans into sending a Sin-Eater, the difference between Brand's story and the *Night Gallery* episode (directed by Jeannot Szwarc) becomes tangible in the scene when the boy, Ian Evans, arrives at the body. He is first struck by the abject corpse, but then his attention is drawn to the brightly colored, delicious-looking food. He is caught between the two—between the collapse of meaning represented by the body, and the promise of sustenance promised by the food. This visual notion is strongly reinforced by the look that director Szwarc and art director Joseph Alves developed for the episode:

> Szwarc and art director Joseph Alves began designing the look of the segment. They developed an organizing visual concept: while the food would have very vivid, bright colors, everything else—the sets, makeup, and costuming—would have subdued colors, predominantly black and white, all designed to heighten the story's central theme.[17]

The notion of the abject is reinforced by this decision in art direction. The ashen, monochromatic look of the face of the corpse, the body covered in a white sheet, contrasts with the vibrancy of the food and is then intercut with the wet, red lips and tongue of Ian as he tries to take in the discordant scene. Although the audience has been included in the suggested deception that Ian will not eat a crumb of the food, but will instead steal it and bring it home, for a moment his expression indicates that he might be overwhelmed by hunger, by the vibrant promise of the food, even in the sight of the corpse. The viewer is suspended in the moment where meaning is on the edge of collapse, and the horror of the situation sets in.

When finally the tension is broken, and Ian chooses in favor of stealing rather than eating, he wails and screams. His reaction is simultaneously overwhelming and pitiable. Ian's intense outcry juxtaposes the real horror of his predicament with the performance that mimicking the ritual requires to deceive the witnesses just outside the room, indicating to them that the sin has passed into the Sin-Eater. This cry is echoed and intensified at the conclusion of the story, when Ian returns home with the food, only to find that he must eat the sins of his Sin-Eater father. Where the earlier cry was part horror in the face of the abject and part performance for the sake of a convincing deception, Ian's concluding moment is a far different matter; it is the fully realized spasm of the abject, fully inhabiting the place where the meaning of self, defined on the difference between inside and outside, of self and other, collapses into the horror of losing all meaning.

In both versions of the story, Ian is presented as a sympathetic subject. He is poised on the precipice of becoming a man, but his life is threatened by the famine. At the beginning of the story, Ian's father, the Sin-Eater, is not dead but is suffering from both illness and starvation. Ian has not come to terms with his father's imminent demise; so at the horrific moment when his mother leads him in to the inner room where his father lies dead, he comes to a parallel moment from earlier in the story. The stranger's corpse has been replaced by his father's corpse, and the deception he perpetrated—pretending to eat the sins of Mr. Craighill—has been replaced by being deceived by his mother into eating the sins of his father. Now he will eat to satisfy his hunger. And his wail as he starts to eat has a parallel double meaning; it is the horror of the realization of his father's death juxtaposed over the abject condition that eating in the presence of his father's corpse places him in. The great power of the story is not lost on the audience even if the transfer of sin is seen as superstition. The story's effects work because of the horrific condition that the character is in, since it is clear that *he* believes that his identity is in grave danger.

The Sin-Eater as scapegoat

The folklore of the Sin-Eater includes the idea that he is a social outcast, a literally unclean person tainted by the process of eating the sins of the deceased. His actions, taken so that the soul of the dead individual can travel to heaven rather than purgatory, make him a threat to the community. It reinscribes the notion of abjection, since he becomes that abject thing that instills revulsion and must be sent away—expelled and separated from the social "body." That expulsion is an exile from the social network.

Both Brand's story and the *Night Gallery* episode emphasize the desperate need for the Sin-Eater, reflected in the hardship the servant endures to find one. The social need to find an undesirable person to act as a scapegoat—to stand in for others and accept blame and responsibility for some occurrence—has, Tom Douglas argues, been part of human culture since it first had to contend with responsibility for its actions under the supposed eye of a divine observer.[18] Douglas traces the origins of the term to William Tyndale, a fifteenth-century scholar who produced one of the earliest translations of the Bible into English, and introduced the term in his rendering of Leviticus 16. Here Aaron

> grabs the head of the live goat, and confess over him all the iniquities of the children of Israel, and all their transgressions in all their sins, putting them upon the head of the goat and shall send him away into the wilderness by the hand of a man who is in readiness. The goat shall bear all their iniquities upon him to a solitary land; and he shall let the goat go into the wilderness.[19]

In "Sins of the Fathers . . ." the desolate cottage where the Evans family lives is quite set apart from the community. Mrs. Evans specifically mentions to the servant how her husband, the Sin-Eater, is sought to perform the task, but then cast away once he has been used.

To get specifically to the term *scapegoat*, Douglas goes into more detail about the ritual invoked in the passage from Leviticus. Among the Hebrews, Mosaic law used two goats in the ritual; "The Lord's goat was sacrificed, the other was the scapegoat; and the high priest having, by confession, transferred his own sins and the sins of the people to it, was taken to the wilderness and suffered to escape."[20] Here the work of the Sin-Eater is located in a specific sanctioned ritual, with the same goals of sanctification and then expulsion into the wild. As a corollary, the suggestion in the idea of "tragedy/goat-song" tied to the celebration of Dionysus sees his domain as the God of the spirit of the wilderness.

The recasting of the scapegoat ritual into the practice of sin-eating is almost satiric in its manipulation of material goods into something more civil. The ritual scapegoating becomes an exchange of goods for services rendered. The food benefits the malnourished, and payment (meager as it might have been) is included as well. In both Brand's version and the *Night Gallery* version, the conclusion of the ritual is simultaneously the moment of payment and the moment of expulsion:

> He let out one startled yell: the door burst open, they all stood gaping: and, hysterically screaming, he thrust his way through them and was out—out into the night air, under the stars and fleeing down the mountain-side to the place he called his home. If they flung gold after him, if the servant recollected his promise of safe conduct, he waited for neither.[21]

In the *Night Gallery* episode, Ian screams and rushes from the room containing Mr. Craighill's corpse. As the witnesses in the next room recoil, Ian races out the door of the home. Mrs. Craighill (played by Barbara Steele), with a disgusted and horrified look on her face, throws the coins into the night after him, but he is already out of range.

The social politics implied in both versions of the story suggest that a transformation of the scapegoat notion has taken place between ancient and more modern times. Douglas notes that there were three essential aspects to the ancient scapegoating process. First, there was a belief that the Hebrews' god had established a set of rules, and that violating those rules was a transgression—a sin—that was bound to be punished, and that required some form of penance—payment, leading to purification—on the part of the transgressor. Second, there was the belief that, at the community level, this cycle of rules, transgressions, and purification required repetition, which caused the "scapegoat" ritual to become an annual event. Third, there was the belief that these transgressions—these sins—had a substantial existence and thus could be transferred through ritual from the original transgressor to the scapegoat or (in a later formulation) through the food to the Sin-Eater. Douglas says that

> this involved a set form of ritual . . . words and ritual actions were regarded as able to effect change—they were instruments of power. Thus it was that the sins of a community could be ceremonially laid upon the selected goat and the animal driven or led out into the wilderness. The sins of the community thus being removed like the disposal of rubbish.[22]

Significantly, in "Sins of the Fathers . . ." the process is less a concern of the community than of the individual. The practice requires means, and exploits those who have little to keep themselves alive. Much as the scapegoat underscored the dominance of humans over animals, the institution of the Sin-Eater represents the dominance of those who could afford to pay to have their sins eaten over those who needed both the food and the money for survival. Like the Catholic practices surrounding indulgences, a monetary or material exchange is constructed to have the power to wipe away the sins of the faithful, to reduce their time in purgatory after death.

Conclusion: scapegoating the community

And what of the sins of the Sin-Eater—the transgressions that accumulated through the practices that fell upon those too materially poor to discharge their own accumulated transgressions? In the story, Brand suggests that the mother, Mrs. Evans, knew all along that the father was not going to survive Ianto's going out to pose as the Sin-Eater. She instructs him:

> "Eat nothing there. Ianto. Not one scrap, not one crumb! Say the prayers. Tell the people to let you alone with the body while you eat. But don't eat. Bring the food away with you."
>
> "And so in that way I shall not eat the sins?" But still the poor, feeble intellect staggered at the thought of the ordeal to be endured. "To see a dead man . . . To say the prayers, to wail and scream . . .! To be left alone with him!" He implored: "Mother! Must I go?"
>
> She bent all her strength to uphold her will against his, "Yes. You must go."
>
> "And bring the food back? Bring it here?" It was dreadful to see the gentle face lose its innocence, the dawn of idiot cunning in his eyes. "But not for myself, Mother? Isn't that it?"
>
> "The money—"
>
> "I don't want the money," he said. "But the food . . ." His thin arm hugged the aching emptiness of his belly.
>
> "I don't want the food," she said. "It's not for me, I shall not touch one crumb of it, not one crumb . . ." But she could not prevent the turn of her anguished heart towards that inner room where her man lay moaning: the turn of her anxious eyes. The boy said "Ah, no—not for you. For him!"
>
> "You shall eat it all," she said; and bent her head guiltily, not meeting the return of his innocent, foolish faith and joy.[23]

The *Night Gallery* episode goes even further, making plain the full extent of Mrs. Evans's understanding of the cycle of abjection and scapegoating. Ian returns to their cottage with the food. Mrs. Evans helps to lay it out on a tray. "Well, son. Now you will eat," she says. But just as he is about to dig in, she takes the tray of food to the inner room of the cottage. "No. It's mine," Ian says. "You promised." He sees her take it toward the inner room where his sick father was laying. "No. You're not giving it all to him," Ian says. "You will have all of it," she replies, and goes into the room for a moment. Then she leads him in: he sees the corpse of his father . . . with the food spread around the corpse. He faints. Mrs. Evans revives him, tells him of all the sins his father has accumulated, and how he needs to be cleansed. "He's your father," she says. "Think of all the sins of the Sin-Eater . . . Hundreds of sins from hundreds of men . . ." She then describes the food to bring his attention back to his hunger . . . then adds, "Ian, don't worry. You'll have a son . . ." (Figure 10.2).

FIGURE 10.2 *In "Sins of the Fathers," Mrs. Evans (Geraldine Page) closes the family circle and tells her son, Ian (Richard Thomas), "Think of your father ... he is not a simple farmer with simple sins ... think of all the sins of the Sin-Eater."*

As the mother she provides sustenance, but at this moment becomes a source of horror, a version of what Barbara Creed describes as the monstrous-feminine.[24] Here the mother becomes abject from the point of view of the attempt of the child—Ian, in this case—to separate himself from his mother. She obliterates this border by using his hunger to keep the family cycle going. She guides him to eat the sins of the father, and he too will be a father one day and can lead his son to do the same. Her actions reinscribe a whole culture of horror: the reproduction of patriarchy, the extension of the scapegoat into the future, the actions of a parent that damn the child through the misplaced manipulation of love and care. In this moment, the critique offered through the story shows what damage is done by a community and its power structure as it tries to purify itself.

It is an important lesson that is taught by this particular horror tale. Consider a community that tries to convince itself that it no longer needs to be responsible for its own historical sins, that it has gone through some sort of purification that has created a scapegoat and then exiled it to be on the outside. Outsiders, foreigners, the unclean and despoiled, the scapegoat, the abject, all having had to consume the sins of history and are paid back by being exiled from the community. The potential horror and darkness comes from a community believing that their processes of purification absolve them from having created a history of victims.

Notes

1 Fred Botting, *Gothic* (London: Routledge, 1996), 12.
2 Inge Nielsen, *Meals in a Social Context: Aspects of the Communal Meal in the Hellenistic and Roman World*, 2nd edn (Aarhus, Denmark: Aarhus University Press, 2001), 67–80.
3 Regina Gee, "From Corpse to Ancestor: The Role of Tombside Dining in the Transformation of the Body in Ancient Rome," in *The Materiality of Death: Bodies, Burials, Beliefs*, ed. F. Fahlander and T. Sestigaard (Oxford: Archaeopress, 2008), 59.
4 "The Church of England Doctrine on the Sacrament of the Lord's Supper." *Church Society*, http://archive.churchsociety.org/publications/tracts/CAT116_CofE-LordsSupper.pdf (accessed October 31, 2015).
5 Jane Aaron, *Welsh Gothic* (Cardiff: University of Wales Press, 2013).
6 Thomas Byers, "Do You Know That Sin Eaters Were Once Real?" *HubPages* (August 17, 2013), http://hubpages.com/religion-philosophy/Do-You-Know-That-Sin-Eaters-Were-Once-Real (accessed October 31, 2015).
7 Mikel J. Koven, *Film Folklore, and Urban Legends* (Lanham, MD: Scarecrow Press, 2008), 26.
8 Virtually every version casts the Sin-Eater as male. For an enlightening exception, see Margaret Atwood, "The Sin Eater," in *Dancing Girls* (New York: Simon and Schuster, 1977), 213–24.
9 Bertram Puckle, *Funeral Customs: Their Origin and Development* (London: T. W. Laurie, 1926).
10 "Last 'Sin-Eater' Celebrated with Church Service," BBC.co (September 19, 2010), http://www.bbc.co.uk/news/uk-england-shropshire-11360659 (accessed October 31, 2015).
11 Christianna Brand, "The Sins of the Fathers . . .," in *What Dread Hand: A Collection of Short Stories* (London: Michael Joseph, 1968), 122–31.
12 Ibid., 122.
13 Julia Kristeva, *Powers of Horror: An Essay on Abjection* (New York: Columbia University Press, 1982), 3.
14 Brand, "The Sins of the Fathers . . .," 127.
15 Ibid.

16 "Sins of the Father" [*Night Gallery*].
17 Scott Skelton and Jim Benson, *Rod Serling's Night Gallery: An After-Hours Tour* (Syracuse, NY: Syracuse University Press, 1999), 285.
18 Tom Douglas, *Scapegoats: Transferring Blame* (New York: Routledge, 1995), 6.
19 Ibid., 7.
20 Quoted in ibid., 8; italics in original.
21 Brand, "The Sins of the Fathers . . .," 130.
22 Douglas, *Scapegoats*, 15.
23 Brand, "The Sins of the Fathers . . .," 126.
24 Barbara Creed, *The Monstrous-Feminine: Film, Feminism, Psychoanalysis* (New York: Routledge, 1993).

Bibliography

Aaron, Jane. *Welsh Gothic*. Cardiff: University of Wales Press, 2013.
Atwood, Margaret. "The Sin Eater." In *Dancing Girls*, 213–24. New York: Simon and Schuster, 1977.
Botting, Fred. *Gothic*. London: Routledge, 1996.
Brand, Christianna. "The Sins of the Fathers . . ." In *What Dread Hand: A Collection of Short Stories*, 122–31. London: Michael Joseph, 1968.
Byers, Thomas. "Do You Know That Sin Eaters Were Once Real?" *HubPages*, August 17, 2013. http://hubpages.com/religion-philosophy/Do-You-Know-That-Sin-Eaters-Were-Once-Real (accessed October 31, 2015).
"The Church of England Doctrine On the Sacrament of the Lord's Supper." *Church Society*. http://archive.churchsociety.org/publications/tracts /CAT116_CofE-LordsSupper.pdf (accessed October 31, 2015).
Creed, Barbara. *The Monstrous-Feminine: Film, Feminism, Psychoanalysis*. New York: Routledge, 1993.
Douglas, Tom. *Scapegoats: Transferring Blame*. New York: Routledge, 1995.
Gee, Regina. "From Corpse to Ancestor: The Role of Tombside Dining in the Transformation of the Body in Ancient Rome." In *The Materiality of Death: Bodies, Burials, Beliefs*, edited by F. Fahlander and T. Sestigaard, 59–68. Oxford: Archaeopress, 2008.
Koven, Mikel J. *Film Folklore, and Urban Legends*. Lanham, MD: Scarecrow Press, 2008.
Kristeva, Julia. *Powers of Horror: An Essay on Abjection*. New York: Columbia University Press, 1982.
Nielsen, Inge. *Meals in a Social Context: Aspects of the Communal Meal in the Hellenistic and Roman World*, 2nd edn. Aarhus, Denmark: Aarhus University Press, 2001.
Puckle, Bertram. *Funeral Customs: Their Origin and Development*. London: T. W. Laurie, 1926.

"Sins of The Fathers." Directed by Jeannot Szwarc. *Rod Serling's Night Gallery* (1972). Season 2, disc 5. United States: Universal, 2008. DVD, 30 min.

Skelton, Scott, and Jim Benson. *Rod Serling's Night Gallery: An After-Hours Tour.* Syracuse, NY: Syracuse University Press, 1999.

PART THREE

The Extreme End of Consumption

11

Coprophagia as Class and Consumerism in the *Human Centipede* Films

Mark Henderson

Along with its two sequels, the 2009 Tom Six film *The Human Centipede (First Sequence)* has gained widespread notoriety as a viscerally repulsive film of the body-horror subgenre. It has even been widely parodied, from the 2011 *South Park* episode "HUMANCENTiPAD" to a skit on Conan O'Brien's TBS late-night show involving a "human centipede menorah." At the heart of the repulsion that it inspires is not only the medical experimentation and nonconsensual surgery on human beings, but the *coprophagia* that is forced upon them through the design of this particular form of surgery. The subjects (or victims) are, after all, surgically sewn together, mouth-to-anus, in sequence, with all but the front "segment" being forced to consume the feces of the person in front of them.

The reason why the premise of coprophagia is so deeply and generally revolting can perhaps be best explained, at least on a psychoanalytic level, by Julia Kristeva, through her theory of the *abject*. According to Kristeva, fecal matter (along with other bodily fluids or other substances discharged as *waste*) is a quintessential object of abjection; as an object "being opposed to *I*,"[1] it is "jettisoned" and "radically excluded"[2] from the individual. The sudden, even convulsive rejection of such loathed objects reveals abjection to be more violent than Freudian uncanniness. Where uncanniness merely spells out the fear "which leads back to what is known of old and long familiar,"[3] abjection involves "a failure to recognize its kin [. . .] even the shadow of a memory."[4] The abject is much less acknowledged and far more denied, even upon sight, than the uncanny. The loathsome "meaninglessness" of the abject arises from its association with death, for the "equivalents" of excrement—"decay, infection, disease, corpse, etc."—stand for the ultimate "danger to identity" that comes from without and threatens the ego's very existence. As Kristeva explains:

> These body fluids, this defilement, this shit are what life withstands, hardly and with difficulty, on the part of death. There, I am the border of my condition as a living being. My body extricates itself, as being alive, from that border. Such wastes drop so that I might live, until, from loss to loss, nothing remains in me and my entire body falls beyond the limit—*cadere*, cadaver.[5]

Excrement, as abject, thus represents a threat to the happy denial of one's true, mortal fragility and a challenge to the "integrity of one's 'own, clean self,'" as Kristeva puts it.[6] The perceived ugliness and uncleanliness of fecal matter, then, is symptomatic of an unwelcome reality.

There exists within abjection, however, something akin to Freud's death drive: a paradoxical fascination with and attraction toward that which one simultaneously finds so threatening to one's existence—"the first instinct [being] to return to the inanimate state."[7] The abject, as Kristeva describes, is like "an inescapable boomerang [or] a vortex of summons and repulsion"[8] that confounds the individual even within his/her horror. Such a contradiction seems to be what makes the obsession with coprophagia experienced by characters in all three of the *Human Centipede* films possible—be it Dr. Josef Heiter's (Dieter Laser) obsession with surgically joining living creatures (first his three Rottweilers, then three human tourists) to share one continuous digestive system in the first film; Martin Lomax's (Laurence R. Harvey) obsessive, emulating fandom of the first film in the second film; or Laser and Harvey's similarities to their respective roles in the previous films, both now in different roles, in the third film.

The very idea of coprophagia is, of course, revolting enough on the level of aesthetics alone, but typically successful horror tropes tend to require a metaphorical dimension. The potential for such a dimension reveals itself when one realizes how coprophagia is literally the *consumption* of *waste*. It then becomes a useful metaphor for consumerism, both in its mandated and "voluntary" forms, thus inviting something of a Marxist interpretation, given the obvious class and economic dimensions of consumerism. Consistent with Kristeva's theory of the abject, a commodity, or a product for consumption, can become "waste" once its production becomes alienated from individual labor and usefulness and devoid of value, content, practical utility, and variation. If, according to Kristeva, the object of abjection "lies there, quite close [yet] cannot be assimilated,"[9] coprophagia monstrously represents the forced assimilation of the unassimilatable—that is, consumption *in spite of* abjection. Applied to consumerism, coprophagia can metaphorically apply to a perversion of the economic model of production–distribution–exchange–consumption that Marx describes in *Grundrise*:

> Production brings forth the objects corresponding to requirements; distribution shares them out according to social laws; exchange further distributes what has been shared out, according to individual need; lastly, in consumption the product leaves this social movement, becomes a direct object and servant of individual need which it satisfies in use [. . .] [T]he concluding act of consumption [. . .] really lies outside the economy, except in so far as it reacts upon the starting point and introduces the whole process afresh.[10]

Such a model assumes a considerable level of independence and vigilance on the part of the consumer. It also assumes that the product to be consumed, the commodity, has a "use-value," or "something useful" about it.[11] But what if the commodity has, in fact, no usefulness, and the consumer is not so autonomous in his/her consumption of that commodity as one might have thought? Hence the twofold indictment provided by coprophagia as socioeconomic metaphor: to expose certain commodities as having no real use-value (useless, worthless, "shit") and to reveal the true, entrapped nature of consumption as not existing outside of the economy at all (enclosed within an unnaturally continuous, prolonged digestive system). Therein lies also the singularity of the films' "human centipede" as a metaphor for consumption.

The *Human Centipede* films are not the first to utilize coprophagia to seemingly provide commentary on class, consumer culture, and cultural hegemony. John Waters and Pier Paolo Pasolini, for instance, were doing it some four decades earlier with *Pink Flamingos* (1972) and *Saló, or the 120 Days of Sodom* (1975), respectively. *Saló*'s portrayal of four wealthy and corrupt fascist libertines in 1944 Italy sadistically humiliating and torturing young victims over the course of four months includes graphic depictions of coprophagia. Not only does the Duke force a young girl he has just raped to eat his feces after defecating in front of her, but the rest of the victims are later served an entire meal of feces within the perverse decorum of upper-class table etiquette. But in spite of such deliberately upsetting aesthetics, and given the gulf of class difference between the upper-class fascists and their much poorer victims, it is not difficult to agree with John Waters's summation of the film as being about "the pornography of power."[12] The infamous conclusion to Waters's own film, *Pink Flamingos*, involves drag queen actor Divine putting fresh dog feces into his mouth and chewing it, which, beyond the pure shock value, provides a tangible confirmation of the "filth politics" described by Divine earlier in the film: "Kill everyone now. Condone first-degree murder. Advocate cannibalism. *Eat shit*. Filth are my politics. Filth is my life." Where the focus of Saló is on class, *Pink Flamingos'* target is consumer culture and mass media's part in it. After his "filth politics" declaration, Divine does, after all, pose voluptuously for the news camera before executing two rivals on live television, with Divine and the news media alike perpetuating the apparent sickness within modern consumerism.

Throughout all three films, the *Human Centipede* series provides commentary on both class *and* consumer culture. Beginning with the first film, which focuses on class difference, a metanarrative on the film series itself as a product for consumption begins to open up through the progression from one film to the next. With this metanarrative expansion also comes increasing levels of tongue-in-cheek self-deprecation and self-incrimination, with the films seeming to acknowledge their own production as wasteful, consumerist "shit." Over the course of all three films, the trope of coprophagia is thus fully developed as a metaphor for consuming cultural waste—not only in the form of consumer products, but in the excesses of the upper classes as well. Dr. Heiter of the first film occupies a higher social position than his victims, the tourists as well as a kidnapped truck driver who is killed for not being a tissue match. In the second film, mentally challenged tollbooth operator Martin, though obviously occupying a lower class, is obsessively influenced by the first film as a consumer product. And just as the second film opens with a viewing of the first film, the third film opens with a viewing of the second, but with the addition of more extensive self-referencing and even an appearance by director Tom Six himself (as himself) later in the film, bringing attention to the series itself as a product for consumption full circle.

The Human Centipede (First Sequence): class and the fetishism of commodities

Near the conclusion of the first film, *The Human Centipede (First Sequence)*, Katsuro, the Japanese tourist (Akihiro Kitamura) who Dr. Heiter captures as a replacement for the killed truck driver within the "centipede," says to Dr. Heiter, "God. Are you God? I'm a puny little insect [. . .] What an insane world we live in." He says this before slitting his own throat with a shard of glass rather than following through on the expected violent showdown with the wounded and scalpel-wielding Heiter, confessing something of a quasi-religious and fatalistic guilt for his having treated his own family so badly. However, further significance can be found in the seeming acknowledgment of class and cultural superiority that "God" (Heiter, versus the "insect" that is himself) connotes, as well as the acknowledgment of class division implicit within that so-called insane world.

The discovery of Dr. Heiter's house at the beginning of the film by American tourists Lindsay (Ashley C. Williams) and Jenny (Ashlynn Yennie) presents the issue of class division immediately and palpably. Stranded and lost due to a flat tire in a foreign country whose primary language is not English, they are unsettlingly positioned as dependent and second-class. In telling Dr. Heiter that he has a "lovely home," Jenny is not only trying to introduce polite conversation into awkward and uncomfortable silence, but calling attention to his superior class position. He outranks them, so to speak, in age, experience, education, wealth, and familiarity with the dominant culture and language (Figure 11.1). Also, his reputation as a world-renowned expert at separating Siamese twins apparently precedes him, as evidenced by the two detectives, Kranz (Andreas Leupold) and Voller (Peter Blankenstein), who acknowledge him as a "first-rate surgeon" and are apologetic for disturbing and "offend[ing]" him even while questioning him about the tourists' disappearances.

Dr. Heiter is quite aware of his superior position and does not hesitate in using it to his own ends. After Kranz becomes increasingly suspicious of Heiter and strikes the sedative-laced glass of water from his hand, Heiter threatens him with firing and a lawsuit in order to buy himself more time. Heiter's chief end, of course, is the construction of his "human centipede," apparently born of a backlash wish to create new creatures by sewing them together rather than separating them, as he had done with so many Siamese twins. As a reflection of Heiter's class superiority, the design of the "centipede" serves as a grotesquely literalized and scatological emblem of the trickle-down design of class-divided consumption, in which the lower classes are left with the waste of what was consumed by the upper classes. The labor that, according to

FIGURE 11.1 *In the first film, Dr. Josef Heiter (Dieter Laser) shows his three victims his design for the "human centipede," a grotesque waste-product of his own upper-class privilege which literalizes both the trickle-down economics of class inequality and the hegemonic classification of the lower-class victims as social waste.*

Marx, forms the "substance of value" is presented as truly alienated from its "individual units" and rendered as "one homogeneous mass of human labour-power."[13] That mass of human labor-power is presented, perhaps mockingly, through the design of the "centipede" as one continuous digestive system. The labor-power is digestion, with each step down on the class-division ladder consuming the waste of the level above it, the "food" becoming less pure, nutritious, and valuable as it passes from one segment to the next.

Furthermore, the realized "centipede" becomes for Heiter an example of what Marx calls the "fetishism of commodities," in which the "values" of the products for consumption are acquired, independent of any actual and practical utility, through merely "being exchanged."[14] For Heiter, the "centipede" is thus the ultimate luxury item, an item of perverse leisure pursued and realized through his own upper-class achievements, misanthropy ("I hate human beings"), and ennui. It is also an emblem of the power of his upper-class position and the abuses that it affords him, perhaps best evidenced by his attempts to train the "centipede" as a pet, insulting Katsuro with class-based racism (calling him a "kamikaze shithole") and Lindsay with class-based misogyny (telling her, "Swallow it, bitch!") while doing so. As a man of wealth and extravagance, he is beyond seeking practical utility, instead seeking something more "mystical" and "transcendent" in consumer products,[15] even if he has to create those products himself, at the domineering and dehumanizing expense of those beneath him on the social ladder.

Also, as the production of the commodities as waste is enclosed within the continuous digestive system and continuous, sewn-together body of the "centipede," Dr. Heiter's "lovely home" encloses and entraps those beneath him in class position, making them vulnerable to his mad whims as well as signifying them as inferior and disposable socioeconomic "shit." The site where Lindsay's attempt to escape before being sewn into the "centipede" begins to be thwarted is, after all, Heiter's indoor swimming pool, where Heiter corners her and designates her position as the middle segment of the "centipede," and an obvious testament to upper-class privilege and extravagance. Later, a second escape attempt (by which time she has already been sewn in) is thwarted due to Lindsay's apparent underestimation of Heiter's financial resources; the large window that he had shattered while pursuing her during the first escape attempt has already been replaced, obviously much sooner than she had expected.

Even more disturbing is the hint of inescapability, even in death, given by the film's conclusion. After Kranz shoots Heiter in the forehead, just before dying from being shot by Heiter and falling into the indoor swimming pool, the resulting scene of dead bodies presents an enduring tableau representing power and acquisition based on class division. Kranz's and Voller's bodies are floating face-down in the pool, positioned in an act of groveling supplication facing the body of Heiter, who, positioned above them in a seated position against a wall on the floor outside of the pool, seems to look above them, with the blood splatter on the wall behind him from Kranz's kill-shot slanting upward and forming the hints of a crown. Also, the fate of Lindsay is left unresolved at the end of the film. After Katsuro has cut his own throat and Jenny has died from blood poisoning, Lindsay is left sobbing and trapped between them in the "centipede." The camera drifts to the house's roof as the credits roll, with no hint, even after Heiter's death, of a third escape attempt. The apparent and horrifyingly pessimistic message here is how, even in death, the likes of Heiter have not necessarily lost—that the grotesque assumptions and abuses within class inequality are destined for perpetuity.

The Human Centipede 2 (Full Sequence): consumerism as class emulation

In an interview which accompanies the DVD of the second film, *The Human Centipede 2 (Full Sequence)*, Tom Six says that a big part of his inspiration for the sequel was the number of people who had expressed concerns over the possibility of mentally disturbed fans trying to copycat the deeds of Dr. Heiter.[16] The second film's protagonist (or "hero," as Six describes him), Martin, is just that—a mentally challenged tollbooth operator who watches the first film obsessively on his laptop at work. He even keeps a scrapbook with images from the film and publicity shots of the cast under his mattress, like porn. Martin also has a considerable axe to grind: he is short, overweight, and asthmatic—and often ridiculed for being so (referred to as "dwarf," "midget," and "retard"); he was sexually abused by his father as a child; the overbearing mother (Vivien Bridson) with whom he lives hates him for having that father, whom she obviously loved in spite of the molestation, imprisoned (even trying to stab Martin in his sleep and often voicing her wish for both herself and Martin to be killed); his psychiatrist, Dr. Sebring (Bill Hutchens), also touches him inappropriately and secretly wishes to sexually abuse him; and a particularly loud and violent neighbor (Lee Nicholas Harris) often beats and belittles him in retaliation for Martin's mother's antagonistic prodding to keep the noisy music down. One is certainly set up to sympathize with Martin (even as he begins to murder those who have wronged him, including his mother) as a bullied underdog and a working-class rebel. However, that is not what Martin wants.

One version of the advertising poster for *The Human Centipede 2 (Full Sequence)* shows an off-center close-up of Martin's face with Dr. Heiter reflected in the lens of his glasses. However, the sunglasses of Dr. Heiter are reflecting the first film's "human centipede." There is, in these reflections, a falling-short of identification. Just as Martin's obsessed gaze is falling not on an actual and present person but a fictional character in a film, he is also, symbolically, looking at a man who does not see him. In terms of class status, one can reasonably assume that Heiter would be disgusted by Martin and might even want to use him for his own "centipede!" But this does not matter to Martin. Through the persona of Heiter, he too is obsessed with the "centipede"; and, perhaps out of desperate wish to transcend his own diminutive stature and lower-class squalor, what he ultimately seeks is to *emulate* Heiter (even donning a lab coat) and thus forego any possibility of working-class rebellion by instead turning to *class emulation*.

The tragedy of Martin coincides with the second film's stark, black-and-white grittiness. It is considerably more graphic and dingier-feeling than the first film, perhaps as a reflection of the impossibility of Martin's "becoming" Heiter due to his vastly inferior levels of education, experience, and resources (Figure 11.2). His "centipede" is even more horrifying than Heiter's not only for the greater number of victims involved (twelve), but for his lack of medical

FIGURE 11.2 *The second film's grittier, black-and-white aesthetic, as well as its more crude and graphic depictions of coprophagia, reflects Martin Lomax's (Laurence R. Harvey) "shittier" lower-class status in spite of his emulation of the upper-class Dr. Heiter.*

knowledge, with Martin having to resort to a staple gun and duct tape rather than Heiter's much cleaner and far more adroit surgical skills. And because of the crude mouth-to-anus stapling, fecal matter is actually *seen* in the second film, pouring out as diarrhea between each stapled segment. The implication is that this second film is "shittier" for its lower-class perpetrator. Such "shittiness," however, also comments further on consumption through the self-reflexive introduction of the metanarrative concerning the film itself as a consumer product.

Not only does the first film itself act as the subject of its sequel through its mere viewed presence, but Ashlynn Yennie, who played Jenny in the first film, appears in the second film as herself, lured by Martin into becoming the first segment of his "centipede" under the bogus pretense of a film audition with Quentin Tarantino. Also, characters other than Martin demonstrate an awareness of the film's cultural impact. Before Martin's construction of the "centipede," one victim, for instance, pleads with him, "You can't do this! It's a film! *The Human Centipede* is a film!" The example of Martin is thus an extreme consequence of the cultural coercion described by Antonio Gramsci through his ideas on hegemony as manufactured consent. Martin's obsession and emulation demonstrates his role, as member of the proverbial "unwashed masses," of "spontaneous consent" to the "general direction imposed on social life by the dominant fundamental group"—such consent being typically inspired by the apparent "prestige [. . .] which the dominant group enjoys because of its position," and whose "deputies" are the "intellectuals."[17] Martin, through his emulation of him, obviously sees in Dr. Heiter that "prestige" (superiority in education, profession, and class) which inspires such consent—a consent manufactured by the "intellectuals," the artists responsible for the film's creation (writer and director Tom Six, as well as the film's actors).

Martin is clearly also succumbing to the "communications" and "cultural" (in both of which cinema is no doubt included) ideologies that Louis Althusser includes in his list of "ideological state apparatuses,"[18] or those repressive social systems that enforce cultural coercion through ideology rather than the more direct violence of "the State apparatus."[19] The majority of his victims are, like him, working-class. He is therefore, within his delusional emulation of the upper class, an unwitting extension of the repressive apparatuses that work "in the interests of the ruling classes [. . .] against the proletariat."[20] Even in his upping the ante of Heiter's depravity and violence—tearing out Ashlynn's tongue with pliers to stop her from screaming, injecting each victim with a laxative, and wrapping his genitals in barbed wire before raping the woman at the end of the "centipede"—Martin is an instrument of the hegemony's proxy-violence upon the lower-class majority.

As Althusser points out, although the "Repressive State Apparatus" works chiefly by violence and idealogical state apparatuses function mainly by ideology, "violence and ideology actually exist in both," with ideological state apparatuses (here, again, in the form of the communications and cultural ideologies) working "predominantly by ideology and secondarily by repression."[21] Martin's proxy-violence is, in fact, proof that there is "no such thing as a purely ideological apparatus"[22]—the pop-culture influence of the first *Human Centipede* driving him toward a delusion of upper-class identification that ultimately diverts from the possibility of a rebellion against that dominant, upper class. Continuing the pessimistic sentiment left by the first film's conclusion, the conclusion of the second film returns Martin to the scene of the film's opening: in his tollbooth, watching the first film on his laptop again. However, just as the audience might be led to think that everything preceding the conclusion was a sick dream or fantasy, the crying of the toddler he had left in the car after kidnapping the parents is heard again, strongly hinting that all events did in fact occur. The circular shape that such repetition lends to the film suggests, again, the triumphant perpetuity of the dominant position's prerogative.

The Human Centipede 3 (Final Sequence): full circle

The last film, *The Human Centipede 3 (Final Sequence)*, adds yet another layer of metanarrative—maintaining the series' continuity by beginning, as the second film did, with the main character's viewing of the previous film's conclusion. Even more so than the second film, the third film wears its metafictional self-reflexiveness on its sleeve. Heiter and Martin are brought together, in a sense, through the costarring of Dieter Laser and Laurence R. Harvey as new characters—and yet not entirely new, for the many tongue-in-cheek references to their previous character manifestations. Laser, now as mad prison warden Bill Boss, drunkenly yells "I hate human beings!" into a trashcan, echoing Heiter's misanthropy; as rioting prisoners are about to break into the office he shares with Boss, Laurence, now as accountant Dwight Butler, asthmatically wheezes and coughs like Martin. Bill, in preparing inmates for the "prison centipede" operation, shoots them with the same kind of tranquilizer gun used by Heiter; Bill, also like Heiter, kills a prisoner for not being a tissue match. In a moment of cross-film referencing, Bill tells a pleading prisoner that his whining only "makes my dick even harder," echoing Martin's father's molestation banter ("Stop them tears. You're just making daddy's willy harder"). Akihiro Kitamura, the Japanese actor from the first film, plays a prison inmate in the third, and the appearance of Eric Roberts (*The Pope of Greenwich Village*, *The Expendables*) as Governor Hughes and Tommy "Tiny" Lister (*Friday*, *The Dark Knight*) as an inmate lend a knowing air of campily employed B-list star power.

The chief metafictional flourish, however, is provided by the appearance of director Tom Six himself (*as* himself) acting as something of a consultant for the construction of the "prison centipede." This appearance, though clearly meant as a light-hearted gimmick, also demonstrates an awareness on the part of Six of his place in the culture industry. The *Human Centipede* films as a franchise are more widely known among the characters in the third film than in the second film: Dwight congratulates Six on the films' becoming "a cultural meme" and brings up the aforementioned *South Park* parody; Bill's secretary/sex-slave Daisy (Bree Olson) is a fan of the films, even asking Six for an autograph; and the prison's doctor, Dr. Jones (Clayton Rohner), enthusiastically recognizes the DVDs of the first two films that Dwight is carrying. Six also demonstrates a good-natured awareness of his own films' status as cultural "shit," hinting at least an initial comfort with Theodor W. Adorno and Max Horkheimer's theory that, as a part of the culture industry, "[f]ilms [. . .] no longer need to present themselves as art," but rather a "business [. . .] used as an ideology to legitimize the trash [it] intentionally produce[s]."²³ Such an awareness of his own "shitty" reputation is evidenced by the sentiment he has communicated by Laser through the character Bill, who is initially resistant to Dwight's calling upon Six as a consultant: "What? That B-movie shit? Impossible! The man [Six] is still in his potty stage, a poop-infatuated toddler! You can call him now and tell him I don't speak with a stupid filmmaker about his poop fetish!"

Six's willingness to lend his services to the prison calls to mind Adorno and Horkheimer's ideas concerning *manufactured* art as a fundamental component of the status quo's culture industry—that industry's primary function being the "control of consumers [. . .] mediated by entertainment,"²⁴ thus creating a "cycle of manipulation and retroactive need"²⁵ in the supposedly independent and free-thinking consumer populace. The goal in creating the "prison centipede" that is to include all non-death row and non-life sentence inmates, in fact, seems continuous with how, according to Adorno and Horkheimer, the goal of films is to create "the illusion the world outside is a seamless extension of the one which has been revealed in the cinema."²⁶ Six portrays himself as initially excited at the prospect of his films having such a direct and incorporating influence on the "real world" and society-at-large. However, things are quickly taken too far even for him.

Six begins to appear genuinely appalled by the effects of his influence as part of the culture industry when, while touring the cells with Bill and Dwight, he encounters an inmate who is eating his own fresh feces and actually wants to be a part of the "centipede." Bill, not wanting anyone who would actually enjoy the experience to be a part of it, immediately shoots the inmate dead. Six appears shaken not only by the sudden murder, but by just what the influence of his films drives people to willingly consume—as a literalized metaphor for his cultural waste, actual fecal matter. He is then driven to projectile vomit upon seeing Bill's "human centipede improvement," the addition to which of "copyright 'The Boss' " by Bill proves his emulation of Six's part in the culture industry: death row inmates and those serving life sentences are not only sewn together mouth-to-anus, but have their limbs removed, forming a "human caterpillar."

Six portrays himself as perhaps underestimating the extent of actual violence that a repressive institution is capable of inflicting under his cultural influence. He also apparently underestimates his role as one of the social hegemony's intellectual "deputies"—the cultural arm of the "apparatus of state coercive power" whose functionary complement is the more directly brutal "juridical" arm,²⁷ exemplified by Bill. More unsettling is how Bill and Six are more similar in appearance than a first glance might have revealed; both are bald, favor tan clothing, and are fond of wide-brimmed hats. Bill, then, is the more violent manifestation of Althusser's repressive State apparatus, which includes "The Police" and "The Prisons,"[28] to Six's more ideological and less direct cultural role. The doubling through hairstyle and clothing, however, implicates Six as a part of the more direct violence more closely, in a way that suggests both playful self-deprecation and self-indictment.

Bill's doubling of Six brings the *Human Centipede* trilogy full circle by superimposing the presence of the ideological "deputy" (as representative of the culture industry) over the film's violent and repressive protagonist. Simultaneously, this doubling provides a return from the metanarrative to the less metafictional focus on class and power inequality present in the first film. However, Bill Boss is not at all the upper-class sophisticate that Dr. Heiter is. He is much louder, lascivious, and more crude. He is also far less independent, even lacking Dr. Heiter's presumptions of superior untouchability; one gets the sense that, as evidenced by his fearful groveling before Governor Hughes, Bill is just as under the thumb of his superiors as his subordinates are to him. His belittling of Dwight and sexual exploitation of Daisy (whose sexual enslavement to Bill is an indentured service for his getting her "asshole father" out of prison) is obviously in part fueled by his own frustrations for not being as much of the "Boss" as his surname implies.

Such an *inferior* position of superiority is perhaps what makes Bill an exaggeration of Dr. Heiter. The misogyny and racism already demonstrated by Heiter is shown more frequently and intensely by Bill. His sexual assaults on Daisy (even while she's comatose) and repeated torturing of nonwhite inmates while also taunting them with racial epithets (calling a black inmate "ape-nigger" and a Native American inmate "Tonto," for example) reveal him to be, because of his obvious wish for greater class superiority, just as much emulating (though less consciously so) of Dr. Heiter as Martin from the second film. The eventual, accidental incorporation of Daisy into the "prison centipede" reinforces the full-circle pattern of the trilogy in its similarity to Lindsay's middle position within the "centipede" of the first film. She too, even before this literal positioning, was being forced to consume the waste of someone above her—be it Bill's loveless semen ("I need my ball sack emptied before lunch") or her accidental ingestion of one of his perverse luxury-delicacies (also misogynistic), dried African clitorises. Through this ultimately successful emulation, thanks to Governor Hughes's smiling conclusion that the "centipede" is "exactly what American needs," as well as Bill's convenient murder of his subordinate Dwight, who had proposed the "prison centipede" in the first place, Bill demonstrates yet again the note of hegemonic perpetuity on which both of the previous films end.

Through the final film, the issues of class division *and* the metanarrative commentary on the equally "shitty" culture industry, which were much separated between the first two films, are more explicitly joined than in the second film, presenting the entire *Human Centipede* series as a neatly cohesive whole. In forming this cohesive whole, it resists the typical watering-down effect of too many sequels, of becoming, as Stephen King describes, "unenlightened imitation."[29] The unifying trope utilized within the trilogy—that of coprophagia—provides a surprisingly poignant social commentary, even satire, on the cruelty within class inequality and the hegemonic nature of the culture industry that dictates consumerism. However, the films' "shitty" aesthetic not only pokes self-reflexive fun at their own extremity and any critical outrage that that extremity would inspire ("These films risk causing harm! They should be banned!" a Jewish inmate yells in the final film), but perhaps more seriously indicts a "shittier" system at large—a system in which, as a product for consumption, the trilogy no doubt soberly includes itself. Promoting consumer awareness, however, is perhaps the aim through which the films hope to transcend that system.

Notes

1 Julia Kristeva, *Powers of Horror: An Essay on Abjection*, trans. Leon S. Roudiez (New York: Columbia University Press, 1982), 1.
2 Ibid., 2.
3 Sigmund Freud, "The Uncanny," trans. Alix Strachey, in *The Norton Anthology of Theory and Criticism*, ed. Vincent B. Leitch (New York: Norton, 2001), 930.
4 Kristeva, *Powers of Horror*, 5.
5 Ibid., 3.
6 Ibid., 53.
7 Sigmund Freud, *Beyond the Pleasure Principle*, trans. and ed. James Strachey (New York: Norton, 1961), 46.
8 Kristeva, *Powers of Horror*, 1.
9 Ibid.
10 Karl Marx, *Grundrise* [extract], in *The Portable Karl Marx*, trans. and ed. Eugene Kamenka (New York: Penguin, 1983), 381–3.
11 Marx, *Capital* [extract], in *The Portable Karl Marx*, trans. and ed. Eugene Kamenka (New York: Penguin, 1983), 438.
12 John Waters, "Why You Should Watch Filth," *BigThink* (June 14, 2011), http://bigthink.com/videos/why-you-should-watch-filth (accessed October 24, 2015).
13 Marx, *Capital*, 442.
14 Ibid., 447.
15 Ibid., 445.

16 "Interview with Filmmaker Tom Six," *The Human Centipede 2 (Full Sequence)*. Dir. Tom Six. IFC Midnight, 2011. DVD.
17 Antonio Gramsci, "The Formation of the Intellectuals," trans. Quintin Hoare and Geoffrey Nowell Smith, in *The Norton Anthology of Theory and Criticism*, ed. Vincent B. Leitch (New York: Norton, 2001), 1143.
18 Louis Althusser, *Ideology and Ideological State Apparatuses* [extracts], trans. Ben Brewster, in *The Norton Anthology of Theory and Criticism*, ed. Vincent B. Leitch (New York: Norton, 2001), 1489.
19 Ibid., 1487.
20 Ibid.
21 Ibid., 1490.
22 Ibid.
23 Theodor W. Adorno and Max Horkheimer, *Dialectic of Enlightenment: Philosophical Fragments*, trans. Edmund Jephcott, ed. Gunzelin Schmid Noerr (Stanford, CA: Stanford University Press, 2002), 95.
24 Ibid., 109.
25 Ibid., 95.
26 Ibid., 99.
27 Gramsci, "The Formation of the Intellectuals," 1142–3.
28 Althusser, *Ideology and Ideological State Apparatuses*, 1489.
29 Stephen King, "What's Scary: A Forenote to the 2010 Edition," in *Danse Macabre* (New York: Gallery, 2010), xv.

Bibliography

Adorno, Theodor W., and Max Horkheimer. *Dialectic of Enlightenment: Philosophical Fragments*. Translated by Edmund Jephcott. Edited by Gunzelin Schmid Noerr. Stanford, CA: Stanford University Press, 2002.
Althusser, Louis. *Ideology and Ideological State Apparatuses* [extracts]. Translated by Ben Brewster. In *The Norton Anthology of Theory and Criticism*, edited by Vincent B. Leitch, 1483–509. New York: Norton, 2001.
Freud, Sigmund. *Beyond the Pleasure Principle*. Translated and edited by James Strachey. New York: Norton, 1961.
Freud, Sigmund. "The Uncanny." In *The Norton Anthology of Theory and Criticism*, translated by Alix Strachey, edited by Vincent B. Leitch, 929–52. New York: Norton, 2001.
Gramsci, Antonio. "The Formation of the Intellectuals." Translated by Quintin Hoare and Geoffrey Nowell Smith. In *The Norton Anthology of Theory and Criticism*, edited by Vincent B. Leitch, 1138–43. New York: Norton, 2001.
The Human Centipede (First Sequence). Directed by Tom Six. 2009. DVD. New York: IFC Films, 2009.

The Human Centipede 2 (Full Sequence). Directed by Tom Six. 2011. DVD. New York: IFC Films, 2011.

The Human Centipede 3 (Final Sequence). Directed by Tom Six. 2015. DVD. New York: IFC Films, 2015.

King, Stephen. "What's Scary: A Forenote to the 2010 Edition." In *Danse Macabre*, xi–xxxi. New York: Gallery, 2010.

Kristeva, Julia. *Powers of Horror: An Essay on Abjection*. Translated by Leon S. Roudiez. New York: Columbia University Press, 1982.

Marx, Karl. *Capital Vol. 1* [extracts]. In *The Portable Karl Marx*, translated and edited by Eugene Kamenka, 432–503. New York: Penguin, 1983.

Marx, Karl. *Grundrise* [extract]. In *The Portable Karl Marx*, translated and edited by Eugene Kamenka, 375–94. New York: Penguin, 1983.

12

Eat, Kill, ... Love? Courtship, Cannibalism, and Consumption in *Hannibal*

Michael Fuchs and Michael Phillips

In the preface to their seminal volume *Foodways and Eating Habits* (1983), Michael Owen Jones, Bruce B. Giuliano, and Roberta Krell stress that food and the rituals of eating reflect the "perceptions of the natural and social environment" of a given society.[1] In view of food's centrality to human existence, they thus conclude that "there is perhaps no more fundamental act than that of sharing food."[2] From the Ingalls gathering around the wooden farmhouse table for a fresh-cooked meal in *Little House on the Prairie*, to Sheldon and friends gathering around the TV to chow down on take-out food in *The Big Bang Theory*, television has not been shy about deploying this potent semiotic device. Indeed, for many television shows, meal scenes offer powerful insights into the world of the show.

Hannibal (2013–15), a television show that reinvents the cannibalistic serial killer known from cinema and books, takes this idea even further by consistently deploying food as a "remarkably concentrated signifier" to communicate a wide variety of messages.[3] Thus, we will argue that *Hannibal*'s eating scenes and cannibalism tap into the operating principle of serialized television narratives, which requires interpretive interaction and speculation on the audience's end. As Richard Dyer has suggested, "[T]he pleasure principle of seriality" has a long history in storytelling: "Bards, jongleurs, griots and yarn spinners . . . have all long known the value of leaving their listeners wanting more, of playing on that mix of repetition and anticipation, and indeed of the anticipation of repetition," as audiences are left wondering, "What will happen next?"[4] In view of this "pleasure principle of seriality," we will suggest that cannibalism and food imagery undermine comfortable assumptions and associations about the characters' desires and motivations. In so doing, we will first show how the TV show creates a Hannibal Lecter different from the incarnations found in earlier literary and cinematic texts. Similarly, we will explore how food imagery helps establish this new Hannibal by contrasting him with other killers in the show. We will then discuss the ways in which Hannibal's gourmet cannibalism functions as a social commentary. Finally, we will examine how food imagery negotiates relationships between Hannibal and other characters in ways that blur the distinction between violence and compassion to maintain the intrigue of Dr. Hannibal Lecter and keep viewers invested in the character and the show.

Rebooting Dr. Hannibal Lecter

Although the character of Dr. Hannibal Lecter first appeared in a minor role in Thomas Harris's novel *Red Dragon* (1981), it was not until the 1991 film version of the sequel, *The Silence of the Lambs* (1988), that the character stepped into the spotlight. Lecter almost instantly "bec[a]me a popular icon,"[5] and strong audience demand prompted two more novels focused on Lecter, which were immediately adapted to the big screen.

Writing about the original incarnation of Hannibal, Maggie Kilgour noted: "Lecter is . . . a man of both cultivated aesthetic as well as crude savage taste, who exposes the affinity between barbarism and civilization."[6] While these original works alluded to Lecter's high-culture predilections, viewer fascination with the character was firmly rooted in the fear of the primitive monster lurking within. This anxiety is reflected in the iconic image from *The Silence of the Lambs*, which depicts Dr. Lecter "[standing] upright on his hand truck, wrapped in canvas webbing and wearing his hockey mask."[7] The removal of the mask releases the instinct-driven animal and leads to the only food scene in the movie, which is also the only graphic, on-screen murder committed by Lecter: To the soothing strains of the *Goldberg Variations*, two police officers bring a caged Lecter a meal of "lamb chops, extra rare."[8] Eventually, Lecter savagely bites off one guard's face before bludgeoning the other guard to death with a police baton. From the choice of meal to the manner of murder, this scene portrays the primitive lust for human flesh that makes this incarnation of Hannibal Lecter so terrifyingly fascinating.

Subsequent texts in different media constructed a back story about Hannibal's forced cannibalism of his sister to endow the character with "a tragic personal history . . . humanizing [him] . . . and making [him] capable of earning our sympathy."[9] However, since the dark allure of the original character was based on the animal lurking within, the suggestion of an underlying moral code that justified Lecter's savage acts diluted the character by introducing a fundamental dissonance. *Hannibal Rising* (2006), in particular, demonstrated that Harris and the filmmakers involved in the adaptation proved unequal to the challenge of creating a prequel that would remain faithful to and consistent with the original character.

In contrast, when Bryan Fuller embarked on the project of transforming Hannibal's story into a television show, he embraced the current fad of reboots, in which the creator of the new version claims the right to take liberties with the story. Before the series even launched, Fuller announced that the creative team would "subvert [Lecter's] legacy and give the audience twists and turns."[10] And, indeed, Fuller went on to alter, omit, or blend episodes from earlier texts (both literary and cinematic), re-sequence and add events, and make significant changes to the dramatis personae by introducing new characters and radically altering inherited characters (e.g., changing gender, modifying race, and merging characters).

A different breed of killer

One of the characters who underwent an important alteration was Hannibal Lecter himself, as Fuller made good on his announced intention to "reinvent Dr. Lecter."[11] An essential element in this reinvention was the rejection of barely controlled savagery as the defining characteristic of Lecter. In fact, *Hannibal*'s version of Dr. Lecter is in complete control over his own emotions and actions, as Anthony Hopkins's wild-eyed, physically menacing presence is replaced by the ominous calm of Mads Mikkelsen. In this way, the tension shifts from a sense of physical danger to psychological horror, for Hannibal's main source of satisfaction is not the killing and consuming of human beings, but rather his ability to use his superior intellect to manipulate people in twisted ways. As Bedelia, Hannibal's psychiatrist, colleague, and occasional love interest, states in the penultimate episode of the entire show, "Hannibal does have agency in the world."[12] To emphasize this cold psychological dimension of the horror of Hannibal, the show uses images of food and consumption to contrast Hannibal with the other killers in the show, who are most often driven by barely controlled desires.

For example, Randall Tier's telling second name ("animal" in German) bespeaks his desire to become an animal. Tier, a monster-of-the-week in season two, constructs an exoskeleton with hydraulic jaws that affords his weak human body superhuman power to stalk and kill. Randall's transformation into an animal manifests the primitive drives generally assumed to guide killers' actions. In contrast, Hannibal uses his intellectual and psychological acumen to manipulate Tier into attacking FBI advisor Will Graham, thereby transforming Tier into Hannibal's pet. In the end, the food imagery takes an unexpected twist when Will ends up killing Tier and dumping his body on Lecter's dining table as a kind of food offering, evoking the feline practice of leaving dead animals on their masters' doorsteps as a token of affection.

Hannibal's powers of psychological manipulation are also evident in his ability to further Francis Dolarhyde's transformation into the inhuman Red Dragon in the second half of season three. Here again, food imagery dramatizes this descent into bestiality. On a ritualistic level, Dolarhyde consumes the ominous Blake painting bite by bite in an effort to assimilate the work's imagined spiritual potency. In a more explicitly cannibalistic scene, Dolarhyde bites off Dr. Frederick Chilton's lips to punish him for his disparaging remarks in the press and to send a message to Hannibal and Will Graham. Although this event is shown in excessively gory detail, Dolarhyde does not actually eat the lips, but rather mails them as a kind of oblation to the imprisoned Dr. Lecter, who quickly swallows one of them. Significantly, the playful way that Hannibal gulps down the lip like an oyster does not suggest submission to a craving for human meat, but rather a considered act by which he both accepts the offering from his disciple and delivers a powerful psychological shock to Dr. Alana Bloom, Lecter's former lover and current keeper.

Despite sending Chilton's lips to Lecter, Dolarhyde fails to connect with the Doctor; rather, the show places killers like Tier and Dolarhyde in stark contrast to Hannibal, whose apparent self-control is so overdone that it even sparks self-reflexive, tongue-in-cheek comments in the diegetic world. In "Secondo," for example, Hannibal serves one of his victims punch romaine, the "cocktail served to first-class guests on the *Titanic* during their last dinner,"[13] as Hannibal informs his guest and viewers before ramming an ice pick into his victim's head. He then calmly opines, "That may have been impulsive," to which Bedelia retorts, "You've been mulling that impulse ever since you decided to serve punch romaine."[14] Indeed, Bedelia's remark highlights that this particular murder had occupied Lecter's mind for a few days, and the cocktail had been carefully selected for maximum symbolic effect; a far cry from the impulsiveness Lecter ascribes to the act.

Of cannibals, class, and consumption

Hannibal's cold rationality breeds his rejection of the fundamental cultural belief in the superiority of human beings over all other animals, which is at the root of the taboo against cannibalism. As he provocatively points out, "[T]he tendency to see others as less human than ourselves is universal."[15] Yet in order to preserve, and even heighten, the audience's attraction to Hannibal, the show normalizes this subversive attitude through the symbolic vehicle of food. To this end, *Hannibal* situates cannibalism within different value systems found in American society to highlight the culturally constructed nature of this taboo and to question its validity.

In "Sorbet," Hannibal's culinary exploits undermine the concept of human exceptionalism. Early in the episode, Hannibal attends an operatic concert, where a banner in the background reveals the performance to be a "concert for hunger relief."[16] The performance scene transitions to a conversation in which a female caricature of the wealthy cultural elite sycophantically takes Hannibal to task for his recent failure to throw one of his dinner parties. The spectacle of a wealthy socialite at a hunger relief concert reminiscing about elaborate dinner parties invites the audience to question the real function of this social event, as well as the sincerity of the participants' concern for the plight of the world's starving masses.

Ultimately, Hannibal does throw one of his dinner parties. In the lengthy food preparation scenes that precede the party, the highly stylized staging, with classical music accompaniment and close-ups of the artful carving maneuvers involved, highlights the artistry of the process and transforms human flesh into a delectable-looking dish. Food's "primacy in our lives," which "precedes literacy,"[17] thus triggers a visceral response in the viewer, and these Pavlovian hunger pains that TV viewers often experience when watching dining scenes take on a particularly disorienting resonance. Thus, situating the act of cannibalism within the elevated signification system of gourmet food destabilizes the presumed symbolic distinction between human and animal meat.

At a mere thirty-eight seconds, the actual dinner party scene consists of little more than a tilting shot of the elaborate dishes Hannibal has prepared, followed by his toast to his guests: "Before we begin, you must all be warned—nothing here is vegetarian."[18] The guests' laughter at this condescending quip reveals that the true purpose of this lavish dinner is a ritual of conspicuous consumption in which the participants celebrate the assumed cultural superiority that makes them too aloof to bother with the mundane concerns behind the vegetarian lifestyle (e.g., animal rights, bodily health, environmental awareness). In fact, their reaction begs the question of whether the diners would even object if they knew the secret ingredient in the dishes before them, thereby tapping into the modern brewing discontent with the growing economic disparities of the world. Indeed, while Jennifer Brown recently concluded that "[t]he cannibal has become the reviled image of overindulgence, overspending, and overexploitation of resources,"[19] *Hannibal* turns the tables, for the show highlights these traits in the non-cannibals at the party, thus calling into question the presumed bonds of affection that unite humanity.

In addition, the veiled reference to cannibalism in Hannibal's remark about vegetarianism functions as a "joke which the viewer is invited to figure out."[20] This device recurs frequently in *Hannibal* and draws viewers into the world of the show. In this way, the viewers' laughter implicates them in another ritual of consumption that carries value connotations, for it serves as a tangible sign of their consumption of an entertainment product about cannibalism and serial murder. And as Ashley M. Donnelly has pointed out in reference to a similar show, *Dexter* (2006–13), watching the show "puts us in an uncomfortable position, as if any enjoyment that we get from the show at all amounts to complicity on our part. If we watch, doesn't our watching amount to endorsement?"[21] This effect is perhaps even more marked in *Hannibal*, which is riddled with cannibalism-based inside jokes between the serial-killing main character and the audience.

Eat, kill . . . love?

Beyond the elements of social criticism, "Sorbet" offers a useful entry point into the role of food imagery in mediating personal relationships. In this case, Hannibal's aforementioned cannibalism-based humor both draws the viewer into the show and provides an insight into Lecter's mind. Not only is he sharp-witted, but he also takes pleasure in amusing himself at the expense of others, a practice which in this case emphasizes his power over the alleged elite of society. However, this episode also makes it clear that Hannibal has tired of toying with the socialites and now wants to move on to more interesting games involving interpersonal relationships. In "Sorbet," the focus is on the preparation scenes, during which he is first assisted by Alana and eventually visited by Will as he puts the final touches on the meal. In these scenes, which reproduce a social practice whereby the host's closest friends or family members arrive early to help prepare for a social gathering, food functions "as the basis of, as well as the justification for, interacting with others."[22] Thus, the monstrous act of carving and seasoning human flesh is transformed into an intimate ritual by which interpersonal bonds are reinforced and perpetuated, leaving the viewer suspended uncomfortably between feelings of tenderness and disgust.

This underlying tension between horror and romance defines the show's entire narrative arc, as the viewers are never certain if Hannibal truly feels anything for any of the other characters, or if he is just simulating emotions as part of his game of manipulation. Although the relationships in *Hannibal* play out largely in both psychological consultations and meal scenes, in keeping with the theme of the present volume, we will exclude the former and focus on some key scenes that employ food imagery to negotiate the relationships in the serial narrative and preserve the fundamental mystery of Hannibal's mind.

Before covering the central interpersonal story between Hannibal and Will, a brief digression into some of the peripheral characters will help demonstrate how food imagery mediates interpersonal relationships. Although the show's main agents are male, there are a few key female characters who serve as accessories. The first to emerge is Abigail Hobbs, the orphaned daughter of the pilot episode's killer-of-the-week whom Hannibal uses to create a family. The essential event for this storyline takes place in the season one episode "Œuf." After an appetizer of hallucinogenic mushrooms designed to prime Abigail's emotional attachment instinct, Hannibal serves her a dinner of sausage and eggs, a classic comfort food that implies a familial intimacy, particularly when contrasted with Hannibal's typical gourmet fare.[23] During the dinner, Alana shows up at the house and Hannibal takes her into the kitchen, where they have a heated argument that almost parodies the conflicts concerned parents have about their children. After seemingly winning the argument (as evidenced by Hannibal's apologetic manner), Alana enters the dining room to find a table set for three. She then takes her place as the mother in this family photo, prompting the drugged Abigail to utter "I see family."[24]

Hannibal eventually engages in a relationship with Alana that features the hallmarks of a healthy relationship. However, the show uses food imagery to demonstrate that Hannibal does not view her as an equal in their relationship or in the game of psychological chess he is playing with Will and Jack Crawford, the head of the FBI's Behavioral Sciences Unit. First, Alana is the only person in the show who drinks beer, a beverage with clear class connotations. Second, there are no scenes of one-on-one meals with Alana, which stresses her function as a tool for Hannibal to reach out to others. In the long run, Hannibal even slips a sedative in her wine to ensure that she will sleep long enough for him to carry out his criminal activities while still using her as an alibi. Here, the ease with which Hannibal can manipulate Alana using ingested substances symbolizes her lack of power. Alana is ultimately nothing more than a minor prop in Hannibal's staged psychodrama.

In contrast, Hannibal's other female "love interest" in the show, Bedelia Du Maurier, is more deeply ensnared in Hannibal's world by her past killing of a patient in "self-defense," orchestrated by Hannibal. Through this event, Hannibal reveals himself to Bedelia, while simultaneously cementing his control over her, as his role as her alibi in that crime precludes her from revealing his criminal acts. Due to this shared knowledge, Bedelia fulfills the requirement of true friendship that Hannibal explains in a later episode: "The most beautiful quality of a true friendship is to understand [and] be understood with absolute clarity."[25]

Although their relationship is staged mostly in therapy sessions, there are a few key meal scenes, as well. First, in the season one finale, after Hannibal has successfully "ended" his "affair" with Will by framing him for murder, he brings dinner to Bedelia. Here, Hannibal fulfills his need to have another person, his one trusted (?) friend, acknowledge and appreciate his complete control over the events in his life. However, the scene also emphasizes Hannibal's power over Bedelia, who consumes the "controversial dish" served to her,[26] despite her implied awareness of its possible origin. Similarly, the season two finale ends with Hannibal sipping champagne on a plane as Bedelia sits (uncomfortably) in the next seat without a drink, thereby reinforcing both her implied complicity and Hannibal's dominance.

In season three, meal scenes completely replace therapy sessions as a tool for dramatizing the relationship between Bedelia and Hannibal. In a move typical of the series, these scenes all play out as common, everyday events, but with an underlying tension caused by the fundamental uncertainty about the possible affection between the two characters. In fact, the violent acts perpetrated during these dinners have less to do with the victims' becoming-food than they do with the effects they have on the relationship between Hannibal and Bedelia. Thus, Hannibal kills one person in front of Bedelia, manipulates her into "technically" killing another, and makes her an unwilling participant in two human-based meals. While her decision to "try not to eat anything with a central nervous system" represents a challenge,[27] Hannibal's acts have clearly bound Bedelia to him as a partner in crime, making her the character that comes closest to a female companion in the series.

However, across the three seasons, the importance of Hannibal's relationship with Bedelia pales in comparison to the one relationship that drives the serial narrative—the convoluted, enigmatic partnership between Hannibal and Will Graham. Indeed, before filming even began, showrunner Bryan Fuller described his intention to create "a love story, for lack of a better description, between these two characters [Dr. Hannibal Lecter and Will Graham]."[28] Leslie Fiedler has traced this trope of homosociality back to American Romanticism in his analysis of various male "couples" in American literature. He argues that these relationships act out the male desire to escape the confines of heterosexual relationships and civilized society by bonding "with [a] comrade of one's own sex" to form "a union which commits its participants neither to society nor to sin."[29] In the present media landscape, this is often labeled "bromance," "in which males symbolically play out romantic attachments to one another while artfully maintaining assiduous control of social and interactional distance."[30]

While the need to maintain distance typically stems from a taboo against homosexuality, in *Hannibal*, this taboo is almost completely subsumed by a host of other taboos that complicate the romance between Will and Hannibal, including prohibitions against relationships between coworkers, patients and doctors, criminals and enforcers of the law, and, ultimately, cannibals and non-cannibals. Although the show certainly contains homosexual overtones, the dramatic tension in the relationship largely stems from the audience's uncertainty about the sincerity of the characters' affections for each other, a typical feature of any love story. Here, questions of food and consumption once again play a central role in blurring the boundaries between Hannibal's affection and manipulation.

Already in the pilot episode, Hannibal's entrance is loaded with food imagery, as he pleasurably consumes (human?) meat alone in his dining room.[31] The scene highlights Hannibal's solitude, but also contrasts the worlds the two characters inhabit at the outset of the show: Hannibal, clad in fine attire, enjoys gourmet fare in his tastefully decorated, dimly lit dining room, while Will stands under garish fluorescent lights in the pathology lab watching the forensic pathologists dissect a corpse. With this juxtaposition of the two settings, the show already begins to undermine comfortable assumptions about the dichotomy between culture and savagery. Furthermore, already in this first episode, food is used to lead the viewers to a false conclusion, as the implied connection between Hannibal and that particular corpse turns out to be false, for Hannibal did not kill that person. Later in the episode, Hannibal pursues his FBI-appointed task of evaluating Graham's psychological fitness by visiting a grumpy Will at his hotel room. In this "first date," Hannibal uses food to penetrate Will's standoffish defenses, as well as to introduce him (unknowingly) to the world of cannibalism, as the visual evidence strongly implies that Hannibal's "little protein scramble" contains human meat (Figure 12.1).[32]

However, for Hannibal, "unknowingly" is insufficient, and he embarks on an elaborate scheme to convert Will using psychological manipulation. As this "love affair" between the two characters plays out, food becomes a vehicle in

FIGURE 12.1 *Hannibal and Will's first shared meal introduces Will to the taste of human meat. Screen shot taken from the episode "Apéritif" (2013).*

the struggle for power between Hannibal and Will (and Jack Crawford). Thus, Hannibal forces a human ear down Will's throat, Will and Jack bring trout to one of Hannibal's dinners to provoke Hannibal, and Will eventually brings Hannibal meat that he suggests is human flesh as a false friendship offering when he is trying to entrap Lecter. This storyline culminates in the scene in which Hannibal plans to feed Will's brains to Will and, presumably, the immobilized Jack, which would represent the ultimate triumph of Hannibal over Will and Jack. However, Hannibal's victory is interrupted by the entry of the police. Here again, food plays a key role, as the police are guided to the scene of the crime by a food trail left by Bedelia and followed by Alana, Hannibal's two "jilted" lovers.

This brings the action back to the mansion owned by Hannibal's nemesis Mason Verger (whom Lecter had previously forced to feed his own face to Will's dogs). Verger is another character whose status is symbolically represented by his relation to food. Where Hannibal's gustatory flair represents his cultured, Old-World aristocratic roots and predilections, Verger's position as the second generation of a family enterprise based on factory farming and producing food for mass consumption highlights his status as a spoiled, nouveau-riche capitalist heir with false aristocratic pretensions. At Verger's dining table, Verger and his chef/surgeon/henchman Cordell chain Will and Hannibal to the chairs in order to feed them samples of the dishes they intend to make out of Hannibal's flesh, only to be interrupted by Will taking a savage bite from Cordell's cheek. However, Will's first conscious taste of human flesh does not seem to convert him, as later in the episode he effectively breaks up with Hannibal using the line "I don't have your appetite."[33]

Of course, this breakup just temporarily postpones the Hannibal/Will love affair until the penultimate scene of the whole show, which is charged with images of consumption. In this scene, Hannibal confesses his "inconvenient" compassion for Will as he opens a bottle of fine wine,[34] the first testament of emotion from Hannibal that seems sincere. However, Will rejects this advance by saying, "If you're partial to beef products, it is inconvenient to be compassionate toward the cow."[35] This moment of romantic tension is interrupted by the Dragon, who shoots both Hannibal and the bottle. This action sets off the transformation from the civilized, quasi-romantic honeymoon scene into an orgy of artistically styled, yet primitive violence in which Hannibal rips the Dragon's throat with his teeth while Will carves him up almost systematically with a knife. Thus, after three seasons, the veneer of gourmet consumption is finally stripped away to reveal the carnal urge that bonds the two characters. The most violent, gory scene depicted in the entire series ends up serving as a shared ritual by which Will and Hannibal finally consummate their relationship and leads to their romantic embrace and dramatic plunge into the Atlantic Ocean.

Doctor, eat thyself

In a chapter about food in *Hannibal*, we would be remiss not to mention the specific scenario of auto-cannibalism. In the course of this chapter, we have demonstrated that Hannibal's culinary expertise neutralizes the horror of cannibalism by masking the source of the food consumed. The fact that the diners are unaware of their own cannibalistic act casts Hannibal as a trickster, who may laugh at his guests but causes them neither physical nor psychological distress. This pushes the viewer toward a realization of the socially constructed nature of the taboo against cannibalism. However, cannibalism takes on a markedly different symbolic value in scenes in which Hannibal feeds Dr. Abel Gideon (the killer who dared to lay claim to some of Hannibal's murders) his own limbs. Gideon's awareness of what he eats, combined with the fact that he is eating himself, transforms Hannibal from trickster to torturer and reveals his complete lack of human empathy. The lack of the violence or gore that typically signals evil in audiovisual horror texts places the focus squarely on Hannibal's extreme cruelty, thereby stripping away any comforting illusions viewers might harbor about Hannibal's redeeming affections for other characters and making these perhaps the most disturbing scenes in the whole series.

FIGURE 12.2 *Hannibal's closing moments invite audience speculation and anticipation. Screen shot taken from the episode "The Wrath of the Lamb" (2015).*

Yet the show saves one more disturbing moment for its final scene, which shows Bedelia clad in alluring eveningwear seated at a table set for three with her own leg prepared as a succulent dish, seemingly waiting in breathless anticipation of something (Figure 12.2). The scene sparked an orgy of speculation among fans and media commentators. Without delving into the many possible interpretations offered, we would suggest that it is the very act of fan speculation that is significant. Since the scene implies Bedelia is sitting at the table of her own free will, viewers are compelled to contemplate how she could still be attached to Hannibal and long for his return. Of course, it is difficult for viewers to ponder these questions for long without realizing that they themselves are experiencing a disturbingly similar feeling—a sadness that the character to whom they have become attached over three seasons is no more. Thus, the postcredit scene highlights one last time the unsettling allure of a character who gains almost godlike powers by exploiting his intellectual superiority and rejecting the constraints imposed by civilized society.

Notes

1   Michael Owen Jones, Bruce B. Giuliano, and Roberta Krell, "Prologue," in *Foodways and Eating Habits: Directions for Research*, ed. Michael Owen Jones, Bruce B. Giuliano, and Roberta Krell (Los Angeles: California Folklore Society, 1983), xii.

2. Michael Owen Jones, Bruce B. Giuliano, and Roberta Krell, "Resources and Methods," in *Foodways and Eating Habits: Directions for Research*, ed. Michael Owen Jones, Bruce B. Giuliano, and Roberta Krell (Los Angeles: California Folklore Society, 1983), 91.
3. Gaye Poole, *Reel Meals, Set Meals: Food in Film and Theatre* (Sydney: Currency Press, 1999), 3.
4. Richard Dyer, *Only Entertainment*, 2nd edn (London: Routledge, 2002), 70–1.
5. Daniel O'Brien, "Foreword," in *Dissecting Hannibal Lecter: Essays on the Novels of Thomas Harris*, edited by Benjamin Szumskyj (Jefferson, NC: McFarland, 2008), 3. Consider the fact that Hannibal had an appearance in the pop culture barometer *The Simpsons* seven months after *Silence*'s theatrical release ("Stark Raving Dad").
6. Maggie Kilgour, "The Function of Cannibalism at the Present Time," in *Cannibalism and the Colonial World*, ed. Francis Barker, Peter Hulme, and Margaret Iversen (Cambridge: Cambridge University Press, 1998), 248–9.
7. Thomas Harris, *Silence of the Lambs* (New York: St. Martin's, 1988), 186.
8. *The Silence of the Lambs* [film].
9. Philip L. Simpson, *Psycho Paths: Tracking the Serial Killer through Contemporary American Film and Fiction* (Carbondale: Southern Illinois University Press, 2000), 11.
10. James Hibberd, "'Hannibal' on NBC: How Bryan Fuller will reinvent Dr. Lecter—EXCLUSIVE." *Entertainment Weekly* (April 19, 2012). http://www.ew.com/article/2012/04/19/bryan-fuller-hannibal (accessed October 2, 2015).
11. Ibid.
12. "The Number of the Beast is 666," written by Jeff Vlaming, Angela Lamanna, Bryan Fuller, and Steve Lightfood, directed by Guillermo Navarro, *Hannibal: Season 3*.
13. "Secondo," written by Angelina Burnett, Bryan Fuller, and Steve Lightfoot, directed by Vincenzo Natali, *Hannibal: Season 3*.
14. Ibid.
15. "Shiizakana," written by Jeff Vlaming, directed by Michael Rymer, *Hannibal: Season 2*.
16. "Sorbet," written by Jesse Alexander and Bryan Fuller, directed by Michael Rymer *Hannibal: Season 1*.
17. Anne L. Bower, "Watching Food: The Production of Food, Film, and Values," in *Reel Food: Essays on Food and Film*, ed. Anne L. Bower (New York: Routledge, 2004), 10.
18. "Sorbet."
19. Jennifer Brown, *Cannibalism in Literature and Film* (Basingstoke: Palgrave Macmillan, 2013), 214.
20. Jonathan Bignell, *An Introduction to Television Studies*, 2nd edn (London: Routledge, 2008), 105.

21. Ashley M. Donnelly, "The New American Hero: Dexter, Serial Killer for the Masses," *Journal of Popular Culture* 45, no. 1 (2012): 22.
22. Jones, Giuliano, and Krell, "Resources," 91.
23. For a detailed discussion of this episode, which makes extensive use of meal scenes to comment on family issues, see Michael Fuchs, "Cooking with Hannibal: Food, Liminality and Monstrosity in *Hannibal*," *European Journal of American Culture* 34, no. 2 (2015): 102–106.
24. "Œuf," written by Jennifer Schuur, directed by Peter Medak, *Hannibal: Season 1*.
25. "Mizumono," written by Bryan Fuller and Steve Lightfoot, directed by David Slade, *Hannibal: Season 2*.
26. "Savoureux," written by Steve Lightfoot, Bryan Fuller, and Scott Nimerfro, directed by David Slade, *Hannibal: Season 1*.
27. "Antipasto," written by Bryan Fuller and Steve Lightfoot, directed by Vincenzo Natali, *Hannibal: Season 3*.
28. Quoted in Hibberd, " 'Hannibal' on NBC."
29. Leslie A. Fiedler, *Love and Death in the American Novel* (Champaign, IL: Dalkey Archive Press, 1997), 348, 339.
30. Murray Pomerance, "The Bromance Stunt in *House*," in *Reading the Bromance: Homosocial Relationships in Film and Television*, ed. Michael DeAngelis (Detroit: Wayne State University Press, 2014), 255.
31. This scene is discussed in more detail in Fuchs, "Cooking with Hannibal," 98–9.
32. "Apéritif," written by Bryan Fuller, directed by David Slade, *Hannibal: Season 1*.
33. "Digestivo," written by Steve Lightfoot and Bryan Fuller, directed by Adam Kane, *Hannibal: Season 3*.
34. "The Wrath of the Lamb," written by Bryan Fuller, Steve Lightfoot, and Nick Antosca, directed by Michael Rymer, *Hannibal: Season 3*.
35. Ibid.

Bibliography

Bignell, Jonathan. *An Introduction to Television Studies*. 2nd edn. London: Routledge, 2008.

Bower, Anne L. "Watching Food: The Production of Food, Film, and Values." In *Reel Food: Essays on Food and Film*, edited by Anne L. Bower, 1–13. New York: Routledge, 2004.

Brown, Jennifer. *Cannibalism in Literature and Film*. Basingstoke: Palgrave Macmillan, 2013.

Donnelly, Ashley M. "The New American Hero: Dexter, Serial Killer for the Masses." *Journal of Popular Culture* 45, no. 1 (2012): 15–26.

Dyer, Richard. *Only Entertainment*. 2nd edn. London: Routledge, 2002.
Fiedler, Leslie A. *Love and Death in the American Novel*. Champaign, IL: Dalkey Archive Press, 1997.
Fuchs, Michael. "Cooking with Hannibal: Food, Liminality and Monstrosity in Hannibal." *European Journal of American Culture* 34, no. 2 (2015): 97–112.
Hannibal: Season 1. Blu-Ray. Santa Monica, CA: Lions Gate, 2013.
Hannibal: Season 2. Blu-Ray. Santa Monica, CA: Lions Gate, 2014.
Hannibal: Season 3. Blu-Ray. Santa Monica, CA: Lions Gate, 2015.
Harris, Thomas. *The Silence of the Lambs*. New York: St. Martin's Press, 1988.
Hibberd, James. " 'Hannibal' on NBC: How Bryan Fuller will reinvent Dr. Lecter— EXCLUSIVE." *Entertainment Weekly*, April 19, 2012. http://www.ew.com/article/2012/04/19/bryan-fuller-hannibal (accessed October 2, 2015).
Jones, Michael Owen, Bruce B. Giuliano, and Roberta Krell. "Prologue." In *Foodways and Eating Habits: Directions for Research*, edited by Michael Owen Jones, Bruce B. Giuliano, and Roberta Krell, vii–xii. Los Angeles: California Folklore Society, 1983.
Jones, Michael Owen, Bruce B. Giuliano, and Roberta Krell. "Resources and Methods." In *Foodways and Eating Habits: Directions for Research*, edited by Michael Owen Jones, Bruce B. Giuliano, and Roberta Krell, 91–3. Los Angeles: California Folklore Society, 1983.
Kilgour, Maggie. "The Function of Cannibalism at the Present Time." In *Cannibalism and the Colonial World*, edited by Francis Barker, Peter Hulme, and Margaret Iversen, 238–59. Cambridge: Cambridge University Press, 1998.
O'Brien, Daniel. "Foreword." In *Dissecting Hannibal Lecter: Essays on the Novels of Thomas Harris*, edited by Benjamin Szumskyj, 1–5. Jefferson, NC: McFarland, 2008.
Pomerance, Murray. "The Bromance Stunt in *House*." In *Reading the Bromance: Homosocial Relationships in Film and Television*, edited by Michael DeAngelis, 255–73. Detroit: Wayne State University Press, 2014.
Poole, Gaye. *Reel Meals, Set Meals: Food in Film and Theatre*. Sydney: Currency Press, 1999.
The Silence of the Lambs. Directed by Jonathan Demme. 1991. Los Angeles: Twentieth Century Fox, 2009. Blu-Ray.
Simpson, Philip L. *Psycho Paths: Tracking the Serial Killer through Contemporary American Film and Fiction*. Carbondale: Southern Illinois University Press, 2000.

13

Catering to the Cult of Ishtar: *Blood Feast*

Rob Weiner and A. Bowdoin Van Riper

Herschell Gordon Lewis's low-budget film *Blood Feast* (1963) weaves together gore, sexuality, and the lore of the "Egyptian" goddess Ishtar to create a cult commentary on madness, obsession, and extremes. Considered by many to be the first "splatter film," *Blood Feast* transposes ancient notions of ritual sacrifice onto the contemporary American suburbs, creating an ideal context for examining the film's links between culinary consumption, religious devotion, and spectacular gore. The screen is filled with blood, breasts, and body parts as a psychopathic caterer, Fuad Ramses, murders young virgins for their vital organs in order to create the titular "blood feast" in honor of Ishtar, the ancient goddess of fertility, war, and carnal love, teasing audiences with the possibility of greater horrors to come.

When wealthy Miami socialite Dorothy Fremont hires Ramses to cater a party for her daughter Suzette, he offers her a feast like none other—one that has not been prepared in 5,000 years—while secretly planning to use the occasion for his own ends. Prowling the city like a grotesque shopper, he gathers his ingredients one murder at a time: brains, limbs, skin, and even more horrifying delicacies—all brutally harvested from beautiful young women—are featured in the culinary array he intends to offer his divine mistress in order to bring about her resurrection. The virginal Suzette will, he intends, be both the guest of honor at the party and the crowning dish in his offering.

Ishtar was, in historical reality, one of the most significant goddesses in Babylonian and Assyrian mythology—the source of all generative powers in nature and mankind—and her cult is often associated with temple prostitution or "sacred sex." It is significant, then, that as he procures the ingredients for his feast in her honor, Ramses commits increasingly brutal acts of misogyny. Throughout the film, the mad caterer is depicted objectifying attractive, virginal women, and then reducing them—literally and figuratively—to "meat": horrifically transforming them into missing ingredients for his bloody banquet.

Blood Feast appeared at, and took full advantage of, a pivotal moment in the history of American cinema and American culture. Shot in just over a week, on an "anorexic" budget,[1] the film was exploitation at its best. Its threadbare narrative has been decried by critics as "senseless," "incredibly crude and unprofessional from start to finish," and "an insult even to the most puerile and salacious of audiences," but its construction of "virtue" as corporeal and consumable remains of particular interest.[2] This chapter, then, will examine *Blood Feast*—with its unique admixture of food, sex, and gore—in light of the film's status as an exploitation classic.

Preparations for a feast

Blood Feast revolves around the Egyptian-born Ramses (Mal Arnold), a grey-haired man with a distinctive, wild-eyed expression to which the film devotes frequent close-ups. Obsessed with the ancient goddess Ishtar, he turns to serial murder in order to gather the ingredients for a "blood feast": a sacrificial meal consisting of a kettle filled with the blood and dismembered body parts of young women. By performing the ancient ritual, Ramses believes, he can bring about Ishtar's resurrection. He believes that winning her gratitude for his faithful service will confirm his status as her "high priest," making him a minor god in his own right.

Ramses claims his first victim in the pre-title sequence, murdering a young woman as she takes a bath in her suburban Miami home, severing her left leg with a machete and carrying it away. Reviewing the case next day with his chief, police detective Pete Thornton (William Kerwin) notes its similarity to four other murder-dismemberment cases from the past two weeks, comparing their brutality to Jack the Ripper's rampage through 1888 London. Thornton suspects a connection between the cases but is unable to establish one, and the chief advises him to continue investigating

Meanwhile, in Ramses' catering shop, Dorothy Fremont (Lyn Bolton) asks him to stage a unique, surprise dinner party for her daughter Suzette

(Connie Mason). Ramses tells her that he has just the thing in mind: a "feast such as one might have attended in Ancient Egypt . . . five thousand years ago." He elaborates and promises her that the date of the event, two weeks hence, will give him time to gather the remaining ingredients he needs. Once Mrs. Fremont leaves, he slips behind a curtain and into the kitchen at the back of his shop, where he has created a shrine to Ishtar. Lighting a torch and explaining to a golden statue of the goddess that he, her "slave," will provide her with a blood feast, he then continues to gather his "ingredients," attacking two young lovers on a deserted beach at night, and stalking another couple outside the cheap motel where they have rented a room for the afternoon. After ensuring that the male half of each couple will not interfere—knocking the man on the beach unconscious, and waiting for the man at the motel to leave temporarily—he overpowers the women and continues his bloody quest.

Elsewhere in the city, Detective Thornton attends a lecture by an Egyptologist, Dr. Flanders, bringing his girlfriend—none other than Suzette Fremont—as a guest. Ishtar (Flanders conveniently explains) was the Egyptian goddess of love and beauty, but also the "mother of veiled darkness," the agent of "an evil love that thrived on violence." The seven-day festival of Ishtar, which occurred each year as spring came to the city of Antioch, was characterized by six days in which the priestesses of Ishtar and the men of the city would indulge in "every kind of lustful vice." On the seventh day, Ishtar's followers would gather for a great feast at her temple "high on the hill" over the city. The young priestesses would be slaughtered, their blood caught in bowls, and their organs and limbs removed and served to the people as the main course of the feast.

Driving home from the lecture, Thornton receives a radio call from the chief, informing him of another attack. The victim, grievously injured and heavily bandaged, tells him—before she dies of her injuries—that her attacker was an old man with gray hair, a limp, and wild eyes, and that he kept repeating something that sounded like "etar."

Ramses, meanwhile, is stalking his final victim: Suzette's friend Trudy Sanders (Christy Foushee), who has written to him expressing an interest in his book *Ancient Weird Religious Rites*. Tracking her down at the Fremont estate, where she is spending time by the pool with Suzette and another friend before the party, he waits until she is walking home alone and knocks her unconscious. Carrying her back to his shop, he chains her to the wall, whips her to death, and collects her blood. Rameses begins work on the feast in earnest in his back-room kitchen, which is now laden with bones, raw meat, blood, and offal representing parts harvested from other victims. He roasts the leg of his first victim, and adds the uncooked bits of others, along with Trudy's blood, to an iron cauldron that he carefully stirs, rendering the harvested body parts of his victims into a ritual meal for Ishtar that, when consumed by Mrs. Fremont and her guests, will bring the goddess to life (Figure 13.1).

Thornton, acting on an as-yet-unexplained hunch that Ramses may be the killer, rushes to the catering shop but arrives too late, finding Trudy Sanders's bloodied corpse on a table in the back room. At the Fremont home, the party is already under way, and Ramses asks a bemused Suzette to come to the kitchen and "humor an old man" by lying on the counter with her eyes closed, and reciting a prayer to Ishtar. Machete in hand, he prepares to sever her head—the final ingredient in the blood feast—but, unable to take his request seriously, she inadvertently thwarts his plan by repeatedly bobbing up and giggling. Before Ramses can dispatch her, Mrs. Fremont bursts into the kitchen with Thornton and the police close behind her. They chase Ramses through the neighborhood and into a garbage dump, where he attempts to hide in the open back of a trash truck and is crushed to death by the compactor. Thornton declares that he met a fitting end, dying "just like the garbage he was."

FIGURE 13.1 *In his kitchen-shrine, Fuad Ramses prepares to remove the roasted leg and foot of his first victim from the oven.*

Ramses' prosaic (if gruesome) death, and Thornton's equally prosaic benediction, seem to frame the dead caterer as a deranged serial killer, but the final scene of the film reintroduces the mythological and supernatural. In the caterer's now-abandoned shrine, the golden statue of Ishtar weeps tears of blood, as if mourning the lost opportunity for a blood feast in her honor.

The cult of Ishtar

The brainchild of screenwriter Allison Louise Downe (then-wife of director Herschell Gordon Lewis), *Blood Feast*'s pseudo-Egyptian-themed plot was intended to capitalize on audiences' enthrallment with exotic Egypt, fostered by films such as *The Mummy* (1932) and its multiple spin-offs throughout the early 1940s,[3] as well as the popular antics of Abbott and Costello in *Abbott and Costello Meet the Mummy* (1955) over a decade later. Tales of "the mummy's curse" had captivated the Western world since the 1920s, when the specter of death seemed to haunt those responsible for disturbing the tomb of King Tutankhamen,[4] and in subsequent years, as Randy Palmer points out, the mummification process, blood vengeance rites, and elaborate surgical techniques held a macabre fascination for readers and viewers.[5] Gruesome accounts of brains being extracted through the nasal passages, organs removed and preserved for the afterlife, and wealth, animals, slaves, and even wives entombed with the dead permeated the lore surrounding Egyptian death rites.

Blood Feast's narrative, while exploiting this popular fascination, has only tenuous roots in Egypt or sacred mythology. The goddess Ishtar is a deity in the Babylonian, rather than Egyptian, tradition—the goddess of sex, love, fertility, and war—the divine personification of the planet Venus.[6] The tale of her descent into the underworld and "resurrection" is seminal in Mesopotamian lore on the alternating of the seasons. While her descent is given various explanations—some suggest that it was intended to rescue her dead lover, Tammuz; others contend that it was to comfort her sister, Queen of the Underworld, after her husband Gugalanna's death—in all cases, her return is fraught with trials and the intrigues of the gods. Her reappearance on earth at the vernal equinox signals the return of prosperity and fertility until her departure again in the fall.[7]

The festival calendar of ancient Egypt includes numerous feast days in honor of its deities. These were elaborate celebrations that included processions, rituals, chants, and speeches, and indulgence in a vast array of food and drink, from waterfowl to wine, celebrating the equinox, the harvest, fertility, and other key periods and events, such as the harvest-time feast of the goddess Isis:

> At this day, in the time of harvest, the inhabitants offer the first fruits of the ears of corn, etc. . . . In some cities also, when they celebrate the feast of Isis in a pompous procession, they carry about vessels of wheat and barley, in memory of the first invention by the care and industry of this goddess.[8]

While Mikita Brottman argues unequivocally that the myths are based on "true events, primal deeds *did* occur" and that "the feast of Ishtar *did* take place" over "five thousand years ago,"[9] the prevalence of human sacrifice to the gods is debated among scholars of the ancient world, with some suggesting that early depictions of the practice exist, while others offer alternative explanations.[10] Cannibalism, however, is another story. Texts and verses referring to the consumption of both men and gods are highly elaborated, such as these utterances from the Pyramid Texts, which describe the pharaoh as "he who eats men and lives on gods":

> It is Grasper-of-topknots who is Kehau
> Who lassos them for the King;
> It is the Serpent with raised head
> Who guards them for him
> And restrains them for him;
> It is He who is over the blood-offering
> Who binds them for him;
> It is Khons who slew the lords
> Who strangles them for the King
> And extracts for him what is in their bodies,
> For he is the messenger whom the King sends to restrain.
> It is Shezmu who cuts them up for the King
> And who cooks for him a portion of them
> On his evening hearthstones.[11]

The conflation of power, resurrection, and bodily consumption found in these utterances is made gruesomely manifest in Ramses' blood feast, as it becomes the pivot point for life, death, resurrection, immortality, celebration, and horror.

As Gary Elbow notes, belief in the transformative nature of cannibalism is well-documented. Ritual cannibalism, he points out,

> is often a way to acquire the attributes of the person whose body parts are being consumed. For example, a victorious warrior who has killed an

enemy may believe he will gain courage or other positive attributes by consuming parts of the victim. This was common among certain tribes of New Guinea, Fiji (once known as the Cannibal Isles), Central Africa, and the Amazon for example.[12]

In both the novel and film, the consumption of human flesh, presented as a blood feast, serves as a means of transformation. The preparations for the blood feast and the subsequent eating of the prepared organs provide the transformative power to bring Ishtar to life and turn Ramses into a god himself—Shamash, the Babylonian god of the sun and justice, who was, in ancient lore, the brother of Ishtar.[13] "The Feast of Ishtar has begun. Henceforth, my name is Shamash," Ramses tells Suzette just before he is about to sacrifice her. She is the final sacrifice he requires in order to finish the feast preparations and transcend his mortal body. This is not consumption for survival, pleasure, vengeance, or even fetish, but rather, for ritual and purpose.

Uniquely, however, *Blood Feast* is a cannibal film where "no actual cannibalism ever takes place."[14] As Brottman observes, Ramses, as the high priest of the cult of Ishtar, "is compelled to re-enact the sacramental feast of the dark goddess," but the feast itself is never consumed.[15] The "fascination of the abomination," described by Joseph Conrad, "inexplicable, mesmerizing evil" draws viewers into the preparation of the feast, as both voyeurs and participants.[16] A brain removed here, a tongue ripped out there, legs cut off, flesh flayed . . . "[t]he meat is cooked, the stew prepared, the flavor added, the table laid, but the sacrament never occurs."[17] The abject is transformed into culinary display, but in the end the goddess is denied her return, Ramses meets his grisly end, and the taboo against consuming human flesh remains intact. The borders of the monstrous—between what may and may not be consumed, the living and the dead, the earthly and the supernatural—remain inviolate.

The invention of "gorror"

The team that created *Blood Feast* includes some of the luminaries of exploitation films. Notorious producer and sideshow entrepreneur Dave Friedman had already teamed with Lewis for a wide range of productions, from the salacious drama of *The Prime Time* (1960) and *Living Venus* (1961) to "nudie cuties" such as *The Adventures of Lucky Pierre* (1961), *Nature's Playmates* (1962), and *Goldilocks and the Three Bares* (1963), to violent "roughies" like *Scum of the Earth* (1963). The pair, having grown bored with their standard fare, was casting about for new, untried approaches to exploitation. Friedman's ongoing passion for carnival sideshows provided the answer:

> In sideshows, I'd seen guys drive nails through their tongues, put hooks in their eyes and pull a car, run a screwdriver up their noses, everything in the world. But it had never been done on film. So, I'm telling Herschell one day about all of the old sideshows, and out of that came the idea for *Blood Feast*.[18]

Allison Louise "Bunny" Downe, Lewis' then-wife, had been featured in several of the pair's earlier nudie-cuties, along with films by director Doris Wishman such as *Blaze Starr Goes Nudist* (1962) and *Gentlemen Prefer Nature Girls* (1963), before joining the Lewis-Friedman production team. Downe is credited with writing the script for *Blood Feast*, as well as with providing the concepts for the story's Egyptian theme and the goddess Ishtar. Stories about this vary, however, as Friedman recalls about the fourteen-page outline that would serve as the script: "I would say the largest scriptwriter was circumstance, in that we would concoct dialogue on the spot. We didn't have time to do much else." He continued:

> Actually Louise Downe and I wrote *Blood Feast* together in tandem, taking turns on the typewriter. When one of us would write because the other had become exhausted from hitting the keys, the other would start fooling around with ideas for gore effects.[19]

Those effects, low budget as they were—theatrical blood, mortician's wax, and animal entrails provided by local meatpacking plants—would catapult *Blood Feast* into cult history. Lewis filled the screen with levels of horror and gore never before seen in theaters: "There were a whole bunch of taboos that we set out deliberately to violate in order to position our picture. I wanted it no that no exhibitor could say, 'Oh, I've seen that before, done better.'"[20]

The film opens with Ramses sneaking into the home of a curvaceous young woman relaxing in a bath. As a voice on the radio warns of a killer on the loose, he stabs her in the eye with a butcher knife. The action pauses—the camera lingering on a mutilated eyeball hanging from the blade—and then the film shifts perspective to a reverse shot, revealing the dead woman's bloody eye socket. As the camera draws away, the killer pulls out a meat cleaver and begins hacking at her lifeless body. When the mutilated corpse is finally revealed, we see that he has amputated her leg. The camera zooms in for a close-up of the tatters of flesh and bone jutting out of the water at the end of the jagged stump.

One by one, beautiful women—several former *Playboy* models[21]—meet gruesome ends at the hand of the mad caterer. As the story unfolds, Ramses fills his hideous shopping list, harvesting a brain from the freshly crushed skull of one victim, tearing the face off another, and in what has become the film's most iconic scene, ripping the tongue from the mouth of a third (Astrid Olsen) in a sleazy motel room. As the pair struggle on the bed, Ramses forces his hand deep into her mouth and the camera cuts to a close-up of a large, ragged tongue being pulled away. Blood and bits of flesh pour onto the sheets as the fiend holds his prize aloft (Figure 13.2). The tongue, taken from a butchered sheep, was large enough that the actor needed to grasp it with both hands, adding a bizarre touch to the already macabre scene. Lewis observed, however, "I think audiences were less sickened by the tongue than they were when she turns her head and all this glob falls out the side. *That's* the part that sickens 'em."[22] The film, as Bob Bankard offers, is "disgusting by suggestion."[23]

FIGURE 13.2 *Herschell Gordon Lewis's trademark stage blood soaks a motel bed in the aftermath of* Blood Feast's *infamous tongue-ripping scene.*

The blood used in this scene and others was a particular point of pride for Lewis, who felt that stage blood was visually ineffective. Over-the-top gore was the film's only claim to fame, and so the blood needed to be as realistic as possible. It also needed to be safe to swallow, as scenes required the actors to "spit, gurgle, and otherwise dribble the stuff from their mouths."[24]

> We needed fake blood, and we needed gallons of it. I hated the kind of blood that was available because in every major film I had seen, the blood never looked right. So, we ended up manufacturing our own.[25]

Lewis's gut-churning blood concoction resulted from a mixture of clear gelatin, red dye, cranberry mix, and Kaopectate (an over-the-counter diarrhea remedy). This formula, which cost a mere $7.50 per gallon, would serve as the director's stage blood for the rest of his career.

Reactions to Lewis's low-budget gore-fest were just as the director had hoped: "I get crank letters to this day about my pictures from people who can't understand at all that something like *Blood Feast* could be made by civilized people."[26] But in the exploitation tradition, any attention is good attention, so when producer Friedman's wife described the film simply as "vomitous," the pair seized the idea and printed vomit bags for screenings that warned "You May Need This When You See *Blood Feast*."

Writing in 1967, Carlos Clarens lamented the film's attempt to bring the "obsolete trickery" of the French *Grand Guignol* to modern audiences, but acknowledged its appeal to more sophisticated tastes.[27] Others, like North Carolina's then-state representative Steve Dolley, not only failed to see the film's charms, but viewed it as a sign of the moral decay of the 1960s, stating "This is one sorry bastard of a picture that needs to be put down for the good of society."[28] There was nothing on the horror horizon at the time that compared with the prolonged, unadulterated violence that the director had packed onto the screen, though Lewis and Friedman would follow this model for several years, rounding out a Blood trilogy, and reuniting in 2002 for a sequel: *Blood Feast 2: All You Can Eat*.[29] *Blood Feast* became the first footfall on the path to the splatter films of the 1970s and 1980s, many of which would evolve into the contemporary slasher film tradition. For better or worse, Lewis had given rise to a new subgenre of blood and thrills that would come to be known as "gorror." The result, perhaps, of Lewis's contention that "[t]hose who have no gods have an easier time creating gods of their own."[30]

Maidens and meat

The appeal of *Blood Feast* to 1963 horror-film audiences, and its subsequent reputation among fans of the genre, rested on its willingness to show—unflinchingly, and in shockingly bright colors—the violence that other horror films merely hinted at. The threat of censorship had, for decades, sustained a set of genre conventions that kept blood and death discreetly off-screen. Even *Psycho* (1960), which pushed harder against them than any mainstream horror film in decades, conveyed Marion Crane's death in the shower with tight shots of wet skin, a flashing knife, and blood swirling in the drain, leaving viewers' imaginations to fill in the rest. Herschell Gordon Lewis set out, in *Blood Feast*, to vigorously and comprehensively trample those conventions. He conceived the film as a departure in content, but not in spirit, from the "nudie-cutie" films that had made his reputation; what they had done for nudity—gratifying audiences by leaving nothing to the imagination—*Blood Feast* would do for violent death and bloody mutilation.

The lurid mythology of Ishtar and her bloody feast provides the film not only with a title, but also with a pretext for its tissue-thin story about beautiful young women stalked, killed, and dismembered by a wild-eyed fiend. Indeed, it sets the stage for considerably more than just death and mutilation. Dr. Flanders, explaining the ancient rituals during his lecture with an odd mixture of professorial sternness and barely disguised relish, describes a six-day orgy followed by a cannibalistic banquet. The virginal priestesses of Ishtar are, in the film's version of the myth, thus consumed twice by the men of the city: first sexually and then, after being sacrificed upon the goddess's altar and carved into tender morsels for the feast, physically.

These salacious hints, however, remain just that. Fuad Ramses' actions drive the plot of the film, and its characterization of him never wavers: He is a cook, both in his real-world occupation as a caterer and in his shadow-world role as a high priest of Ishtar. His interest in the women he victimizes is, therefore, not sexual but culinary: they are the sources of the ingredients that he must harvest in order to properly prepare the feast he longs to offer to his goddess-patron. The fact that they are young and beautiful—even the fact that they are women—is relevant to him only because they must be so to fulfill their role as priestesses, sacrifices, and (ultimately) ingredients. He encounters four of his five victims in intimate settings, wearing revealing clothes or no clothes at all, and two as they are on the verge of offering themselves to their lovers, but his interest remains that of a chef choosing the freshest meat or produce from a market. Their sexual availability is, for him, merely an outward sign of their suitability as food for Ishtar.

Lewis's camera, acting on behalf of the audience, *does* sexualize and objectify the women—up to a point. It ogles the first victim as she undresses and then relaxes in her bath with legs outstretched and a tenuous veil of soapsuds clinging to her breasts. It peers at the second as she embraces her boyfriend on a deserted beach, determined to meet his challenge to "prove that you love me," and the third as she prepares for midday sex in a cheap motel room. Before Trudy is whipped to death and Suzette nearly beheaded, they cavort with a third friend in and around the Fremonts' pool as the camera roves over their bikini-clad bodies, lavishing particular attention on Trudy's cleavage. Once Ramses appears in the scene, however, the camera's gaze becomes detached rather than salacious, its focus shifting to the body parts that he bloodily harvests and the grotesque wreckage—gaping eye sockets, bloody stumps, and sheared-off skulls—he leaves behind. The film's "money shots," though they involve beautiful women in explicitly sexualized poses, are not just un-erotic but, for most in the audience, likely *anti*-erotic.

The infamous tongue-ripping scene, for example, begins when the victim and her would-be lover arrive at their rented room for an alcohol-fueled tryst. The lover stumbles away in search of another bottle, and the woman—mistaking Ramses' knock for his return—answers the door in her brassiere, her tight wool skirt unfastened and slid partway over her hips. Ramses wrestles her onto the bed and pins her with his body as she writhes and screams beneath him, but his attention is focused solely on her tongue. His fingers are already in her mouth as he forces her down, and once he claims his prize he gives her no more attention than he would the carcass of a just-filleted fish. Later, after whipping Trudy to death in his kitchen-shrine, he thrusts a silver chalice between her parted legs as she hangs from her manacles, but once again it is a purely functional act: a careful chef, determined not to waste a drop of the precious blood he has worked so hard to gather. The whipping scene ends with her dead, but still dressed and (except for her back) unmarked. When the police find her body, however, it is lying face down and all but naked on Rameses's kitchen work table, smeared with blood and surrounded by utensils and unidentifiable chunks of flesh that hint at her further transformation from woman to meat.

Lewis calls the audience's attention to the convergence of human and meat throughout *Blood Feast*. Animal flesh—most infamously, the sheep's tongue—substitutes for human flesh on screen; the severed leg of Ramses' first victim, after hours in his back-room oven, has the color and texture of roast pig; the flesh in the stewpot that Ramses is periodically shown stirring could be . . . anything. Trudy's blood-smeared body, the most dehumanized corpse in the film, has a bowl of fresh green salad positioned between its ankles, highlighting her status as food. Even the penultimate line of dialogue, delivered by Thornton, underscores the connection: "Lust . . . murder . . . food for an ancient goddess who received life through the perverted death of others."

The film's relentless emphasis on the reduction of maidens to meat, and its foregrounding of an arch-fiend for whom their youthful beauty and sexual availability are significant only as evidence of their suitability as food, masks *Blood Feast*'s final irony. The great event for which Rameses prepares with such devotion, and for which Lewis relentlessly primes the audience—the cannibalistic feast that will bring Ishtar, in all her blood-and-lust-fueled glory, to terrible life—never happens.

Conclusion: selling the sizzle

Herschell Gordon Lewis once boasted that *Blood Feast* was a more profitable film than *Star Wars*. With its miniscule budget of $24,500 and box-office receipts of $4,000,000, however, he was right. The film's outrageous financial success was, at least in part, the result of Lewis and Friedman's experience and skill as exploiteers—their ability to, as Friedman put it, "sell the sizzle, not the steak."[31] Audiences flocked to see "adult horror" never before featured on screen, from a director and producer well known for thumbing their noses at both censors and sensibilities. From *Playboy* pin-ups to vomit bags, the pair pulled out all the stops in the production and promotion of a film that violated conventions, taboos, and good taste. In good exploitation fashion, advertising for *Blood Feast* drew its viewers in with promises like:

> NOTHING SO APPALLING IN THE ANNALS OF HORROR!

> WHILE HIS NUBILE YOUNG GIRL VICTIMS SCREAMED OUT THEIR LIFE BLOOD HE PREPARED THE MOST HORRENDOUS OF ALL FEASTS

> A WEIRD, GRISLY ANCIENT RITE HORRENDOUSLY BROUGHT TO LIFE IN BLOOD COLOR

What audiences actually *saw*, however, fell short of these promises. Once in the theater, they found a film that was as coy in its depiction of sex as it was brazen in its depiction of gore, and in which the villain—with one beautiful, scantily clad woman after another in his grasp—could think only of turning them into a stew that he never quite got around to serving. Breasts remain covered, tantalizing victims remain chaste, and the Feast of Ishtar—the motivation for the whole gruesome mess—remains uneaten. With this, *Blood Feast* joins the ranks of Lewis and Friedman's over-the-top fare—selling the sizzle, without a steak in sight—and in good exploitation fashion, it winks at its guests from across the bloody banquet table and says: "Well, maybe next time."

Notes

1. Randy Palmer, *Herschell Gordon Lewis, the Godfather of Gore: The Films* (Jefferson, NC: McFarland, 2006), 40.
2. *Variety* (May 6, 1964), http://www.liquisearch.com/blood_feast/critical_reception (accessed April 11, 2016).
3. *The Mummy's Hand* (1940), *The Mummy's Tomb* (1942), *The Mummy's Ghost* (1944), and *The Mummy's Curse* (1944)
4. For more on the mummy's curse and the deaths surrounding the archeological team, see Bob Brier, *Egyptomania: Our Three-Thousand Year Obsession with the People of the Nile* (New York: St. Martin's, 2012), 161–92; and Jasmine Day, *The Mummy's Curse: Mummymania in the English-Speaking World* (New York: Routledge, 2006).
5. Palmer, *Herschell Gordon Lewis*, 12.
6. Felix Guirand, "Assyro-Babylonian Mythology," in *New Larousse Encyclopedia of Mythology* (London: Hamlyn, 1968), 58.
7. See Joshua J. Mark, "Inanna's Descent: A Sumerian Tale of Injustice," *Ancient History Encyclopedia* (February 23, 2011), http://www.ancient.eu/article/215/ (accessed April 11, 2016); and Timothy Stephany, *The Descent of Ishtar: Both the Sumerian and Akkadian Versions* (CreateSpace, 2015).
8. J. F. Lake Williams, *An Historical Account of Inventions and Discoveries Which Are of Utility or Ornament to Man* (London: T. and J. Allman, 1820).
9. Mikita Brottman, *Offensive Films: Toward an Anthropology of Cinema Vomitif* (Westport, CT: Greenwood Press, 1997), 84; emphasis in the original.
10. See, for example, Ian Shaw, *The Oxford History of Ancient Egypt* (New York: Oxford University Press, 2004), 68; and Jacques Kinnaer, *The Ancient Egypt Site*, www.ancient-egypt.org (accessed April 11, 2016).
11. Jimmy Dunn [writing as Taylor Ray Ellison], "The Pyramid Text," utterance 173–4, http://www.touregypt.net /featurestories/pyramidtext.htm (accessed April 11, 2016).
12. Gary Elbow, Professor of Human Geography, Texas Tech University (Oral History Interview, December 1, 2015).
13. David Leeming, *The Oxford Companion to World Mythology* (New York: Oxford University Press, 2005), 390.
14. Brottman, *Offensive Films*, 81.
15. Ibid., 86.
16. "The Fascination of the Abomination," *The New York Times* (February 1, 1989), http://www.nytimes.com/1989/02/01/opinion/the-fascination-of-the-abomination.html (accessed April 11, 2016).

17 Brottman, *Offensive Films*, 81.
18 Michael H. Price and John Wooley, *Forgotten Horrors to the Nth Degree: Dispatches from a Collapsing Genre* (CreateSpace, 2013), 32.
19 Palmer, *Herschell Gordon Lewis*, 41.
20 Ibid.
21 Connie Mason, Ashlyn Martin, and Astrid Olsen.
22 Palmer, *Herschell Gordon Lewis*, 53.
23 Quoted in David Konow, *Reel Terror: The Scary, Bloody, Gory Hundred-Year History of Modern Horror Films* (New York: St. Martin's, 2012), 94.
24 Ibid., 39.
25 Ibid., 38
26 Ibid.
27 Carlos Clarens, *Illustrated History of Horror and Science Fiction Films: The Classic Era 1985–1967* (1967. New York: De Capo Press, 1997), 154.
28 Quoted in Price and Wooley, *Forgotten Horrors to the Nth Degree*, 31.
29 Palmer, *Herschell Gordon Lewis*, 46; Price and Wooley, *Forgotten Horrors to the Nth Degree*, 27–50.
30 Konow, *Reel Terror*, 93.
31 *Mau Mau Sex Sex*.

Bibliography

Brier, Bob. *Egyptomania: Our Three-Thousand Year Obsession with the People of the Nile*. New York: St. Martin's, 2012.

Brottman, Mikita. *Offensive Films: Toward an Anthropology of Cinema Vomitif*. Westport, CT: Greenwood Press, 1997.

Clarens, Carlos. *An Illustrated History of Horror and Science Fiction Films: The Classic Era 1985–1967*. 1967. New York: De Capo Press, 1997.

Day, Jasmine. *The Mummy's Curse: Mummymania in the English-Speaking World*. New York: Routledge, 2006.

Dunn, Jimmy [writing as Taylor Ray Ellison]. "The Pyramid Text." http://www.touregypt.net /featurestories/pyramidtext.htm.

Guirand, Felix. "Assyro-Babylonian Mythology." In *New Larousse Encyclopedia of Mythology*. London: Hamlyn, 1968.

Konow, David. *Reel Terror: The Scary, Bloody, Gory Hundred-Year History of Modern Horror Films*. New York: St. Martin's, 2012.

Leeming, David. *The Oxford Companion to World Mythology*. New York: Oxford University Press, 2005.

Mark, Joshua J. "Inanna's Descent: A Sumerian Tale of Injustice." *Ancient History Encyclopedia*. Last modified February 23, 2011. http://www.ancient.eu/article/215/.

Mau Mau Sex Sex. Directed by Ted Bonnitt. 2001. Water Valley, TX: Seventh Planet Entertainment Group. 2004

The New York Times. "The Fascination of the Abomination," February 1, 1989. http://www.nytimes.com/1989/02/01/opinion/the-fascination-of-the-abomination.html (accessed April 11, 2016).

Palmer, Randy. *Herschell Gordon Lewis, the Godfather of Gore: The Films.* Jefferson, NC: McFarland, 2006.

Price, Michael H., and John Wooley. *Forgotten Horrors to the Nth Degree: Dispatches from a Collapsing Genre.* North Charleston, SC: CreateSpace, 2013.

Shaw, Ian. *The Oxford History of Ancient Egypt.* New York: Oxford University Press, 2004.

Stephany, Timothy. *The Descent of Ishtar: Both the Sumerian and Akkadian Versions.* North Charleston, SC: CreateSpace, 2015.

Williams, J. F. Lake. *An Historical Account of Inventions and Discoveries Which Are of Utility or Ornament to Man.* London: T. and J. Allman, 1820.

14

From Gourmet to Gore: Jean-Pierre Jeunet's *Delicatessen*

Karen A. Ritzenhoff and Cynthia J. Miller

Black milk of daybreak we drink you at night
We drink in the morning at noon we drink you at sundown
We drink and we drink you
A man lives in the house he plays with the serpents he writes

—Paul Celan, "Death Fugue" (1948)[1]

In 1945, the Romanian-born Jewish writer Paul Celan wrote the "Death Fugue" (published as *"Todesfuge"* in German), using food imagery to depict the horrors of the death camps during the Holocaust.[2] In it, the "black milk"—a toxic drink that destroys instead of nourishing—symbolizes the deaths of the Jews under Nazi rule. Jean-Pierre Jeunet's film *Delicatessen* (1991)[3] likewise uses food to signify the horrors of the Holocaust, but with meat, rather than milk, as a source of the abject[4] and an object of deathly consumption. Jeunet's film is concerned not only with horrors, however, but also with the ways in which they are hidden, by those complicit in perpetrating them, beneath a veil of normality and a shroud of silence.

Delicatessen is a dark French comedy that depicts the end of the world by focusing on a dystopian society in miniature: an apartment building where food shortages are exacerbated by the tenants' determination to maintain their former way of life. Craving meat, but no longer able to obtain it, they obstinately refuse to consider changing their diet. Instead, they turn to cannibalism, consuming strangers and, ultimately, each other even as they pretend that nothing has changed. The film is set, as Stephen Infantino notes, in "a post-scarcity economy where nothing and no one can escape the cutting edge."[5] Jeunet, however, evokes the horror of this world without ever portraying his central character—the butcher who runs the shop of the title—actually dissecting bloody human flesh, or the residents of the building actually consuming the body parts of their former neighbors. The dystopian French society breeds gore, not gourmets, but although every character understands the horrors that are taking place, only a handful speak of—let alone oppose—them. The grotesque community of collaborators in *Delicatessen*'s apartment building thus becomes, in Jeunet's hands, an allegory for the dark history of France under Nazi occupation, and for the nation's gradual, painful acknowledgment of the crimes against humanity in which it had been silently complicit.

The political economy of meat

Delicatessen takes place amid a postapocalyptic cityscape: barren, grey, isolated, dirty, and poor. The sky is dreary and cloudy; the air seems thick, overwhelmed by the residue of death and decay.[6] The "environment of scarcity and rationing," as Infantino observes, is "cast in hues of nuclear disaster."[7] The film opens with a wide shot of two buildings: one that is barely standing, with only one wall in place, and a second, less decrepit structure where several windows are faintly illuminated. A large fence circles the properties, and a gate can be spotted in the background. Jeunet and his codirector Mark Caro focus on the second building, an apartment complex, and the bizarre, eccentric characters who inhabit it. The delicatessen of the title is a butcher shop, located on the first floor of the complex, whose owner, Clapet (Jean-Claude Dreyfus), provides the residents with a suspiciously steady supply of meat (Figure 14.1).

The opening scene of the film shows the butcher's latest assistant being trapped and killed. Listening through the ventilation ducts in the building, which serve as a makeshift intercom system, he has overheard the butcher's ritual of sharpening his dull blades. Realizing that he may be next on the menu, the young man wraps himself with paper and duct tape in his apartment and tries to hide in the trash can along with the other garbage, hoping to be picked

FIGURE 14.1 *The French butcher Clapet (Jean-Claude Dreyfus) supplies his clients with human meat in* Delicatessen *(1991)*.

up by a truck. However, the disguise fails, and the scene ends with Clapet lifting the lid of the waste container with a greedy look, butcher knife in hand.

With the dawning awareness of the sort of "meat" that is central to the political economy of the building, viewers gradually learn the backstory of the butcher, his tenants, and his wares. Clapet's means of securing meat for his tenants is to lure in outsiders with promises of work ("room and board; southern exposure . . . in exchange for odd jobs"), kill them, butcher them in accordance with his trade, and then engage in an exclusive system of exchange with his tenants, who trade bags of grain for cuts of meat. The butcher's tenant-patrons thus literalize the notion of a "consumer society"— one whose members are distanced by choice, rather than circumstance, from that which they consume.

The residents of the apartment building nearly all consent to participate in the grotesque ritual of human slaughter and distribution orchestrated by the butcher. Perhaps predictably, the only objection to this carnivalesque consumption is voiced by his adult daughter Julie (Marie-Laure Dougnac), a vegetarian. The gentle, isolated young woman takes pity on her father's victims, straddling the line between her duty to (and dependence on) her father and her sense of morality. Narrative tension in the film is provided when the larger question of cannibalism is brought to a head by the butcher's latest potential victim: the child-like Louison (Dominique Pinon), an unemployed clown who wins Julie's heart and those of the other tenants as well. A gentle soul, Louison left his previous job when the circus director butchered his companion, the beloved chimpanzee "Livingston." He and Julie thus represent the moral and ethical counterpoint to Clapet and his tenants in this *crise alimentaire*.

When Louison's demise seems imminent, Julie contacts members of a local resistance movement, hoping to enlist their aid in saving him from her father. The *Troglodistes*, subterranean vegetarian "terrorists" who reject the surface-dwellers' cannibalism, function as a gastronomic counterculture—a true "underclass"—in contrast to those above. In seeking their help, Julie transgresses not only her father's and neighbors' foodways, but the film's clear social boundaries as well, crawling under a sewer cover in search of help.

As the meat-fueled tensions rise in the apartment building, Louison and Julie are cornered by hungry neighbors, led by the butcher himself, and must barricade themselves in the bathroom for temporary safety. Louison, who cannot bring himself to fight off his attackers, resolves to use water, similar to the flood in the biblical story of Noah's Ark, as a nonviolent way of purging the antagonists. He pulls pipes out of their sockets, plugs openings—the bathtub drain, the crack under the bathroom door, and eventually the vents high on the wall—with his clothing and waits for the bathroom to fill to the ceiling.

As the lovers, clad only in their undergarments, wait for the room to fill, they embrace and finally kiss under water. This interlude is contrasted with the pounding and screaming of the frenzied mob outside, desperate to satisfy their hunger for meat. Clapet encourages brute force, and the thuggish crowd—equipped with sticks, axes, and other heavy tools—angrily breaks down the doors to find their prey. Seemingly turning into beasts, they roar like wild animals.

As this assault takes place, the secret underground army of *Troglodistes* is approaching, arising from the watery world below the surface to rescue the pair. The men are dressed in uniforms and wearing headlamps, anticipating the look of characters that reemerge in Jeunet's later films. Contrary to Clapet's meat-hungry crowd, the "trogs" appear coordinated and rational.

By the time Clapet's mob finally breaks down the outer door of Julie's apartment and approaches the bathroom, Louison and Julie can barely breathe. Clapet carefully turns the knob of the door and the floodgates open, unleashing a tsunami. The wall of water sweeps out and washes all the antagonists down the stairwell, cleansing the house of the assault.

The water, however, weakens the building's structure and the floor of the bathroom comes tumbling down, allowing an opening through which Clapet can again attack the defenseless couple. Clapet brandishes a new weapon—a circus knife designed to work like a boomerang—but meets his end when the murder weapon, flung at Louison, returns and embeds itself in his head. Clapet's own cannibalistic aggression, not Louison's defense, kills him.

A finite universe of archetypes

In "*Delicatessen*: Slices of Postmodern Life," Stephen Infantino explores the theatricality of Jeunet's film, particularly in terms of its staging and characters, citing the influences of French street theater and Italian *commedia dell'arte*—both art forms intended for the "common folk." In the universe of the film, there exists no other location; everywhere outside of the apartment building and the subterranean depths below has become a hostile wasteland, a nowhere. Thus, the characters in this finite universe are elevated to the status of archetype: *Boucher* (the butcher), *Facteur* (the mailman), *Clown* (Louison), each apparently the last of his kind, with an established role and function.[8] Infantino suggests that Louison, in particular, echoes the character of the *Arlequin*, the light-hearted, romantic trickster, drawn from these historic traditions.[9]

Jeunet, however, credits Georges Méliès, the great visionary of French silent film, as one of the significant inspirations for his cinematography and imagery.[10] Méliès is well known for his use of fantasy, science fiction, play, and elaborate costuming to visualize and bring to life the inner worlds of his characters. Following Méliès, Jeunet crafts a dark, postapocalyptic fairy tale in *Delicatessen*, full of grotesque imagery and bizarre occurrences that would be impossible in "real" life. The film signals this approach in the very first scenes, first as Clapet's assistant tries to wrap himself in paper and tape without assistance—and, impossibly, succeeds—and then as Clapet discovers him. The image of the butcher sharpening his knives as he looks hungrily at his cowering victim would, in a realistic film, be unbearably horrifying. In Jeunet's hands, however, the horror becomes surreal fantasy. Like Hänsel and Gretel roasting the Witch in her own oven, or the Giant declaring that he will grind Jack's bones for flour, it is too far removed from everyday reality to disturb. A similar surrealism mutes the horror of Clapet's own death: the cartoon-like behavior of the trick knife, and the karmic justice of the killer caught in his own trap, distance it from quotidian experience.

The interior of the apartment building itself is a surreal, fairy-tale world and thus an homage to Méliès' intricately mobile, multilayered sets. Early in the film, in the scenes showing the first victim listening to Clapet sharpening his butcher knife from his apartment, Jeunet's camera traces the intricate passageways of the venting system like a doctor performing a colonoscopy. The insides of the venting ducts are meandering, slimy, and wet, reinforcing the image and creating the illusion that the building is a fantasy-world of its own. In time, the film reveals that the stairwell, the underground tunnels, and the venting system that allows Clapet to follow conversations in the entire apartment all intersect, forming a world within the world. Finally, in the "flood" scene, the building behaves as no real structure could, with the bathroom door holding back the water even as the room fills to the ceiling.

As Jack Zipes concludes in his study *The Enchanted Screen: The Unknown History of Fairy-Tale Films*, however, fairy-tale films can be "more realistic than so-called realistic fictional films" and are capable of "addressing social realities through imaginative metaphors." The films "engage with social realities as storytellers, who are in touch with the mysteries of life, and if we watch these fairy-tale films closely, perhaps a tiny bit of wisdom will rub off on us."[11]

The "social reality" that Jeunet addresses in *Delicatessen* is clearly that of France under Nazi occupation during the Second World War. The world of the film, choked with dust and rubble, resembles a bombed-out European city and is photographed in a sepia-tinted light that evokes the wartime past rather than a postapocalyptic future. The characters' clothes and the furnishings of their apartments likewise evoke both the styles and the austerity of the early 1940s. The organized resistance that operates in the sewers, on the inhospitable fringes of the "civilized" world, much like the wartime *maquisards* who hid in the rural scrublands of southern France, spiriting downed Allied fliers and Jewish refugees to safety.

The specific moment in French history that the film thus evokes—the "dark years" between 1940 and 1944—remained controversial, and emotionally fraught, at the time the film was made. France had, for nearly thirty years after the war, embraced an image of itself as a nation of resisters, fiercely and uniformly opposed to the Nazi occupation. That comforting interpretation of the past was shattered, however, by American historian Robert Paxton's book *Vichy France: Old Guard and New Order*, which appeared in 1972. Drawing on French and German wartime records, Paxton argued that soon after the Nazi invasion "the urge to return to home and job started many Frenchmen down a path of everyday complicity that led gradually and eventually to active assistance with German measures undreamed of in 1940."[12] The majority of the French population that accommodated their occupiers were, Paxton contended, like the "good Germans" who performed their routine functions within the Nazi regime, carefully averting their eyes from the regime's larger, horrific goals. Such individuals, he argued,

[p]erform jobs that may be admirable in themselves, but are tinctured with evil by the overall effects of the system. Even Frenchmen of the best intentions, faced with the alternative of doing one's job, whose risks were moral and abstract, or civil disobedience, whose risks were material and immediate, went on doing the job. The same may be said of the German occupiers. Many of them were "good Germans" . . . dutifully fulfilling some minor blameless function in a regime whose cumulative effect was brutish.[13]

The "everyday complicity" into which the Vichy government led France extended, Paxton concluded, even to "the Third Reich's final, desperate paroxysms: the Final Solution, forced labor, reprisals against a growing resistance."[14]

Later historians argued that Paxton had merely replaced a myth of near-universal resistance with one of near-universal collaboration, and argued for a more complex picture.[15] The argument, however, was about the degree and duration of collaboration, rather than the fact of it. That fact—long buried and un-discussed—was now a matter of public record, continually under scrutiny. Marcel Ophüls's two-part documentary film *The Sorrow and the Pity*, completed in 1969 and nominated for a 1971 Academy Award, finally reached French television (which had commissioned, but then declined to even consider showing, it) in 1981.[16] Historian Tony Judt would later refer to the film as the "*locus classicus* of shame and denial in the long civil war that is French contemporary history."[17] Four years later, Claude Lanzman's epic documentary *Shoah* (1985) depicted Poles as knowingly complicit in the Final Solution, drawing an uncomfortable (if unspoken) parallel with his native France.

The 1987 trial of Klaus Barbie, "The Butcher of Lyon," which took place just prior to the making of *Delicatessen*, brought wartime collaboration to the forefront of French culture once again. Barbie, an SS captain who served as head of the Gestapo in Lyon from 1942 to 1944, was one of the most notorious Nazi war criminals to survive the war, known for his extensive deportations of local Jews to the concentration camps, his ruthless war against the Resistance, and the brutal torture techniques he practiced on prisoners held at the "Hôtel Terminus." In one particularly infamous act, he arranged for 44 orphaned Jewish children to be sent to Auschwitz. Barbie, thought to be personally responsible for the deaths of 4,000 individuals and the deportation of more than 7,500 others, was tracked down in Bolivia by "Nazi hunters" Serge and Beate Klarsfeld and finally extradited to France in 1983. Charged with 341 counts of crimes against humanity, Barbie pleaded innocence, but was found guilty on all counts and sentenced to life imprisonment. He passed away in his prison cell in 1991, the year *Delicatessen* was released.

Barbie's team of lawyers, led by Jacques Vergès, attempted to defend him by indicting France. They argued, for example, that his crimes were no different than the crimes committed by French soldiers in North Africa, and by French bureaucrats of the Vichy government, and those who carried out their policies. "Barbie has been promoted to the rank of an expiatory victim, a scapegoat so that France can try and shed its own responsibility,"[18] Vergès argued. The strategy failed to save Barbie but the charges stung. Marcel Ophüls chronicled the trial in detail in *Hôtel Terminus: The Life and Times of Klaus Barbie* (1988), forcing audiences to confront not only Barbie's crimes but France's complicity in them. André Fontaine, editor of *Le Monde*, declared: "It's a time in France where people are more and more conscious of the necessity of knowing something about history and especially about recent history."[19] *Delicatessen*, released the same year that Barbie died in prison, was part of that process of "knowing," but its portrayal of "ordinary" French citizens was even more damning. Its central characters are not just passively complicit in a monstrous evil (as Ophüls, Paxton, and Lanzman suggested to varying degrees) but active participants who (literally) feed on the results of the horrors they facilitate.

The banality of cannibalism

Cannibalism is among the most intense, and most strictly observed, of all Western taboos. Even when committed unknowingly, it is horrifying. Transgressions of it are excused only by extreme need, as in the case of plane-crash survivors or shipwrecked sailors struggling to avoid death by starvation. Jeunet makes it absolutely clear, however, that the residents of the apartment building—his microcosm of wartime France—have deliberately *chosen* cannibalism. Worse, they have done so not out of desperation or as a last resort, but because they want to keep eating meat and the butcher offers them the opportunity to do so.

The opening scenes of the film make clear that the cannibalism is deliberate, systematic, and ongoing. Clapet, sharpening his large knives and thinking lustfully of his next victim, is engaged in a familiar process—almost a ritual. He already knows what will be involved in the killing, carving-up, and parceling-out of the victim and takes pleasure in anticipating it. The frantic actions of the intended victim, his petrified assistant, in attempting to disguise himself and escape, implies that he, too, has recognized an established process at work. The shocked look on his face when Clapet thwarts his plan and corners him suggests that he understands, all too well, what will happen to him. The scene is shot from the subjective point of view of the victim, looking up at Clapet's triumphant grimace: it is as if the viewer is indeed next.

The contrast between Clapet and his assistant in the scene mirrors the photographs and film with which Allied troops documented the liberation of the Nazi concentration camps. Specifically, it recalls scenes from Alain Resnais's documentary *Night and Fog* (1955) when the doors to the camps are opened. The guards, men and women whose well-fed bodies are evoked by the beefy Clapet, emerge under the gaze of their emaciated former captives. The prisoners in *Night and Fog*, transformed in that moment from incipient victims to survivors, share the wide-eyed, tortured expression of Clapet's assistant. Jeunet, in *Delicatessen*, focuses his attention on those who are absent from the footage documenting the liberation of the camps: those for whom (like Clapet's assistant) rescue came too late, and the many whose actions made them complicit in those deaths.

The other tenants of the apartment building—whose ground floor houses Clapet's dingy shop—are not only participants in the gore, but the reason for it. Resources like water are still available in this apocalyptic world, but meat is scarce. Faced with this shortage, which leads to restrictions and rationing like those imposed during the war, they refuse to change their diets. The possibility of eating vegetarian fare is unthinkable to them; of all the characters in the film, only Julie, Louison, and the revolutionaries in the sewage system—all outsiders—do so. Hunger could easily be eradicated within the building if the tenants cooked the grain in their possession. Instead they starve themselves and trade their bags of grain to Clapet and wait patiently for him to supply them with their next slice of meat.

The title of the film and of the butcher store, *Delicatessen*, is as misleading as the inscription at the entrance of Auschwitz and other concentration camps that stated "Work Sets You Free" (*Arbeit Macht Frei*). The store appears to be selling fine foods, but the butcher is only seen distributing meat when another human victim has been killed. The butcher divides each human body into delicious bites, and his customers request specific body parts in language (such as "the shoulder") that does not disguise their origin. They are no more furtive or ashamed than if they were purchasing beef or pork, and show no qualms about asking for their share, obediently and quietly waiting in line until it is their turn. Strangers and less-favored tenants become, like animals, raised for their meat, a commodity. They exist only to be "processed" by the butcher and distributed to their fellow tenants. Each time a new tenant moves into the building to work at the delicatessen, the countdown begins: how long will it take until the new inhabitant is killed and consumed?

The audience hardly ever sees anybody eating, except for a crazy man who is surrounded by toads and delights in snails, but it is assumed that every carnivore participates in the uncivilized feast. The breakdown of the miniature society within the building is complete: The tenants have lost their ability to sustain themselves, and parents have ceased to think about engaging in a trade that would feed their families and children, let alone model any kind of moral compass for them. Man eats man. The butcher slaughters his subordinates, growing rich in seeds he never thinks about planting and grains he never thinks about cooking. He counts the bags that accumulate in the back room of his shop, profiting while the world around him descends into barbarism and members of a close-knit community turn on one another, choosing to embrace carnage instead of compassion.

The choice "not to know" as political metaphor

The abject conflation of meat packages and human body parts, as they are delivered to patient customers in the butcher shop in *Delicatessen*, points to a darker political metaphor. Their repression of guilt suggests a connection to a larger psychosocial mechanism for coping with atrocities. Jeunet's satire not only questions the connection between capitalism and carnage but also underscores issues of complicity in the sense that citizens, while aware of murder, nevertheless look the other way. Rather than revolt against injustice, the film suggests, society encourages repression, denial, and complicity in state-sanctioned crimes, effectively rewriting history even as it is being lived.

Scholars focused on historical memory in conflict-torn nations have observed that frequently fear has "provided the glue that cemented the willingness" of their citizens to leave atrocities of the past behind.[20] As historian Rahman Haghighat observes:

> Historical memories may be pushed back for social cohesion or denial of responsibility. When they return to the consciousness in full, and facing their truth is too painful, people may try to disavow them... Why remember what you cannot heal? Thus, in a selective amnesia for a troubled past, some people may deny the whole story.[21]

War crimes enacted or sanctioned by *L'État Français* and the collaborationists, and met with silence or denial by much of the nation's citizenry, return here in Jeunet's world of grim fairy-tale parable, in search of justice and resolution, bringing to life Haghighat's warning that "[r]emnants of the foregone, shards of broken hopes, fragments of ruins—these are likely to return like nightmares."[22]

Early in the film, Clapet, echoing historical figures such as Henri Philippe Pétain and Pierre Laval, assures Louison that there are no neighbors meddling in his affairs and no visitors—and so no external constraints or regulations to limit his authority. He is confident in his role as benevolent dictator, knowing that none of his "charges" will challenge him either. Thus we see that throughout the apartment building owned and overseen by *Le Boucher*, there is a conspiracy of silence. Some are silent because they benefit from the consumption of "meat" that they know is deeply taboo; others are silent because they fear becoming victims themselves. Throughout the film, the building's inhabitants periodically grapple with the practicalities of their cannibalistic system of exchange: welcoming outsiders to avoid "eating their own"; debating whether it is more appropriate to eat the elderly to prolong the lives of those with more years to live; shielding loved ones from the butcher's cleaver; and, in the case of one unfortunate resident, refusing to eat one's own severed "meat"; but the larger moral issues surrounding such consumption are almost never entertained.

Those who are consumed are peripheral members of this postapocalyptic community—newcomers, outsiders, strangers, and the elderly in the world of the film, evoking the immigrants, Jews, and gypsies of history—and most of those lured to the building by the promise of employment are already exploited, depersonalized commodities when they enter through the door. These individuals are killed and eaten, not only because they are not valued players in the building's political economy—they are, even while living, objects rather than individuals. It is easy "not to know" what's happening to them because the residents don't know *them*—their histories, their hopes, their idiosyncrasies. Only Julie, whose ethics cause her to abstain from eating meat at all, empathizes with and protects the butcher's would-be victims, out of a higher-order respect for life. She cannot avoid knowing, and thus, cannot avoid taking action against the residents' atrocities.

Louison disrupts the status quo of the building, first for Julie, then for other residents, by removing himself from the category of stranger/outsider/other and making himself into a Person (in their eyes). As a clown, *he* is the one who speaks the uncomfortable truth . . . by staging a scene for Julie with his head on a platter with a trick knife stuck into it (Figure 14.2). This tableau, created in an act of innocent, creative whimsy, takes what is (by agreement) Not Known and Not Said in the world of the apartment building and makes it manifest.

In her monograph *Jean-Pierre Jeunet*, Elizabeth Ezra investigates the motifs of the clown and the circus, and links them to a form of interpersonal decay, arguing that "[t]he circus in Jeunet's film functions as a key site of nostalgia whose eclipse signaled a decline in communal values and social

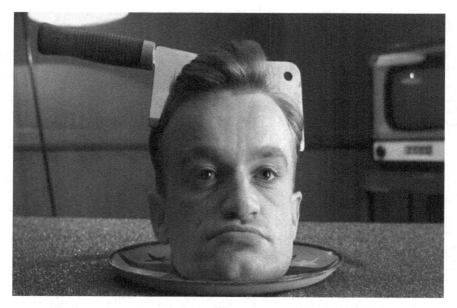

FIGURE 14.2 *The larger question of cannibalism is brought to a head by the butcher's latest potential victim: the child-like Louison (Dominique Pinon). He is a retired clown who practices a circus trick where his head is served on a platter.*

cohesion—in other words, a 'loss of authenticity' that spawned a 'nostalgia for intimate contact.' "[23] Ezra argues that the circus (and by extension, the figure of the clown) belongs to a nostalgic past, of "childlike wonder and slapstick humor, with all the ambiguity that these entail."[24] Louison evokes both sides of this equation, innocent slapstick and gruesome ambiguity, in his butchered-head tableau. When Julie reads his comic creation in the context of the building's dark history, however, she is frozen in terror. Louison opens his eyes and smiles at her, leaving his pose and apologizing for frightening her. Little does the clown know that he has inadvertently made manifest what all in the house (except Julie) have managed to repress.

Ezra explains that the film's viewers only see glimpses of disconnected body parts, such as a bloodied hand in a brief scene during the opening credits, evoking horror more in the audience's imagination than the actual visual display on screen:

> The merging of mutilation with that which has been discarded creates an overdetermined image that points to repression on a number of levels: repression of the memory of physical violence; repression of the ideological and political divisions between collaborator and resistants; and

repression of the fact of the repression itself. That the severed member has been discarded suggests a failure to recognize that repression has occurred, a denial of the severing ties with the past—the mutilation or cutting off of the past is itself discarded, repressed, and unacknowledged.[25]

This circus-trick-scene between the clown and the butcher's daughter begins to unlock the unspoken, and thus strengthens their bond.

The clown's offer of his own head on a platter is a visualization of Julie's worst nightmare. Louison's incorporation of her father's butcher knife into his macabre "still life" heightens the effect, creating a dissonance of fantasy, cruelty, and humor that is at the core of Jeunet's parable about repression and violence. The head's gaze provides another layer of horror that, unlike the meat handed out by the butcher to his clientele—the building's cannibals—cannot be concealed in neat wrappings of opaque brown paper. The act of concealing the origin of the crime—or in this case, of the meat—is part of the rules of the tenants' game of complicity, similar to that which shrouds war crimes in mutually, tacitly agreed-upon silence, often for decades after the crimes themselves have been committed.

Conclusion

The horrors of life in Nazi-occupied Europe were not circumscribed by the fences surrounding the death camps, or by the boundaries of other sites where atrocities were calmly and efficiently carried out. They also occurred—quietly and subtly, all but invisibly—in the ordinary spaces where ordinary men and women, Germans and citizens of the occupied nations alike, did their best to carry on as if nothing had really changed. Doing their jobs, minding their business, they chose to avoid the larger questions that, if asked, could only lead to uncomfortable conclusions. Physically separated from the sites of the atrocities their work helped—however indirectly—to facilitate, they also practiced conceptual separation by choosing *not to know*.

So it is in the microcosmic world within which Jeunet invites his audiences to see the macrocosm of occupied France (and, perhaps, of any society where war forces life-or-death choices on individuals ill-prepared to make them). The horror in *Delicatessen* lies not so much in the actual depiction of food and human meat as abject but in the complicity of the consumers. Throughout the film, Jeunet emphasizes the extent to which, within the building, cannibalism has been naturalized as an everyday occurrence, and the abject quality of raw human meat undermined. When the inhabitants dine on their latest meat allotment they are neither innocent nor skeptical: they consent, fully and knowingly, to the horror of consumption. All who conform to the rules of repression, holding knowledge and guilt equally at bay, thus become, through their silence, collaborators in the crimes themselves.[26]

Notes

1. *Deathfugue* ("Todesfuge") by Paul Celan, translated by Michael Hamburger.
2. The poem was published in 1948.
3. The term *Delikatessen* is of German origin. It is not per se used as a term for butcher/meat market but as an umbrella term for a store that offers delicacies that are rare.
4. The "abject" is referred to in the psychoanalytical tradition of the abhorrent. See Barbara Creed, *The Monstrous-Feminine: Film, Feminism, Psychoanalysis* (London: Routledge, 1993).
5. Stephen Infantino, "Delicatessen: Slices of Postmodern Life," *Arachné* 4, no. 1 (1997): 92.
6. This view of the world after a disaster is reminiscent of Chris Marker's apocalyptic Paris in *La Jetée* (1962). In Jeunet's satire, there are no dictators or malignant scientists who use humans for their experiments as in Marker's film, but it is the average little people in the building who witness atrocities and refuse to stand up against them because they may profit from the crimes themselves. In this way, consuming meat is parallel to being bystanders to crimes against humanity. The threat is not coming from a force outside but is generated and tolerated from within.
7. Infantino, "Delicatessen," 92.
8. Ibid., 94–5.
9. Ibid., 97.
10. Another parallel can be found in Terry Gilliam's work, especially in *Twelve Monkeys* (1995), based on Chris Marker's *La Jetée* (1962).
11. Jack Zipes, *The Enchanted Screen: The Unknown History of Fairy-Tale Films* (New York: Routledge, 2011), 366.
12. Robert O. Paxton, *Vichy France: Old Guard and New Order, 1940–1944* (New York: Columbia University Press, 2001), 19.
13. Ibid., 383.
14. Ibid., 382. See also Deborah Dwork and Robert Jan van Pelt, *The Holocaust: A History* (New York: Norton, 2002).
15. See, for example, John F. Sweets, "Hold That Pendulum! Redefining Fascism, Collaboration, and Resistance in France," *French Historical Studies* 15, no. 4 (Fall 1988): 731–58; and Phillipe Burrin, *Living with Defeat: France under German Occupation, 1940–1944* (London: Hodder, 1996). Chris

Millington, "Vichy France: Collaboration and Resistance," French History Online, https://frenchhistory.files.wordpress.com/2012/12/vichy-france-millington.pdf (accessed February 8, 2016) is a useful overview.

16 Sian Reynolds, "*The Sorrow and the Pity* Revisited or Be Careful, One Train Can Hide Another," *French Cultural Studies* 1, no. 2 (1990): 149.
17 Tony Judt, "Review of *The Sorrow and the Pity, Shoah*, and *Heimat*," *Radical History Review* 41 (Spring 1988): 130.
18 Frederick M. Schweitzer, "Antisemitism and Law," in *Antisemitism in North America: New World, Old Hate*, ed. Stephen K. Baum et al. (Leiden: Brill, 2016), 252.
19 Quoted in "On This Day: 3 July 1987," BBC.co, http://news.bbc.co.uk/onthisday/hi/dates/stories/july/3/newsid_2492000/2492285.stm (accessed February 8, 2016).
20 Omar G. Encarnacion, *Democracy without Justice in Spain: The Politics of Forgetting* (Philadelphia: University of Pennsylvania Press, 2014), 103–104.
21 Rahman Haghighat, *Historical Memories in Culture, Politics and the Future: The Making of History and the World To Come* (New York: Peter Lang, 2014), 80.
22 Ibid.
23 Elizabeth Ezra, *Jean-Pierre Jeunet* (Urbana: University of Illinois Press, 2008), 37.
24 Ibid., 36.
25 Ibid., 29.
26 The authors would like to thank Clémentine Tholas-Disset and Aimee Pozorski for their invaluable feedback.

Bibliography

Burrin, Phillipe. *Living with Defeat: France under German Occupation, 1940–1944*. London: Hodder, 1996.
Creed, Barbara. *The Monstrous-Feminine: Film, Feminism, Psychoanalysis*. London: Routledge, 1993.
Delicatessen. Directed by Jean-Pierre Jeunet. 1991. Santa Monica, CA: Miramax, 2006.
Dwork, Deborah, and Robert Jan van Pelt. *The Holocaust: A History*. New York: Norton, 2002.
Encarnacion, Omar G. *Democracy without Justice in Spain: The Politics of Forgetting*. Philadelphia: University of Pennsylvania Press, 2014.
Ezra, Elizabeth. *Jean-Pierre Jeunet*. Urbana: University of Illinois Press, 2008.
Haghighat, Rahman. *Historical Memories in Culture, Politics and the Future: The Making of History and the World to Come*. New York: Peter Lang, 2014.
Infantino, Stephen. "Delicatessen: Slices of Postmodern Life." *Arachné* 4, no. 1 (1997): 91–100.

Judt, Tony. "Review of *The Sorrow and the Pity, Shoah,* and *Heimat.*" *Radical History Review* 41 (Spring 1988): 129–44.

Millington, Chris. "Vichy France: Collaboration and Resistance." *French History Online.* https://frenchhistory.files.wordpress.com/2012/12/vichy-france-millington.pdf (accessed February 8. 2016).

Paxton, Robert O. *Vichy France: Old Guard and New Order, 1940–1944.* New York: Columbia University Press, 2001.

Reynolds, Sian. "*The Sorrow and the Pity* Revisited or Be Careful, One Train Can Hide Another." *French Cultural Studies* 1, no. 2 (1990): 149–59.

Schweitzer, Frederick M. "Antisemitism and Law." In *Antisemitism in North America: New World, Old Hate,* edited by Stephen K. Baum *et al.,* 225–99. Leiden: Brill, 2016.

Sweets, John F. "Hold That Pendulum! Redefining Fascism, Collaboration, and Resistance in France." *French Historical Studies* 15, no. 4 (Fall 1988): 731–58.

Zipes, Jack. *The Enchanted Screen: The Unknown History of Fairy-Tale Films.* New York: Routledge, 2011.

15

Who Can Be Eaten? Consuming Animals and Humans in the Cannibal-Savage Horror Film

Erin E. Wiegand

Low budget, formulaic, and largely produced in Italy, the "cannibal-savage" exploitation horror genre encompasses fewer than two dozen films released between 1972 and 1988, with its peak years between 1977 and 1981 (the so-called cannibal boom). These films follow a standard narrative in which a party of "civilized" urban protagonists enters the jungle (whether in South America, the Caribbean, or Southeast Asia) and encounters "savage" indigenous people, who subsequently attack, capture, kill, and devour them. In many cases, one or more of the "civilized" protagonists are revealed to have selfish motives for entering the jungle, exploiting indigenous resources and occasionally committing violent acts against the people themselves. Cannibal-savage films, especially before 1982, are also well known for a peculiar and disturbing genre trope: the real killing and, usually, consumption of animals.[1]

This chapter focuses on the relationship between consuming animals and consuming humans in the cannibal-savage genre. On one level, these films make manifest a neocolonial anxiety about Western consumption of the jungle and its inhabitants—that is, within the narrative, colonizers "consume" indigenous land and its resources metaphorically; indigenous people exact revenge by consuming the colonizers literally. But by juxtaposing scenes in which real animals are killed and eaten with scenes in which human beings appear to be killed and eaten—often using real animal entrails to simulate human organs—these films also draw attention to Western cultural anxieties about what it means to be human, the violence inherent in the acquisition of meat, and which animal species are acceptable as part of the human diet—in other words, the questions of who can be eaten and what it says about us.

The savage cannibal

Cannibal-savage films place "civilized" protagonists in opposition to indigenous "cannibal" Others, who are cast in these films as being closer to animals than to human beings. (Among other things, both animals and humans are shown eating raw viscera; additionally, both lack language.) However, as Cary Wolfe and Jonathan Elmer point out, species significations form a kind of grid rather than a simple dividing line, a grid in which we find quadrants of the "animalized animal," the "humanized animal," the "animalized human," and finally, the "wishful category of the *humanized human*, sovereign and untroubled."[2] The distinction, however, only becomes meaningful with a "humanized human"— the nonindigenous outsider—present in the film to create opposition, as well as to observe and comment upon the animalized human others.

This category of "humanized human," however, is nearly always troubled in cannibal-savage films, as "civilized" outsiders reveal themselves be quite "savage" in their treatment of the native people they encounter. The protagonist of *Last Cannibal World* (1977), after escaping from the tribe that has held him captive, rapes one of the tribeswomen, then kills their chief, tears out his heart, and eats it. Similarly, the documentary crew in *Cannibal Holocaust* (1980), who have come to find and film a "savage cannibal" tribe, end up torching a peaceful village, killing their livestock, and raping a woman. (Upon viewing the found footage of the crew's behavior, one character muses, "I wonder who the *real* cannibals are.") Like many horror films, cannibal-savage films explore the fear that "civilization" is merely a mask for an underlying brutal savagery (cannibalism) that lies at the heart of all human animals. While we are clearly positioned to identify with the Western protagonists over the indigenous characters, it is suggested that "we" are nevertheless equally or *more* savage than "them."

In *Cannibal Ferox* (1981), Gloria, a graduate student researching cannibalism, is eager to prove that, as she states in the film, "cannibalism as an organized practice of human society does not exist, and historically has never existed . . . let's say it was an invention of racist colonialism, which had a vested interest in creating the myth of the ferocious, subhuman savage fit only for extermination. The mythical lie of 'cannibal ferox' was only an alibi to justify the greed and cruelty of the *conquistadores*." The film sets up this analysis only to reveal it as well-intentioned naïveté, once Gloria encounters the real cannibals she had sought to disprove the existence of. After she emerges as the only survivor of her party's trek into the jungle, the film cuts to a final scene in which she receives an award for her now-published thesis, *Cannibalism: The End of a Myth*. It is revealed that Gloria has lied about the true fate of her companions and is receiving accolades for having (somehow) disproven the myth of cannibalism.

Perhaps more than any other film, *Cannibal Ferox* gestures toward real-life debates among anthropologists about the extent—or even the very existence—of ritual cannibalism. Gloria's thesis echoes the name and topic of a book by the anthropologist William Arens: *The Man-Eating Myth*, published just two years before the release of *Cannibal Ferox*. Arens's claim was that most if not all reports of ritual cannibalism (as opposed to survival cannibalism, which he acknowledges) were unfounded due to the absence of credible eyewitnesses; his book directly indicted the field of anthropology for being lackluster in gathering clear supporting evidence for claims of cannibalism, inciting a furious debate among anthropologists and garnering attention from the popular press as well. Reflecting on the way in which *Cannibal Ferox* borrows from Arens's book and the controversy around it, Gavin Weston et al. write:

> The irony of using Arens's idea regarding the fabrication of cannibalism as a starting point to show a cannibalistic "other" is perhaps lost on the those who set out to make films where the sine qua non is shot after shot of mud-caked people eating intestines. While there is sympathy for the cannibals across these films, and while the anthropologists are shown to be "on their side," it is hard to watch the films without feeling that their primary objective is to shock viewers rather than to make them question the ethnocentric construct of a cannibalistic or savage Amazonian "other."[3]

While cannibal-savage films do gesture toward the underlying savagery of their "civilized" protagonists, actual indigenous people are still relegated to the role of the savage other; even if their violence is justified retribution, they are still cast as dangerous and predatory. What's more, indigenous actors remain voiceless and nameless within the films' narratives and absent from the credits, accorded the same status within the film as animals and other "natural" features of the films' settings.

Animal violence and consumption

Cannibal films exhibit a simultaneous desire for and fear of the "wild and uncontaminated world" of the jungle (as *The Mountain of the Cannibal God* [1978] proclaims in its opening credits), which they locate in "exotic" locales such as Papua New Guinea, the Amazon, and the Philippines. Several films (including *Cannibal Ferox, Eaten Alive* [1980], and *Cannibal Holocaust*) open with establishing shots that visually juxtapose the city with the jungle: as the protagonists leave their urban environments to enter the jungle, these films frequently include sweeping aerial shots of thick trees and, notably, shots of wildlife.

The inclusion of animal inhabitants of the jungle in these "arrival scenes" might seem to simply flesh out the establishing shots that situate the narrative in a particular place: they are part of the scenery, part of what establishes the jungle as not-city. But throughout these films, animals continue to make their presence felt at incongruous, shocking moments, primarily in scenes of violence and consumption. As human characters make their way through the jungle, the action is interrupted by spliced-in footage of a snake devouring a monkey (*Mountain of the Cannibal God, Eaten Alive*) or lizard (*Last Cannibal World, Primitives* [1980]), or a leopard eating a coati (*Cannibal Ferox*). There are also numerous scenes of humans killing and eating animals ranging from insects and grubs to monitor lizards and turtles to mammals such as monkeys, coatis, and pigs.

These scenes of animal violence and consumption may initially seem to be completely superfluous interruptions of the narrative. In fact, several DVD and Blu-ray releases of the best-known film of the genre, *Cannibal Holocaust*, offer viewers the option of watching the film with the animal death scenes omitted, since the film still works as a coherent whole without them. The scenes, however, serve two critical functions: first, authenticating the narrative, and second, confronting audiences with violations of food taboos, and thus underscoring the ultimate food taboo—cannibalism—that is at the heart of the genre. Taken together, they force viewers to reflect on what it means to be both "human" and "civilized."

The authentic animal death

Cannibal films are frequently invested with the illusion of authenticity and realism: *Last Cannibal World* and *The Man from Deep River* inform the audience in the opening credits that they are "based on a true story," while *Mountain of the Cannibal God* proclaims New Guinea to be "the last region on earth which still contains immense unexplored areas, shrouded in mystery, where life has remained at its primordial level." In this sense, they gesture toward ethnographic and nature documentaries, as well as toward the "mondo" exploitation documentary films of the 1960s and 1970s (e.g., *Mondo Cane* [1962], *Africa Addio* [1966], *Savana Violenta* [1976]), which are often considered to be direct predecessors of the cannibal-horror genre. The "mondo" films pasted together unusual and shocking clips from around the world, many of which were staged or completely faked. Scenes of real animal slaughter, ranging from snakes being skinned in a Singapore marketplace to foie gras production in France, are also commonly found in these films.

Cannibal-savage genre films, like mondo films, use scenes of unsimulated animal slaughter to help authenticate the film and produce a sense of realism—as Erik van Ooijen puts it, they "[rely] on the ability of the indexical body to break through the layers of fictional meaning."[4] Jonathan Burt concurs that violence toward animals in film "breaks the boundary between image and reality . . . the idea that animals represent an insertion of the real or the natural into film is crucial to the question of violence."[5]

The association of animal death with a realist aesthetic was perhaps first articulated by Sergei Eisenstein: about the use of slaughterhouse footage as metaphor for the slaughter of (human) workers in his film *Strike* (1925), Eisenstein explained that the animals stand in for human actors who would—without actually dying—be unable to achieve the desired quality of realism for the greatest impact. He wished "to extract the maximum effect of bloody horror" by filming the actual slaughter of animals, in order to "excise from such a serious scene the falseness that the screen will not tolerate but that is unavoidable in even the most brilliant death scene."[6] In other words, the visceral impact of the animal death sends a more powerful message than a faked human death ever could. Akira Lippit argues, "The actuality of the animal slaughter supercedes the metaphor and imposes from outside the diegesis a taste of death, of the real."[7]

While directors of cannibal-savage films are presumably less invested in conveying political messages to an audience than Eisenstein was—real death is used in these films exploitatively, for "shock" entertainment—the desire of provoking a powerful "effect of bloody horror" remains the same. Here, as in mondo films, the murder and gruesome dismemberment of animals on screen is intended to both add an element of authenticity and elicit visceral reactions from the film's audiences. An infamous scene in *Cannibal Holocaust* in which the filmmakers slaughter a giant river turtle, for example, is really not focused on the *death* of the animal. The death itself happens rather quickly: the turtle's head is chopped off with one stroke of a machete. The focus of this scene

FIGURE 15.1 *In* Cannibal Holocaust, *a character is disgusted by the sight of the turtle's evisceration . . .*

FIGURE 15.2 *. . . but nevertheless eats its cooked flesh.*

is, rather, on the slow dismemberment and disembowelment of the carcass, along with the reactions of the characters watching (one of whom turns away in disgust and vomits) (Figure 15.1). The flesh of the turtle is then cooked and eaten (Figure 15.2).

The same pattern is evident in other films in this genre: in *Eaten Alive* and *Mountain of the Cannibal God*, a monitor lizard is quickly gutted, then skinned;

the camera then zooms in as the body cavity is spread open and the animal's entrails scooped up with bare hands. The camera lingers on this shot, as the human fingers explore the innards of the lizard.[8] A similar scene occurs with a caiman in *Last Cannibal World*. Scenes of animal death are also captured primarily through long takes and with a single camera, with as little editing as possible.

Both academic scholarship and popular writing on cannibal-savage films have all-but-universally connected scenes of animal slaughter to the genre's investment in realism and authenticity (as well as pure shock value) and argue that the inclusion of real death scenes in these films helps boost audience credibility when it comes to simulated human death scenes.[9] In large part, this is also due to the fact that most scholarship on the genre has focused exclusively on *Cannibal Holocaust*, a film that—unlike others in the genre—self-consciously explores questions of veracity and ethics in filmmaking.

Frequently cited as a forerunner of the "found footage" horror film, *Cannibal Holocaust* tells the story of a lost group of documentary filmmakers through a framing story in which their recovered film is screened for a group of television executives. In this recovered footage, filmmakers are shown fomenting an intertribal war and committing acts of rape and murder in the process of making their "documentary." Reflecting on the film's animal death sequences, Neil Jackson argues that

> [b]y blankly recording the bodily contractions and contortions of a body in extremis, the film documents mortal states which reinforce and echo . . . the various instances of simulated human death. The mimetic aspects of the film's violence are therefore absorbed into a discourse which frequently blurs the distinctions to be drawn between simulation and actuality, seeking to further tease the viewer into believing that the human slayings are as genuine as those enacted upon the jungle creatures.[10]

In other words, the role of the animal in the cannibal-savage film is to *stand in* for the human. Especially in films like *Cannibal Holocaust*, which maintains the pretense of containing human snuff footage,[11] authentic animal deaths gesture toward the suggested shock of witnessing real human death. While what is desired by these films' audiences and filmmakers is the witnessing and capturing of the human death, the animal serves as a sufficient substitute.

How is this act of substitution—animal for human—satisfactory? In his book *Violence and the Sacred*, René Girard explores this question as it relates to ritual sacrifice, which has always relied on diverting violence onto a sacrificeable body. He writes that while sacrifice must "conceal the displacement upon which the rite is based," the sacrifice must also bear some resemblance to the original object—he cautions, "this resemblance must not be carried to the extreme of complete assimilation, or it would lead to disastrous confusion. In the case of animal victims the difference is always clear, and no such confusion is possible."[12]

The "horror" of the cannibal-savage film is that it does not abide by these rules of sacrifice—the difference is *not* clear, as human and animal become confused in scenes of cannibalistic violence, when human beings are suddenly "food" as previously only animals had been. What's more, real animal viscera are frequently used in scenes of cannibalism to stand in, convincingly, for human viscera; the effect is potent precisely because it's difficult to tell the difference. When we identify scenes of animal slaughter, as Mikita Brottman does, as having "associated implications of a vicious and abhorrent attitude toward living human beings"[13] as well as having a certain power over our perception of scenes of cannibalism as real and authentic, we acknowledge that there is an uncanny resemblance—too close of a resemblance—between the shrieks of a dying coati and the screams of a dying human, between eating the entrails of a lizard and eating our own.

Clearly, a distinction should be made between violence against animals/humans and the *consumption* of animals/humans—humans may behave violently toward animals for reasons other than food acquisition, such as fear, revulsion, or self-defense. (In several cannibal films, tarantulas and snakes are killed without being eaten.) But because these films deal explicitly with questions of food and consumption—by virtue of their being about cannibalism—it is important to acknowledge a second role played by scenes of animal slaughter: the foregrounding of cultural food taboos.

Food taboos in the cannibal-savage film

Previous scholarship on animal snuff (as well as the accidental killing of animals in the process of filmmaking) has explored questions of when the practice is considered acceptable or justifiable, and when it is seen as revolting and worthy of condemnation.[14] "Acceptable" instances typically fall into two categories. The first applies when the film is considered to possess "redeeming social or artistic value" (as US obscenity laws define it), often because it is the work of a well-regarded "art" director. Examples include Jean-Luc Godard's *Weekend* (1967) and Jean Renoir's *The Rules of the Game* (1939), both of which include scenes of hunting or slaughtering rabbits. The second applies when animals killed in the film were intended for slaughter with or without the camera present; that is, when they are part of an existing animal agricultural system. Examples of scenes covered by the second exemption include the slaughter of a cebu in Francis Ford Coppola's *Apocalypse Now* (1979) and the filming of a cattle slaughterhouse in Rainer Werner Fassbinder's *In a Year of 13 Moons* (1978).[15] Related to this, I would propose that animal slaughter in film is also only considered acceptable when abiding by cultural food taboos dictating *which* animals may be eaten.

In cannibal films, part of what turns the common practice of animal slaughter for meat into a horrific, shocking act is the fact that with few exceptions, the animals being killed and eaten are not commonly considered "food" by Westerners: caimans, snakes, turtles, and monkeys. For Western viewers, these animals are not part of a recognizable system of animal agriculture, despite the fact that they are considered part of an acceptable diet in many other parts of the world. This includes, often, the regions where the cannibal films are made; Deodato, among others, has pointed out that all of the animals killed in his films were indeed eaten by the indigenous actors.

What's more, the disgust provoked by some scenes of animal slaughter and consumption hinges on what parts of the animal are eaten, and how they are eaten. Meat is used, in this instance, to demonstrate the animal-like savagery of indigenous characters and to juxtapose them with "civilized" protagonists. While the latter may kill animals for food as well, they are usually only shown eating cooked meat, which often no longer resembles their prey; both animals and indigenous people, in contrast, are portrayed eating raw viscera with their bare hands. In *Mountain of the Cannibal God*, for example, an indigenous man is shown skinning a snake with his teeth, while in another scene, others eat the raw organs of a disemboweled lizard. These displays of "savagery" echo earlier scenes in which a small monkey is devoured alive by a snake and a crocodile eats a monitor lizard: human predators are depicted similarly to animal ones. The "civilized" protagonists, in contrast, eat only the cooked meat of crabs they have caught—fare that would not be out of place in an expensive restaurant. Moreover, in this as well as most of the other films surveyed here, animal viscera are prominently displayed and sometimes eaten by indigenous characters.

Following Claude Levi-Strauss's work on "the raw and the cooked," anthropologist Nick Fiddes argues that cooking is a primary characteristic distinguishing nature (raw) from culture (cooked). In particular, he identifies the importance of the cooking of meat: "Raw meat, dripping blood, is what is eaten by wild, carnivorous animals, not by civilised humans . . . Raw meat is bestial and cooking sets us apart."[16] What's more, cooking meat also may serve to distance ourselves from its origins. "Cooking ameliorates the stark animality of the flesh, by altering its colour, imposing a human hallmark since we are the only species to possess this skill, and confirming, beyond doubt, the death of the beast."[17] In other words, the transformation of beast to meat, and thus the dissociation of meat from a living creature who was slaughtered and butchered, is made complete with the transformation of the flesh from red to brown, from raw to cooked.[18]

Finally, and perhaps most importantly, these scenes foreground the process of butchering as a part of the meat-acquisition process, making explicit the violence contained within the practice of meat consumption, no matter what animal is the source of the meat. By showing in gruesome detail animals being killed, disemboweled, and eaten, these films reveal what Carol Adams calls the absent referent of meat: "that which separates the meat eater from the animal and the animal from the end product. The function of the absent referent is to keep our 'meat' separated from any idea that she or he was once an animal . . . meat becomes unanchored by its original referent (the animal), becoming instead a free-floating image."[19]

Norbert Elias points out that this disassociation between "meat" and "slaughtered animal" arises as part of what he calls the "civilizing process." In the upper classes of medieval European society, he notes, the entire dead animal or large portions of it were served and carved at the table. But over time, a shift occurred, and indications that meat comes from a dead animal began to be avoided. Elias writes:

> In many of our meat dishes the animal form is so concealed and changed by the art of its preparation and carving that while eating one is scarcely reminded of its origin . . . people, in the course of the civilizing process, seek to suppress in themselves every characteristic that they feel to be "animal." They likewise suppress such characteristics in their food.[20]

Among the lower classes, however—those who must slaughter the animals and pluck or dismember them in order to turn them into "food"—the connection between animal and meat remains palpable.

In an ethnographic study of slaughterhouse work and the politics of sight, Timothy Pachirat draws upon Elias's work to point out that what kind of violence against animals human beings are capable of "standing the sight of" varies across cultures and time periods. Pity and other emotions, such as disgust, are "an emotive response that becomes increasingly refined and widespread . . . [with] the advancement of a civilizing process that has as its central mechanism concealment and distance."[21] Our shock at the sight of slaughter and our pity for the animals killed is not a "natural" response but one generated by unfamiliarity—the product of a culture in which slaughter is generally concealed from sight. For those who are accustomed to treating living animals as incipient food products—those on the farm or in the slaughterhouse—shock is usually nullified. When "civilized" humans react with shock to the sight of an animal's slaughter, "it is a reaction predicated on the operations that remove from sight, without actually eliminating, equally shocking practices required to sustain the orbit of their everyday lives."[22]

When asked during an interview about the slaughter of animals in *Cannibal Holocaust*, Ruggero Deodato admitted that he would not do it again were he to make a film today. He reasons that "times have changed. When I was a child I lived in the country and it was normal to see a chicken, a rabbit, or a pig being killed. Today my daughter sees it and becomes distressed."[23] That is, like Elias and Pachirat, Deodato identifies a "modern" disconnect between the killing of an animal for food and its consumption as meat.

Erik van Ooijen argues that while films like *Cannibal Holocaust* are condemned for their cruelty to animals, in fact they may draw back the curtain on meat as a "reification of violence":

> We may actually find an ethical and political potential in the depicted dismembering of animals as contrasted to the purely reified presentation of a steak or a hamburger in, for example, a seemingly harmless romantic comedy. In both cases, deadly violence is an inevitable part of movie production, but while the mainstream comedy conceals real violence in the reified props of fictional meaning, exploitation cinema uses indexical presence in making strange our ideological relationship to food as pure commodity.[24]

That is, van Ooijen identifies a certain hypocrisy at work in ethical critiques of scenes of animal slaughter, when we consider that they simply show first-hand what most people participate in on a daily basis through eating meat. Of course, it is unlikely that most viewers of cannibal-savage films are aware of the cognitive dissonance provoked by these scenes, or that they change their behavior or mindset accordingly—that is, by becoming vegetarian or by becoming more closely attuned to where their meat comes from. In part, this is due to the breaking of food taboos mentioned earlier: eating the raw brains of a monkey may simply be too far removed from eating a cooked hamburger for most viewers to make a connection between the two. Still, van Ooijen's observation raises questions about *how* such scenes could be read politically when cultural attitudes about diet—as well as attitudes about the ethical considerations human beings should have for animals in general—are so resistant to challenges.

Who can be eaten?

Jeremy Bentham famously proposed changing the form of the question used to judge what rights humans should provide nonhuman animals. Rather than asking whether animals can reason, he argued, we must ask: "Can they suffer?" Jacques Derrida notes that Bentham's question shifts the issue from an active to a passive stance; to suffer implies incapacity, an inability to act, a lack of power. " 'Can they suffer?' amounts to asking 'can they *not be able?*' . . . Being able to suffer is no longer a power; it is a possibility without power, a possibility of the impossible. Mortality resides there, as the most radical means of thinking the finitude that we share with animals, the mortality that belongs to the very finitude of life."[25]

It is in part because of this that we disavow our connection with other animals, with our shared vulnerability and mortality. Yet one of the most important lessons we might take from Derrida is that any disavowal still leaves a trace of itself. We find this trace returning in the cannibal film in two ways: first, in parallels between human and animal savagery (as problematic as that may be); and second, in the highlighting of what Derrida calls "the possibility of nonpower"[26] shared by humans and nonhumans—the presentation of human beings as "able to be eaten" in the same way that animals are. As a hunter proclaims in *Emanuelle and the Last Cannibals* (1977), "You have to share risks with the animals. Man, too, can be hunted." (Subsequently, he and his wife are captured, killed, and eaten by an indigenous tribe.)

What the cannibal films trouble—violently and horrifically—is what is normally taken for granted: the animal can be eaten while the human cannot be. Cora Diamond argues that meat eating is a core element of learning what it is to be human—that is, to be different from animal. "We learn what a human being is in—among other ways—sitting at a table where *WE* eat *THEM*. We are around the table and they are on it."[27] In this sense, the fear of being food for another—of being the one on the table—is linked to a fear of not being human.

Interestingly, this fear does not seem to exist—at least, not in the same way—within the actual indigenous cultures portrayed in the cannibal-savage films. The anxieties that these films attempt to work through may only be those of the filmmakers and their audiences, not of the "savages" being filmed and represented.[28] In his work with the Runa of Ecuador's Upper Amazon, anthropologist Eduardo Kohn finds that when the Runa hunt animals for food, they enter into a "web of relations" with those animals as well as everything else in our shared environment with them. "One's ability to destroy other selves rests on and also highlights the fact that one is an ephemeral self—a self that can all too quickly cease being a self."[29] Similarly, Tim Ingold argues that hunter-gatherer societies understand how "humans are, indeed, just like other animals . . . by virtue of their mutual involvement, as undivided centers of action and awareness, within a continuous life process."[30] And Eduardo Viveiros de Castro notes that in some Amazonian societies, nonhumans are considered to have a sort of spirit or personhood equal to that possessed by humans—they simply have different bodies and thus different perspectives. He writes:

> All of the inhabitants of the cosmos are people in their own department, potential occupants of the deictical "first person" position in cosmological discourse: interspecies relations are marked by a perpetual dispute surrounding this position, which is schematized in terms of the predator/prey polarity, agency or subjecthood being above all a capacity for predation.[31]

This inverts the common message of the cannibal-savage film, which is that human beings are little more than savage animals at heart. Instead, we are all people—though people whose basic mode of relating to each other is rooted in predation. What the cannibal-savage films cast as terrifying and horrific, then, is what the indigenous cultures they depict take as a given: we can *all* be eaten.

Notes

1. The parameters of the genre are somewhat nebulous: not all films associated with what I am here calling "cannibal-savage" horror actually show graphic depictions of cannibalism; they are alternately referred to as "jungle" films, connecting them with a long tradition of Western obsession with the savage, the uncivilized, and the untamed. (For example, the colonial fiction of Edgar Wallace and H. Rider Haggard, Tarzan and Sheena stories, early travel documentaries, and adventure films.) Additionally, not all films of the genre contain scenes of animal slaughter, although they can be found in the most popular and best-known examples of the genre: *Last Cannibal World* (Ruggero Deodato, 1977); *Mountain of the Cannibal God* (Sergio Martino, 1978); *Cannibal Holocaust* (Ruggero Deodato, 1980); *Eaten Alive* (Umberto Lenzi, 1980); and *Cannibal Ferox* (Umberto Lenzi, 1981).
2. Cary Wolfe and Jonathan Elmer, "Subject to Sacrifice: Ideology, Psychoanalysis, and the Discourse of Species in Jonathan Demme's *Silence of the Lambs*," *boundary 2* 22, no. 3 (Autumn 1995): 147.
3. Gavin Weston et al. "Anthropologists in Films: 'The Horror! The Horror!'" *American Anthropologist* 117, no. 2 (2015): 321.

4. Erik Van Ooijen, "Cinematic Shots and Cuts: On the Ethics and Semiotics of Real Violence in Film Fiction," *Journal of Aesthetics and Culture* 3 (2001): 10.
5. Jonathan Burt, *Animals in Film* (London: Reaktion Books, 2002), 136.
6. Quoted in Akira Lippit, "The Death of an Animal," *Film Quarterly* 56, no. 1 (2002): 14.
7. Ibid.
8. It is, in fact, *exactly* the same scene in these two films—the footage in *Eaten Alive* has been reused from the earlier film, along with another scene of a monkey being swallowed by a snake.
9. Cf. Neil Jackson, "Cannibal Holocaust, Realist Horror, and Reflexivity," *Post Script: Essays in Film and the Humanities* 21, no. 3 (2002): 32–55; Julian Petley, "Cannibal Holocaust and the Pornography of Death," in *The Spectacle of the Real*, ed. Geoff King (Bristol, UK: Intellect Books, 2005), 173–85; Carolina Jauregui, "'Eat It Alive and Swallow It Whole': Resavoring Cannibal Holocaust as a Mockumentary," *Invisible Culture* 7 (2004), https://ivc.lib.rochester.edu/eat-it-alive-and-swallow-it-whole-resavoring-cannibal-holocaust-as-a-mockumentary (accessed January 6, 2016); Ed Morgan, "Cannibal Holocaust: Digesting and Re-digesting Law and Film," *Southern California Interdisciplinary Law Journal* 16 (2006): 555–70; David Kerekes and David Slater, *Killing for Culture: An Illustrated History of Death Film from Mondo to Snuff* (London: Creation Books, 1995).
10. Neil Jackson, "Cannibal Holocaust, Realist Horror, and Reflexivity," *Post Script: Essays in Film and the Humanities* 21, no. 3 (2002): 41.
11. Director Ruggero Deodato intentionally fostered rumors that several actors had been killed during the making of the film, and he was actually brought to trial for allegations that *Cannibal Holocaust* was in fact a snuff film. Charges were thrown out when the ostensibly murdered actors appeared in court (Andrew DeVos, "The More You Rape Their Senses, the Happier They Are: A History of *Cannibal Holocaust*," in *Cinema Inferno: Celluloid Explosions from the Cultural Margins*, ed. Robert G. Weiner and John Cline (Lanham, MD: Scarecrow Press, 2010), 76–100). Interestingly, the court then replaced the murder charges with ones of animal cruelty, invoking a little-used law that had initially been intended to outlaw bullfighting; in court as well as in the film itself, animals are used as substitutes for humans.
12. René Girard, *Violence and the Sacred* (Baltimore: Johns Hopkins University Press, 1977), 11.
13. Mikita Brottman, *Meat Is Murder! An Illustrated Guide to Cannibal Culture* (London: Creation Books, 2001), 138.
14. Cf. Simon Hobbs, "Animal Snuff," in *Snuff: Real Death and Screen Media*, ed. Neil Jackson et al. (New York: Bloomsbury, 2016); and van Ooijen, "Cinematic Shots and Cuts."
15. Both films, of course, would likely fall into the first category as well.
16. Nick Fiddes, *Meat: A Natural Symbol* (London: Routledge, 1991), 89.
17. Ibid., 114.

18 Of course, many "civilized" cuisines contain raw meat dishes, such as sushi or steak tartare. However, these are still carefully prepared and are often associated with sophisticated culinary skills; the raw meat is thus still transformed in order to distinguish it from its original form. To eat a plate of sushi is quite different from eating an entire raw fish.
19 Carol J. Adams, *The Sexual Politics of Meat* (New York: Continuum, 2010), 13.
20 Norbert Elias, *The Civilizing Process* (New York: Urizen Books, 1978), 120.
21 Timothy Pachirat, *Every Twelve Seconds: Industrialized Slaughter and the Politics of Sight* (New Haven: Yale University Press, 2011), 251.
22 Ibid.
23 Quoted in van Ooijen, "Cinematic Shots and Cuts," 11.
24 Ibid., 11–12.
25 Jacques Derrida, *The Animal That Therefore I Am* (New York: Fordham University Press, 2008), 28; italics in original.
26 Ibid.
27 Cora Diamond, "Eating Meat and Eating People," *Philosophy* 53, no. 206 (1978): 470.
28 Director Eli Roth reports that in the process of filming his homage to the genre, *The Green Inferno* (2015), he showed *Cannibal Holocaust* to the tribe he had hired to act in his movie. According to Roth, "They thought it was the funniest thing that they had ever seen." See Ali Plumb, "Eli Roth Talks *The Green Inferno*," *Empire Online* (February 5, 2013), http://www.empireonline.com/movies/news/eli-roth-talks-green-inferno (accessed December 9, 2015), paragraph 6.
29 Eduardo Kohn, *How Forests Think: Toward an Anthropology beyond the Human* (Berkeley and Los Angeles: University of California Press, 2013), 17.
30 Tim Ingold, "Hunting and Gathering as Ways of Perceiving the Environment," in *Animals and the Human Imagination*, ed. Aaron Gross and Anne Vallely (New York: Columbia University Press, 2012), 49.
31 Quoted in Pierre Clastres, *Archaeology of Violence* (Cambridge: Semiotext(e), 2010), 47.

Bibliography

Adams, Carol J. *The Sexual Politics of Meat*. New York: Continuum, 2010.
Brottman, Mikita. *Meat Is Murder! An Illustrated Guide to Cannibal Culture*. London: Creation Books, 2001.
Burt, Jonathan. *Animals in Film*. London: Reaktion Books, 2002.
Clastres, Pierre. *Archaeology of Violence*. Cambridge: Semiotext(e), 2010.

Derrida, Jacques. *The Animal That Therefore I Am*. New York: Fordham University Press, 2008.

DeVos, Andrew. "The More You Rape Their Senses, the Happier They Are: A History of *Cannibal Holocaust*." In *Cinema Inferno: Celluloid Explosions from the Cultural Margins*, edited by Robert G. Weiner and John Cline, 76–100. Lanham, MD: Scarecrow Press, 2010.

Diamond, Cora. "Eating Meat and Eating People." *Philosophy* 53, no. 206 (1978): 465–79.

Elias, Norbert. *The Civilizing Process*. New York: Urizen Books, 1978.

Fiddes, Nick. *Meat: A Natural Symbol*. London: Routledge, 1991.

Girard, René. *Violence and the Sacred*. Baltimore: Johns Hopkins University Press, 1977.

Hobbs, Simon. "Animal Snuff." In *Snuff: Real Death and Screen Media*, edited by Neil Jackson, Shaun Kimber, Johnny Walker, and Thomas Joseph Watson, 63–80. New York: Bloomsbury, 2016.

Ingold, Tim. "Hunting and Gathering as Ways of Perceiving the Environment." In *Animals and the Human Imagination*, edited by Aaron Gross and Anne Vallely, 32–54. New York: Columbia University Press, 2012.

Jackson, Neil. "Cannibal Holocaust, Realist Horror, and Reflexivity." *Post Script: Essays in Film and the Humanities* 21, no. 3 (2002): 32–55.

Jauregui, Carolina. "'Eat It Alive and Swallow It Whole': Resavoring Cannibal Holocaust as a Mockumentary." *Invisible Culture* 7 (2004). https://ivc.lib.rochester.edu/eat-it-alive-and-swallow-it-whole-resavoring-cannibal-holocaust-as-a-mockumentary (accessed January 6, 2016).

Kerekes, David, and David Slater. *Killing for Culture: An Illustrated History of Death Film from Mondo to Snuff*. London: Creation Books, 1995.

Kohn, Eduardo. *How Forests Think: Toward an Anthropology beyond the Human*. Berkeley and Los Angeles: University of California Press, 2013.

Lippit, Akira. "The Death of an Animal." *Film Quarterly* 56, no. 1 (2002): 9–22.

Morgan, Ed. "Cannibal Holocaust: Digesting and Re-digesting Law and Film." *Southern California Interdisciplinary Law Journal* 16 (2006): 555–70.

Pachirat, Timothy. *Every Twelve Seconds: Industrialized Slaughter and the Politics of Sight*. New Haven: Yale University Press, 2011.

Petley, Julian. "Cannibal Holocaust and the Pornography of Death." In *The Spectacle of the Real*, edited by Geoff King, 173–85. Bristol, UK: Intellect Books, 2005.

Plumb, Ali. "Eli Roth Talks *The Green Inferno*." *Empire Online*, February 5, 2013. http://www.empireonline.com/movies/news/eli-roth-talks-green-inferno (accessed December 9, 2015).

Van Ooijen, Erik. "Cinematic Shots and Cuts: On the Ethics and Semiotics of Real Violence in Film Fiction." *Journal of Aesthetics and Culture* 3 (2001): 1–15.

Weston, Gavin, Jamie F. Lawson, Mwenza Blell, and John Hayton. "Anthropologists in Films: 'The Horror! The Horror!'" *American Anthropologist* 117, no. 2 (2015): 316–28.

Wolfe, Cary, and Jonathan Elmer. "Subject to Sacrifice: Ideology, Psychoanalysis, and the Discourse of Species in Jonathan Demme's *Silence of the Lambs*." *boundary 2* 22, no. 3 (Autumn 1995): 141–70.

PART FOUR

You Are What You Eat

16

"You Are What Others Think You Eat": Food, Identity, and Subjectivity in Zombie Protagonist Narratives

LuAnne Roth

Few figures have evolved to meet the American appetite for monsters like the zombies that shuffle across the cultural landscape. While the shambling undead might seem to be one-dimensional, there is far more depth to them than first meets the eye. Zombies are "symbolically prolific and textually ubiquitous,"[1] functioning as a barometer of social and psychological preoccupations.[2] Since the earliest days of legends about zombies, the living dead have functioned as a means of addressing societal fears and anxieties. In many ways, zombies seem to be empty screens onto which the fantasies and fears of the living are projected. Since their cinematic debut in *White Zombie* (1932), they have served as metaphors for such cultural fears as aging/death/decay, bioterrorism, cannibalism, capitalist consumption, communism, contagion, immigration, racism, and slavery, among others. In fact, as zombies evolve from decade to decade, they rise ironically to feed the seemingly insatiable hunger of the living (and respond to current fixations).[3]

As a folklorist and scholar of foodways, I am particularly intrigued by food-related aspects of the current zombie craze, a heretofore-unexplored area of study. "Foodways" refers to the system of cultural, social and economic practices relating to the production and consumption of food. The goal of studying foodways is to make *explicit* what is otherwise *implicit* about a society's food,[4] and this chapter examines contemporary cinematic discourse surrounding the foodways of the living dead.[5] One of the characteristics oft-noted by the living about zombies is their *unheimliche* (unhomey/unfamiliar) nature.[6] In fact, as the zombified parody of Norman Rockwell's iconographic *Freedom From Want* painting suggests, the consumption behaviors of this folk group, as imagined by the living, are actually quite familiar (Figure 16.1).[7] Complex and contested, zombie foodways embody many of the same concerns that plague the living.

FIGURE 16.1 Freedom From Want (of Brains) *parodies Norman Rockwell's 1943 patriotic painting* Freedom From Want.

Zombie foodways on screen: a brief history

In the first thirty years of zombie cinema, zombies were seen as being under the control of their creators and masters. Nothing was said about what, whether, or how zombies ate. Discourse about zombie foodways did not enter the mainstream until 1968, when George Romero's cult classic *Night of the Living Dead* famously liberated zombies from their roots in slavery, transforming them from docile, mind-controlled bodies into relentless cannibalistic ghouls that attack humans and replicate through infection and death.[8] One scene, shot in lurid detail, shows zombies feasting on the bodies of teenage lovers Tom and Judy, who are killed when a truck explodes.[9] Upon seeing the charred leftovers of the couple, the Sheriff quips, "Somebody sure had a cookout here."

Another scene depicts the inevitable moment when the zombies break into the farmhouse where the living characters have been hiding. Barbra (Judith O'Dea) is dragged by her zombified brother, Johnny (Russell Streiner), into the middle of a zombie mob where, one can assume, she is devoured. Back in the cellar, Helen (Marilyn Eastman) encounters her newly zombified daughter, Karen (Kyra Schon), who is busy eating her father's arm, her mouth dripping with blood. Karen drops the arm and turns to pursue her mother instead. Even in black and white, the scene oozed gruesomeness, shocking audiences, arousing disgust and revulsion, and immediately shifting the paradigm of zombie narratives to follow. Close-up shots of the "marauding ghouls" eating human flesh made stomachs turn, and the macabre picnic twisted Anthelme Brillat-Savarin's claim, "You are what you eat" into "you are *who* you eat." Today, scenes of zombies consuming bodies of the living have become a genre motif, so that modern audiences approach zombie films with expectations of the living as prey for the dead.

Threats to personal, social, and national security are often depicted as outsiders or Others. "Whether in reference to criminal outsiders, sexual 'deviants,' or international 'terrorist' threats," Sasha Cocarla explains, "the representation of this other is always-already made monstrous."[10] The "Other-as-monster" enables creative, even playful, expression of general social anxieties and fears. "On a more insidious level," Cocarla adds:

> [T]he filmic monster lurking in the closet or eating your neighbor's brain is imbued with traits that are already deemed culturally deviant/strange/excessive/unnecessary. In this respect, this symbolic representation further vilifies, marginalizes, and ostracizes real people and experiences, while at the same time it further perpetuates mainstream, hegemonic ideals.[11]

Throughout time, people have been similarly "Othered" according to the food they are presumed to eat, the relevant equation being "strange people equals strange food."[12] In fact, one of the things that most distinguishes modern zombies as monsters (besides, of course, their undeadness) is their "strange" food behavior. Drawn to the sound (and smell) of other zombies feeding, zombies are like living humans in that they like to gather in groups when feasting. Beyond such accusations of "horde-like behavior," zombies are charged with having "nasty table manners, turning everything into finger food."[13]

In Romero's series of zombie films (and the plethora that followed), zombies become identified with consumption. As soon as the zombie developed into a flesh-eater, and became conflated with the "ravenous corporeality" of the cannibal, this new configuration "proved so effective that flesh eating was quickly established as the core trait of the cinematic zombie."[14] Following the success of *Night of the Living Dead*, countless scenes in film (and other cultural texts) have depicted zombies in gory close-up, ripping, grasping, pulling, and chewing flesh, in defiance of "civilized" manners, eating utensils, meal conversation, or cleanliness.

Diverse theories have been posited to explain why zombies specifically crave brains, revealing a high degree of uncertainty among the living regarding the Other's foodways. Actually, this preoccupation with brains has not always been the case. Romero's "marauding ghouls" were not picky, gnawing on a variety of body parts ranging from fingers to viscera, and even an insect. The idea that zombies crave brains came later, seemingly introduced in Dan O'Bannon's *Return of the Living Dead* (1985), a film that also broke with Romero by featuring zombies that can talk and cannot be killed by a well-placed shot to the head.[15] O'Bannon's zombies verbalized their cravings with the now-iconic line of dialogue "more brains" and explained—in a memorable scene showing the torso of a female zombie being interrogated while tied to a gurney—that zombies can feel themselves rotting and brains help "relieve the pain of being dead."

The notion of zombies specifically craving brains persisted and has subsequently been reinforced in myriad forms of popular culture, but O'Bannon's notions of zombies as rational eaters, consuming brains for a *reason*, more or less faded away, replaced by zombies that eat mindlessly and compulsively. Romero's second zombie film, *Dawn of the Dead* (1978), had already established the idea that "the ghouls . . . represent consumers on the most fundamental and primitive level (all they do is take, and what they take is food),"[16] and that idea remained powerfully resonant. The numerous disgusting scenes in *Dawn* and subsequent films showing close-up shots of zombies eating reinforce the idea that zombies eat not for sustenance, but "simply for the sake of eating."[17] As the ultimate consumers, therefore, zombies search for satisfaction through compulsive material acquisition.[18] If the Haitian zombie represents the slave of colonialism, *Dawn of the Dead*'s zombies "are a gross exaggeration of the late-capitalist bourgeoisie: blind consumption without any productive contribution."[19] These zombies are infected with Aristotle's *pleonexia*, "the disposition to have more."[20] Zombies devour human beings in lieu of televisions, computers, or clothing. "They can be understood to be an embodiment of the id," ruled entirely by their appetites.[21] Zombie foodways, in that respect, reveal something about the culture of the living.[22]

Beyond brains: food and the comedic zombie

Recently, zombie film narratives have been moving beyond the compulsive-brain-eating stereotype, developing more nuanced protagonists who reflect on, struggle with, or are empowered by their relationship to food and eating. Kyle William Bishop notes that in pre-Romero zombie narratives, no attempt was made to encourage psychological connection between zombie and audience.[23] "Romero employs a variety of filmmaking techniques over the course of his zombie films," explains Bishop, "to shift the loyalty of his viewers from character to character and ultimately from human to zombie, causing the audience to consider the role of the living dead in progressively different ways."[24] These narratives bestow the "evolved zombies" with identities, personalities, motivations, and humanity. The humans in these stories are not necessarily humane, and the zombies are not necessarily monstrous. Cinematic and editing techniques foster audience identification with and sympathy for zombies, while narrative and dialogue "attempt to align audience sympathies with the zombies instead of the rather inhuman humans."[25] Bishop, drawing in particular upon Kaja Silverman's theory of psychological suture, points out scenes in which the filmmakers' placement of the camera and composition of individual shots encourage viewers to take the camera's perspective as their own.[26] This process also occurs through editing and the assembly of shots—for example, the shot/reverse shot construction, eyeline match, and the use of "i-camera"—allowing the viewer to identify with the fictional character through subjective points of view and functioning, ultimately, to enable audience members to experience genuine sympathy for the characters on-screen. The result of these narrative, cinematic, and editing developments is "a steady increase in audience sympathy for zombies," which even enables living audiences to root for the plight of the zombies.[27]

In fact, scholars such as Dave Beisecker take issue with the common assumption that zombies represent the Other, arguing that

> far too much has been made of the zombie as "Other," not just because the idea isn't literally true, but also because it has become increasingly uninteresting and unproductive. To think of them as some unredeemable alien threat only serves to excavate an unacceptable moral gulf between us that threatens to disconnect us from the potential zombie lurking within each and every one of us. After all, the whole poignancy of a zombie rebellion . . . is that the zombies really are us (or at least what remains of us after we've changed).[28]

Many scholars of zombie films claim that, unlike their undead vampire cousins, zombies are asexual. "In spite of the obvious analogies," notes Darren Elliott-Smith, "the exposure of internal bodily spaces, bodily fluids and primal urges, it [the zombie] has remained largely an anti-erotic object."[29] Yet the connection between eating, hunger, and sexuality must be considered in the case of zombies. "Eating is not really a metaphor for the sexual act," writes feminist scholar Susan Bordo, "rather, the sexual act . . . is imagined as itself an act of eating, of incorporation and destruction of the object of desire."[30] Although writing specifically about perceptions of female sexuality, Bordo's argument becomes relevant to zombies since, in many zombie stories, the act of eating is equated with sexual desire.[31] Steven Shaviro argues, in this vein, that Romero's "postmodern zombie as a critique of the Western capitalist system perpetuated on mindless consumption" may also be read erotically.

> In terms of erotic pleasure, it is via the viewers' identification with the victims on film during the zombies' attacks that they are subjected to both a threat of penetration and of being devoured. This can be paralleled with the subject's fear of his/her body being penetrated or consumed by another (sexually or otherwise) or, worse still, a fear of *actually enjoying* it . . . [T]he voyeuristic anticipation of watching and waiting for the zombies to attack their victims provides an erotic frisson of passive pleasure as a spectator which works to titillate the viewer, encouraging enjoyment in the implied orgasmic intensity of the climatic attack.[32]

While Elliot-Smith, following Shaviro, theorizes that erotic pleasure stems from the audience's identification with the living victims who experience bodily violation, I argue that zombie-as-protagonist narratives just as readily stimulate erotic pleasure through eating behavior, as several examples from heterosexual and homosexual zombie romance narratives reveal.

In the film *Graveyard Alive: A Zombie Nurse in Love* (2003), for example, this connection between food and sexual craving is made explicit. The female protagonist, a shy nurse named Patsy Powers (Anne Day-Jones), becomes "a flesh eating sex kitten" after being bitten by a zombified male hospital patient. Before-and-after scenes depict Patsy's changing relationship with both food and sex. Before becoming a zombie, Patsy's diet is shown to be as dull and empty as her social life. She either sits in her basement apartment joylessly eating frozen dinners while watching televised hospital soap operas or, during her breaks at the hospital, munches on raw carrots while reading romance novels. This food behavior contrasts with that of her coworkers, who laugh and heartily socialize during lunch breaks. Ironically, becoming undead allows Patsy to come alive, empowering her with a sense of sexual confidence that quickly catches the attention of men around her. In one scene, Dr. Dox (Karl Gerhardt) courts Patsy by preparing a romantic home-cooked spaghetti meal. However, Patsy now finds herself repulsed by the food of the living and refuses to eat even one bite of the pasta. In a subsequent scene, Patsy invites the amorous doctor to her apartment, where the camera peers through the window to show that her dinner preparations involve running raw meat through a grinder. Scenes elsewhere suggest that this meat derives from a deceased patient at the hospital's morgue. During their dinner, brief images show Patsy and Dr. Dox eating and drinking with gusto, an act equating Patsy's newly awakened sexuality with her new appetite for fleshy food. She goes from mindlessly eating the bland food of the living to mindfully eating food made *from* the living.

The sexual appetite of zombies may also be framed through narratives about deliberate abstinence. In the musical *Zombie Love* (2007), the 200-year-old zombie protagonist Dante (Brad Culver) comes to realize while eating human flesh that there is more to life than eating. This revelation occurs just prior to his "love at first sight" moment with a mortal woman. Dante's attraction to Claudia (Esme Allen) compels him to reflect upon, and then resist, his ravenous hunger for living flesh. Similarly, in the Irish high-school comedy *Boy Eats Girl* (2005), the teenage male lead, Nathan (David Leon), is accidentally killed and then resurrected as a zombie through his mother's pagan magical rituals. Unaware of his new undead condition, Nathan awakens hungry and goes to the fridge. He tries to eat "healthy" foods—carrots, apples, and yogurt—but spits them out in disgust because they taste rotten to his changing taste buds. The rest of the film balances Nathan's attraction and desire for Jessica (Samantha Mumba) with his efforts to avoid succumbing to his physical hunger. As the zombie epidemic spreads throughout the high school community, "Nathan's life as a zombie both allows him more agency (he controls his hunger better than anyone else in the film, and remains intelligent and aware) and is eventually cured."[33] In the end, as with Patsy in *Graveyard Alive*, Nathan's zombification creates a new beginning.

While these three narratives reinforce the post-Romero stereotype that zombies crave human flesh, they also problematize that assumption with thoughtful, self-reflexive zombies who struggle with their bodily cravings and personal food choices. Similarly, in *Warm Bodies*, the 2010 novel from which the 2013 Hollywood blockbuster was adapted, the protagonist, R, reflects on his personal foodways early on: "Eating is not a pleasant business. I chew off a man's arm, and I hate it. I hate his screams, because I don't like pain. I don't like hurting people, but this is the world now. This is what we do. Of course if I don't eat all of him, if I spare his brain, he'll rise up and follow me back to the airport, and that might make me feel better. I'll introduce him to everyone, and maybe we'll stand around and groan for a while."[34]

In the world of *Warm Bodies*, zombies will eat any flesh, but they do, in fact, specifically crave brains because eating brains causes intensely realistic flashbacks of the victim's life. "As always, I go straight for the good part, the part that makes my head light up like a picture tube. I eat the brain, and for about thirty seconds, I have memories. Flashes of parades, perfume, music . . . life. Then it fades, and I get up, and we all stumble out of the city, still cold and gray, but feeling a little better. Not 'good,' exactly, not 'happy,' certainly not 'alive,' but . . . a little less dead. This is the best we can do."[35] R's self-reflection addresses important epistemological and ontological concerns. Early on, R kills and takes a bite from the brain of Julie's boyfriend, Perry. R decides to bring Julie and the leftovers of Perry's brain back to the airport. Sasha Cocarla's analysis of this scene reveals the complex motivations behind R's craving:

> Instead of instantly devouring every morsel of it, embracing his zombie instincts, R instead decides to ration Perry's brain and savor each bite he takes. As he slowly consumes it, he is continuously flooded with Perry's memories, including moments from his childhood, the moment he first met Julie, the deepening of their romantic feelings for one another, his father's death, and the moment that R killed him. With each influx of new memories, R longs for more, but it is not more brains that he is longing for. Instead, he longs for the familiarity of Perry; his memories seem so familiar in that it is detailing a life that R once had himself. Through the consumption of Perry's brain, Perry's memories become R's memories; Perry's feelings and emotions begin to become R's feelings and emotions. It is almost a complete envelopment of one into the other.[36]

Literary theorist Sarah Sceats writes that although "[u]neaten food is 'other,' part of the world outside," at some point, "its status changes as it is taken in to the mouth, is chewed, swallowed, digested. At what point does it become part of us?"[37] In philosopher Carolyn Korsmeyer's view, as "[t]he objects of taste are taken into one's own body; they become one."[38] Eating, therefore, is not only biological, but also symbolic.[39] Similarly, Sceats argues that the act of eating is linked to subjectivity formation within the individual.[40] The orality of eating, in this view, is the first libidinal zone and focus of desire, and the oral site is directly implicated in ego-identity.[41] In light of these insights, it is no surprise to find the reverse of the "strange people equals strange food" formula, where zombies are repulsed by the food the living eat. For instance, R ruminates in great detail on his disgust for the food the living eat, especially when compared with the stimulating taste and mood-altering effect of eating fresh human flesh. For instance, after helping Julie find some frozen Pad Thai, R's internal monologue reveals his feelings: "I don't want any of the Dead to see Julie eating this lifeless waste, these empty calories [. . .] She jabs at the frozen-solid noodles with a plastic fork. She looks at me. 'You really don't remember much, do you? How long has it been since you ate real food?' I shrug."[42] Despite his desire and longing for living flesh, R decides to abstain from eating it in order to impress Julie. As the relationship progresses, R gradually becomes less undead through some inexplicable magical process. He becomes better able to speak and begins to retain more than fleeting memories, moreover, his instincts to eat the living subsides. He eats only one living human after meeting Julie and beginning this transformation, and he ends up vomiting in disgust because, it appears, he now sees himself through the eyes of the living.

Similar concerns occur in *American Zombie*, a pseudo-documentary about a community of zombies residing alongside humans in the greater Los Angeles area. The film follows four "high-functioning" zombies wrestling with their new identities in a world where many zombies are victims of exploitation, oppression, and violence. The film's subjects challenge genre-fed expectations, to the chagrin of filmmaker John (John Solomon), who is obsessed with uncovering "the truth" about whether zombies eat human flesh. Convinced they are hiding something, John asks to film the inside of the zombies' refrigerators. Ivan (Austin Basis), a convenience store clerk who fittingly works "the graveyard shift," explains that he has adopted the motto "carpe diem" (seize the day) since he can never know when his body will start to decay. When Ivan opens his fridge door, the contents inside are sparse—a small pizza box, some cans of beer, and some mysterious blue vials.[43] "That's one of the perks of the job, free food," he says and then proudly explains his food philosophy: "I try to get as many preservatives into my body as possible. You know, they give me all the expired food from the minimart . . . Those foods have a shelf life of almost 57½ years, so I figure that's what I'm after."

Ironically, as we see here, Ivan seeks the very foods the living are advised to avoid—highly processed foods full of preservatives.

Ivan's food philosophy is soon contrasted with that of Judy (Suzy Nakamura), who is introduced in the opening montage through a close-up of her biting into an organic tomato grown in her own backyard. Explaining that she keeps worms as pets since she is allergic to cats, and because it helps to develop compost for the garden, Judy then recites a well-rehearsed food philosophy as John rifles through her fridge: "I follow a vegan, organic lifestyle; I believe in a healthy diet" (Figure 16.2). Ignoring polite social conventions, John blurts out, "Is that 'cause your flesh is kind of rotting, or, why is that? Like, sorry, like how does it all work? Do you digest stuff? Or do you eat regular food?" Startled by questions that position her as Other, Judy responds innocently: "I don't eat any refined sugars. I don't eat anything from animals. I go to the farmer's market." Standing next to a box of hemp granola atop Judy's fridge, John persists: "What about, like, human flesh? Do you eat that?" Uncomfortable and confused, Judy tries to change the subject: "You know what, I have some soynut butter and some wheat-free crackers right here. Do you guys want some? I can make it."[44] John does not seem to notice that, while Judy's refrigerator is packed with healthy food, some of it is visibly moldy, making astute audience members wonder whether she actually eats

FIGURE 16.2 *In* American Zombie *(Grace Lee 2007), Ivan (Austin Basis) shows the documentary filmmaker the contents of his fridge, explaining "I try to get as many preservatives into my body as possible." Later, Judy (Suzy Nakamura) (pictured here) boasts about her contrasting food philosophy, saying, "I follow a vegan, organic lifestyle."*

any of the food she appears to be hoarding. By the end of the film, however, Judy sheds her shame and finally accepts, even embraces, her inner zombie. She allows her plants to die, sports heavy cosmetic make-up, and tousles her hair. Moreover, she munches mindlessly on cheese puffs, food containing the refined sugar and preservatives she previously avoided.[45] As these scenes illustrate, zombie foodways remain poorly understood by the living, reinforcing folklorist Robert Georges' claim that "you often eat what others *think* you are" and, in the case of zombies, the proverb further becomes, "You *are* what others *think* you eat."[46]

Food and conflicted identity in zombie dramas

The fact that all of the texts discussed thus far—*Graveyard Alive, Zombie Love, Boy Eats Girl, Warm Bodies*, and *American Zombie*—are comedies might suggest that the foodways of zombies surface, as a subject, only in comic pastiches.[47] However, similar dynamics occur in zombie-as-protagonist dramas as well. The characters in *Zombies Anonymous*, for example—like those of *American Zombie*—live in a world where the living and dead coexist and where zombies are often victims of hatred and violence.

The film focuses on Angela (Gina Ramsden), who awakens as a zombie after being murdered by her abusive boyfriend. Ashamed of her new social status, she joins a support group "for the mortally challenged," where Lewis (Kevin T. Collins), who introduces himself as "undead and proud," inquires as to her newfound food cravings: "Whatcha been eating? Italians? Mexicans? Chinese?" Smiling, Angela responds coyly, "I used to be a vegetarian." Lewis persists, "A zombie vegetarian—that's funny. [. . .] You ever walk through the supermarket and find yourself standing in the meat department, looking at all those packages of raw beef?" "Yeah, I have," Angela says, startled, as Lewis continues: "Staring at those drops of blood and juice that seep out of the meat and pool up at the bottom? And you just wanna rip that shit right open and sink your teeth into that cold flesh right there in front of everybody?" The camera cuts to a close-up of Angela's face. "Yeah, I have," she responds, mesmerized.

Uncomfortable with this degree of candor, the group leader tries to change the subject, saying cheerfully: "I think this is a good time for a coffee and donut break." At this prompt, each group member pulls out a trashcan with his/her name on it. After partaking of the donuts, they vomit into the cans. When Angela asks why they would eat something that they know will make them sick, the leader responds, "Because that's what normal people do at group meetings."

While "normal" people, hopefully, do not have personal trashcans for vomiting, the repeated scenes of eating and purging here, and in other zombie films, do resemble the real-life eating disorders that plague the living. An intense scene, set in the privacy of Angela's apartment, makes this parallel clear by showing the extent of her disordered relationship with food. Angela eats raw ground meat with her fingers while surfing an online dating site for the undead. The camera cuts to Angela in the bathroom, examining her face in the mirror, and later kneeling over the toilet, into which she deposits her undigested dinner. Cold, bloody ground beef may be an acceptable substitute, but she really craves warm, living flesh. Hence, when she hears a mouse in the kitchen, she hurries to set a trap. Upon catching it, she ravenously devours the mouse. Then, seeing her own behavior through the eyes of "normal" living society, Angela slumps to the floor, crying in self-pity and despair.

This tragic scene demonstrates the parallels between humans and zombies, and supports Beisecker and Pafenroth's observation about zombies not being so "Other" after all.[48] Like people with eating disorders for whom "food is at the same time a friend and an enemy,"[49] Angela's eating habits follow a "circular pattern in which people indulge themselves, feel momentary pleasure followed by guilt, anxiety, frustration and self-disgust, then attempt to diet and deny themselves their favourite foods, and then feel the need for pleasurable release again."[50] In living humans, this tendency toward compulsive eating might result in feelings of being overwhelmed by their relationship with food, finding the food dangerous and frightening.[51] Dietitians and nutrition counselors Evelyn Tribole and Elyse Resch state that "eating can be one of the most emotionally laden experiences that we have in our lives," and there are myriad ways food is used to cope with feelings—not as a component of biological hunger, but of emotional hunger, the most extreme form of coping involves numbing or anesthetizing eating.[52]

"The inside of a binge," writes Geneen Roth, "is deep and dark. At the core . . . is deprivation, scarcity, a feeling that you can never get enough."[53] For dieters, living in a state of perpetual denial, food is a persistent, beckoning force. Hunger, for them, is "represented as an insistent, powerful force with a life of its own."[54] Zombie food scenes might reflect the grim actualities of contemporary Westerners' eating problems. That is, many living humans, like zombies, fear that once they start eating, they will be unable to stop.

Along the lines of disordered eating, the avant-garde Canadian/German film *Otto; or, Up with Dead People* is a particularly complex exploration of the zombie-as-protagonist narrative. Actually a film about the making of two films—hence its undecided title—it defies generic classification: part satirical comedy, part melodrama, part pseudo-documentary, part horror film, part music video, and part gay pornography. Half of the narrative follows the protagonist Otto (Jey Crisfar)—a young zombie with an identity crisis, who has only fleeting memories of his previous life—and, as in other zombie-as-protagonist films, addresses the central character's conflicted relationship with food. In *Otto*, "the undead metaphor is deployed to sound issues of homosexuality, homelessness, social disenfranchisement, and emotional alienation."[55]

The film "critiques homosexual culture as much as heterosexual capitalism."[56] Medea Yarn (Katharina Klewinghaus), the elitist maker of the film-within-a-film, explains that, following the outbreak, those zombies that were not exterminated managed to evolve.[57] Hence, a new wave of gay zombies emerged: "When it was discovered that the gay undead craved the flesh of man, they were hunted down and eliminated even more ruthlessly than the previous generation. Gangs of marauding street youth stomped on the heads of zombies and set them on fire until they ceased to exist." One of the human characters, an actor named Fritz (Marcel Schlutt), comments to the camera about Otto's function as a tabula rasa: "I knew that Otto was the perfect subject for Medea. He was a Hollow Man. The empty signifier upon which you could project a political agenda." Fritz believes Otto is "homeless, delusional, and possibly schizophrenic." Furthermore, Fritz speculates, Otto "seems to have some kind of eating disorder."

The film does, in fact, reveal some unusual food behaviors on Otto's part. For example, he repeatedly finds himself drawn to a butcher shop where he stares longingly through the window. At first the audience might assume that this is because of a craving for raw meat, but the convoluted narrative later reveals, through flashback, that Otto used to date the shop-owner's son. In another scene, Otto sits on a park bench watching a series of living people pass by while eating handheld fast food, and reflects, through a voiceover monologue: "I wanted to consume the living, to devour human flesh, but I couldn't bring myself to do it. At first I thought it might have something to do with the time before, when I was alive. It occurred to me that I might have been vegetarian or, worse, a vegan. But that wasn't exactly it."

Otto's personal food system is, in fact, much more complicated than traditional zombie-film tropes might suggest. In another scene, he stands in front of the refrigerated meat section of a grocery store, picks up a package of raw meat and begins eating it. A young girl holding a chocolate bar approaches Otto; the two stand facing and watching each other while eating their own foods. This scene, like others, plays with viewer assumptions about what is real and what is constructed for the camera, as Medea interrupts—"Get out of here, you snot, you're ruining my shot!"—and chases the girl away. Offering Ottto-as-actor motivation for the retake, Medea says: "I want you to focus on meat because the world is meat. We are meat. Do you understand?" As such, the film's "self-reflexive presentation of fake gay zombies" and "ambiguous performances" deliberately confuses the audience.[58] Otto's status as zombie is likewise ambiguous, in fact, he leads the audience "to question the actual existence of zombies by portraying the central undead figure as a suicidal metaphor for gay disenfranchised youth, while never offering or discounting either a supernatural or rational conclusion."[59]

Another scene involves Medea taking Otto to a slaughterhouse. "In this scene," she tells him:

> I want you to imagine that you are drawn to the slaughterhouse like the prince of the dead returning to his beloved homeland. As a zombie, you are intoxicated by the lurid perfume of bloody carnage. The sweet systematic slaughter that could only have been devised by the diabolical mind of modern man. For you, it is a lotus land, an idol of truth and beauty, a symbol of mankind's quest to turn the earth into an industrialized wasteland of casual extermination and genocide. Do you understand?

Although Otto nods silently, it seems doubtful that he does understand. "Just think of it as a metaphor for the heartless corporate technocracies that govern the earth, and you'll be fine," Medea adds as attempted clarification.

Shortly thereafter, while filming in a garbage dump, Medea delivers a speech in which she reports with disgust that Americans discard 200,000 tons of edible food every day and produce 220 million tons of garbage each year: "It's the gluttonous, mindless consumers of developed industrial countries who are burying the third world in an avalanche of putrescence and decay." After listening silently to all of Medea's soliloquies, Otto finally asks a question, "Why did you bring me here?," to which Medea responds, "Because, my dead darling, this is the earth you will inherit."

By the end of the film, audiences are as confused as Otto about whether he is actually a zombie (or just believes he is), and about which scenes are real (as opposed to reenacted for the film).[60] Despite his speculation on the park bench, Otto's eating problems seem to be rooted not in latent vegetarianism or veganism, but in psychological problems. In fact, we learn from his former boyfriend that Otto was at one point hospitalized for "eating disorders, melancholia, schizophrenia"—so-called disorders of the soul. Both Medea and Fritz attempt to diagnose Otto's pathology. Neither seem to regard him as a "real" zombie; they understand his zombie-ism as "a reaction against an oppressive, capitalist system from which they believe he is retreating into a narcoleptic state."[61] In fact, Medea sees Otto as both a victim of capitalist society and a "revolutionary subject" within this society, reflecting: "A person who functions normally in a sick society is himself sick, while it is only the non-adjusted individual who can achieve a healthy 'acting out' against the overly strict restraints and demands on the dominant culture. Clearly as a homeless vagabond who believed he was dead, Otto was conducting his own one-man revolution against reality." In this trajectory, only those people who are already "sick" themselves (aka conformists to capitalism) would consider Otto sick.[62]

Whether configured as conformist capitalist or revolutionary hero, "the idea of Undeath problematizes our everyday notions of what it means to be alive in the first place," note philosophers Richard Greene and K. Silem Mohammed. "[I]n a literal sense, we are all, as living beings, 'Undead.' It is only a short step from this idea to the suggestion that the state of non-death (otherwise known as 'life') we privilege as authentic might itself be subject to the same doubts that attend our apprehension of Undeath."[63] The revelation of Otto's mental illness, the film-within-a-film structure, and the film's genre ambiguity all combine to render Medea, Fritz, and Otto unreliable narrators. As such, the film ends without resolution, drawing attention to Otto's ambiguous status and suggesting "that death is neither an end nor answer."[64] Otto wanders outside of the city and closes his monologue ironically, with a remark that reverses the traditional life/death binary—"Maybe I will find a whole new way of death."

Conclusion

Despite the lack of genuine belief in zombies among the living, at least in the West, the discourse surrounding zombie foodways has become ubiquitous and contested. Since pleasure may result from violating social norms, through zombies, the living can pretend to violate the most universally transgressive of human social norms—from "poor" etiquette to killing and cannibalism.[65] Zombie foodways, from methods of procurement and debates about nutrition to the symbolism of food preferences, actually reflect on the living's relationship to food, showing that "you often eat what others think you are" and "you are what others think you eat."[66]

Cinematic depictions of zombie foodways thus reveal the contested relationship of food stereotypes, food philosophies, and actual food behavior. Such scenes move beyond the one-dimensional brain-eating zombie, problematizing our cultural preoccupation with how and what zombies eat and offering more nuanced renderings of taste, cravings, and personal identity. Zombie foodways are thus complex and contested, sharing many of the same concerns plaguing the living. Countering the brain-eating stereotype, zombie-as-protagonist narratives produce rich insights into personal food systems with complex characters struggling with food, consumption, and identity just like the living. This trajectory toward zombie subjectivity reflects our own problematic relationship to food, linking the act of eating with other offal/awful anxieties and identities. Because humans project their own anxieties onto the undead, therefore, such examples of zombie foodways hold up a mirror to us, the living, reflecting our fear of our own incessant cravings and our own unruly bodies. Discourse about whether, what, how, and why zombies eat actually signals our association of the act of eating with anxieties about personal food philosophies, identity, sexuality, and the tenuous boundary between life and death.[67] This insight returns us, inevitably, to the final refrain that "Zombies Are Us."

Notes

1 Cory James Rushton, "Race, Colonialism, and the Evolution of the 'Zombie,'" in *Race, Oppression and the Zombie*, ed. Christopher M. Moreman and Cory James Rushton (Jefferson, NC: McFarland, 2011), 1.

2 Kyle William Bishop, *American Zombie Gothic: The Rise and Fall (and Rise) of the Walking Dead in Popular Culture* (London: McFarland, 2010); Shawn McIntosh, "The Evolution of the Zombie: The Monster that Keeps Coming Back," in *Zombie Culture: Autopsies of the Living Dead*," ed. Shawn McIntosh and Marc Leverette (Lanham, MD: Scarecrow Press, 2008), 1–17. There are parallels to vampires—both creatures are driven by hunger and return from the dead to feed on the living—yet zombies aren't sexy like vampires, whose "razor-sharp fangs complement their razor-sharp refinement" (Matthew Walker, "When There's No More Room in Hell, the Dead Will Shop the Earth: Romero and Aristotle on Zombies, Happiness, and Consumption," in *The Undead and Philosophy: Chicken Soup for the Soulless*, ed. Richard and K. Silem Mohammad (Chicago: Open Court Publishing, 2006), 81), nor are they exotic. Romero's zombies rise out of contemporary America, not some distant past or place.

3 Bishop, *American Zombie Gothic*; Sasha Cocarla, "A Love Worth Un-Undying For: Neoliberalism and Queered Sexuality in *Warm Bodies*," in *Zombies and Sexuality: Essays on Desire and the Living Dead*, ed. Shaka McGlotten and Steve Jones (Jefferson, NC: McFarland, 2014), 36–51; Peter Dendle, "The Zombie as Barometer of Cultural Anxiety," in *Monsters and the Monstrous: Myths and Metaphors of Enduring Evil*, ed. N. Scott (New York: Rodopi, 2007), 33–43.

4 Charles Camp, *American Foodways: What, When, Why and How We Eat in America* (Little Rock, AR: August House, 1989), 24; Michael Owen Jones, Bruce Giuliano, and Roberta Krell, "Foodways and Eating Habits: Directions for Research," *Western Folklore* 40, no. 1 (1981): 134–7; LuAnne Roth, *Talking Turkey: Visual Media and the Unraveling*

of Thanksgiving, PhD dissertation, University of Missouri, 2010; Jacqueline S. Thursby, *Foodways and Folklore: A Handbook* (Westport, CT: Greenwood Press, 2008).

5 Despite their extreme popularity in the present, zombies are not a recent phenomenon. The legend originates during the colonial period of the African slave trade, in which the zombie functions as a powerful allegory for slavery itself. Since their beginnings as a figure associated with Haiti, and the Vodou religious system, zombies are perhaps best understood as a postcolonial figure, saying as much about Western fears, anxieties, and racism as they reflect on Haitian reality (Rushton, "Race, Colonialism, and the Evolution of the 'Zombie,' " 1). While food does not play a significant part of these early narratives, when food *is* mentioned during the colonial period, such mentions focus mainly (and briefly) on what zombies should *not* eat. For example, in his sensationalist *The Magic Island* (1929), William Seabrook presents one such legend in which a group of zombie slaves are accidentally "freed" when, pitying "the poor brutes," the plantation owner's wife gives them candy containing salt.

6 Bishop, *American Zombie Gothic*; Kim Paffenroth, *Gospel of the Living Dead: George Romero's Visions of Hell on Earth* (Waco, TX: Baylor University Press, 2006).

7 This chapter is based on papers presented at the annual meetings of the American Folklore Society (October 2011 and November 2014), and profited from audience feedback.

8 Bishop, *American Zombie Gothic*, 236; R. H. W. Dillard, "*Night of the Living Dead*: It's Not Like Just a Wind That's Passing Through," in *American Horrors: Essays on the Modern American Horror Film*, ed. Gregory A. Waller (Chicago: University of Illinois Press, 1987), 14–29; Barry Keith Grant, "Taking Back the 'Night of The Living Dead'—George Romero, Feminism and the Horror-Film," *Wide Angle* 14, no. 1 (1992): 64–76.

9 Paffenroth, *Gospel of the Living Dead*, 32.

10 Cocarla, "A Love Worth Un-Undying For," 52.

11 Ibid., 53–4.

12 Susan Kalčik, "Ethnic Foodways in America: Symbol and the Performance of Identity," in *Ethnic and Regional Foodways in the United States: The Performance of Group Identity*, ed. Linda Keller Brown and Kay Mussell (Knoxville: University of Tennessee Press, 1984), 37–65; Lucy M. Long, "Culinary Tourism: A Folkloristic Perspective on Eating and Otherness," *Southern Folklore* 55, no. 3 (1998): 181–204; LuAnne Roth, "Beyond *Communitas*: Cinematic Food Events and the Negotiation of Power, Belonging, and Exclusion," in *Folklore/Cinema: Popular Film as Vernacular Culture*, ed. Sharon R. Sherman and Mikel J. Koven (Logan: Utah State University Press, 2007), 197–220.

13 Walker, "When There's No More Room in Hell."

14 Darren Elliott-Smith, " 'Death Is the New Pornography!': Gay Zombies, Homonormativity and Consuming Masculinity in Queer Horror," in

  Screening the Undead: Vampires and Zombies in Film and Television, ed. Leon Hunt and Sharon Lockyer (London: I.B. Tauris, 2013), 141.

15 Bishop, *American Zombie Gothic*, 15.

16 Ibid., 236.

17 Ibid., 237.

18 This critique of consumerism echoes Greek philosopher Aristotle from more than two millennia ago (Walker, "When There's No More Room in Hell," 82). "Despite the historical distance that separates Romero from Aristotle," reflects Walker, Aristotle isn't above providing gross-out descriptions of cannibalistic mayhem. For instance, in the fifth chapter of Book VII of the *Nicomachean Ethics*—Aristotle's major treatise on ethics—the philosopher serves up some memorably gag-inducing accounts of 'bestial' vice so far beyond the pale that it seems simply to fall outside the boundaries of humanity. In these odd pages, Aristotle introduces us to feral women who devour unborn fetuses, Black Sea tribes who sacrifice babies and munch on raw human flesh, and mad slaves who feast on other people's livers" (ibid.).

19 Bishop, *American Zombie Gothic*, 237.

20 Walker, "When There's No More Room in Hell," 84.

21 Elliott-Smith, "Death Is the New Pornography!" 144.

22 Encouraging zombies to eat mindfully, Austin cautions that gorging can lead to a ruptured stomach, so that "it is important that you eat responsibly." In yet another parallel between zombies and the living, it appears that some zombies are striving for small portions. The self-help book *Zombies for Zombies* advertises a delivery food company, Putrisystem Plus, which eliminates the unpleasantries of food procurement, providing home delivery of nutritional ready-to-eat meals that emphasize portion control, much like the pre-packaged "snack size" foods marketed to the living. Sometimes, it seems, zombie food behavior mimics that of the living.

23 Bishop, *American Zombie Gothic*, 159. Notable exceptions would include zombies Madeleine (Madge Bellamy) from *White Zombie* (1932) and Jessica (Christine Gordon) from *I Walked with a Zombie* (1943), although these are pre-Romero and therefore pre-cannibal zombies.

24 Ibid., 168–9.

25 Ibid., 166–7.

26 Ibid., 167–8.

27 Ibid., 167.

28 Dave Beisecker, "Bye-Gone Days: Reflections on Romero, Kirkman and What We Become," in *"We're All Infected": Essays on AMC's* The Walking Dead *and the Fate of the Human*, ed. Dawn Keetley (Jefferson, NC: McFarland, 2014), 201–14; Paffenroth, *Gospel of the Living Dead*, 209–10.

29 Elliott-Smith, "Death Is the New Pornography!" 142.

30 Susan Bordo, "Hunger as Ideology," in *Eating Culture*, ed. Ron Scapp and Brian Seitz (Albany, NY: State University of New York Press, 1998), 20–1.
31 For notable exceptions to the assumption that zombies are asexual, see McGlotten and Jones, *Zombies and Sexuality*.
32 Ibid., 142–3; emphasis in original.
33 Cory James Rushton, "Eating Ireland: Zombies, Snakes and Missionaries in *Boy Eats Girl*," in *Race, Oppression and the Zombie: Essays on Cross-Cultural Appropriations of the Caribbean Tradition*, ed. Christopher M. Moreman and Cory James Rushton (Jefferson, NC: McFarland, 2011), 157.
34 Isaac Marion, *Warm Bodies: A Novel* (New York: Emily Bestler Books, 2011), 7.
35 Ibid.
36 Cocarla, "A Love Worth Un-Undying For," 63–4.
37 Sarah Sceats, *Food, Consumption and the Body in Contemporary Women's Fiction* (Cambridge, UK: Cambridge University Press, 2000), 1.
38 Carolyn Korsmeyer, *Making Sense of Taste: Food and Philosophy* (Ithaca, NY: Cornell University Press, 1999), 189.
39 Sceats, *Food, Consumption and the Body*.
40 Julia Kristeva, *Powers of Horror: An Essay on Abjection* (New York: Columbia University Press, 1982); Sceats, *Food, Consumption and the Body*; Susanne Skubal, *Word of Mouth: Food and Fiction after Freud* (New York: Routledge, 2002).
41 Skubal, *Word of Mouth*.
42 Marion, *Warm Bodies*, 42.
43 John spots the blue vials in the butter compartment, but just then Ivan's roommate Glenn charges in, slams the fridge door shut, and says, "Mind your own f_cking business." Glenn's response suggests there might actually be something to hide in regards to this blue "zombie speed."
44 Prompted by the contents of Ivan's fridge, John asks Judy, "Do you have any injectable stuff in here, like blue vials and stuff, or . . .?"
45 In the end, after snacking on cheese puffs, Judy attacks John and bites him on the neck, presumably to convert him into the zombie club she has finally joined. In doing so, the film ends up reinforcing the "flesh-eating" zombie stereotype it initially tries to dismantle.
46 Robert Georges, "You Often Eat What Others Think You Are," *Western Folkore* 43, no. 4 (1984): 249–56; LuAnne Roth, "Foodways in the Zombie Zeitgeist: The Offal Truth about the Undead's Eating Habits," paper presented at the American Folklore Society Conference, Bloomington, Indiana, 2011.
47 Elliot-Smith, "Death Is the New Pornography!"
48 Beisecker, "Bye-Gone Days"; Paffenroth, *Gospel of the Living Dead*.

49. N. Charles and M. Kerr. "Food for Feminist Thought," *Sociological Review* 34, no. 3 (1986): 570.
50. Deborah Lupton, *Food, the Body and the Self* (1996. London: Sage Publications, 2011), 149.
51. Bordo, "Hunger as Ideology," 17.
52. Evelyn Tribole and Elyse Resch, *Intuitive Eating: A Revolutionary Program That Works* (1995. New York: St. Martin's, 2012), 149–50; see also Brian Wansink, *Mindless Eating: Why We Eat More than We Think* (London: Bantam, 2007).
53. Geneen Roth, *Feeding the Hungry Heart* (New York: New American Library, 1982), 15.
54. Bordo, "Hunger as Ideology," 14.
55. Dendle, "The Zombie as Barometer of Cultural Anxiety."
56. Elliot-Smith, "Death Is the New Pornography!" 2.
57. Medea Yarn is apparently an anagram for Maya Deren, avant-garde experimental filmmaker (e.g., *Meshes of the Afternoon* [1943]) and author of *Divine Horsemen: The Living Gods of Haiti* (1953) about Haitian Vodoun.
58. Elliot-Smith, "Death Is the New Pornography!" 4.
59. Ibid., 3.
60. Ibid., 4–5.
61. Ibid., 5.
62. Ibid., 6.
63. Greene and Mohammed, *Undead and Philosophy*, xiii–xiv.
64. Eliott-Smith, "Death Is the New Pornography!" 10.
65. McIntosh, "Evolution of the Zombie," 13.
66. Georges, "You Often Eat What Others Think You Are."
67. Presuming that readers of this chapter will be living humans, not zombies, I use the second person "we," "us," and "our" here.

Bibliography

Beisecker, Dave. "Bye-Gone Days: Reflections on Romero, Kirkman and What We Become." In *"We're All Infected": Essays on AMC's The Walking Dead and the Fate of the Human*, edited by Dawn Keetley, 201–14. Jefferson, NC: McFarland, 2014.

Bishop, Kyle William. *American Zombie Gothic: The Rise and Fall (and Rise) of the Walking Dead in Popular Culture*. London: McFarland, 2010.

Bordo, Susan. "Hunger as Ideology." In *Eating Culture*, edited by Ron Scapp and Brian Seitz, 11–35. Albany, NY: State University of New York Press, 1998.

Camp, Charles. *American Foodways: What, When, Why and How We Eat in America*. Little Rock, AR: August House, 1989.
Charles, N., and M. Kerr. "Food for Feminist Thought." *Sociological Review* 34, no. 3 (1986): 537–72.
Cocarla, Sasha. "A Love Worth Un-Undying For: Neoliberalism and Queered Sexuality in *Warm Bodies*." In *Zombies and Sexuality: Essays on Desire and the Living Dead*, edited by Shaka McGlotten and Steve Jones, 36–51. Jefferson, NC: McFarland, 2014.
Dendle, Peter. "The Zombie as Barometer of Cultural Anxiety." In *Monsters and the Monstrous: Myths and Metaphors of Enduring Evil*, edited by N. Scott, 33–43. New York: Rodopi, 2007.
Dillard, R. H. W. "*Night of the Living Dead*: It's Not Like Just a Wind That's Passing Through." In *American Horrors: Essays on the Modern American Horror Film*, edited by Gregory A. Waller, 14–29. Chicago: University of Illinois Press, 1987.
Elliott-Smith, Darren. "'Death Is the New Pornography!': Gay Zombies, Homonormativity and Consuming Masculinity in Queer Horror." In *Screening the Undead: Vampires and Zombies in Film and Television*, edited by Leon Hunt and Sharon Lockyer, 148–72. London: I.B. Tauris, 2013.
Georges, Robert. "You Often Eat What Others Think You Are." *Western Folklore* 43, no. 4 (1984): 249–56.
Grant, Barry Keith. "Taking Back the 'Night Of The Living Dead'—George Romero, Feminism and the Horror-Film." *Wide Angle* 14, no. 1 (1992): 64–76.
Greene, Richard, and K. Silem Mohammad, eds. *The Undead and Philosophy: Chicken Soup for the Soulless*. Chicago: Open Court, 2006.
Jones, Michael Owen, Bruce Giuliano, and Roberta Krell. "Foodways and Eating Habits: Directions for Research." *Western Folklore* 40, no. 1 (1981): 134–7.
Kalčik, Susan. "Ethnic Foodways in America: Symbol and the Performance of Identity." In *Ethnic and Regional Foodways in the United States: The Performance of Group Identity*, edited by Linda Keller Brown and Kay Mussell, 37–65. Knoxville: University of Tennessee Press, 1984.
Korsmeyer, Carolyn. *Making Sense of Taste: Food and Philosophy*. Ithaca, NY: Cornell University Press, 1999.
Kristeva, Julia. *Powers of Horror: An Essay on Abjection*. New York: Columbia University Press, 1982.
Long, Lucy M. "Culinary Tourism: A Folkloristic Perspective on Eating and Otherness." *Southern Folklore* 55, no. 3 (1998): 181–204.
Lupton, Deborah. *Food, the Body and the Self*. 1996. London: Sage Publications, 2011.
Marion, Isaac. *Warm Bodies: A Novel*. New York: Emily Bestler Books, 2011.
McGlotten, Shaka, and Steve Jones, eds. *Zombies and Sexuality: Essays on Desire and the Living Dead*. Jefferson, NC: McFarland, 2014.
McIntosh, Shawn. "The Evolution of the Zombie: The Monster that Keeps Coming Back." In *Zombie Culture: Autopsies of the Living Dead*," edited by Shawn McIntosh and Marc Leverette, 1–17. Lanham, MD: Scarecrow Press, 2008,

Paffenroth, Kim. *Gospel of the Living Dead: George Romero's Visions of Hell on Earth.* Waco, TX: Baylor University Press, 2006.

Roth, Geneen. *Feeding the Hungry Heart.* New York: New American Library, 1982.

Roth, LuAnne. "Beyond *Communitas*: Cinematic Food Events and the Negotiation of Power, Belonging, and Exclusion." In *Folklore/Cinema: Popular Film as Vernacular Culture*, edited by Sharon R. Sherman and Mikel J. Koven, 197–220. Logan: Utah State University Press, 2007.

Roth, LuAnne. *Talking Turkey: Visual Media and the Unraveling of Thanksgiving.* PhD dissertation. University of Missouri, 2010.

Roth, LuAnne. "Foodways in the Zombie Zeitgeist: The Offal Truth about the Undead's Eating Habits." Paper presented at the American Folklore Society Conference, Bloomington, IN, 2011.

Rushton, Cory James. "Eating Ireland: Zombies, Snakes and Missionaries in *Boy Eats Girl*." In *Race, Oppression and the Zombie: Essays on Cross-Cultural Appropriations of the Caribbean Tradition*, edited by Christopher M. Moreman and Cory James Rushton, 149–61. Jefferson, NC: McFarland, 2011.

Rushton, Cory James. "Race, Colonialism, and the Evolution of the 'Zombie.'" In *Race, Oppression and the Zombie: Essays on Cross-Cultural Appropriations of the Caribbean Tradition*, edited by Christopher M. Moreman and Cory James Rushton, 1–14. Jefferson, NC: McFarland, 2011.

Sceats, Sarah. *Food, Consumption and the Body in Contemporary Women's Fiction.* Cambridge, UK: Cambridge University Press, 2000.

Skubal, Susanne. *Word of Mouth: Food and Fiction after Freud.* New York: Routledge, 2002.

Thursby, Jacqueline S. *Foodways and Folklore: A Handbook.* Westport, CT: Greenwood Press, 2008.

Tribole, Evelyn, and Elyse Resch. *Intuitive Eating: A Revolutionary Program that Works.* 1995. New York: St. Martin's, 2012.

Walker, Matthew. "When There's No More Room in Hell, the Dead Will Shop the Earth: Romero and Aristotle on Zombies, Happiness, and Consumption." In *The Undead and Philosophy: Chicken Soup for the Soulless*, edited by Richard Greene and K. Silem Mohammad, 81–90. Chicago: Open Court Publishing, 2006.

Wansink, Brian. *Mindless Eating: Why We Eat More Than We Think.* London: Bantam, 2007.

17

From Sugar-Fueled Killer to Grotesque Gourmand: The Culinary Maturation of the Cinematic Serial Killer

Mark Bernard

The presence of a serial killer alone does not automatically categorize a film as horror. Serial killers, according to Bruce Kawin, only truly "become the province of the horror film when their deeds and their reasons for committing them are not merely criminal but especially frightening, revolting, graphic, disturbing and shocking."[1] The sadistic whims of the serial killers that populate horror cinema "attack the body and the spirit," their deeds going "well beyond ordinary experience" and entering the "level of the unspeakable."[2] A film's narrative does not always have to graphically depict the violence unleashed by these human monsters, however, especially when audiences can be just as disturbed, shocked, horrified, and disgusted by a serial killer's food behaviors.

Seemingly banal and unexceptional, the eating process is actually made up of a complicated traffic of materials into and out of the body, as human beings must partake of substances from the world around them in order to survive. When one seriously considers this process, eating can seem grotesque. To help shield ourselves from the potential disgust and strangeness of eating, human societies have established complex systems of what Carole M. Counihan calls "etiquette and food rules" that "[govern] what, with whom, when, and where one eats."[3] A violation of these etiquette and food rules can easily push people into an unspeakable realm that lies beyond ordinary experience. One can be revolted by someone not washing their hands before eating, someone not showing up for a planned dinner date, or someone eating a non-breakfast food in the morning, just as by scenes of blood and guts in the movies. Perhaps for this reason, food often seems to play a significant role in the mise-en-scene and the meaning-making process of serial killer films.

Some cinematic serial killers violate food rules in splashy, obvious ways; perhaps the most well known and iconic of all cinematic serial killers, Hannibal Lecter (Anthony Hopkins) of *Silence of the Lambs* (1991) expresses his contempt for society and its restrictions by practicing cannibalism and eating those who offend him. Other cinematic serial killers break food rules in ways less obvious, but no less significant. This chapter explores how attending to the specifics of food and its representation in serial killer films—more specifically to what, how, and when serial killers eat—illustrates how the serial killer film has evolved and what the sociological implications of these changes may be.

Beginning with *M* (1931), a classic of German cinema that Robert Cettl identifies as "the earliest full demonstration of the serial killer film formula,"[4] serial killers in cinema are often represented as child-like and their murders connected to a childish abandonment of "proper" meal cycles. This image of the serial killer largely held sway over films for the next several decades, with two potent examples emerging from the films of Alfred Hitchcock: *Shadow of a Doubt* (1943) and *Psycho* (1960).

The image of the serial killer begins to shift, however, with *Silence of the Lambs*, which became a "central point of reference" for subsequent serial killer films.[5] In *Silence*, the serial killer matures from a sugar-fueled child to a grotesque gourmand. The influence of Lecter can be seen in subsequent films, such as *Se7en* (1995), in which a sophisticated serial killer (Kevin Spacey) uses food behaviors to express his contempt for the world around him, and *American Psycho* (2000), in which a budding serial killer (Christian Bale) fails to master food behaviors and appear powerful and sophisticated. The serial killer's culinary maturation reveals how, as Alzena MacDonald puts it, "representations of the serial killer function to address concerns and preoccupations specific to their context of production."[6] In this case, food behaviors in the serial killer film reveal how tastes and audiences' positioning in relation to serial killers change over time.

"Frantic indulgence of childish appetites": Hans Beckert and *M*

Many commentators have praised *M*'s bravura opening scenes and the ways in which Lang innovatively utilizes film form—specifically sound and editing—to establish the horrors of living in a city terrorized by a rash of child murders.[7] The centrality of food to these scenes, however, has been relatively unexplored. The film opens with a circle of children playing a game in a tenement courtyard, as one of the child sings a macabre song: "Just you wait, it won't be long / The man in black will soon be here / With his cleaver's blade so true / He'll make mincemeat out of you!"[8] Thus, the film begins with a song that only not conflates serial killing and food behaviors, but also associates these activities with the world of childhood. As the children play their game, a woman carrying laundry on an upper level of the tenement scolds them and tells them to stop, making clear that the song also stands outside of the prohibitions that adults attempt to impose on children. Many prohibitions that adults impose upon children are food-related, as artifacts of "culturally and socially determined meal systems that identify 'correct' versus 'incorrect' food behaviors."[9] To venture outside of the regulations of established meal systems is to court danger, as this forbidden territory is the province of the serial killer.

The danger of abandoning meal cycles is emphasized in the film's next scenes. Inside the tenement, Frau Beckmann (Ellen Widmann) prepares lunch for her daughter Elsie (Inge Landgut) as she waits for the child to return home from school. The mother's meal preparations are crosscut with the child-murderer Hans Beckert (Peter Lorre) approaching Elsie as she leaves school, playfully bouncing a ball. Beckert tempts her from her path with promises of a balloon and candy; later, a candy wrapper is the only clue police are able to turn up when investigating Elise's disappearance (Figure 17.1).

Elise's mother becomes anxious when the child does not return home, and eventually leans out of the kitchen window and calls out to her. As she shouts Elise's name, a series of five shots reveals to the viewer that Elise has been murdered. These shots are of the tenement's empty staircase, an empty attic (the tenement's laundry room), Elise's empty chair at the table, Elise's ball rolling away through the grass, and the child-shaped balloon that Beckert bought for her, caught for a moment in the power lines above. The third shot of Elise's empty place at the table provides an ominous turning point. As Tom Gunning observes, the first two shots of empty locations within the tenement building are accompanied by a voiceover of Frau Beckmann calling Elise's name, but the last three shots are silent, an auditory cue that signals

FIGURE 17.1 *A candy wrapper is a murder investigation's only clue in* M *(1931).*

Elise's murder.[10] Thus, the sight of Elise's empty chair at the table comes at a pivotal moment that underscores the terrible fate that awaits those who abandon meal cycles and society's rules concerning how one should eat.

Beckert's juvenile appetites are juxtaposed with the more mature tastes of the adult world throughout the film. Desperate to capture the murderer, the police raid a speakeasy where criminals congregate; amid the scene of the raid, there is a telling shot of a speakeasy table, littered with half-full or broken beer mugs and shot glasses, overflowing ashtrays, and spilled beer, emphasizing that the deviant, but nonetheless adult, tastes of the criminal underworld have been disrupted by Beckert's indulgence of his childish urges. The city's criminals scheme to catch Beckert themselves by enlisting the help of beggars and other street dwellers and giving them assigned sections of the city to watch. Fittingly enough, the criminals hand out these assignments in a room above a sandwich shop. While the rough-and-tumble patrons of the shop eat sandwiches, drink beer, and admire the aroma of aged cheese, Beckert avoids the workaday world by wandering the streets, snacking on fruit, and window-shopping. This juxtaposition reflects the ways in which cinematic serial killers are often "cast free of the labors of workplace discipline," giving them an "unbalanced mind" that is often "contrasted to the detective proclivities of an uncouth but also working investigator kept earthy by daily routine."[11] The criminals and beggars fulfill the role of detective in *M*; the criminals want to catch the killer so they can get back to "work," and the beggars admire the pungent odor of aged cheese compared to the sweet fruits preferred by Beckert.

Childish appetites drive Beckert until they doom him, just as Elise's abandonment of the table her mother set for her leads to her death. When Beckert sees a young girl on the street and is tempted by his unhealthy appetites, he attempts to calm himself with an "adult" culinary activity; he dashes into a sidewalk café and orders two cognacs in rapid succession. These two drinks fail to satisfy him, however, and he picks up another girl, buying her a balloon from the same blind street vendor he patronized with Elise. The blind man recognizes Beckert because of his repetitive whistling, and his childish food behaviors allow him to be marked by the blind man's accomplice so others can pursue him. As Beckert peels oranges and tosses the peels on the sidewalk, his pursuer walks by, feigns slipping on the peels, grabs onto Beckert, and marks a chalk "M" on his shoulder. Thus, Beckert's "frantic indulgence of childish appetites" leads to his capture.[12] If Lang's film lays the groundwork for the serial killer genre by crossbreeding the crime film with the horror film,[13] it also establishes food and food behaviors as central elements of the subgenre.

Sandwiches, milk, and candy corn: Hitchcock's killer children and their descendants

Over the next few decades, serial killer films began to emerge in American cinema, including two notable examples in which food plays a prominent role: *Shadow of a Doubt* and *Psycho*, both directed by Hitchcock. *Shadow of a Doubt* tells the story of Charlie Oakley (Joseph Cotten), a serial killer who flees from the police to his sister's (Patricia Collinge) home in sleepy Santa Rosa, California, and lives with her family in hopes of eluding the authorities. At first, Charlie seems worldly and sophisticated, especially in the eyes of his adoring niece and namesake, Young Charlie (Teresa Wright), but cracks in his façade begin to show when Young Charlie learns that her uncle is a murderer on the run. As Charlie's evil nature begins to show through, it becomes apparent that he is still a child. When his sister rushes to meet him as he first arrives in town, Charlie raises his hand to stop her and commands, "Don't move. Standing there, you don't look like Emma Newton. You look like Emma Spencer Oakley . . . of St. Paul, Minnesota, the prettiest girl on the block," as if he hopes to travel back in time to their childhood. Later in the film, Emma tells Young Charlie about a serious injury her uncle sustained as a young boy that seemed to completely change his personality, intimating that this childhood injury set him on the path of becoming a murderer, forever frozen in time as a selfish child.

Charlie's true nature is most powerfully revealed during scenes in which food is prominent. Early in the film, family dinners with the Newtons are times of nurturing communion; as the film progresses, however, Charlie's personality shines through during meal times, so much so that Charlie's little sister, Ann (Edna May Wonacott), does not want to sit beside him at dinner. Ann's apprehension foreshadows a severely uncomfortable meal during which Charlie denounces the "useless" women he has met (and murdered) as "fat wheezing animals." When a neighbor (Hume Cronyn) stops by to tell Charlie's father (Henry Travers)—his friend and fellow crime-story enthusiast—that poisonous mushrooms would make an ideal murder weapon, it is all too much for Young Charlie, who angrily gets up from the table and storms out of the house. Uncle Charlie then realizes he will have to kill his niece to protect his secret.

These scenes centered on food and the ways in which serial killers' improper food behaviors can betray their motives are emblematic of Hitchcock's cinema.[14] *Psycho*'s Norman Bates is, perhaps, the exemplar of the serial killer with childish appetites. Norman's attack on Marion Crane (Janet Leigh) in the much-celebrated shower scene is one of the most iconic moments in film history, making it easy to overlook two crucial scenes featuring food that bookend her murder. When Marion arrives at the Bates Motel, Norman invites her to share his unexciting, but supposedly wholesome meal of "sandwiches and milk." As they have dinner in the hotel parlor, however, Norman does not eat, but instead uses the meal as an opportunity to watch Marion.[15] In this scene, Norman rejects "proper" nutrition in favor of indulging his unhealthy appetite for voyeurism, a hunger that will only grow in intensity as, like a naughty child, he spies on her in the shower. Afterward, he goes back up to the Bates house (where "Mother" supposedly is), walks into the kitchen, and sits down at the table, as if awaiting the arrival of his real meal: Marion's murder.

The fact of Marion's murder begins to come to light in another pivotal scene featuring food. Arbogast (Martin Balsam), a private investigator, shows up at the Bates Motel looking for Marion. When he arrives, Norman sits outside the motel office door, reclining in a lawn chair, reading a magazine, and snacking on candy corn. Raymond Durgnat describes Norman as exuding "contentment" at the beginning of this scene and cites the candy as a signal of Norman's emotional state.[16] Norman even confidently offers some to Arbogast. His confidence begins to slip, however, when Arbogast catches him in a few lies, and Norman begins to stumble under the investigator's questioning. As Durgnat explains, "Norman's the child, Arbogast is the father" in this scenario.[17] As Arbogast recognizes Marion's handwriting in the register, Norman leans to look over his shoulder, and a low-angle shot emphasizes Norman's jaw as he nervously chews; Durgnat describes Norman's jaw and neck here as looking "like a bird's gizzard."[18] Like Marion, Arbogast also suffers a nasty death at Norman's hands, and Norman is revealed as a prototypical perverse serial killer, driven by childish appetites.

Serial killer films became a regular fixture of horror cinema in the wake of *Psycho*'s success, with many of these films—prestige pictures as well as low-budget drive-in and grindhouse programmers—featuring killers stuck in an adolescent state of arrested development. Such is the case with *The Sadist* (1963), a gritty, low-budget picture that tells the story of Charlie Tibbs (Arch Hall, Jr.), a psychopathic, teenaged murderer, and his mute girlfriend Judy (Marilyn Manning) as they ambush a trio of schoolteachers—an older man named Carl (Don Russell), a younger man named Ed (Richard Alden), and a young woman named Doris (Helen Hovey)—when their car breaks down at a junkyard outside of Los Angeles. Ed tries to fix the car as Carl looks around the junkyard for help. He goes into the living quarters for the family that supposedly runs the place, and immediately knows something is wrong when he finds a dinner table set with still-warm, half-eaten food. Charlie, gun in hand, and Judy accost the trio, and Ed recognizes them as murderers who have been on a killing rampage from Arizona to California.

Charlie terrorizes his victims in ways that are perversely food-related. For example, at one point, he shoves Doris to the ground and grinds her face into the earth, commanding: "Taste it! Taste it! Eat that dirt!" The most striking conflation of murder and food in *The Sadist* comes, however, when Charlie murders Carl. As Doris and Ed watch helplessly, Charlie makes Carl get on his knees in front of him. In one hand, Charlie holds a gun, in the other, a bottle of soda, the quintessential high-sugar, youth-oriented beverage. Charlie says to Carl, "As soon as I finish this [he holds up the soda bottle], you're gonna be through talkin.'" Carl pleads for his life while Charlie takes huge swigs from the bottle. Charlie finishes the soda, drops the bottle, and shoots Carl in the face (Figure 17.2).

Over the next twenty-five years, a wide range of films featured serial killers whose childish tastes drive their murders. In *Targets* (1968), mad sniper

FIGURE 17.2 *Crazed killer Charlie Tibbs (Arch Hall, Jr.) chugs a soda before gunning down a victim in* The Sadist *(1963).*

Bobby Thompson (Tim O'Kelly) munches on Baby Ruths and sips soda while drawing a bead on his prey from atop a water tower overlooking the freeway. Loosely based on the life of Ed Gein, the infamous serial killer, necrophile, and cannibal, *The Texas Chainsaw Massacre* (1974) features a family of cannibal killers whose violence seems to stem less from malice than from twisted childish glee. Also based on Gein, *Deranged* (1974) tells the story of Ezra Cobb (Roberts Blossom), a deadly child-in-a-man's-body who lives with his mother's corpse and eats at a kitchen table made of human bones. In *Maniac* (1980), memories of his abusive mother lead Frank (Joe Spinell) to become an overweight, slovenly killer who snacks on Cracker Jacks before a particularly brutal murder.

Even though his parents abused him, the eponymous killer in *Henry: Portrait of a Serial Killer* (1986) exhibits food behaviors that seem to suggest he may be trying to grow up. The film opens with Henry (Michael Rooker) finishing his meal at a diner and politely paying his check. The viewer quickly learns, however, that all of Henry's food behaviors are not so civil, when a montage of Henry's victims reveals a woman who has met a ghastly end by having a broken bottle shoved into her face. Henry shares a small, dingy apartment with his friend Otis (Tom Towles) and Otis's sister, Becky (Tracy Arnold), who has fled her abusive husband. Many scenes take place around the kitchen table as the trio share meals. Even if these meals are very uncomfortable,[19] the fact that these subaltern characters eat a "proper" meal in a "proper" space offers their lives a bit of stability. When Henry and Otis venture away from the table, however, terrible things happen: Henry introduces Otis to the world of serial killing, and Otis later rapes and tries to strangle Becky in the living room. Henry intervenes, leading to a brawl in which Becky stabs Otis in the eye with the sharp handle of a comb. Henry takes the implement from her, fatally stabs Otis in the chest, and later dismembers his body. As the pair flees town to avoid the law, Becky professes her love for Henry, who hesitantly reciprocates her sentiment. But with no domestic dining space to connect them, their tenuous relationship cannot last. After they check into a motel for the night, Henry leaves alone the next morning, the implication being that he murdered Becky.

After Lecter: the serial killer grows up

Silence of the Lambs "legitimized" the serial killer genre and lent it prestige.[20] Just as the genre's respectability grew, so did its killers, with Hannibal Lecter representing a new breed of serial killer: highly intelligent and well-educated with refined tastes in art, music, and, most importantly, food—even if he does often enjoy human flesh with his fine wines and sophisticated dishes. Lecter is a far cry from baby-faced Hans Beckert, mama's boy Norman Bates, or soda-slurping Charlie Tibbs.

The maturation of the cinematic serial killer has implications that extend outside of the film's diegesis and reveal a great deal about the audiences for these films. Discussing serial killer films, Louis Bayman argues that "despite apparent narrative disavowals of the serial killer's tastes, the films' styles are coherent with the tastes of the killer . . . [drawing] the spectator into the same realms of the killer, creating an identification with the killer and an ambiguous attitude toward his crimes."[21] In other words, the style of a serial killer film is closely related to the degree to which the viewer identifies with the serial killer. Lang's style in *M*, for example, creates a viewpoint that exists "outside the consciousness of any character"[22]; thus, the audience feels little identification with Beckert, but rather observes him from an analytical distance. Similarly, Hitchcock's *Psycho* is a narrative shell game, with the point-of-view skipping from character to character while ultimately keeping everyone in the dark. The unaffected style and mundane settings of *Henry* all but dare the viewer to try to understand Henry's thoughts and motivations. These films, in short, do not encourage much audience identification with their childish serial killers.

Things begin to change with *Silence*, as the film's well-known actors and high production values made it appealing for mainstream audiences and positioned Hannibal as a relatable character. Ian Olney, in fact, observes that Hannibal Lecter "has emerged as something of a cult hero in contemporary American cinema."[23] According to Olney, the valorization of Lecter is problematic because this character does not call into question the cannibalistic qualities of white male privilege, but instead invites identification with this figure so that audiences embrace the privileged cannibal in themselves, proving that "the project of imperialism . . . has been reinvented and perfected."[24] In other words, the tastes of the serial killer, the ways these tastes are depicted, and the tastes of the audience are now aligned, making the serial killer a character with which the audience (particularly those of privilege) can safely relate because the "tastefulness" of the film allows them to feel as cunning and sophisticated as the killer. There are other examples of this transformation of cannibal killers in recent American cinema, as well. For example, the cannibal clan of *The Texas Chainsaw Massacre* franchise may have started out as demented, inchoate children, but over the course of the franchise, their evolving depiction leads the audience to identify with them as they begin to look more like a middle-class family whose values have been adjusted to incorporate cannibalism as a way to thrive in a capitalistic "dog-eat-dog" society.[25] Slickly produced films with sophisticated serial killers allow the audience "to identify with the 'best' sides of a serial killer" as the killer emerges as a "a superb mind hunter who is hyper intelligent."[26] These sophisticated killers allow audiences to identify with them—and admire their wits—in a way they never would with a blubbering man-child like Hans Beckert.

The sophistication and intelligence of this new breed of serial killer are often conveyed through food behaviors, and Jonathan Doe from *Se7en* provides an example of the post-Lecter serial killer. While Doe is far from being a cult hero like Lecter, the intricate design of his murder cycle based on the seven deadly sins is what draws the viewer into the film. Similar to Lecter, Doe's food behaviors show his contempt for those around him whom he sees as crude and pedestrian. For instance, he writes in his journal about a man who approached him on the subway and tried to make conversation. When the man gives Doe a headache with his "banality," Doe vomits on him and laughs. Doe's regurgitation on the stranger is an inversion of the social function that food is expected to have in our culture, and his continued violation of these rules comes into clearer focus when considered alongside how food brings people together in other key moments of the film. For instance, when they first meet, veteran detective Somerset (Morgan Freeman) does not bond with Mills (Brad Pitt), the young, hot-headed detective who is to replace Somerset after his retirement, until Mills's wife, Tracy (Gwyneth Paltrow), invites Somerset to their apartment for dinner. Food and drink also provide a connection between Tracy and Somerset when she asks him to meet her at a diner, confiding to him that she is pregnant (which she has not told Mills) and has serious misgivings about their new life in the city.

When juxtaposed with these scenes of people bonding over food, Doe regurgitating food on a stranger powerfully communicates his contempt for the world. His food-related contempt finds its fullest expression with the first victim in his cycle of murders. Representing the sin of gluttony, Doe's victim is an obese man (Bob Mack) whom he ties up, force-feeds spaghetti, and then kicks in the stomach, causing him to hemorrhage internally and die a painful death. Doe's cycle of murders beginning in this manner further emphasizes the centrality of food to the serial killer genre. When Doe turns himself in to the police near the end of the film, he sits in a confession room and, as Mills and Somerset watch him behind a two-way mirror, slowly steeps tea with measured strokes. Doe's calm mastery of food behaviors conveys that he is in total control of his environment and his worst deeds are still to come.

Conversely, an example of a post-Lecter serial killer whose lack of control and mastery over his environment are conveyed through food behaviors is Patrick Bateman in *American Psycho* (2000). In this satiric film set in the late 1980s, Bateman and his facile Wall Street associates talk shop over meals and obsess over obtaining reservations at the city's trendiest restaurants, the crown jewel of which is Dorsia. A table at Dorsia is the apex of alpha-male achievement; Bateman's coworker Paul Allen (Jared Leto) is the most-envied broker at the firm because, in addition to having the most tastefully designed business card, he is able to score a reservation at Dorsia for 8:30 on a Friday night. Bateman tries in vain to assert his masculinity through food behaviors and book an ever-elusive table at Dorsia, but the best he can do are second-tier venues like Pastelles, a restaurant where the film's opening scenes takes place.

From this first scene, Bateman's masculinity-in-peril is intimately linked to food and food behaviors. The décor of Pastelles is dominated, appropriately enough, by soft pastels; its waiters delicately deliver dishes to tables and smilingly inform customers about their menu, which contains such eco-friendly dishes as "grilled free-range rabbit with herb french-fries." Sitting at one of the tables are Bateman and two of his friends, Timothy Bryce (Justin Theroux) and Craig McDermott (Josh Lucas), who fidget nervously over their drinks. Brice complains, "God, I hate this place. It's a chicks' restaurant. Why aren't we at Dorsia?" McDermott snickers and replies, "Because Bateman won't give the maitre d' head." McDermott's haranguing is interrupted as the fourth member of their party, David Van Patten (Bill Sage), returns to the table and complains that the restaurant does not "have a good bathroom to do coke in."

This opening reveals a great deal about how the men in this narrative think about food and conceptualize food spaces. First, food and food spaces are explicitly gendered, as Brice dismisses Pastelles as a "chick's restaurant," a space that is too "soft" and "feminine" to contain their "manly" habits like drinking liquor straight up and doing coke in the bathroom. Second, their conversation alludes—albeit in a joking way—to Bateman being unable to procure reservations at Dorisa, a restaurant that, within the context of the film, represents the apex of both social standing and manliness. This highly desirable food space is apparently inaccessible to Bateman and would only become accessible if Bateman would perform fellatio on the maitre d', the most "unmanly" of actions within the hyper-heterosexist world of these Wall Street power players. This is only the first of many times that Bateman will fail to perform his masculinity in the arena of food. With food spaces and the ability to nab reservations at the trendiest restaurants looming so large in the identities of the film's characters, Bateman's failure to "effectively" perform in terms of food behaviors and masculinity presents him with an identity crisis.

Repeatedly, Bateman's feelings of powerlessness are conveyed through his failure to master food environments. In one scene, Bateman has a dinner date with associates at a restaurant called Espace that is "masculine," with industrial-themed décor dominated by exposed brick and black and grey colors. Even the flower arrangement—a single flower jutting up, erect in the middle of the table—is masculine. Although this is an environment more fitting for Bateman's hypermasculine fantasies, it is also one in which Bateman cannot see himself or bring his fantasies to fruition. When Bateman arrives, Bryce hands Bateman a copy of Espace's menu, which is engraved on a piece of metal. When Bateman looks at the menu, his reflection is blurry and distorted, suggesting that Espace is a place where Bateman, quite literally, cannot "see himself." This blindness is underscored by Bryce's comment that "the menu's in Braille."

Failing to assert himself through food behaviors, Bateman turns to torture and murder. However, his acts of brutality are still intimately tied to food behaviors, and he eventually tries the ultimate combination of food behaviors and murder: cannibalism. He stores a woman's head in his freezer by the sorbet, bites into another female victim, and kills a third with a chainsaw. He finally spirals out of control and, hysterically, calls his lawyer and tearfully records a full confession of his ghastly deeds on the answering machine. He sobs, "I even . . . I ate some of their brains . . . [gags] and I tried to cook a little." The presence of cannibalism illustrates the complete confluence of food behaviors and murder in Bateman's attempts to assert his masculinity. But his slight gagging during his confession demonstrates his continued failure to be "manly" in his food behavior. The conclusion of the film reveals all of Bateman's efforts have been for naught. It turns out that, in all likelihood, none of his murders even took place, and he fails to cement an identity and assert his masculinity on all fronts, scoring neither a table at Dorsia nor a headline in the newspaper. Consistent with its sardonic tone and satirical intent, *American Psycho* breaks with other post-*Silence* serial killer films by encouraging the viewer to laugh at, rather than identify with, Bateman's callow and pedestrian taste in music, food, and his hesitancy (even in the depths of his madness) to embrace murder and cannibalism. He is, essentially, a failed Hannibal Lecter.

The evolution of the cinematic serial killer is not wholly linear, with only childish serial killers appearing before *Silence of the Lambs* and only sophisticated ones (or ones failing at sophistication) afterward. Murderous preacher Harry Powell (Robert Mitchum) in *Night of the Hunter* (1955), for example, is far from juvenile and decidedly not consumed with childish appetites. Indeed, he spends most of the film playing boogeyman to a group of children. Conversely, it would be difficult to argue that the white-trash killer couple played by Brad Pitt and Juliette Lewis in *Kalifornia* (1993) has sophisticated tastes. Nevertheless, looking at how cinematic serial killers deviate from accepted food behavior demonstrates how much importance our culture places upon proper food behaviors and meal cycles. If human monsters "attack our body and spirit" as Kawin suggests, cinematic serial killers do so by making a mockery of the ways we are supposed to eat. Childish killers like Hans Beckert, Norman Bates, and Charlie Tibbs thumb their bratty noses at appropriate mealtimes and food decorum, refusing to follow the culinary rules of the adult world. Sophisticated killers like Hannibal Lecter—and even wannabes like Patrick Bateman—take these rules way too far. It would appear that if humans hope to not become monsters, they must follow a narrow path between these two extremes: neither too childish, nor too adult; neither too fat, nor too thin. Still, the potential of becoming a monster never completely goes away because, ultimately, everyone has to eat.

Notes

1   Bruce Kawin, *Horror and the Horror Film* (London: Anthem Press, 2012), 174.
2   Ibid., 152.
3   Carole M. Counihan, *The Anthropology of Food and Body: Gender, Meaning, and Power* (New York: Routledge, 1999), 19.

4 Robert Cettl, *Serial Killer Cinema: An Analytical Filmography with an Introduction* (Jefferson, NC: McFarland, 2003), 268.

5 Philip Jenkins, *Using Murder: The Social Construction of Serial Homicide* (New York: Aldine De Gruyter, 1994), 75.

6 Alzena MacDonald, "Dissecting the 'Dark Passenger': Reading Representations of the Serial Killer," in *Murders and Acquisitions: Representations of the Serial Killer in Popular Culture*, edited by Alzena MacDonald (New York: Bloomsbury Academic, 2013), 7.

7 Tom Gunning, *The Films of Fritz Lang: Allegories of Vision and Modernity* (London: British Film Institute, 2000), 165.

8 This English translation is from the Criterion Collection's 2004 DVD release of the film.

9 Cynthia Baron, Diane Carson, and Mark Bernard, *Appetites and Anxieties: Food, Film, and the Politics of Representation* (Detroit: Wayne State University Press, 2014), 28.

10 Gunning, *Films of Fritz Lang*, 171.

11 Louis Bayman, "Do Serial Killers Have Good Taste?" in *Murders and Acquisitions: Representations of the Serial Killer in Popular Culture*, ed. Alzena MacDonald (New York: Bloomsbury Academic, 2013), 153.

12 Ibid., 148.

13 Cettl, *Serial Killer Cinema*, 8.

14 Baron, Carson, and Bernard, *Appetites and Anxieties*, 172–4.

15 Ibid., 175.

16 Raymond Durgnat, *A Long Hard Look at "Psycho"* (London: British Film Institute, 2002), 165.

17 Ibid., 158.

18 Ibid., 165.

19 Shaun Kimber, " 'Meat's Meat, and a Man's Gotta Eat.' (*Motel Hell*, 1980): Food and Eating Within Contemporary Horror Cultures," in *Food, Media and Contemporary Culture: The Edible Image*, ed. Peri Bradley (London: Palgrave Macmillan, 2015), 131.

20 Cettl, *Serial Killer Cinema*, 413.

21 Bayman, "Do Serial Killers Have Good Taste?," 158.

22 Gunning, *Films of Fritz Lang*, 166.

23 Ian Olney, *Euro Horror: Classic European Horror Cinema in Contemporary American Culture* (Bloomington: Indiana University Press, 2013), 195–6.

24 Ibid., 197.

25 Mark Bernard, "Cannibalism, Class and Power: A Foodways Analysis of *The Texas Chainsaw Massacre* Series," *Food, Culture & Society* 14, no. 3 (2011): 415–16.

26 Victoria L. Smith, "Our Serial Killers, Our Superheroes, and Ourselves: Showtime's *Dexter*," *Quarterly Review of Film and Video* 28 (2011): 391.

Bibliography

Baron, Cynthia, Diane Carson, and Mark Bernard. *Appetites and Anxieties: Food, Film, and the Politics of Representation*. Detroit: Wayne State University Press, 2014.

Bayman, Louis. "Do Serial Killers Have Good Taste?" In *Murders and Acquisitions: Representations of the Serial Killer in Popular Culture*, edited by Alzena MacDonald. New York: Bloomsbury Academic, 2013.

Bernard, Mark. "Cannibalism, Class and Power: A Foodways Analysis of *The Texas Chainsaw Massacre* Series." *Food, Culture & Society* 14, no. 3 (2011): 413–32.

Cettl, Robert. *Serial Killer Cinema: An Analytical Filmography with an Introduction*. Jefferson, NC: McFarland, 2003.

Counihan, Carole M. *The Anthropology of Food and Body: Gender, Meaning, and Power*. New York: Routledge, 1999.

Durgnat, Raymond. *A Long Hard Look at "Psycho."* London: British Film Institute, 2002.

Gunning, Tom. *The Films of Fritz Lang: Allegories of Vision and Modernity*. London: British Film Institute, 2000.

Jenkins, Philip. *Using Murder: The Social Construction of Serial Homicide*. New York: Aldine De Gruyter, 1994.

Kawin, Bruce. *Horror and the Horror Film*. London: Anthem Press, 2012.

Kimber, Shaun. "'Meat's Meat, and a Man's Gotta Eat.' (*Motel Hell*, 1980): Food and Eating within Contemporary Horror Cultures." In *Food, Media and Contemporary Culture: The Edible Image*, edited by Peri Bradley, 125–43. London: Palgrave Macmillan, 2015.

MacDonald, Alzena. "Dissecting the 'Dark Passenger': Reading Representations of the Serial Killer." In *Murders and Acquisitions: Representations of the Serial Killer in Popular Culture*, edited by Alzena MacDonald, 1–13. New York: Bloomsbury Academic, 2013.

Olney, Ian. *Euro Horror: Classic European Horror Cinema in Contemporary American Culture*. Bloomington: Indiana University Press, 2013.

Smith, Victoria L. "Our Serial Killers, Our Superheroes, and Ourselves: Showtime's *Dexter*." *Quarterly Review of Film and Video* 28 (2011): 390–400.

18

Consumption, Cannibalism, and Corruption in Jorge Michel Grau's *Somos lo que hay*

Stacy Rusnak

Jorge Michel Grau's 2010 film *Somos lo que hay* (We are what we are) focuses on a modern day cannibalistic family whose patriarch dies in the opening moments of the story, leaving his economically disenfranchised family the burden of providing for their "ritual" feast. Unlike other cannibal-horror films, *Somos lo que hay* represents the eating of human flesh as a banal, everyday occurrence—more alluded to than seen on screen. Within the context of the film, the theme of cannibalism expresses the difficulties that face the citizens of Mexico's ever-growing metropolis.

Key debates on Mexican cinema have focused on Mexico's uncomfortable relationship to its violent colonial past and its current neocolonial relationship to the United States. From this tension, a discourse on *mexicanidad* (Mexican national identity) has come to define a significant portion of representations of Mexico on screen. However, these representations of national identity often completely erase the presence of those marginalized citizens that suffer the most. *Somos lo que hay* brings the focus back onto the urban poor through the representations of cannibalism, or cannibal-like behaviors, that play out on the screen. This chapter, then, looks at how *Somos lo que hay* captures the raw and gritty ramifications of Mexico's political and economic failures for its citizens. Temporal and spatial locations in the film form dialectical relationships that encourage us to reconsider the importance of historicization through the association with cannibalism and consumption, while more traditional taboos allegorize the repressive patriarchal structures that construct Mexican society. These structures become manifest in the rise of "urban tribes"—from prostitutes and alienated youth to cannibals—as a means of survival. As these "tribes" align with contemporary notions of social change, they devour and eat away at the typically powerful and corrupt entities that control Mexican society.

Somos lo que hay focuses on a poor family of five whose economically precarious existence in present-day Mexico City is endangered when the father (Humberto Yáñez) dies unexpectedly. Alfredo (Francisco Barreiro), the socially awkward eldest son, and his hot-headed younger brother Julián (Alan Chávez) are forced to provide for their mother and sister—a role that, it soon becomes clear, they are ill-equipped to fill. "Providing," however, means more than tending the family business in one of the city's street markets; they are a family of cannibals, who require a steady supply of victims to ritually kill and consume. The brothers' attempts to bring home human "meat"—first a homeless boy, then a prostitute, and finally a young gay man Alfredo picks up in a club—fail in a variety of ways, humiliating them and forcing their sister Sabina (Paulina Gaitan) and mother Patricia (Carmen Beato) to take action to secure the family's food supply. Patricia, having had sex with a cab driver and brought him home for the night, beats him to death with a shovel the next morning, then watches approvingly as Sabina butchers his corpse in preparation for a feast.

Before the family members can satisfy their hunger, however, their world begins to disintegrate. The brothers' clumsiness as kidnappers, the authorities' discovery of a human finger in the father's stomach, and Patricia's arrogance stir even Mexico City's notoriously corrupt authorities to action. At the climax of the film, Patricia insists on completing the ritual feast, even as police converge on the family's small apartment. Both brothers are gunned down, and Patricia—though she escapes into the city—is soon beaten to death by prostitutes seeking revenge for her role in the murder of one of their own. Only Sabina—mistaken by the police for a victim, rather than a member, of the family—survives to continue a cycle in which Mexico City's underclass feeds, literally, on itself.

Historicization, poverty, and consumption

In "Theses on the Philosophy of History," Walter Benjamin states that to articulate history is not to recognize events from the past as they were per se, but rather "to seize hold of a memory as it flashes up at a moment of danger . . . The danger affects both the content of the tradition and its receivers. The same threat hangs over both: that of becoming a tool of the ruling classes."[1] Images of the past do not simply belong to their specific time, but can be blasted out of the continuum of history. When the past and present come together in these moments, they produce a dialectical relationship. This relationship requires that two moments in history be brought together in such tight tension that a productive stasis results, opening up a gap in the text that offers an alternative understanding of history (self, identity, etc.).

In *Somos lo que hay*, past and present collide in the space of the shopping mall, a quintessential icon of American consumerism, and the *tianquis*, the open-air markets whose history stretches back to Aztec times. This collision allows us to investigate the connections between consumerism, classism, poverty, and violence. In the opening scene, the father emerges from the bowels of a shopping center, shot from a high, disorienting angle. The mall is a sterile-looking structure of gray steel and glass, which stands in stark contrast to the dirty, disheveled man stumbling through it. He is a modern-day *flâneur*, ambling through the open-air passages of the mall like one of George A. Romero's zombies from *Night of the Living Dead* (1968). Unlike the classical Benjaminian *flâneur*, who negotiates the physical confines of urban topographies and the traces of local histories, the father is connected to the unconscious walking dead and to mindless consumers.

The father's emergence into the city center visually establishes the theme of starvation, which is echoed later in the film by the family's desperate measures to secure a cannibalistic meal without his assistance. As he comes up an escalator from the lower level of a shopping mall, he is tightly framed on both sides by the walls of the passageway that leads outside. The gaping space works like a mouth that opens out into everyday life—spitting him out into the city center, where he walks past a display of bikini-clad mannequins, stumbling away from their mockingly blank stares. They are a reminder of his marginalized position in society: that he will never have the means to shop in this mall, let alone take a luxurious vacation to the beach. He takes a few steps and falls to the ground, clutching his belly as he spews black bile onto the concrete (Figure 18.1). The black vomit tells us that he is suffering from the effects of starvation. At his death, we simply assume that he is yet another victim of poverty. However, we will later learn that the he has fallen behind on his duties to provide for his family. Instead of hunting for their next prey, he has given in to his carnal desires, spending his "leisure" time with the local prostitutes.

The father's appearance is like a stain. He makes "dirty" the space of the mall, and therefore, must be expelled quickly. However, he makes his

FIGURE 18.1 *Modern-day flâneur: Humberto Yáñez as the cannibal father.*

mark on the film by his grotesque display of poverty through his suffering body, illustrating Julia Kristeva's notion of the abject—human waste, blood, corpses, bodily disfigurement, and so on—as a site where meaning collapses, threatening the symbolic structure because it does not obey rules or respect borders, and disturbing identity and order.[2] The father's dirty appearance and public vomiting are both examples of abjection, but it is his economic marginalization that is most threatening. His presence disturbs the consumer dream, provoking a sense of anxiety. The authorities' swift erasure of his death by the removal of his body ensures a speedy return to the numbing rhythms of distracted consumer consumption.

Once death removes the father from the story, the focus of the film shifts to the impact of his absence on the family. His sons Alfredo and Julián, thrust into the role of provider, must open the family's stall in one of Mexico's *tianguis*. The history of these markets extends far back into the pre-Hispanic era, when they were considered the most important form of commerce. Makeshift shops are set up early in the morning and then broken down at the end of the day. The appearance of the *tianguis*, in comparison with the opening images of the shopping mall, functions as a bridge that links the past to the present. Bringing these disparate spatial and temporal moments together in the film sparks the creation of a dialectical image that holds the two moments in tension. In the resulting gap, the past can be reimagined with "the possibility of a radicalized relationship to history, in which the present as much as the past can be reimagined, re-experienced, and critiqued."[3] In this case, allowing for a critique of Mexico's legacy of classism.

The scenes in the *tianguis* demonstrate how the inequality in socioeconomic conditions drives a wedge between different classes. The sequence begins with Julián and Alfredo waiting in line to rent a table to display their wares (the family is too poor to afford their own) and then cuts to the boys tightly framed within their booth at the end of the row of stalls. The tight framing and staging of their booth reflect the pressures of society and their marginalization in it. A man approaches and asks about a Mido watch that he left with the father for repair. From its inception, Mido (in Spanish, "I measure") was associated with technical innovation and modern sophistication.[4] When the boys look up at the customer, Julián gives a quick, snide laugh at the man's shaved head, baggy t-shirt, and hoodie jacket. Offended, the customer looks at Julián and says, "*¿De qué te ríes pinche escuincle?*" (What are you laughing at, you fucking punk?). The term *escuincle* comes from the Nahuatl, *itzcuintli*, which literally means dog in English. Julián lunges at the customer in a vicious attack. He throws stab-like punches into the upper part of his opponent's body, as if he were literally slicing into the man's flesh. On a literal level, Julián's outburst of violence (the first we see from him in the film) prefigures the all-out slaughter that the family will eventually engage in to secure a human body for their cannibalistic consumption. On another level, it is a metaphor for the bubbling over of class tensions—a reminder that in neoliberal Mexico, upward mobility is not always achieved through work and effort. Julián, like his father before him, knows that he will never be able to afford such luxury. The "good life" therefore becomes synonymous with the symbolic display of material possessions rather than with productivity, an association that directly conflicts with the cannibal family's drive to find a meal and survive.[5]

In addition to the outburst of violence, the next sequence opens with a second subtle hint about the kind of family featured in the film. The boys return home to a small apartment in the "Bicentennial Projects," a housing unit for poor, urban families. Patricia, their mother, is alone preparing the ties with which they will later bind the arms and legs of their victims. A medium close-up captures the movement of Patricia's hands as she pulls each tie to ensure its strength. There are perhaps twenty such ties on the table in front of her, clearly indicating that the family's capture and consumption of humans is nothing new. Patricia expresses anger at the news of the boys' confrontation in the *tianguis*, but it is the sudden arrival of the daughter, Sabina, that really turns things on end. Sabina reveals the news about their now-dead father, which sends Patricia into a rage as she blames his ineptitude as a provider on the prostitutes with whom he spent his time. Satisfying the desires of the flesh clearly does not put food on the table.

Meanwhile, the siblings gather in the hallway, and Sabina announces that they *must get something* for the next day. It is interesting to note that the apartment in the Bicentennial Projects is where the siblings drop the first hint about food. The name of the place is symbolic, since in September 2010 Mexico celebrated the bicentennial anniversary of its independence from

Spain. A series of projects were organized across Mexico City with the hope of highlighting its progress as a modern, global city.[6] Eventually, this space will witness the slaughter of the family's ritual feast, echoing the Aztec struggle against Spanish colonialism and critiquing the present neoliberal moment. Despite Mexico's attempt to present itself as a modern, progressive country, many of its citizens are forced to rely on their ancestors' "barbaric" customs to survive in the so-called civilized world. People resort to violence when they have nothing to lose, and in *Somos lo que hay*, this violence is articulated through a fundamental, primitive drive to sustain the human body.

Christina Jacqueline Johns suggests that any discussion of violence in Mexican society requires a return to the sixteenth century and the Spanish Conquest. During this time, "Mexico was assigned a position within the capitalist world system. Mexico is still in a basically colonial position 400 years later, subordinate within the capitalist world system."[7] Society suffers from the heritage of the colonial era and the persistence of political forms and ideologies with their foundations in the economic inequalities of that era. Even with a radical change in economic structure, Mexico would still have to struggle "against Colonial values and attitudes ingrained within the lives of the people."[8] Any real change would require redemption from this preconceived sense of inferiority—a redemption that, Benjamin suggests, comes at a high cost, in a crucial moment of recognition. He writes, "[O]ur image of happiness is indissolubly bound up with the image of redemption. The same applies to our view of the past, which is expressed through history. The past carries with it a temporal index by which it is referred to redemption."[9] *Somos lo que hay* appears, at first, to shut down any possibility of this redemption, leaving us to mourn the future, which is already lost.

This "loss" is reflected in the family's drive to secure their next victim, in order to complete the grand finale of their ritual feast. The two brothers are next in line to follow in their father's footsteps, but they prove hopeless at providing for the family. After one night of hunting for prey, the boys return with a female prostitute, just the kind of "meat" that Patricia abhors. As the prostitute lies tied to a large wooden table, Julián, like his father, is overcome by his carnal desire and begins to run his hands all over the woman's body. When Alfredo tries to stop him, a fight breaks out between the brothers, ended only by the sudden appearance of Patricia, who uses a large mallet-like weapon to bludgeon the defenseless prostitute. The "whack" of the instrument striking the body chills the viewer and causes the boys to cower in fear. Patricia's savagery is uncannily fascinating, as she has remained fairly passive through the first half of the film. She rejects the prostitute's "meat" as nonchalantly as one might dismiss an overdone steak. Her "pickiness" demonstrates that the family's cannibalism is about more than survival. The poverty-stricken family, with which we may once have sympathized, turns monstrous right before our eyes.

The sense of "loss," and of the boys' inability to provide, is repeated when Alfredo's choice of meat—a young gay man named Gustavo (Miguel Ángel Hoppe)—manages to flee the cannibal family. As the siblings stand around trying to decide whether they should chase him, the cab driver—Patricia's lover from the night before—walks into the room and turns to run away from the scene himself. At that exact moment, however, Patricia hits him in the face with a shovel and—for the first time in the film—the family comes together as they descend ravenously upon her lover-turned-victim. Patricia, Julián and Sabina hold the prey down, while Alfredo picks up a wooden tool and savagely beats the man's face in, then takes a bite out of his eye and shoves the tool into his mouth. The camera slowly zooms out, and we see that *this* meal will not get away. Working collectively, the family has finally secured an "appropriate" victim to sustain and nourish them.

However, this jubilant moment is brief. Patricia immediately sends the boys in search of Gustavo, and as they leave, she begins the ritual preparation of their victim by handing over the sacrificial knife to Sabina. There is a cut to an extreme close-up of the tip of the knife as Sabina slices into the man's belly, completely at ease performing her duties. She continues by taking a hammer to the man's body with a loud "whack," and after she pulls out the tool that Alfredo lodged in the man, a second "whack" is heard, followed by a cut-away to Patricia's blood-splattered face. Neither woman flinches. The camera tilts downwards as the two women take hooks and pull apart the man's body at the sternum, accompanied by the sound of viscera being torn asunder.

This scene, along with the boys' inability to lead or provide, is suggestive of a shift in the carefully constructed notions of gender passed down through postrevolutionary rhetoric. According to Armida De La Garza, typical postrevolutionary iconography codes macho men as violent and abusive, while women are envisioned as caregivers and are tied to the domestic sphere.[10] Although the women in the film prepare the body in the space of the home, the brutality of the scene as Sabina tears the body apart—accented by blood splattering and the sounds of breaking bones, piercing skin, and wrenching intestines out—all work to rip apart simple binary notions of gender.

The women's dismemberment of the body also signals the banality of everyday violence in Mexico, where kidnappings, drug-related murder, and human trafficking are all too common. In the media, various factors account for the violence that plagues the country: the shift in North America's market for drugs, personal enmities between crime bosses, government inaction or mis-action, and so on.[11] None of these explanations, however, account for

Mexico's violent past, and the redemptive moment that Benjamin speaks of is therefore lost.

In the film, Alfredo alone experiences this moment of recognition, albeit only on the verge of his own death. As he is about to be shot by police, Alfredo pounces on his sister and takes a ravenous bite out of her throat, causing blood to spew everywhere. His attack is not about ingesting her flesh, but is, rather, a sacrifice designed to save her and allow her to continue the family legacy. He knows that his gesture will be misinterpreted by the authorities, who will think she is just another one of the family's victims, and he is proven correct. A final close-up of Sabina at the end of the film shows her scanning the crowded Mexico City streets for her next victim. The cycle of violence continues, and she carries the family heritage forward.

Cannibalism, youth culture, and disaffection

The dystopian vision presented in *Somos lo que hay* prefigures an equally dismal future for Mexico's youth culture, as the theme of cannibalism becomes manifest in a kind of cultural feasting, where the youth are "invited" to devour themselves. We see this self-consumption in the ways in which the family members' predatory behaviors reduce all interactions with the outside world to acts of indulging in the flesh, all in an attempt to fulfill the emptiness in their individual lives. As a sociopolitical category, "youth" culture is influenced by a variety of discourses (legal, psychological, sociological, filmic) and institutions (family, state, church, school). For this reason, any discussion of youth culture "must be situated historically and geographically in particular times and particular spaces."[12] Laura Podalsky suggests that the acute socioeconomic polarization within Mexico, and in relationship to its northern neighbor, becomes manifest in youth films as an intense feeling of de-centeredness.[13] In *Somos lo que hay*, the themes of cannibalism and self-consumption transform the family into a symbolic, integrated digestive system, one that eats indiscriminately but cannot process what it has consumed. The more the family members attempt to feed, the more disconnected they become from themselves and from each other.

After failing to abduct a street kid and being wounded by the would-be victim's posse, Alfredo returns home so that Sabina can tend to his wounds. The viewer senses Alfredo's insecurity and feeling of entrapment through the tightness of the pair's framing in the claustrophobic space of their bathroom. Alfredo is shot with his back toward the camera in medium close-up, head hanging dejectedly downwards. He looks over his shoulder at Sabina and there is a cut to his point-of-view. The image is then reversed and Alfredo is looking at his reflection in the mirror. Sabina is in the foreground, slightly off center to the left and somewhat out of focus. For the first time, Alfredo's expression changes to one of conviction as he tells Sabina, "*No puedo*" (I can't do it). He cannot provide the ritual feast. The camera tilts up, and Sabina is brought into focus while Alfredo becomes a blur. This movement of the camera and the rack focus foreshadow the ending of the film, when Sabina will emerge as the head of the family. In the intimate space of the bathroom, patriarchal conservatism is literally "flushed away" as the cinematography underscores Sabina's emerging status as the leader of the family.

In Mexico, where the national symbol of masculinity is the nation-state, a tacit agreement between the male and the state is forged via the socially understood role of the *macho* empowered by the state. In turn, allegiance to and identification with the patriarchy guarantees the state a position of power. Despite his failure, Alfredo makes one final attempt to find a suitable feast for the family as he stalks the unwitting Gustavo, but his choice of a gay man as his prey defies the image of the strong, *macho* patriarch and earns his mother's disdain. Not only does his preference alienate him from the social norm, it also drives a wedge between mother and son, demonstrating the unraveling of the patriarchal family.

Alfredo finds Gustavo in the transitory space of the subway and follows him to a local nightclub. Strobe lights filter through the space of the club and techno music pumps out of loudspeakers. The camera's gaze, and so the viewers' eyes, moves over the crowd, mimicking Alfredo's search for Gustavo. The pounding techno music and the surging bodies match the anticipation we experience with Alfredo as he literally stalks Gustavo. When the two finally come together, Gustavo kisses Alfredo, and a medium close-up reveals a look of bewilderment on Alfredo's face, as he is not there to "pick up" Gustavo but to bring him home for the family's next buffet. Unsure and anxious about the kiss, Alfredo flees the club.

The camera follows Alfredo into the subway, where he is shot in a medium close-up with tears in his eyes as a lady on the subway begins to sing:

> I don't care about life / Nothing is important to me / It's suffering / Those who have nothing / Don't cry over love / They live happy / All of the disappointments / Within a broken soul / They don't hurt or harm you / They make you stronger / Life is so thankless / It puts you on / Bitter paths / Of trouble / And of suffering / But when the evening / Of our hard life comes / The voice of our mother / Is light / Is light dear.

As the song plays out, a series of cuts shift our attention to other family members, who display their sense of detachment. The first shows Julián at home, a low-key, side lighting illuminating half of his face in a medium close-up shot. He looks lost, quite literally "in the dark" about his family's future and his own. Another reveals Sabina, submerged up to her nose in the bathtub, looking like a hungry alligator ready to snap at any available victim. Julián enters the bathroom and sits on the edge of the tub, and because there have been several moments of sexual tension between these two, one is led to believe that Julián might be having sex with his own sister. The song continues to play over these images, breaking down the boundaries between the film and the viewer, plunging us into the feelings of hopelessness that link the three. Finally, there is a cut to the back of a taxi. The camera zooms out, and Patricia pops up in the window, bobbing back and forth as she is fucked from behind by the taxi driver—the same man who will become the family's ritual sacrifice, which they never actually get to eat.

At the end of the song, Alfredo returns to the club and passionately, yet violently, kisses Gusatvo. In this moment, Alfredo recognizes the power of seduction. He becomes aware of his sexuality and uses it as a weapon to draw in the unsuspecting victim. He has officially challenged the patriarchy, while still bringing home the bacon, so to speak. Jon Towlson writes that "cannibalism is seen as a monstrous extension of patriarchal family values and a way of holding the family unit together in the face of social change."[14] For this family, cannibalism is presented as the social norm, not a deviation from the norm. Like cannibalism, Alfredo's homosexual transgression, Sabina and Julián's implied incest, and Patricia's spur-of-the moment coupling with the taxi driver are all taboo subjects. Their individual desires actually drive them away from socially accepted behavior and from each other, which ultimately leads to their downfall. The disintegration of the family unit illustrates the weakening of the repressive patriarchal structures that secure the perpetuation of the *macho* nation state.

Corruption, community, and urban tribes

Mexico has a long history of corruption. *Mordidas* ("bribes" in the colloquial, "little bites" in the literal) are commonly used with corrupt police or bureaucrats. Judges can be paid off at the right price, and high-ranking government officials have been known to pocket millions. This climate of political corruption has fostered a sense of public distrust and cynicism.[15] *Somos lo que hay* demonstrates how this distrust manifests itself in the construction of what we might call "urban tribes." Coined by Michel Maffesoli, the term refers to the recent appearance of micro-groups in urban areas, which are considered tribe-like because of their shared philosophies, styles, and behavioral patterns. Individuals in these groups form informal, emotional connections with one another, which function as alternatives to traditional family structures.[16] In the film, the urban tribes are like pack animals. The cannibal family is one of them, but the other two groups—the street kids and prostitutes—are markedly different. They are not seeking the flesh of their fellow members. Instead, their presence in the film reveals the ways in which cannibalism and capitalism are intimately connected and work together to expose the failing infrastructure and corruption that plagues society.[17]

The street kids would appear to be the most vulnerable urban tribe in the film. The elimination of state protection for children in Mexico is a direct result of the state's capitulation to a neoliberal agenda.[18] Without state assistance, children who are already economically marginalized are left exposed to the ravages of global capitalism. For this reason, Alfredo and Julián see the street kids as an easy food source, and they pick off two little boys just as casually as one would choose an apple in the store. Their plan is quickly foiled, however, as the other kids spring into action and protect one another. One little girl pulls on the legs of the child that Alfredo is trying to drag away while another grabs hold of Alfredo's leg, creating an the image reminiscent of lions ripping apart prey in the wild. The savagery of the scene becomes mesmerizing as the tables turn and the children erupt into violence, throwing rocks and chasing Alfredo and Julián away. The scene ends with a medium close-up of the kids flanking their friend on either side, assessing his well-being. The children's ability to work together contrasts sharply with the disintegration of the cannibal family. Collective action proves to be more advantageous than the ideology of individualism and self-interest—dominant features of capitalist societies.

The other economically disenfranchised urban tribe is the prostitutes, whose function in the film is to expose police corruption. After Patricia brutally murders the prostitute her boys bring home as the family meal, she takes the battered, lifeless body and dumps it on the street, directly in front of the other prostitutes, who call the police, willing to pay them to kill the perpetrators. A close-up of one of the prostitutes registers a distinct look of surprise when the officer turns down their *mordida*. She whistles, and two women bring out a young girl of about fifteen as a more attractive "offering" to him. In a medium long shot, we witness the officer simply "eat her up" as he caresses her hair. However, the officer gets a call and rushes away from the scene and toward the Bicentennial Projects—the family's home—from which Patricia has fled, leaving the rest of her family behind. Her disloyalty to her children contrasts with the prostitutes' loyalty to the tribe. In a long shot, we see

FIGURE 18.2 *A heap of flesh: Patricia's murder by the prostitutes' urban tribe.*

Patricia sitting alone on a slide at a playground. The scene is dimly lit by one lamppost. From off-screen, the prostitutes file into the frame, and the camera cuts away from the action, then back to Patricia's bloody, lifeless body on the ground (Figure 18.2). Reduced to a pile of meat, unfit to consume, Patricia's body is simply left to rot. The prostitutes have transgressed the law through murder, but their act symbolizes the new generation devouring the old. In an increasingly global culture, the traditional, patriarchal family represented by the cannibals is difficult to sustain, while the constructed family of the urban tribe becomes a viable means of survival.

Conclusion

The theme of cannibalism in *Somos lo que hay* plays a central role in highlighting the presence of the urban poor, who are often dismissed in cinematic representations because their presence reminds us of our own inadequacies and of the state's failures. The urban tribes of cannibals, street kids, and prostitutes demonstrate a sense of fatalism about urban poverty in Mexico. Since the establishment of NAFTA, many filmmakers have expressed the depreciation of the lives of the poor, evidenced in the decreased services, lack of basic infrastructure, and the inability to articulate a hopeful future for the poor.[19] *Somos lo que hay* reflects these conditions, depicting one group (the cannibals) that literally consumes society to survive, while the other two, instead of succumbing to the misery of the streets, have learned to navigate life by forming alternative structures that provide them with new mechanisms for survival. Moving away from the individualizing rhetoric of neoliberalism, the film suggests that in a Mexico that lacks state support and infrastructure, citizens are left to depend on each other for security and protection.

Notes

1. Walter Benjamin, "Thesis on the Philosophy of History," in *Illuminations*, ed. Hannah Arendt, trans. Harry Zohn (New York: Shocken Books, 1968), 255.
2. Julia Kristeva, *The Powers of Horror: An Essay on Abjection* (New York: Columbia University Press, 1982), 53.
3. Rosalind Galt, *The New European Cinema: Redrawing the Map* (New York: Columbia University Press, 2006), 73.
4. "History," *MIDO: Swiss Watches Since 1918*, http://www.midowatch.com/en/content/1918-0 (accessed October 9, 2015).
5. Susana Rotker, "Cities Written by Violence: An Introduction," in *Citizens of Fear: Urban Violence in Latin America*, ed. Susana Rotker (New Brunswick, NJ: Rutgers University Press, 2002), 12–13.
6. Chris Hawley and Sergio Solache, "Mexico Falling behind on Grand Bicentennial Plans," *The Arizona Republic*, September 18, 2009, http://archive.azcentral.com/arizonarepublic/news/articles/2009/09/18/20090918bicentennial0918.html (accessed October 6, 2015).
7. Christina Jacqueline Johns, *The Origins of Violence in Mexican Society* (Westport, CT: Praeger Publications, 1995), 199.
8. Ibid., 200.
9. Benjamin, "Theses on the Philosophy of History," 254.
10. Armida De La Garza, *Mexico on Film: National Identity & International Relations* (LaVergne: Arena Books, 2006), 151.
11. Pamela Starr, "Mexico's Big, Inherited Challenges," *Current History* 111, no. 742 (2012): 46–7.
12. Laura Podalsky, *The Politics of Affect and Emotion in Contemporary Latin American Cinema: Argentina, Brazil, Cuba, and Mexico* (New York: Palgrave Macmillan, 2011), 102.
13. Laura Podalsky, "The Young, the Damned, and the Restless: Youth in Contemporary Mexican Cinema," *Framework* 49, no. 1 (2008): 151.
14. Jon Towlson, *Subversive Horror Cinema: Countercultural Messages of Films from Frankenstein to the Present* (Jefferson, NC: McFarland, 2014), 98.
15. Stephen D. Morris, "Corruption and the Mexican Political System: Continuity and Change," *Third World Quarterly* 20, no. 3 (June 1999): 623.
16. Frank Iovene, "Sociologist: Descartes Created the Crisis of Modernity, and 'Urban Tribes' Will Fix It," *Business Insider*, October 7, 2014, http://www.businessinsider.com/afp-urban-tribes-thriving-in-modern-society-2014-10 (accessed November 5, 2015).

17 Towlson, *Subversive Horror Cinema*, 148.
18 Roger Magazine, "An Innovative Combination of Neoliberalism and State Corporatism: The Case of a Locally Based NGO in Mexico City," *The Annals of the American Academy of Political and Social Sciences* 590 (2003): 245.
19 Misha MacLaird, *Aesthetics and Politics in the Mexican Film Industry* (New York: Palgrave Macmillan, 2013), 111.

Bibliography

Benjamin, Walter. "Thesis on the Philosophy of History." In *Illuminations*, edited by Hannah Arendt, translated by Harry Zohn, 253–67. New York: Shocken Books, 1968.

De La Garza, Armida. *Mexico on Film: National Identity & International Relations*. LaVergne: Arena Books, 2006.

Galt, Rosalind. *The New European Cinema: Redrawing the Map*. New York: Columbia University Press, 2006.

Hawley, Chris, and Sergio Solache. "Mexico Falling Behind on Grand Bicentennial Plans." *The Arizona Republic*, September 18, 2009. http://archive.azcentral.com/arizonarepublic/news/articles/2009/09/18/20090918bicentennial0918.html (accessed October 6, 2015).

"History." *MIDO: Swiss Watches Since 1918*. http://www.midowatch.com/en/content/1918-0 (accessed October 9, 2015).

Iovene, Frank. "Sociologist: Descartes Created the Crisis of Modernity, and 'Urban Tribes' Will Fix it." *Business Insider*, October 7, 2014. http://www.businessinsider.com/afp-urban-tribes-thriving-in-modern-society-2014-10 (accessed November 5, 2015).

Kristeva, Julia. *The Powers of Horror: An Essay on Abjection*. New York: Columbia University Press, 1982.

Johns, Christina Jacqueline. *The Origins of Violence in Mexican Society*. Westport, CT: Praeger Publications, 1995.

MacLaird, Misha. *Aesthetics and Politics in the Mexican Film Industry*. New York: Palgrave Macmillan, 2013.

Magazine, Roger. "An Innovative Combination of Neoliberalism and State Corporatism: The Case of a Locally Based NGO in Mexico City." *The Annals of the American Academy of Political and Social Sciences* 590 (2003): 243–56.

Morris, Stephen D. "Corruption and the Mexican Political System: Continuity and Change." *Third World Quarterly* 20, no. 3 (June 1999): 623–43.

Podalsky, Laura. "The Young, the Damned, and the Restless: Youth in Contemporary Mexican Cinema." *Framework* 49, no. 1 (2008): 144–60.

Podalsky, Laura. *The Politics of Affect and Emotion in Contemporary Latin American Cinema: Argentina, Brazil, Cuba, and Mexico*. New York: Palgrave Macmillan, 2011.

Rotker, Susana. "Cities Written by Violence: An Introduction." In *Citizens of Fear: Urban Violence in Latin America*, edited by Susana Rotker, 7–22. New Brunswick, NJ: Rutgers University Press, 2002.

Scholefield, Joanna. "Under the Skin: How Filmmakers Affectively Reduce the Space between the Film and the Viewer." *Film Matters* 5, no. 1 (2014): 44–53.

Somos lo que hay. Directed by Jorge Michel Grau. 2010. MPI Media Group, 2011. DVD.

Starr, Pamela. "Mexico's Big, Inherited Challenges." *Current History* 111, no. 742 (2012): 43–9.

Towlson, Jon. *Subversive Horror Cinema: Countercultural Messages of Films from Frankenstein to the Present*. Jefferson, NC: McFarland, 2014.

19

Sinister Pastry: British "Meat" Pies in *Titus* and *Sweeney Todd*

Vivian Halloran

In 2004, three years before the trial of Canada's worst serial killer—pig farmer Robert (Willie) Pickton—finally started, a series of billboards sponsored by People for the Ethical Treatment of Animals (PETA) started appearing along the roads around Toronto and Edmonton. Featuring a head-shot of a serious blond young woman on the left and a rather cheerful looking pig on the right, the message linking both images together was an unmistakable reference to the horrific killings: "Neither of us is meat." Not only was Pickton convicted of killing and dismembering his victims, whose skeletal remains were scattered around the grounds, but according to reporter Colin Perkel: "The province's medical officer of health said recently meat products from Pickton's farm may have contained human remains."[1] When challenged by the victims' families about the questionable ethics of exploiting this crime to promote its vegetarian ideology, PETA refused to apologize for its shock-value tactics. News of the ad campaign went viral, with news outlets around the world showing the image and interviewing victims' relatives. The PETA ads not only invoked the taboo subject of cannibalism to promote their radical animal rights agenda, but their self-righteous, faux-feminist equation of meat consumption with the sexual exploitation of women appeared to blame the victims for their own unsavory end, since most of them were sex workers.

An editorial condemning the organization's ad campaign in the *Toronto Star* quoted PETA's campaign director, Bruce Friedrich, as stating: "A corpse is a corpse, whether it formerly belonged to a pig, a cow, a chicken or a human."[2] As indefensible as this statement may sound at face value, there is an eerie resonance between the notion of regarding all corpses as equally bestial, and the long-standing culinary tradition in the Anglophone world of describing filled pie crusts as "coffins."

When Pickton finally went on trial in 2007, the *Daily Mail* once again reminded its readers of the distasteful fate of his young victims with its headline "Did farmer turn 28 women into pies?" However, no definitive proof was ever found that he either put human flesh into the pies or fed his victims to his pigs and then stuffed pork pies with them. Pickton was eventually convicted of murder and sentenced to life in prison.[3]

Covering the events surrounding the first day of the trial, a *Daily Mail* reporter noted that: "The judge has warned jurors the case would be 'as bad as a horror movie.'"[4] Cannibalism had long been a staple of low-budget exploitation-horror films, such as Tobe Hooper's *Texas Chainsaw Massacre* (1974), Eli Roth's *Cabin Fever* (2002), and Alexandre Aja's *The Hills Have Eyes* (2006), or perhaps the transformation of unwitting travelers into sausage in Kevin Connor's *Motel Hell* (1980), but by the time of Pickton's trial it had also begun to appear in mainstream films with prestigious theatrical pedigrees, such as *Titus* (1999) and *Sweeney Todd* (2007).

Julie Taymor's stylized adaptation of Shakespeare's earliest tragedy and Tim Burton's adaptation of Stephen Sondheim's musical, itself based on a successful penny dreadful, both exact much bloodier revenge upon their protagonists, but the specter of unwitting cannibalism haunts both films, as it did the legal proceedings surrounding Pickton. While both films may be effectively read through a range of psychological interpretations, I would like to advance a different reading—culinary in nature—to better understand the significance of the making and eating of fleshy "meat pies" that is central to each.

Sins of the flesh

Titus Andronicus begins with the titular Roman general returning from a long campaign with Tamora, queen of the newly defeated Goths, as his captive. She swears vengeance on him and his family after he sacrifices her first-born son to the gods, touching off a cycle of violent retribution that includes the rape and mutilation of Titus's daughter Lavinia, and the murder of her husband, by Tamora's surviving sons. The story culminates in a banquet where Titus, having killed her sons, cooks their flesh into a meat pie and forces her to eat it before she, too, is dispatched. *Sweeney Todd* tells the story of Benjamin

Barker, a London barber exiled to Australia on a trumped-up charge by corrupt Judge Turpin, who then takes advantage of Barker's absence by raping his wife Lucy and appointing himself guardian of their daughter Johanna (who he also covets). Returning after fifteen years, Barker resumes his old profession under the name "Sweeney Todd," plotting revenge while venting his anger by slitting the throats of customers with a straight razor. The bodies of his victims become filling in the meat pies baked by his landlady, Mrs. Lovett, in her disreputable basement shop, removing the incriminating evidence while providing her with a steady, no-cost supply of fresh "meat."

As they follow a dishonored general's and a grief-stricken barber's descent into madness, each of these movies demand that their audiences confront the two-stage transformation of frightened, living people first into inanimate corpses, and then into savory pastry. The emphasis on the culinary aspect of this transfiguration downplays the cold-blooded horror of the murders themselves, because of the deep associations people have between food and nourishment. By showcasing (or parodying) the cooking process that goes into producing meat-filled delicacies, these films evoke a primal fear associated with all covered foods—the pies' lack of transparency means that the cook has all the power and diners are at his or her mercy. The fear of being randomly killed thus seems unlikely, compared to the gnawing paranoia viewers suddenly experience about what they (may) have eaten, especially for audience members who do not routinely prepare their own food. By showing how the body is reduced to mere flesh, both films contrast their own intangibility as visual media with the embodied, three-dimensional reality of their audiences' physical heft.

The meat pie's iconic value as a symbol of British comfort food renders its perversion through the addition of human flesh intensely shocking for the viewer. The audience's awareness of Titus Andronicus and Mrs. Lovett's willful adulteration of the food-supply chain elicits feelings of the uncanny—once the integrity of the familiar meat pie has been called into question, the idea of it does not seem quite as comforting as it once was.

Food and corruption

Writing in a 2012 op-ed essay in the *New York Times*, investigative journalist Eric Schlosser argued that

> [w]ithout tough food safety rules, a perverse economic incentive guides the marketplace. Adulterated food is cheaper to produce than safe food.

Since consumers cannot tell the difference between the two, companies that try to do the right thing are forced to compete with companies that couldn't care less.[5]

Although *Sweeney Todd* is set in nineteenth-century London, rather than in Schlosser's twenty-first-century United States, the same dynamic is at work. The unscrupulous baker Mrs. Lovett, played with relish by Helena Bonham Carter, is a widowed businesswoman who is mindful of the unfair marketplace and resentful of corrupt companies guilty of the same price-fixing Schlosser criticizes in present-day America. Throughout the song "The Worst Pies in London," she frequently alludes to the scarcity of meat, blaming the slim fillings ("it's nothing but crusting," "Only lard and nothing more") for the unappetizing nature of her wares: "And no wonder with the price of meat/ What it is/When you get it."[6] She informs her only customer, Sweeney Todd (Johnny Depp)—whom she has not yet recognized as her upstairs lodger and long-ago object of desire Benjamin Barker—that a rival pasteler, Mrs. Mooney, has resorted to filling her pies with cat meat from her neighbors' pets. She croons "Have to hand it to her—/Wot I calls/Enterprise/Popping pussies into pies/Wouldn't do it in my shop."[7] The innuendo is present in both the song and the film, and Mrs. Lovett's frequent jealous references to Mrs. Mooney, whom we never see, contrast with her quick dismissal of an old woman whom we later learn is Barker's wife Lucy, long thought dead, when she enters the shop to call the safety of the food into question. With the scene's dim lighting, the prevalence of insects crawling out of meatless pastries and all over the floured surface upon which Mrs. Lovett rolls out the pie's top crust, the musical insists that the sudden infusion of human flesh into the food chain is a definite improvement upon both the freshness of the pie offerings and the general hygiene of the pie shop.

Todd, a barber driven to madness by a corrupt judge's abuse of his family, vents his rage at the world by slitting the throats of his customers. Mrs. Lovett first proposes using the unfortunate victims of his sharp blades as a sustainable meat source during the song "A Little Priest." Bonham Carter's Lovett shows Depp's Todd a beautiful, golden meat pie fresh out of the oven looking so scrumptious that the barber pauses and asks what it is, to which the pie maker replies "priest." By the time the pair have looked out the window and imagined how the different types of tradespeople they see walking outside would taste, the camera pans out to show that the counter top behind them is now spic and span, with clean mixing bowls and various different styles of pies, including "shepherd's pie," bearing its namesake. The lasting horror of *Sweeney Todd* lies in its taunting reminder that the industrial food-supply chain is both inherently insecure and vulnerable to sabotage from external and internal agents regardless of their cannibalistic tendencies. Mrs. Lovett's playful reference to religion, in the form of envisioning juicy pies made out of both priests and vicars, in no way deters her from carrying out her sinister plan since her primary motivation is to make a profit.

Morality is much more complicated in the pagan, war-torn world of Taymor's *Titus* where the household deities are as bloodthirsty as the generals and demand the satisfaction of fresh entrails upon the achievement of a victory at battle. The spectacle of the vanquished Goth queen and distraught mother Tamora (Jessica Lange) first witnessing Roman general Titus Andronicus (Anthony Hopkins) offering the entrails of her firstborn son Alarbus as a sacrifice upon her arrival in Rome and then being served her two younger sons, baked into a pie, demands a reckoning with the troubling notion of ingestion as the means through which, in *Titus*, humans commune with gods and gods accept human sacrifice (Figure 19.1). Tamora denounces the Romans' "cruel, irreligious piety," as they offer up the entrails of her firstborn to feed the unholy appetites of their household gods. As David Fredrick points out, "The perfumed odor of Alarbus's roasted entrails, together with the references to consumption and eating, allow this passage to anticipate the cannibal feast at the end of the play."[8] So, appetite is an undeniable attribute of godliness, one that Tamora, in a complex plot twist, takes on after replacing Titus's daughter Lavinia as the wife of the newly crowned emperor, Saturninus. The wedding celebration features countless trays of fresh fruit piled high, as well as wait staff offering trays of delectable appetizers to the assembled guests. Arguably the most grotesque suggestion of cannibalism in the whole film, however, is the floating food sculpture of a Janus-headed

FIGURE 19.1 *Hung like game in the kitchen of their vengeful enemy, Tamora's sons await entombment in Titus's meat pies: in the British vernacular, pastry-crusted "coffins."*

bust bearing the likeness of Tamora on one side and her Roman lord on the other. The shot then focuses in as Tamora reaches in and plucks an eye out of her husband's culinary effigy and feeds it to him.

The horror of this scene is its blatant suggestion of self-consumption, which recalls the opening scene, set in the present day, in which the young Lucius takes a bite out of a hot dog pierced through with a fork and then plops it down upon a plate which also contains a hamburger on a bun, French fries, and ketchup. As he plays with his toy Roman soldiers and war planes and tanks, Lucius makes a huge mess, spilling food, drink and condiments all over and shoving a toy fighter jet into a piece of chocolate cake. The abandon with which he plays and his lack of regard for etiquette or decorum highlight the absence of a mother figure from such a domestic setting. The intensity of his playing renders the sustenance before him into carnage—he squirts ketchup over the toy figurines to mimic blood. This childish waste and virtual bloodlust anticipates the sheer multitude of corpses that will grace the filmic stage before the closing credits roll. But, it also makes the very visual connection between sustenance and death.

As Fredrick points out, critics have long recognized how Shakespeare's play sexualizes death through its repeated suggestion of anthropophagy: "The opening scene of *Titus Andronicus* establishes a fundamental connection between the tomb and eating the corpse. This connection will be sexualized over the course of the play, so that the earth as receptacle comes to equal the female body and the vagina the mouth."[9] I want to offer two slightly different readings of the symbolism between the tomb and the corpse as featured in Taymor's film, which depicts an alimentary, rather than sexual, vocabulary. After Alarbus's entrails are fed to the gods, the next shot is of the corpses of Titus's sons, fallen warriors encased in their funereal wrappings and bearing their battle armor atop them, being inserted into the individual sepulchers within the family vault. Meera Jagannathan suggests that this interaction between the earth and body is comestible rather than copulative, not unlike the shadows' ingestion of Alarbus's innards: "The tomb in its role as 'the receptacle,' which swallows his sons, again and again, creates the repetitive incursion of the original trauma that will eventually swallow him."[10]

According to this calculus, human remains sustain the earth's metabolism. While this digestive metaphor is closer to my meaning, I want to advance a reading of this scene in the film through the lens of culinary, not merely alimentary, processes, since the ritual offering to the household gods that preceded it could be seen as religious cookery and the pie making that culminates Tamora's utter humiliation definitely involves some kitchen skills. The general motion of sliding the bodies into each semicircle shaped opening cut into the rock wall recalls the action of sliding pastries into a brick oven to cook, thereby once more invoking the trope of cannibalism. Early bakers recognized this similarity, so I want to now pause to consider the etymological implications of describing entombment as baking and piecrusts as "coffins."

Culinary etymology and the English housewife

Food columnist Mark Morton traces the origin of "coffin" as a culinary term back to the fifteenth century in one of his quarterly columns for *Gastronomica*, arguing that it is a more fitting translation of the original Greek source than is our modern funereal usage:

> Coffins are not something you expect to read about in a cookbook, and yet *A New Booke of Cookerie* refers to them often. That word had denoted, since the fifteenth century, a pie mold, a meaning that persisted until the eighteenth century. Indeed, the culinary sense of the word is etymologically more accurate than the funereal sense: "coffin" derives from the Greek kophinos, meaning "basket."[11]

Morton offers his helpful etymology in the context of his review of the 1615 tome *A New Booke of Cookerie*. Another British cookbook published to much acclaim that same year was Gervase Markham's *The English Housewife*; it outlined the housewife's virtues as the paragon of the English nation. Chief among these was her skill as a pastry-maker:

> Next to these already rehearsed, our English housewife must be skillfull in pastry, and know how and in what manner to bake all sorts of meat, and what paste is fit for every meat, and how to handle and compound such pastes. As, for example, red deer venison, wild boar, gammons of bacon, swans, elks, porpoise, and such like standing dishes, which must be kept long, must be baked in a moist, thick, tough, coarse, and long lasting crust, and therefore all other your rye paste is best for that purpose: your turkey, capon, pheasant, partridge, veal, peacocks, lamb, and all sorts of water fowl which are to come to the table more than once (yet not many days) would be baked in a good white crust, somewhat thick; therefore your wheat is fit for them: your chicken, calves' feet, olives, potatoes, quinces, fallow deer, and such like, which are most commonly eaten hot, would be in the finest, shortest, and thinnest crust; therefore your fine wheat flour which is a little baked in the oven before it be kneaded is the best for that purpose.

This lengthy quotation illustrates the huge range and variety of animal proteins English people used to consume in pie form.[12] As was the case in *A New Booke of Cookerie*, *The English Housewife* also uses "coffin" as a culinary term related to pies at least sixteen different times. The recipe for chicken pie illustrates how much violence must be perpetrated upon the carcass to make it fit within the pie mold: "after you have trussed your chickens, broken their legs and breast bones, and raised your crust of the best paste, you shall lay them in the coffin close together with their bodies full of butter."[13] Leaving the bones in a chicken pie adds its own level of danger in terms of a potential choking hazard. Then again, the crusts were not always part of the finished meal, but rather, in some instances their function was to preserve the pie's contents and keep them from spoiling, much as actual coffins do by keeping the elements away from embalmed corpses. According to Gillian Goodwin, during the Renaissance, "pastry was essentially packaging: either just for cooking—where we might use foil, or talk of a flan, earlier cooks put their ingredients in a paste 'coffin'—or for keeping game, meat, poultry, or fish. Although it could be and was eaten some varieties were far too hard and coarse and were merely for protection as pies were sent round the country."[14] This preservative aspect of the pie as coffin is something that *Titus* plays with in its funereal imagery, but *Sweeney Todd* relies on the integrity of both crusts of the human meat pies to obfuscate and deter prying eyes from discerning the "secret ingredient" that made the pastries so suddenly delectable.

Unlike small fish and fowl, the flesh of larger animals must undergo yet further transformation in order to make them fit, usually involving mincing or grinding. Both *Titus* and *Sweeney Todd* evoke the grinding process on-screen to heighten the sense of the uncanny—the former through close-up shots of the grotesquely large slices of medium-rare ground beef pie Titus serves to Tamora and Saturninus at the macabre banquet in Taymor's film, and the latter through a none-too-subtle shot of an industrial-size meat grinder extruding red ground meat. Mrs. Lovett's ward, Toby, stands next to the machine, simultaneously providing scale and eliciting fear and suspense in the audience, since he is both ignorant of the nefarious dealings that fuel the shop's sudden prosperity and is small enough to be especially vulnerable to the gigantic contraption. As grotesquely oversized as grinder appears—a perception reinforced by Toby's child-sized proportions—its size matches the demand for meat typical of a successful restaurant or eating-house. It also nicely fits large cuts of meat, such as those from full-fledged adult males, the nearly exclusive source of the meat for Mrs. Lovett's cottage industry (Figure 19.2). The nearby oven is likewise oversized, so it can accommodate multiple trays full of pies, invoking fairy tale images of cannibalistic witches, eager to feast on the flesh of plump young boys.

FIGURE 19.2 *Mrs. Lovett's giant meat grinder: symbol of the industrial food-supply chain's insatiable, indiscriminate hunger, and its capacity for hiding uncomfortable realities.*

The scale of the machinery visually links Mrs. Lovett's basement bakery to the modern, industrial food-supply chain, while the film's imagery of grinders and grinding underscore PETA's point that once ground up, indeed, it is hard to distinguish between the flesh of a pig, cow, deer, or human, thus adding to the fear of the cook as an agent of adulteration and of the eater's own possible complicity in unwitting cannibalism. As the recent (2012–15) global panic surrounding the routine use of the additive known as "pink slime" in ground beef has demonstrated, the eating public still has deep ambivalence regarding their desire to know exactly what they are ingesting, and their instinct to rely primarily on taste as a reassurance that everything on the plate is good enough to eat.[15]

Professional cooks and the absent housewives

As was true in the Pickton case, the meat pies in both *Titus* and *Sweeney Todd* are prepared in locales that blur the line between the domestic and the professional: the kitchen of the Andronici manorial estate and Mrs. Lovett's World Famous Meat Pies store front/bakery/living quarters/upstairs barber shop on Fleet Street. Titus and Mrs. Lovett are the only two characters openly depicted as being adept in the kitchen, and they both cook in a professional, rather than domestic, capacity. When, in *Titus*, the vengeful general tells his victims—Tamora's sons, who have raped and mutilated his daughter Lavinia—how he will prepare them for the banquet, his recitation reads both as a description of his skills and as an anti-recipe: "Hark, villains. I shall grind your bones to dust and with your blood in it, I'll make a paste and of the paste a coffin. I will rear and make two pasties of your shameful heads." Once he has slit their throats and bid Lavinia collect her rapists' blood in a basin, Titus assumes charge of his ersatz kitchen staff, commanding: "Come, come, be everyone officious to make this banquet, which I wish may prove more stern and bloody than the Centaur's feast."

Titus dons a chef's uniform, complete with a toque, and when questioned by a surprised Saturninus, he does not tell the Emperor what he has uttered in the privacy of his own kitchen, "I shall play the cook." Instead, he assures his guest that his uniform conveys his dedication to the success of the evening: "I would be sure to have all well to entertain Your Highness and Your Empress." Thus, his statement conveys the power that official garments have vested upon them to confer authority to those who wear them without apology. A similar endorsement of Mrs. Lovett's culinary prowess takes place in *Sweeney Todd* through three distinct authentication mechanisms: first, the camera focuses on a poster glued to the alley wall advertising the pie shop's "grand reopening"; next, the shot pans out and moves upward, pausing on the image of her name adorning the bustling store front; and finally, Toby's enticing promotional jingle, "God, That's Good." The films highlight the absence of the "good housewife" from both Titus's and Mrs. Lovett's domestic worlds, and thus the tragic breakdown of the family unit which must be avenged.

While the humans consumed in pie form are male in both films, *Titus* and *Sweeney Todd* divide the female characters into two distinct groups of "housewives": those whose virtue remained unstained by their marital vows (the newlywed Lavinia in *Titus* and the barber's wife, Lucy, seen mostly through flashbacks in *Sweeney Todd*) and those whose lasciviousness extends beyond the bounds of matrimony, such as the Goth queen/Roman empress Tamora and the savvy restaurateur and landlady Mrs. Lovett. Both films depict the wanton victimization of the ideal housewives at the hands of corrupt agents of power who ravish them, while the lusty widows are construed as traitors to their gender, since they actively work against the interests of the virtuous female characters. Both women are denied their housewifely roles by the absence of their husbands—Lavinia's is killed by Tamora's sons before they attack her, and Lucy's is lost to her when Judge Turpin exiles him to Australia in order to have free access to her.

In contrast to Tamora's and Mrs. Lovett's unrestrained appetites, Lavinia and Lucy are examples of negative consumption in their respective texts, thereby resisting the trend toward repulsive or obscene overeating exhibited by the masses. The first time we see the family's formal dining room in use, Lavinia refuses her father's entreaties to be nourished: "Now sit, and look you eat no more than will preserve just so much strength in us as will revenge these bitter woes of ours." She informs her father that she prefers to only drink her own tears. Her taut restraint stands in sharp contrast to Titus's extravagant hunger for violent revenge. Young Lucius, general's grandson, is also present at the dining table, and when he kills a fly Titus first menaces him and then takes a dagger and pretends to kill both Tamora and her servant (and secret lover) Aaron the Moor. This mimicked murder, in turn, prefigures two actual killings that will later occur at that same table: Titus's murder of the queen by stabbing her in the neck to prevent her from regurgitating the pie stuffed with her sons' flesh, and his own death at Saturninus's hand as the emperor impales him with a chandelier and pins him to the table top.

Lucy is likewise defined by her restrained consumption. Todd/Barker learns, in the song "Poor Thing," that she was raped, during his long absence, by the same corrupt judge who exiled him, and in the ensuing conversation Mrs. Lovett tells him that Lucy poisoned herself with arsenic. The information she conveniently leaves out is that the poison did not kill Lucy, but left her ruined and impaired. Lucy's survival, and her debilitated state, resulted from consuming too little of the poisonous cocktail to end her life.

Todd does not recognize the aged Lucy until after he has killed her in the middle of battling the judge's henchmen as they conduct a trumped-up food inspection of the bakery. When he confronts Mrs. Lovett and she confirms her omission, Todd retaliates in a way that is distinct from his other killings, but very fitting for the "witch" Lucy (as the old woman) had charged Mrs. Lovett with being: he throws her into the industrial oven and locks the door. Though no one eats her, this punishment simultaneously inverts the logic of her culinary undertaking (baking) and reasserts proper funereal rites through incineration of her remains. Rather than baking pies in "coffins," the oven itself becomes Mrs. Lovett's tomb, an image that parallels the entombment of Titus's warrior sons in Taymor's Shakespearean tragedy. Todd and Lucy are reunited in death, as Toby fulfills his earlier vow to his foster mother of confronting the evil Mr. Todd by slitting the barber's throat with his beloved "friend," the razor.

Conclusion

As gruesome as the events they depict are, both *Titus* and *Sweeney Todd* present societies in which murder is driven by revenge, rather than satisfying an innate need for bloodshed. Thus, viewers are hardly likely to experience much personal fear of being randomly dispatched by either highly decorated army generals or even their local barber. The real horror these films evoke is in the alienation effect they produce upon their audience, who suddenly fear to think upon the meals they have enjoyed that day, and each time they have purchased food made by others. The opportunistic alignment between cannibalism and cuisine both films depict leads to utter revulsion, precisely because hunger and appetite are such undeniably strong urges that must be routinely satisfied if one is to remain alive. The alienation effect produced by these films endures long after the lights go back on in the theater; it is the little voice of doubt each audience member hears whenever they so much as think about enjoying a pastry or eating a fast food burger.

Notes

1 Colin Perkel, "Anti-meat Ads Referencing Pickton Case 'Grotesque,'" *The Canadian Press* (April 6, 2004), http://www.missingpeople.net/anti_meat_ads.htm (accessed September 16, 2014).

2 *Toronto Star*, "PETA Goes Too Far" (April 8, 2004), http://lists.envirolink.org/pipermail/ar-news/Week-of-Mon-20040405/023533.html (accessed June 12, 2016).

3 *CBC News*, "Pickton Gets Maximum Sentence in Murders" (December 11, 2007), http://www.cbc.ca/news/canada/british-columbia/pickton-gets-maximum-sentence-for-murders-1.650944 (accessed September 16, 2014).

4 *Daily Mail*, "Did Farmer Turn 28 Women Into Pies?" 9 *Regional Business News* (January 22, 2007).

5 Eric Schlosser, "Unsafe at Any Meal," *The New York Times* (July 24, 2012), http://www.nytimes.com/2010/07/25/opinion/25schlosser.html?_r=3&ref=opinion (accessed June 12, 2016).

6 Stephen Sondheim, "The Worst Pies in London," in *Sweeney Todd: The Demon Barber of Fleet Street* (New York: Applause Theatre Book Publishers, 1991), 35–6.

7 Ibid.

8 David Fredrick, "Titus Androgynous: Foul Mouths and Troubled Masculinity," *Arethusa* 41, no. 1 (2008): 205–33.

9 Ibid., 209.

10 Meera Jagannathan, "Trauma of Death and Decorum in *Titus Andronicus*: The Tomb as Ahistorical Reality," *Plaza: Dialogues in Language and Literature* 4, no. 1 (Fall 2014): 11. https://journals.tdl.org/plaza/index.php/plaza/article/viewFile/7025/pdf (accessed June 12, 2016).

11 Mark Morton, "Coffins, Pipkins, and Pottles," *Gastronomica* 3, no. 4 (Fall 2003): 6–7.

12 Gervase Markham, *The English Housewife*, ed. Michael R. Best (Montreal: McGill-Queen's Press, 1994), 101.
13 Ibid., 100.
14 Gillian Goodwin, "Simple Simon," *History Today* 35, no. 9 (1985): 60.
15 Daniel Engber, "The Sliming: How Processed Beef Trimmings Got Rebranded Again and Again and Again," *Slate* (October 25, 2012), http://www.slate.com /articles/news_and_politics/food/2012/10/history_of_pink_slime_how_partially_defatted_chopped_beef_got_rebranded.html (accessed June 12, 2016).

Bibliography

CBC News. "Pickton Gets Maximum Sentence in Murders." December 11, 2007. http://www.cbc.ca/news/canada/british-columbia/pickton-gets-maximum-sentence-for-murders-1.650944 (accessed September 16, 2014).
Daily Mail. "Did Farmer Turn 28 Women Into Pies?" 9 *Regional Business News*, January 22, 2007.
DiManno, Rosie. "Jury Gets Glimpse of Pickton's Mind." The Star.com, January 24, 2007. http://www.thestar.com/news/2007/01/24/jury_gets_glimpse_of_picktons_mind.html.
Engber, Daniel. "The Sliming: How Processed Beef Trimmings Got Rebranded Again and Again and Again." Slate, October 25, 2012. http://www.slate.com/articles/news_and_politics/food/2012/10/history_of_pink_slime_how_partially_defatted_chopped_beef_got_rebranded.html (accessed June 12, 2016).
Fredrick, David. "Titus Androgynous: Foul Mouths and Troubled Masculinity." *Arethusa* 41, no. 1 (2008): 205–33.
Goodwin, Gillian. "Simple Simon." *History Today* 35, no. 9 (1985): 60.
Jagannathan, Meera. "Trauma of Death and Decorum in *Titus Andronicus*: The Tomb as Ahistorical Reality." *Plaza: Dialogues in Language and Literature* 4, no. 1 (Fall 2014): 1–18. https://journals.tdl.org/plaza/index.php/plaza/article/viewFile /7025/pdf (accessed June 12, 2016).
Markham, Gervase. *The English Housewife*. Edited by Michael R. Best. Montreal: McGill-Queen's Press, 1994.
Morton, Mark. "Coffins, Pipkins, and Pottles." *Gastronomica* 3, no. 4 (Fall 2003): 6–7.
Perkel, Colin. "Anti-meat Ads Referencing Pickton Case 'Grotesque.'" *The Canadian Press*, April 6, 2004. http://www.missingpeople.net/anti_meat_ads.htm (accessed September 16, 2014).
Schlosser, Eric. "Unsafe at Any Meal." *The New York Times*, July 24, 2012. http://www.nytimes.com/2010/07/25/opinion/25schlosser.html?_r=3&ref=opinion (accessed June 12, 2016).
Sondheim, Stephen. "The Worst Pies in London." In *Sweeney Todd: The Demon Barber of Fleet Street*, 35–6. New York: Applause Theatre Book Publishers, 1991.

Sweeney Todd. Directed by Tim Burton. 2007. Universal City, CA: Dream Works Pictures and Warner Bros. Pictures 2008. DVD.

Titus. Directed by Julie Taymor. 1999. Beverly Hills, CA: Twentieth Century Fox Home Video, 2000. DVD.

Toronto Star. "PETA Goes Too Far." April 8, 2004. http://lists.envirolink.org/pipermail/ar-news/Week-of-Mon-20040405/023533.html (accessed June 12, 2016).

20

All-Consuming Passions: Vampire Foodways in Contemporary Film and Television

Alexandra C. Frank

In *Our Vampires, Ourselves*, feminist literary critic Nina Auerbach proposes that the titular mythical creatures have maintained their popularity throughout Anglo-American history because each new vampire reflects the times in which it was reinvented.[1] Our fascination with (im)mortality, fear of the "Other" in society, the thrill of forbidden romance, and the connection between technology and modernity can all be used to explore and explain those changes, but this essay views early twenty-first-century vampire narratives through a different analytical lens: representations of vampires' relationship to their food—that is, blood. Recent vampire movies and television programs encourage audience sympathy for the mythic killer by emphasizing the ways in which the vampire protagonists negotiate various facets of their identities—notably gender, sexuality, and religion—through their relationships to eating or, more accurately, to drinking blood.

This trend in portrayals of vampires on screen transcends national boundaries, budgets, and filmmaking styles. Films such as the blockbuster *Twilight* franchise (2008–12), the auteurist art-house picture *Only Lovers Left Alive* (2013), the Korean morality tale *Thirst* (2009), and the dystopic sci-fi thriller *Daybreakers* (2009) as well as the American television shows *Moonlight* (2007–08), *True Blood* (2008–14), and *The Vampire Diaries* (2009–present) all accentuate the methods by which their vampire characters procure and ingest their life-sustaining blood-drink. These range from the mythic beings' traditional method of taking their victims by force, to more modern solutions, such as forming partnerships with willing mortals, looting hospital blood banks, or (in tales where vampires are an acknowledged subculture within society) seeking out synthetic blood on the open market. Some postmillennial vampires even abstain from drinking human blood altogether, preferring to subsist on the blood of animals or go hungry if none is available. These "vampire foodways"—played out in narratives that incorporate elements of non-horror genres such as mystery, romance, comedy, and science fiction—disrupt long-established horror conventions and contribute to a new, more complex and nuanced representation of vampire characters on-screen.

This new focus on the diversity of ways in which vampires consume blood reflects our society's current fascination with the interplay between food and culture, as well as individuals' pressing concerns about what they eat, and how. It is part of a broad cultural movement that includes the emergence of "food studies" as a field of scholarship; the rise of "foodie" cultures that both reconfigure and reinforce the relationship between food and social class; the growth of concerns about the industrial food system and its "implications in health problems, ecological devastation, and social injustices"[2]; and the rising popularity of celebrity chefs, featured on cable television cooking and reality competition shows. Food, in short, has become a topic of broad and serious interest, no longer taken for granted due to its seemingly innocuous ubiquity. The makers of vampire films and television shows are arguably aware of this contemporary fascination with the relationship between food and those who consume it, and they manipulate it in order to make their vampires' food-related existential crises more relevant to contemporary audiences.

Blood and identity

You are what you eat. This well-circulated proverb reminds us that what we choose to ingest (or not) reveals much about us as individuals and as members of certain communities, announcing our cultural affiliations to others.[3] As food scholar Fabio Parasecoli writes: "The social, economic, and even political relevance [of food] cannot be ignored. Ingestion and incorporation constitute a fundamental component of our connection with reality and the world outside our body."[4] In other words, one of the primary ways we make sense of ourselves and the world is through our relationships to food. It is no different for the vampires considered here, whose diets and foodways not only define them, but carry strong implications for the social, economic, and political identities of the humans in their lives as well. As Parasecoli observes, "Vampires' victims [who may also be their romantic and/or sexual partners] seem to experience a deep and uncontrolled pleasure in becoming food themselves, revealing a profound ambivalence towards devouring and being devoured."[5]

Vampires' distinctive food culture revolves, of course, around the drinking of blood. Given its many shapes and incarnations over the years, the modern vampire does not have a set description or list of character traits, but it remains rooted in eighteenth- and nineteenth-century fiction—particularly gothic fiction—which gave rise to the eponymous villain of Bram Stoker's classic 1897 novel *Dracula*. These tales portrayed the vampire as an undead human who, having turned into a vampire just before dying, can potentially live forever subsisting only on (preferably human) blood. While other iconic elements of the genre have changed over time—such as the vampires' nocturnal lifestyle, shape-shifting abilities, and aversion to sunlight, garlic, and crosses—blood-drinking remains the single defining characteristic of this monstrous species.[6] It has pervaded on-screen depictions of vampires since Bela Lugosi, in the genre-defining *Dracula* (1931), stared hungrily at the blood on a dinner guest's cut finger and, a few moments later, intoned: "I never drink . . . wine."

Recent vampire movies and TV shows can, therefore, be seen as food films, where characters express their emotions and personal and cultural identities through preparing and presenting exquisite offerings of food, over which the camera lingers lovingly.[7] Many scenes in such productions are set in food-centric locales such as kitchens, restaurants, or dining rooms, with the procurement and ingestion of blood emphasized in ways that echo the details of preparing, presenting, and consuming more traditional cuisines. While the on-screen vampires of old hid their biting attacks on humans under swooping capes, today's "children of the night" openly discuss and display their eating habits in front of the audience. Like the characters in more mainstream food films, the vampires question "identity, power, culture, class, spirituality, or relationships through food."[8]

Vampire food films are part of a larger trend toward the "domestication" of the vampire. Narratives across literature, film, and television now privilege the "outsider" or "Other" point-of-view of the vampire rather than those of the humans seeking to expel the evil menace.[9] The sympathetic vampire of the twenty-first century struggles to fit into society, and nowhere is that struggle more pronounced than in matters related to diet. In fact, less violent or more humane vampire foodways are often a metaphor for something else—such as an "unhealthy" sexual appetite or addiction to drugs—and can also be read as a political allegory for gay rights and, by extension, basic human rights.

The consumption of "fresh" human blood in vampire food films entails biting a live human and sucking nourishment directly from their veins. Even though the vampire characters discussed here are most notable for the nonbiting methods they use, drinking human blood directly from the source is always presented as the ultimate gratifying feeding experience. The issue is not merely "freshness," or even taste, but something more visceral: biting and drinking from the human body also satiates vampires' sexual appetites. In fact, eating and fornicating are presented as so inextricably linked in the lived experiences of vampires and their human sexual partners that they become one and the same. Becoming food for the vampire during sex is compelling to humans in these narratives, because it is an opportunity to lose oneself, to merge with an exotic Other. Describing the corporeal fusion between vampire and human, Fabio Parasecoli writes:

> In the moment of the embrace, followed by the . . . bite . . . [the vampire and human] temporarily lose their individuality; as a matter of fact, they seem to experience sensual pleasure precisely because they get lost in a sort of blurring of their boundaries, a feeling that provokes both bliss and panic.[10]

If, according to Sally Miller, "sexual activity for the vampire is both polymorphously perverse and inseparable from the ingestion of food,"[11] then the choice *not* to feed on live humans—whether voluntary or enforced by circumstances—becomes particularly complex.

Abstinence from feeding on humans precludes having sex with them, while simultaneously ostracizing sympathetic vampires from their vampire brethren. Such self-denial of the vampire's alimentary and sexual drives thus constitutes an unhealthy lifestyle and a rejection of the vampire identity as a whole. In the case of the short-lived CBS crime procedural *Moonlight*, the reluctant vampire protagonist Mick St. John's (Alex O'Loughlin) feeding habits are presented as diametrically opposed to those of other vampires—including the humane drinking customs of his friends—and render his gender identity and sexuality aberrant. Working as a private investigator in Los Angeles, he polices the tenuous, invisible line between human and vampire cultures, often dispatching vampires in the interest of maintaining order and balance. Mick's ability to straddle both worlds prevents his full assimilation into either one, but he holds onto his humanity through abstaining from drinking fresh human blood. Instead, he relies on his vampire friend Guillermo (Jacob Vargas), who works in a hospital morgue, for his supply of blood bags, preferring to pour the refrigerated contents into a tall glass and indulge in private.

Mick's references to "six-packs" of blood bags, and preference for blood type A-positive (rather than O-positive, which Guillermo insists "has got a much better finish") align him with familiar symbols of virile American masculinity, like the copious consumption of cheap domestic beer. Blood, for him, is fundamentally straightforward: a source of nourishment and pleasure, rather than a tool for self-definition. Guillermo, meanwhile, displays the qualities traditionally associated with male vampires. Sexual, sophisticated, and intellectual, he pointedly dismisses Mick's taste as unsophisticated and déclassé, while displaying his own refined tastes by using the language of wine connoisseurs to discuss blood. Mick's older vampire friend Josef (Jason Dohring), a successful businessman, also teaches him proper blood-drinking habits, continually offering him a "freshie"—a human who willingly allows vampires to feed on their body for mutual sexual gratification. Josef, too, affects the language of a wine connoisseur, referring to his attractive yellow- and red-haired female companions as if they were bottles of "white" and "red," and musing that some (birth) years are more pleasurable than others. He sees the combined pleasures of feeding on and having sex with humans as central to vampire identity, and considers Mick's self-denial to be evidence of his friend's self-loathing—an expression of Mick's wishful thinking that he can be something other than vampire, and of his desire to be human.

Films and television shows adapted from young adult literature often frame the vampire's abstinence from drinking fresh human blood as a metaphor for chaste romance. According to Anna Silver, "[M]uch YA literature has a tendency to moralize and instruct adolescents"[12] and is often specifically designed, as Roberta Trites writes, "to curb teenagers' libido."[13] This tendency is especially pronounced in Stephenie Meyer's bestselling *Twilight* saga, in which the sexual tension between human teenager Bella Swan and ageless (but youthful-looking) vampire Edward Cullen amounts to "abstinence porn," a "new sub-genre" that offers readers a "sensational, erotic, and titillating" teen romance that possesses those qualities "precisely because it [is] unconsummated."[14] In the films, as in the books, Edward (Robert Pattinson) can hardly bear to face his beloved, because she is his hunger—alimentary and sexual—personified. To give in to temptation would lower his opinion of himself, since he prides himself on being able to stay close to her and remain firmly in control of his intertwined sexual urges and primal vampire bloodlust. Bella (Kristen Stewart) and Edward's much-admired chaste relationship thus appears unrealistically old-fashioned, most troublingly in the fact that—although

Bella's all-consuming passion for Edward matches his for her—she must rely on Edward's capacity for self-denial in order to remain safe.

The long-running supernatural romance series *The Vampire Diaries* presents a more complex depiction of the relationship between drinking blood and having sex. Like Edward Cullen of *Twilight*, who hunts deer instead of humans, Stefan (Paul Wesley) subsists on a "vegetarian" diet, drinking the blood of animals such as rabbits, but his struggle to maintain control over his bloodlust weaves in and out of the narrative. Shunning vampires' regular foodways, he initially resorts to procuring human blood from hospitals and blood banks. Later, with the help of his teenaged human girlfriend Elena (Nina Dobrev) and his brother Damon (Ian Somerhalder), who satisfies his own more robust vampire appetites by biting his sexual partners, Stefan detoxes from human blood—but not without first going through withdrawal.

Stefan avoids contact with Elena, including sexual encounters, because he fears he will be unable to resist the temptation to bite her during sex. When the couple does eventually have sex (after much talk around it), however, his control of his thirst for human blood is so complete that he is even able to resist biting and drinking from her in the middle of their passion. The struggle that Stefan endures in order to control his bloodlust during sex is an expression of self-preservation and love for a human romantic partner as well as a constant attempt to transcend the vampire foodways and, hence, identity.

Blood as a drug

Stefan's attempt to overcome his reawakened hunger for human blood in *The Vampire Diaries* evokes drug-abuse rehabilitation programs, and, similarly, in *Twilight* Edward warns Bella that her scent is "like a drug to me. You're like my own personal brand of heroin." The act of drinking human blood as a metaphor for drug-taking runs even deeper in recent vampire-food films. When introducing Guillermo through voiceover narration in the first episode of *Moonlight*, for example, Mick likens his friend to a drug dealer. Since most of these films portray mainstream human society as unaware of vampires' existence, the humane, nonbiting methods by which vampires procure blood are as incontrovertibly illicit as the sale of drugs such as heroin or cocaine.

Only Lovers Left Alive, director Jim Jarmusch's soulful and comically deadpan meditation on the philosophical and earthly pleasures of immortality, provides the most nuanced treatment of the blood-as-drug analogy. Reclusive vampire musician Adam (Tom Hiddleston) opposes biting and draining humans because he feels that killing is barbaric and outdated. Instead, he purchases Thermos bottles filled with blood in the darkened laboratory of a Detroit hospital at night—exchanges recalling the sales of illegal substances that might take place in a park or on a street corner. Meanwhile, Adam's wife Eve (Tilda Swinton), half a world away in Tangier, walks the city's labyrinthine streets on her way to a rendezvous with her own dealer in a café. Drug pushers try to tempt her along the way, promising that they have what she needs. Their proclamations are ironic (they clearly do not intend to sell her blood), and scenes of Eve carrying her illicit goods home in a pharmacy bag compound the irony of the blood/drug's provenance.

Jarmusch and editor Affonso Gonçalves intercut, step-by-step, scenes of the pair. They first pour the liquid into Victorian longneck flute glasses, savoring the first sip as if it were wine (Figure 20.1). The camera follows Adam, Eve, and her dealer, the long-presumed-dead playwright Christopher Marlowe (John Hurt), as they feel the effect of the blood and slump backward into the cushions of their furniture. Close-ups capture the blissfully ecstatic looks on their faces, their teeth stained red with blood. They are all careful not to overdose, however, for having more than an ounce or two would mean drinking to excess. Ingesting blood is thus framed simultaneously as a historic, civilized ritual—a shared experience that transcends time and space—and as an experience, pleasurable but fraught with danger, with overtones of addicts getting their latest fix.

Given the range of foods reputed to induce sexual desire or enhance virility, from oysters and chocolate to asparagus and avocados, it is not a stretch to assume that blood is an aphrodisiac drug for the vampires of film and

FIGURE 20.1 *Adam (Tom Hiddleston), savoring blood as if it were wine.*

television. Indeed, according to Miriam Hospodar, "People have ingested the blood of everything from bulls to blondes in the hope that it would increase strength, potency, and libido."[15] The vampire thus achieves, through a regular diet of blood, the god-like powers of "energy, ecstasy, and immortality," qualities for which humans have searched throughout history.[16] While the disgust evoked by consuming blood is strong, Mandy Aftel observes that "the precarious balance between arousal and disgust is sexual in its very nature, creating erotic tension and heightening arousal."[17] Perhaps this accounts for the vampire's everlasting appeal as a product of our cultural imagination: we are simultaneously seduced and repulsed by their monstrous relationships with "the quintessential liquid of life."[18]

Menstrual blood in particular has long been considered a "powerful aphrodisiac,"[19] and *Thirst*, a fanciful Korean adaptation of Émile Zola's *Thérèse Raquin*, from the genre-bending director Park Chan-wook, comically explores its drug-like quality. *Thirst* transposes the story of *Thérèse Raquin* from nineteenth-century France to the Catholic minority of contemporary Korea, focusing on the struggle of a young Catholic priest-turned-vampire, Sang-hyun (Song Kang-ho), as he comes to terms with his new vampiric diet and foodways. The film posits that not even the most devout among us are immune to moral corruption. Sang-hyun's own personal corruption begins when he smells the onset of a young woman's menstrual period. This moment triggers his all-consuming passion for Tae-ju (Kim Ok-bin), the long-suffering wife of his childhood friend Kang-woo (Shin Ha-kyun), and begins his descent into a life of sin. Determined to lead as moral a life as possible, given his newfound hunger, Sang-hyun drinks the blood of comatose hospital patients, vowing never to kill anyone for food. The sounds of Sang-hyun's enthusiastic slurping of the IV drips echoes his impassioned lovemaking with Tae-ju, as they kiss and suck each other's skin, seemingly in an effort to eat one another. The soundtrack's effect on the viewer walks a precarious line between arousal and disgust, as the noise is unpleasant but erotically charged. When Sang-hyun bites Tae-ju for the first time, mid-coitus, she wonders aloud if the pleasure she feels makes her a "pervert." Her sudden existential crisis recalls Fabio Parasecoli's earlier notion that the victims of vampires feel both ambivalent about and aroused by the prospect of becoming food.

Thirst also illustrates that the relationship between vampire foodways and vampire sexuality does not play out in a vacuum. Instead, both influence how the vampire simultaneously negotiates other parts of their identity. In the case of *Thirst*, the events leading up to his transformation reveal that Sang-hyun's newfound bloodlust significantly challenges his religious identity. Feeling restless at home and wishing to "save people" from suffering, the Catholic priest sacrifices himself when he submits to vaccine trials in Africa aimed at preventing the spread of an aggressive blood blistering disease known as the Emanuel Virus (EV). After he contracts EV and dies on the operating table, a blood transfusion miraculously revives him, but curses him with vampirism. In order to keep EV at bay, he must drink blood.

Sang-hyun initially chooses to feed off comatose patients in the hospital where he works (Figure 20.2), but he gradually loses his moral compass, and his affair with Tae-ju progresses to the point where they kill Kang-woo. Eventually, Sang-hyun turns Tae-ju into a vampire, whose feeding habits are at odds with his own. Lacking fangs that would puncture the skin, Tae-ju revels in stabbing scissors into her male victims' throats. Having felt imprisoned by her husband and mother-in-law, and enslaved in the family fabric store, Tae-ju's violent attacks on unsuspecting men reflect her vengeful, anti-patriarchal stance. She disavows humanity, embracing what Sang-hyun cannot: the transformation into "human-eating beasts." Although Sang-hyun feels lost, defeated, remorseful, and suicidal at several points during his fall from grace, he only succeeds in putting a stop to their shared murderous ways when he subjects Tae-ju to a murder-suicide: death by sunlight.

While such an act is certainly a violation of his faith, Sang-hyun retains the audience's sympathy because his claims of victimhood are well founded: he didn't choose his vampire affliction. Tae-ju further victimizes him by manipulating his protective concern for her well-being: presenting her self-inflicted bruises as evidence of her husband's abuse, and leading him down a vengeful path that culminates in Kang-woo's murder. Tae-ju becomes an evil menace who even influences Sang-hyun to abandon his humanity, finally killing a woman for her blood, and raping a devout Catholic.

FIGURE 20.2 *Sang-hyun (Song Kang-ho), feeding on blood in the hospital.*

Blood and the social order

The wider implications of vampire foodways need not be solely personal, however; they can also be political. HBO's long-running supernatural soap opera *True Blood*, for example, uses its vampires to frame a political allegory about civil rights and social justice, while the science fiction neo-noir horror-thriller *Daybreakers* uses their rapacious hunger for blood as the basis for its critique of the unsustainable foodways of the industrialized West.

Based on the series of bestselling novels by Charlaine Harris and set in the small fictional town of Bons Temps, Louisiana, the show achieves this effect through its food-centric conceit: in an alternate reality, vampires have "come out of the coffin" in 2006, thanks to the introduction of a synthetic blood drink, TruBlood. It is marketed in a glass beer bottle and sold, in all blood-type varieties, everywhere from convenience stores to bars. The drink is an apt symbol for vampires' desire to be recognized as equal citizens, for it allows them to come out of the shadows and seek assimilation by practicing humane feeding habits. This integration of vampires into mainstream culture extends, in the *True Blood* universe, to campaigns for vampires' legal right to marry humans (and vice versa) and recalls real-life political struggles to end bans on same-sex marriage.

Vampires in the *True Blood* universe are clearly stand-ins for oppressed queer people, as the parallel language of "coming out of the coffin" and "coming out of the closet" illustrates. Many main and supporting vampire characters in the series are queer themselves, and in some cases, humans embrace and act upon their homosexual desires only after they have been turned into vampires. Vampires in *True Blood* and other texts in this study (and beyond) exhibit preferences for the sex of their sexual partners/meals, and these appetites run the gamut of human sexuality.

In a further nod to the real-world queer community, the vampire subculture depicted in *True Blood* is itself diverse and complex—a sharp departure from the monolithic, single-minded beings of traditional horror tales. Assimilation, and the desire to assimilate, are thus far from universal in the fictional world of Bon Temps. Those individuals determined to remain separate from the society of the living see it as impossible that humans and vampires will ever overcome their extreme prejudice and live together peacefully. On the one hand, outspoken, hate-fueled Christian fundamentalists believe vampires are abominations; signs reading "God Hates Fangs," which echo the real-life hate-speech slogan "God Hates Fags," are sprinkled throughout the show's Deep South setting. On the other hand, nonassimilating vampires revel in their bloodlust and the violence with which they satisfy it.

The moral panic regarding vampires' foodways, intensified by their inextricable link to sexuality, effectively lays the groundwork for the first season of *True Blood*'s overarching narrative. While telepathic waitress Sookie Stackhouse (Anna Paquin) embarks on a relationship with TruBlood-drinker Bill Compton (Stephen Moyer), learning from him the ins and outs of marginalized vampire cultures (including but not limited to the vampires' tendency to bite during sex), several women in Bon Temps wind up brutally murdered. Townspeople suspect that vampires are to blame, because the victims were "fangbangers" or at least "vampire sympathizers." In reality, however, a mortal newcomer killed the women, after first murdering his own sister because she fraternized with vampires. The show's continued emphasis on the split between "good" and "bad" (i.e., nonassimilating) vampires continued into the second season, troubling some queer academics, who felt that it associated gay men and women with sexually deviant and "parasitic" vampires.[20] The show's reality, however, is more complicated, with humans who are drawn to the vampires' Otherness—achieving sexual pleasure by serving as their food, or financial gain by turning vampire blood into a potent black-market drug to feed the addictions of thrill-seeking mortals.[21]

Much as *True Blood* uses attitudes toward vampire foodways to critique real-world prejudice, intolerance, and even misogyny, the vampire foodways of *Daybreakers* present an uncanny reflection of our own. Set in a not-so-distant future where a virus has transformed more than 95 percent of the world's population into vampires and human blood is a scarce commodity, the film presents vampire foodways not simply as a symbol of a larger social crisis, but as the focus of a crisis in their own right. Everyone in society risks devolving into starved, demented, bat-like creatures—"class four" citizens, informally referred to as "subsiders," who live on the streets, begging for blood, and are driven underground or into a life of crime. Hematologist Edward Dalton (Ethan Hawke) is an outsider among his vampire brethren, because he abandons his professional obligation to develop a synthetic blood substitute, instead joining a group of human survivors and discovering a cure for vampirism. For Edward, the political is personal, and vice versa. His refusal to drink human blood goes hand-in-hand with his moral opposition to his employer's practice of treating humans like livestock by exploiting them in "blood-farming" operations.

Like Mick's strange feeding habits in *Moonlight*, Edward's self-denial isolates him from his vampire brethren, especially his younger brother Frankie (Michael Dorman). Although Edward and Frankie both work for the pharmaceutical corporation Bromley/Marks (Frankie is a soldier who hunts humans), they possess opposing worldviews, which they express through their foodways. For example, Frankie brings an expensive (wine) bottle of "100% pure" human blood for Edward's birthday, a present that the older

Dalton pours down the kitchen sink. Frankie naïvely believes that vampire society's blood diet and foodways are sustainable, despite all evidence to the contrary. The thirst for "pure" blood that drives Frankie and others like him provides the financial incentive for the Bromley/Marks's decision to continue blood-farming, even as the company had been preparing to market a synthetic-blood drink. Company executive Charles Bromley (Sam Neill) understands that people will pay exorbitant prices in order to drink "the real thing," and seeks to capitalize on the collapsing food-supply chain by offering wealthy customers a more gourmet food experience. Bromley's approach makes it seem that the filmmakers are critiquing the fetishization of whole and organic foods, but in fact his assertion demonstrates that the diets and foodways of the vampire elite are unethical, inhumane, and even tyrannical.

The future foodscape that Bromley imagines will help him maintain his wealth and power is unsustainable, much like the state of our own food industrial complex. Whereas our food system relies on the cultivation and manufacturing of cheap, highly processed foods that erode health and shorten lifespans, the one in *Daybreakers* depends on the rapid depletion of natural (i.e., human) resources. *Daybreakers* makes the moral corruption of its fictional food economy explicit, showing Bromley/Marks's military operatives arresting "subsiders" in droves with the intent of burning them alive. It thus blends a critique of capitalist excesses—the criminalization of poverty and elevation of the conspicuously wealthy to the status of an anointed elite—with echoes of the Nazi obsession with purity of blood and the Third Reich's "final solution" for those who lacked it.

Committed to overturning this system, Edward and the band of human rebels forcibly infect unrepentant vampires with a cure as they infiltrate Bromley/Marks's corporate headquarters. Edward allows Bromley to bite him and drink his treated blood—knowing that it will cure him of his vampirism, rendering him mortal—then kills the evil (and now vulnerable) former tycoon, causing the Bromley/Marks regime to topple. At the end of the film, Edward, now a leader in the human resistance movement, turns his attention to crafting a more humane, sustainable alternative to both the blood shortage crisis and its by-product, the prevalence of "subsiders" and the perceived need to commit genocide against them.

The rebel group's method of repopulating the human race may ultimately bring their society into a closer relationship with nature, by fostering a realization that it is necessary to channel more resources—both money and labor—into agriculture to restart and sustain a human diet based on plant and animal products. Other than the unidentified ultramodern city where most of the film's action takes place, all landscapes are barren and deserted, suggesting that in the ten years since the outbreak of the vampire virus, agriculture has fallen by the wayside. The final scene, in which a cured vampire speeds through the arid country landscape in a Trans Am decorated with a phoenix on the hood, also symbolizes the vampires' claim to humanity and rebirth through a return to nature, with foodways based on plants and animals rather than human blood-farming. This renewed diet is the true equalizer in *Daybreakers*.

Conclusion

Much like their human counterparts, what vampires consume—and how they consume it—is part of a complex set of broader values, beliefs, and behaviors that combine to both create and express individual and group identities. The choices that vampires make about food, and how to procure it, likewise defines their place in the spectrum of what we may broadly refer to as "vampire culture." From predator, to dilettante, to activist, vampires' patterns of consumption establish their relationships with others of their kind, as well as with humans, as they make decisions about the circumstances of their feeding. And, as in human culture, those decisions regulate social interactions, establish hierarchies, and play a key role in power, privilege, and political economy.

These similarities with human culture, along with vampires' adaptability to and reflectivity of their times, is part of their enduring appeal.[22] The concern of recent vampire films and television with their undead characters' feeding habits reflect our own concerns—increasingly pressing and increasingly complex—about our relationships with food. In exploring how vampires and their human companions negotiate different facets of their identities—especially their gender, sexuality, and religion—through food, they position the vampire characters as dynamic, sympathetic, sexual subjects, and reflecting on them provokes more thoughts on the subject of vampire foodways in cinema and television throughout history.

Notes

1 Nina Auerbach, *Our Vampires, Ourselves* (Chicago: University of Chicago Press, 1995), 1.
2 Josée Johnston and Shyon Baumann, *Foodies: Democracy and Distinction in the Gourmet Foodscape* (New York: Routledge, 2010), xvii.
3 For more on how food reflects society's organization, see Sherrie A. Inness, ed., *Cooking Lessons: The Politics of Gender and Food* (Lanham, MD: Rowman & Littlefield, 2001).

4 Fabio Parasecoli, *Bite Me: Food in Popular Culture* (Oxford: Berg, 2008), 2.
5 Ibid., 44.
6 Tim Kane, *The Changing Vampire of Film and Television: A Critical Study of the Growth of a Genre* (Jefferson, NC: McFarland, 2006), 7–8.
7 Anne L. Bower, "Watching Food: The Production of Food, Film, and Values," in *Reel Food: Essays on Food in Film*, ed. Anne L. Bower (New York: Routledge, 2004), 5.
8 Ibid., 6.
9 Joan Gordon and Veronica Hollinger, "Introduction," in *Blood Read: The Vampire as Metaphor in Contemporary Culture*, ed. Joan Gordon and Veronica Hollinger (Philadelphia: University of Pennsylvania Press, 1997), 2.
10 Parasecoli, *Bite Me*, 45.
11 Sally Miller, " 'Nursery Fears Made Flesh and Sinew': Vampires, the Body, and Eating Disorders: A Psychoanalytic Approach," Beastly Publications, 1999. homepages.nildram.co.uk /~beast/publications/vamp_paper/index.html (accessed October 17, 2010).
12 Anna Silver, "*Twilight* Is Not Good for Maidens: Gender, Sexuality, and the Family in Stephenie Meyer's *Twilight* Series," *Studies in the Novel* 42, no. 1 & 2 (Spring & Summer 2010): 123.
13 Roberta Trites, *Disturbing the Universe: Power and Repression in Adolescent Literature* (Iowa City: University of Iowa Press, 2000), 85.
14 Christine Seifert, "Bite Me! (Or Don't)," *Bitch: Feminist Response to Pop Culture* 42 (2009): 23. However, Bella and Edward do consummate their relationship after marriage in the final installment of the book series, *Breaking Dawn*.
15 Miriam Hospodar, "Aphrodisiac Foods: Bringing Heaven to Earth," *Gastronomica* 4, no. 4 (Fall 2004): 90.
16 Ibid., 82.
17 Mandy Aftel, *Essence and Alchemy* (New York: North Point Press, 2001), 167.
18 Hospodar, "Aphrodisiac Foods," 90.
19 Ibid.
20 Maxine Shen, "Flesh & 'Blood': How HBO Series Has Turned Hot Vampires Into Gay-Rights Analogy," *New York Post* (June 23, 2009), nypost.com/2009/06/23/flesh-blood (accessed December 11, 2015).
21 David Bianculli, " 'True Blood,' Tasty New TV From Alan Ball And HBO," *National Public Radio* (September 5, 2008), npr.org/templates/story/story.php?storyId=94320825 (accessed December 11, 2015).
22 Auerbach, *Our Vampires*, 1; Gordon and Hollinger, "Introduction," 3.

Bibliography

Aftel, Mandy. *Essence and Alchemy*. New York: North Point Press, 2001.
Auerbach, Nina. *Our Vampires, Ourselves*. Chicago: University of Chicago Press, 1995.
Bianculli, David. "'True Blood,' Tasty New TV From Alan Ball And HBO." *National Public Radio*, September 5, 2008. npr.org/templates/story/story.php?storyId=94320825.
Bower, Anne L. "Watching Food: The Production of Food, Film, and Values." In *Reel Food: Essays on Food in Film*, edited by Anne L. Bower, 1–13. New York: Routledge, 2004.
Gordon, Joan, and Veronica Hollinger, "Introduction." In *Blood Read: The Vampire as Metaphor in Contemporary Culture*, edited by Joan Gordon and Veronica Hollinger, 1–7. Philadelphia: University of Pennsylvania Press, 1997.
Hospodar, Miriam. "Aphrodisiac Foods: Bringing Heaven to Earth." *Gastronomica* 4, no. 4 (Fall 2004): 82–93.
Inness, Sherrie A., ed. *Cooking Lessons: The Politics of Gender and Food*. Lanham, MD: Rowman & Littlefield, 2001.
Johnston, Josée, and Shyon Baumann. *Foodies: Democracy and Distinction in the Gourmet Foodscape*. New York: Routledge, 2010.
Kane, Tim. *The Changing Vampire of Film and Television: A Critical Study of the Growth of a Genre*. Jefferson, NC: McFarland, 2006.
Miller, Sally. "'Nursery Fears Made Flesh and Sinew': Vampires, the Body, and Eating Disorders: A Psychoanalytic Approach." Beastly Publications, 1999. homepages.nildram.co.uk/~beast/publications/vamp_paper/index.html (accessed October 17, 2010).
Parasecoli, Fabio. *Bite Me: Food in Popular Culture*. Oxford: Berg, 2008.
Seifert, Christine. "Bite Me! (Or Don't)." *Bitch: Feminist Response to Pop Culture* 42 (2009): 23–5.
Shen, Maxine. "Flesh & 'Blood': How HBO Series Has Turned Hot Vampires Into Gay-Rights Analogy." *New York Post*, June 23, 2009. nypost.com/2009/06/23/flesh-blood (accessed December 11, 2015).
Silver, Anna. "*Twilight* Is Not Good for Maidens: Gender, Sexuality, and the Family in Stephenie Meyer's *Twilight* Series." *Studies in the Novel* 42, no. 1 & 2 (Spring & Summer 2010): 121–38.
Trites, Roberta. *Disturbing the Universe: Power and Repression in Adolescent Literature*. Iowa City: University of Iowa Press, 2000.

About the Editors

Cynthia J. Miller is a cultural anthropologist, specializing in popular culture and visual media. Her writing has appeared in a wide range of journals and anthologies across the disciplines. She is the editor of *Too Bold for the Box Office: The Mockumentary, From Big Screen to Small* (2012) and *The Silence of the Lambs: Critical Essays on Clarice, a Cannibal, and a Nice Chianti* (2016) and coeditor of *Steaming into a Victorian Future* (2012, with Julie Anne Taddeo) and *Border Visions: Identity and Diaspora in Film* (2013, with Jakub Kazecki and Karen A. Ritzenhoff). She is also film review editor for the journal *Film & History* and series editor for Rowman & Littlefield's *Film and History* book series; she also serves on the editorial advisory boards for *The Journal of Popular Television* and Bloomsbury's *Guide to Contemporary Directors* series.

A. Bowdoin Van Riper is a historian who specializes in depictions of science and technology in popular culture. His publications include *Science in Popular Culture: A Reference Guide* (2002), *Imagining Flight: Aviation and the Popular Culture* (2003), *Rockets and Missiles: The Life Story of a Technology* (2004; rpt. 2007), and *A Biographical Encyclopedia of Scientists and Inventors in American Film and Television* (2011). He was guest editor, with Cynthia J. Miller, of a special two-issue themed volume (Spring/Fall 2010) of *Film & History* ("Images of Science and Technology in Film") and the editor of *Learning from Mickey, Donald, and Walt: Essays on Disney's Edutainment Films* (2011).

Miller and Van Riper are coeditors of *Undead in the West: Vampires, Zombies, Mummies, and Ghosts on the Cinematic Frontier* and its "sequel" *Undead in the West II: They Just Keep Coming* (2012, 2013), *1950s "Rocketman" TV Series and their Fans: Cadets, Rangers, and Junior Space Men* (2012), *International Westerns: Re-locating the Frontier* (2014), *Horrors of War: The Undead on the Battlefield* (2015), and *The Laughing Dead: The Horror Comedy Film from Bride of Frankenstein to Zombieland* (2016).

Notes on Contributors

Ralph Beliveau is an associate professor at the Gaylord College at the University of Oklahoma. He is the coeditor of *International Horror Film Directors: Global Fear* (2016) and coauthor of *Digital Literacy* (2016). His research focuses on documentary, critical media literacy, popular culture, and rhetoric. He has written about Guillermo del Toro, documentary rhetoric, horror media, *The Wire*, African American biographical documentaries, Alex Cox, *Supernatural*, Richard Matheson, and Paolo Freire. At the University of Iowa he completed his PhD and a Certificate in the Rhetoric of Inquiry, and received a BS in media production from Northwestern University.

Mark Bernard is an instructor of American studies at the University of North Carolina at Charlotte. He is the author of *Selling the Splat Pack: The DVD Revolution and the American Horror Film* (2014) and coauthor of *Appetites and Anxieties: Food, Film, and the Politics of Representation* (2014, with Cynthia Baron and Diane Carson). He has written about food in horror cinema and race in serial killer cinema, among other topics. He is currently writing about acting and stardom in horror cinema and television.

Bart Bishop received his MA in English from Xavier University and has a background in teaching and journalism. He has taught at Greenville Technical College and the University of South Carolina Upstate, and now teaches online composition classes at Cincinnati State Technical and Community College. He is a scopist for Thomson Reuters, and has edited two published novels. His writings on the theater, pop culture, food, and literature have appeared in the *Spartanburg Herald-Journal*, *CityBeat*, *Cincinnati Magazine*, and *LitReactor*. His interests include feminist criticism, gender/queer studies, and critical race theory. He lives with his wife and daughter in Cincinnati, Ohio.

Alexandra C. Frank received her master's degree in cinema studies from New York University. While there, she wrote a thesis about vampire foodways in contemporary film and television. Now an independent film scholar, she blogs semi-regularly at www.cinefeelyeah.net. You can follow her on Twitter @cinecurator—she'd love to talk movies with you. She is interested in representations of food, gender, and sexuality on-screen. She wants to write a memoir about how the movies have shaped her outlook on the world.

Michael Fuchs is an assistant professor in American studies at the University of Graz in Austria. He has coedited three books (most recently *ConFiguring America: Iconic Figures, Visuality, and the American Identity* [2013]) and authored more than twenty published and forthcoming journal articles and book chapters on horror and adult cinema, video games, American television, and contemporary American literature. Currently, he is coediting three other books and working on three monographs. For more information on his past, current, and forthcoming work, check out his website at www.fuchsmichael.net.

Vivian Halloran is associate professor of English and American studies at Indiana University Bloomington. She is the author of *The Immigrant Kitchen: Food, Ethnicity, and Diaspora* (2016). The book examines food memoirs by immigrants and their descendants and reveals how their treatment of food deeply embeds lingering twenty-first-century concerns about immigrant identity in the United States. Other recent food publications include "After Forty Acres: Food Security, Urban Agriculture, and Black Food Citizenship" in *Dethroning the Deceitful Pork Chop: Rethinking African American Foodways from Slavery to Obama*, ed. Jennifer Jensen Wallach (2015).

Mark Henderson earned his bachelor and master of arts in English from the University of Louisiana at Monroe, and then his PhD in English with concentrations on nineteenth-and twentieth-century American literature and psychoanalytic theory from Auburn University in 2012. He currently teaches at Tuskegee University. His research interests include the American Gothic, American modernism, film, and surveillance studies. His film interests include horror, film noir, science fiction, dystopia, and disaster. He has published works on the significance of fire and diabolism in Richard Wright's *Native Son* and *Dark Nature as Metaphor in the Works of Edgar Allan Poe* (forthcoming).

Tom Hertweck is assistant director of the Core Writing Program and lecturer of English at the University of Nevada, Reno, where he also earned his PhD in program for Literature and Environment. The editor of *Food on Film: Bringing Something New to the Table* (2014) and coeditor of the book series *Cultural Ecologies of Food in the 21st Century*, he is currently completing a manuscript about the literary and spatial construction of food commodities entitled "Narredibility: Postwar Literature and the Spaces of American Food Consumption."

NOTES ON CONTRIBUTORS

Jennifer L. Holm received her bachelor's degree from Grinnell College and her master's and doctoral degrees from the University of Virginia. She is an assistant professor of French and head of the French Program at the University of Virginia's College at Wise. Her research examines gastronomy in twentieth- and twenty-first-century French literature and film.

Sue Matheson is an associate professor of English literature at the University College of the North in Manitoba, Canada. She teaches in the areas of American film and popular culture, Canadian literature, and children's literature. Her interests in film, culture, and literature are reflected in more than forty essays published in a wide range of books and scholarly journals. She the editor of *Love in Western Film and Television: Lonely Hearts and Happy Trails* (2013) and the author of *The Westerns and War Films of John Ford* (2016).

Salvador Jimenez Murguia is associate professor of sociology at Akita International University, Japan, and Paul Orfalea Center Fellow in Global Studies at the University of California, Santa Barbara. His research interests include popular culture, deviant behavior, and food and foodways among prison populations. Professor Murguia is the editor of the *Encyclopedia of Japanese Horror*, and is currently working on several other books including *Diets of the Disrepute: Control and Resistance within Prison Dining*.

Michael Phillips is a senior lecturer in English at the University of Graz in Austria. He has coedited *ConFiguring America: Iconic Figures, Visuality, and the American Identity* (2013). His research interests include cult media, fan cultures, and the interrelations between sports and culture, as evidenced in his essays on *Star Wars* fandom and the stardom of basketball superstar LeBron James.

Alex Pinar is assistant professor of intercultural communication and Spanish in undergraduate and graduate programs at Akita International University (Japan). He holds a PhD in applied linguistics and MA in research in language and literature from University of Barcelona and is enrolled in a doctorate program in Theory of Literature and Comparative Literature, writing a dissertation about world literature adaptations in Japanese cinema. His research interests are world literature and world cinema, literature film adaptations, and cultural studies. He is currently working on an encyclopedia of contemporary Spanish cinema, coedited with Salvador Jimenez Murguia.

Thomas Prasch is professor and chair of the Department of History at Washburn University. Assistant editor for film reviews for the *American Historical Review* from 1994 to 2004, he has edited a biennial selection of film reviews for *Kansas History* since 2001. His recent publications include

NOTES ON CONTRIBUTORS

" 'Radiation's Rising, but One Mustn't Grumble Too Much': Nuclear Apocalypse Played as Farce in Richard Lester's *The Bed Sitting Room* (1969)" in Karen A. Ritzenhoff and Angela Krewani (eds.), *The Apocalypse in Film: Dystopias, Disasters, and Other Visions about the End of the World* (2016); " 'All the Strange Facts': Alfred Russel Wallace's Spiritualism and Evolutionary Thought" in Alisa Clapp-Itnyre and Julie Melnyk (eds.), *"Perplext in Faith": Essays on Victorian Beliefs and Doubts* (2015); and " 'Strange Things Happen in a War-Torn Land': Cat Demons, Samurai, Victims' Vengeance, and the Social Costs of War in Kaneto Shindo's *Kuroneko* (1968)" in Cynthia J. Miller and A. Bowdoin Van Riper (eds.), *Horrors of War: The Undead on the Battlefield* (2015). He received his PhD from Indiana University.

Karen A. Ritzenhoff is professor in the Department of Communication at Central Connecticut State University. She is affiliated with the Women, Gender, and Sexuality Studies Program and cinema studies. In 2015 she coedited *The Apocalypse in Film* with Angela Krewani (Germany), *Selling Sex on Screen: From Weimar Cinema to Zombie Porn* with Catriona McAvoy (United Kingdom), and *Humor, Entertainment, and Popular Culture during World War I* with Clémentine Tholas-Disset (France). Ritzenhoff is also coeditor of *Heroism and Gender in War Films* (2014) with Jakub Kazecki; *Border Visions: Diaspora and Identity in Film* (2013) with Jakub Kazecki and Cynthia J. Miller; *Screening the Dark Side of Love: From Euro-Horror to American Cinema* (2012) with Karen Randell.

LuAnne Roth is an assistant teaching professor in the English Department at the University of Missouri, where her courses revolve around the topics of folklore, foodways, contemporary legend, and critical theory. Roth's current research focuses on media representations of food and culture (especially Thanksgiving), for which she maintains a digital archive of scenes related to food/culture, legend/rumor, and the undead. The latter archive comes in handy for her "Zombies 'R' Us" film genre course. Surely, if we (the living) better understood the eating habits of zombies, she surmises, we would be more tolerant of our undead neighbors.

Stacy Rusnak is an assistant professor of film at Georgia Gwinnett College. She holds a PhD from Georgia State University in moving image studies and an MA in Spanish language and literature. Her interests include: Spanish language cinema, popular culture, and politics of identity. Dr. Rusnak has directed two short films and has served as a film judge for various festivals, including Atlanta's Buried Alive Film Festival. She has published on Agamben's 'State of Exception' in *Children of Men* in *The Postnational Fantasy* and on MTV and the Satanic Panic in *Satanic Panic: Pop Cultural Paranoia in the 1980s*.

Hans Staats received his PhD in comparative literature and cultural studies at Stony Brook University. Excerpts from his dissertation "Don't Look Now: The Child in Horror Film and Media" have appeared in *Offscreen, the Irish Journal of Gothic and Horror Studies, Journal of the Fantastic in the Arts*, and the recent anthology *War Gothic in Literature and Culture* (eds. Steffen Hantke and Agnieszka Soltysik Monnet, 2016). Forthcoming publications include a chapter on the media interface between the golden age of American horror comics, television news, and the early slasher film cycle, to be included in the anthology *The Representation of Cruel Children in Popular Texts* (eds. Monica Flegel and Christopher Parkes, 2017).

Rob Weiner is popular culture/humanities librarian and honors college professor at Texas Tech University. He is author, editor, or coeditor of numerous volumes, including: *Marvel Graphic Novels* (2007); *The Joker: A Serious Study of the Clown Prince of Crime* (2016); *Perspectives on the Grateful Dead* (1999); *From the Arthouse to the Grindhouse* (2010); *Cinema Inferno* (2010); *Marvel Comics into Film*; and *Web-Spinning Heroics* (2012). His work has also been published in journals and volumes such as *ImageText, International Journal of Comic Art, The Journal of Pan-African Studies, Movies in American History*, and *Global Glam*. He has been featured on A&E's Biography, and in documentaries related to West Texas music.

Erin E. Wiegand received her MA in cinema studies from San Francisco State University. She is currently a senior editor at North Atlantic Books. Her previously published work includes the articles "Marriage Bites: Lesbian Vampires and the Failure of Heterosexual Monogamy in *Daughters of Darkness*" and "The Unfilmable: Bringing Lovecraft to the Screen," both published in *Paracinema* magazine. For more, visit http://erinewiegand.com.

Index

301/302 (film) 7, 137–53

abject, the 53
  as concept 8, 160, 172, 174–6, 189–91
  consumption of 9, 21, 176–8, 227, 237
  individuals as 163–4, 181–3
  meat eating and 155, 246, 249
abstinence 277, 342–4
abuse 194–5, 300, 328
  physical 100, 109, 114, 138, 150, 347
  psychological 144, 150
  sexual 140–1, 143, 196, 199, 328
  (*see also* rape)
addiction 3, 7, 67, 82, 84, 88–92, 342, 345, 349
Adorno, Theodore and Max Horkheimer 23, 199, 200
aesthetics 2, 190, 206
  of film 66, 100–1, 103, 106, 107, 112, 115, 197, 202, 257
  of food 177, 192
Africa Addio (1966) 257
African Americans 123–36, 356, 357
Aftel, Mandy 346
Alemany-Galway, Mary 106
Althusser, Louis 198, 200
American Dream 32, 35–7, 40
American Psycho (2000) 9, 194, 303–5
American Zombie (2007) 279–81
anorexia 138, 139, 147, 152 n.13
anthropologists 2, 254–5, 261, 264, 355
anxieties
  food-related 1, 26
  political 65
  projected onto the undead 271, 283, 286, 287 n.5
  social 9, 25, 50, 254, 264

appetite 43, 215, 336
  childish 295–301, 305
  control of 4, 55, 56–8, 60
  monstrous 3, 5, 42, 52, 56, 113, 129, 275, 329, 334
  sexual 140, 142–5, 152nn.11–12, 277, 342, 344, 348
Arens, William 255
Auerbach, Nina 339

Bad Taste (film) xi, 2, 3, 6, 15–30
Bakhtin, Mikail 51
Bankard, Bob 229
banquets 51, 107
  cannibalistic 222, 231, 234, 326, 332, 334
  funerary 170–1, 176–8
Barbie, Klaus 243–4
Barratt, Jim 20, 21, 23
belief systems 1, 25–6, 69, 75, 160, 172, 174, 180, 209, 226, 351
Beliveau, Ralph vii, 8, 169–85, 356
Bell, Dorian 156
Beloved (1998) vii, 7, 18, 123–36
Bishop, Bart vii, 7, 123–36, 356
Bishop, Kyle William 51, 53, 275, 335
blood 105, 108, 115, 160–1, 221, 225, 238, 330
  as abject 19, 27, 34, 51, 53, 157, 174, 261, 294, 312
  as aesthetic element in cinema 129, 140, 229, 230–4, 248, 257
  as byproduct of violence 17, 22, 25, 27, 33, 54, 55, 56, 99, 127, 148, 195, 232, 315–16, 320
  as food 5, 66, 69, 171, 273, 281–2, 284, 334, 339–53
  as sacrifice 8, 10, 222–4, 226–8, 231, 232, 329

blood (cont.)
    as symbol 159, 162, 171
    synthetic 10, 340, 348, 350
Blood Feast (1963) 2, 4, 8, 10, 221–36
Blood Feast 2: All You Can Eat (2002) 230
Bordo, Susan 276
Botting, Fred 170
Bousquet, Mark 2
Boy Eats Girl (2005) 277–8
brains 15, 17, 20, 56, 229
    as abject 19, 27
    as food 24, 66, 69, 82, 214, 221, 227, 263, 272, 273, 275, 278, 285, 304
Bramen, Lisa 31–2, 44
Brand, Christianna 173, 176–80
Brecht, Bertolt 106, 107, 119 n.19
Britton, Andrew 36
Brottman, Mikita 19, 226–7, 260
Brown, Jennifer 210
burial grounds 38
    Native American 16, 18, 26, 35, 37, 45n.11, 83
Butcher, The (1970) (see *Le Boucher*)
butcher shops 81, 139–40, 143, 158–9, 248, 250n.3, 283
butchers 7, 9, 155–65, 238–41, 245, 246
butchery
    of animals 16, 17, 81, 163, 229, 240, 262
    of people 17, 148, 239, 310
    (see also carving, dismemberment)

cadaver 160–1, 190 (see also corpse)
Cannibal Ferox (1981) 254–5, 256, 265
Cannibal Holocaust (1980) 2, 3, 254, 256–9, 263, 265, 267 n.28
cannibal-horror films 253–68, 309
cannibalism
    as cultural critique 10, 38–40, 50, 61, 66, 69–72, 99–100, 103, 109–10, 115, 206–10, 274, 285, 288n.18, 294, 302, 3045, 309–21, 325
    as metaphor 8–10, 53–5, 238, 240–1, 244, 247–9, 271
    as taboo 4–5, 21, 55, 192, 213, 215, 226–7, 254–61, 264–5, 326, 336
    types of 72–6, 146–7, 150, 333

capitalism 6, 26, 65, 246, 283, 285, 319
    and consumption 50, 61, 74, 139
    in Asia 70, 78n.21, 149, 150–1
    and social order 35–6, 45n.11, 46n.17, 139–40, 145, 147
Cardullo, Bert 101
"carnal gaze" 155
Caro, Mark 238
Carroll, Nöel 125
Carson, Diane 3, 138, 151, 152n.4, 156
carving 158, 160–1, 209, 211, 244, 262 (see also butchery, dismemberment)
Catholic Church 171, 180, 346–7
Cettl, Robert 294
Chabrol, Claude 7, 155–7, 158, 159, 163
Chan, Fruit 65, 68, 69, 70, 72–74, 76
chefs 6, 214, 334
    celebrity 340
    skills of 102, 241, 232
children 36, 45n.11, 58, 69, 83, 319, 332, 341
    eating habits of 5, 25, 34, 57, 330
    monstrous 7, 19, 32, 85, 125–34
    parenting of 67, 83, 86–7, 127–34, 152n.6, 158, 182, 211, 263
    serial killers compared to 299, 300–2, 305
    violence against 109, 123–4, 161, 196, 233, 246
Christianity 36, 62n.17, 129, 171, 173, 348
cinéma vomitif 19
civilization 1, 5, 52, 55, 106–7, 113–14, 206, 254–5
Clarens, Carlos 230
class 2, 58, 61, 341
    conflict 41–2, 61, 110–14, 190–204, 209–10, 313
    signifiers of 49, 52, 85–6, 110, 114, 209–10, 211, 302, 341
Cocarla, Sasha 273, 278
Cohen, Larry 82
comedy
    dark 22, 38, 155, 210, 237, 248
    genre hybridization with horror 20, 27, 50–5, 68, 248–9, 281–2, 277, 344, 346

romantic 263, 277, 344
satirical 81–95, 282
commodification 6, 24, 32, 37, 48n.6, 72–6
consumerism 50, 61, 76, 93n.5, 102–3, 112, 190–204, 288n.18, 311
  consumption 1–4, 6, 10, 31, 38, 41, 126, 140, 142, 150, 158, 160, 208–9, 213–15, 239, 278, 286, 310, 332, 342, 351
  excessive 54 (*see also* gluttony)
  of fast food 15, 19, 25–6, 81
  horrific 82, 170, 183, 237, 250, 256, 260–63, 325, 329
  mindless 24, 54, 58, 90–92, 125, 271–2, 274–5, 276, 312
  restrained 146, 334–5
  self- 147, 313, 316, 330
  as self-definition 70, 75, 77, 81, 103, 106, 108, 110, 145
  symbolic 8, 74, 152n.8, 162, 191–4, 197, 200, 210, 221, 226–7
  of taboo substances 7, 8, 20–21, 67, 70, 74–6, 148, 190–204, 247, 283
  of women 152 n.8
Cook, the Thief, His Wife and Her Lover, The (film) 7, 99–122
cookbooks 331
cooking 10, 68, 71, 73, 245–6, 340
  emotional dimensions of 137, 138, 142, 144, 146–7, 163, 218
  at home 68, 163, 205, 277
  of humans 137, 223, 226–7, 304, 326–7, 330–31
  as transformation 57–8, 59, 84, 261–3
cooks 101, 103, 109, 111, 231, 332–4 (*see also* chefs)
coprophagia 8, 189–204
Cornand, André 162
corpses 3, 4, 45n.11, 178, 325–6, 330, 332
  as abject 174–6, 177, 190, 312
  dehumanized quality of 224, 228, 234, 327
  interactions with 8, 43, 104, 155, 172, 178, 180–81, 213, 300, 310
Counihan, Carole 166, 294

Creed, Barbara 182
cuisine (*see* food, haute cuisine)
culture 142, 157, 169, 270, 316, 320, 348
  consumer 57, 68, 70, 106–7, 191–2, 200–2
  defined by foodways 2–5, 16, 23–6, 171, 179, 182, 261–2, 274–5, 283, 285, 302, 351
  influence 163, 302, 305
  high v. low 110, 112–14, 213

Daniels, Stephen V. 131
Davis, Blair 3
Dawn of the Dead (1978) 36, 50, 54, 274–5
Daybreakers (2009) 340, 348–51
Delicatessen (1991) 2, 9, 155, 237–52
Demetrakopoulos, Stephanie 127, 131, 132, 133
Deranged (1974) 300
Derrida, Jacques 264
devouring mother 125, 131–3, 134
diet
  healthy 6, 86
  individual identity and 142, 245, 277, 341, 344, 346, 350–1
  socially constructed 1, 70, 254, 261, 263
dinner party (*see* banquet)
disgust 44, 160, 211, 229, 262, 294
  directed at individuals 180, 196, 284, 293
  objects of 21, 31, 34, 38, 74, 258, 261, 273, 274, 277, 346
  self- 282
  (*see also* abject, the)
dismemberment 4
  of animals 2578, 262–3
  of humans 20, 39, 54, 59, 138, 140, 147, 222, 231, 301, 315, 325
documentary film 72, 169, 257, 356
  fictional device in dramatic films 254, 259, 279–80, 282
  Holocaust depicted in 243–4, 245
Donnelly, Ashley M. 210
Douglas, Mary 2, 4, 73
Douglas, Tom 179–80

Dracula (film; 1931) 32, 85, 341
Dracula (novel; 1897) 341
DuMaurier, Bedelia 212
Dumplings (2004) 4, 6, 65–79
Durgnat, Raymond 299
Dyer, Richard 205

Eaten Alive (1980) 256, 258, 266 n.8
eating
  as gluttony 54, 56–7, 126, 142, 288 n.22
  as pleasure 31, 34, 86–7, 142, 267n.17, 296
  as self-definition 41–2, 44, 69, 144–5, 147–8, 212, 261, 264, 273–4, 277–81, 285–6, 300, 302, 305, 335, 340
  as social activity 59–60, 86, 90, 171–3, 175, 192, 247, 298, 346
  as torture 100, 102, 106, 326–7
  as trauma 131, 177–8, 181–2, 192
eating disorders 137–9, 146–7, 152–3n.13, 283
Ebert, Roger 101, 111
economy, market 23–6, 68–69, 111–12, 238–9, 247, 350 (*see also* capitalism)
Elbow, Gary 226
Emanuelle and the Last Cannibals 264
excess 3, 144, 170, 273
  cinematic 54, 101, 208, 227–30
  consumerist 8, 99–100, 102, 113, 192, 245
  societal 7, 106, 109, 350
exploitation 8, 26, 201, 210, 279, 325
exploitation film 20, 221–34, 253–68, 326

families
  bonding rituals of 59–61, 210, 218 n.23
  broken 123, 125, 127–8, 132, 193, 326, 328, 334–5
  critique of 41–4, 309–23, 347
  monstrous 10, 38–41, 84–91, 139, 173–4, 179–82, 300, 302, 309–323
  nuclear 31–8, 41–4, 46n.17, 49, 50–53, 297–9, 320

family horror film cycle 31–49
farm-to-table 6, 32–3, 37–41, 57, 81
Fasso, Phil 22
fast food 6, 15–30, 50–1, 52, 55–9, 61, 283, 336
feces (*see also* coprophagia)
  abject 174–5, 190–1
  consumption of 105–6, 189, 192, 194, 200
  metaphorical 194, 195, 197, 199, 200–2
femininity 130, 152n.9, 182, 304
feminism 68, 76, 137–8, 140, 145–6, 149, 165n.14, 276, 325, 339, 356
festa stultorum 54
fetus, consumption of 4, 65–79, 288 n.18
Fiddes, Nick 261
Fiedler, Leslie 213
Fleischer, Ruben 50, 52, 54–5
folklore 8, 32, 65, 69, 126, 171–3, 178, 272, 281, 359
food (conceptual)
  aesthetics 102, 105–7
  as allegory 41–3, 102, 106, 139–41, 159, 209, 237, 348–9
  as comfort 1, 7, 52, 124, 129–30, 132
  and cultural norms 4, 178–85, 238, 240, 293–5, 297–300, 304–5, 330
  and the fantastic 4, 15–30, 31, 81–96, 271–92, 339–53
  as gift 138, 142–6, 162–3, 208, 230–31
  and identity 9, 38–9, 43, 49, 142–6, 149, 238, 272–5, 277–86, 303–5, 339–53
  as indulgence 1, 2, 31, 57, 88, 124, 240, 245, 348, 350–51 (*see also* gourmet, haute cuisine)
  and loss of control 35, 50–51, 85–90 (*see also* hunger)
  as Other 34, 36
  processed 6, 81–2, 280, 327–8, 350–52 (*see also* fast food, food industry)
  sharing of 42–3, 59–62, 85–7, 210–15, 302–3, 330 (*see also* family)

INDEX

taboos 1, 2–3, 8, 10, 54–5, 62, 65–6, 73–5, 194, 233, 256, 260–64 (*see also* abject, cannibalism, coprophagia)
and transformation 18–19, 91–92, 171–4, 178–80, 260–64, 333–5
food (specific varieties)
candy 125, 295–6, 297, 299
eggs 19, 34, 176, 177, 211
fried chicken 18, 28n.15, 59, 148–9
milk 9, 35, 42, 100, 125–7, 130–2, 134, 237, 298
oranges 297
sandwiches 9, 42, 59, 296, 298
soda 19, 299–301
Twinkies 58, 61
food industry (*see also* fast food)
abrogation of responsibility by 6, 23–6, 31–3, 37, 44, 87–90
documentary films about 24–5
satire of 7, 15–30, 81–95
sustainability of 340, 348–50
vulnerability to sabotage 90–92, 328–9, 332–3
foodways 240, 356, 358, 359
social construction of 1, 3, 4, 9, 205
traditional 23, 27, 38, 52
vampire 10, 339–53
zombie 50, 272, 273–5, 278, 281, 285–6
Foodways and Eating Habits (1983) 205
found footage film 254, 259
France 9, 107, 238, 242–4, 249, 257, 346
Franco, Dean 133
French Revolution, The 107–9
Freud, Sigmund 25, 74, 190
Friedman, Dave 227–8, 233
Fuller, Bryan 207, 212
funerary rites (*see* banquets – funeral)

Gee, Regina 170
gender 2, 123, 207, 339, 342, 351
roles 132, 138, 139, 174, 315, 334
spaces 129, 152, 304
ghosts 7, 34–5, 124–7, 130–1
Girard, René 74, 259
Giuliano, Michael B. 205
gluttony 55, 57, 101, 303, 334

Goddard, Jean Luc 106, 116–17n.18, 260
gourmets 8, 99, 102, 155, 206, 209, 211, 213, 215, 340, 343
Gramsci, Antonio 197
Grand Guignol 230
Grande Bouffe, Le (1973) 2
Grant, Barry Keith 20
Gras, Vernon 102, 107
Grau, Jorge Michel 10, 309
Graveyard Alive (2003) 277–8, 281
greed 102, 111, 132, 239, 255
Greenaway, Peter 7, 99–122
Gunning, Tom 295

Hannibal (TV series; 2013–2015) 8, 205–19
Hannibal Rising (2006) 207
Harris, Trudier 129, 130
Harvey, Lawrence R. 190, 197, 199
haute cuisine 99, 102
health 130
diet and 70, 86, 210, 277, 280, 285, 340, 350
fast food and 6, 23–5, 89
public 90, 101, 325
Henry: Portrait of a Serial Killer (1986) 300–1
Hertweck, Tom xi, 7, 10, 137–53, 357
hierarchies 1, 52, 74, 351
Hightower, Jim 25
Hinson, Hal 111
Hitchcock, Alfred 3, 4, 41–3, 85, 156, 297–9, 301
Holm, Jennifer L. 7, 155–67, 357
Holocaust, the 237–8, 242–4, 249–50
Hong Kong 6, 66
economy 67
film industry 65, 68, 70
sovereignty 65, 68–9
Hooper, Tobe 31, 32, 36, 38–9, 326
Horkheimer, Max 23, 199–200
horror film
genre boundaries of 20, 70, 293
history 31–49, 77, 85, 227–31
politics of 32–3, 36, 38, 40
(*see also* cannibal-horror film, exploitation film, splatter film)

INDEX

Hospodar, Miriam 346
Howe, Desson 107
Human Centipede films (2009–2015) 9, 189–204
Humor (*see* comedy)
hunger 4, 37, 42
  and cannibalism 2, 4–5, 17
  insatiable 5, 85–7, 90–91, 102, 127, 129, 132, 134, 143–5, 282
  monstrous 45n.11, 55–6, 276–7, 286n.2
  and poverty 8, 173–8, 181–2, 209, 240–1, 245, 309–23
  for specific foods 57–8, 60–61, 297, 298
hunting 42, 260, 311–14
Hurston, Zora Neale 126

ideology 319, 325
  bourgeois-patriarchal 26, 32–35, 36, 40, 42, 45n.11, 45 n.17
  socialist 69
  unlimited growth as 90–1
immortality 226, 344, 346
imperialism 24, 302
indigenous peoples 253–5, 261, 264, 265
inequality, social 32–3, 36–40, 76, 194–5, 201–2, 312
Infantino, Steven 238
intertexts 31
Ishtar (deity) 8–9, 221–36

Jackson, Neil 259
Jackson, Peter xi, 6, 15, 16–17, 20, 21, 26
Jacobean era 108–10, 112, 115, 118 n.33
Jagannathan, Meera 330
Jameson, Fredric 36
Jeunet, Jean-Pierre 9, 156, 237–52
Johnston, Ian 68
Johnston, Ruth 108
Jones, Michael Owen 205

Kang, Nancy 130, 135n.14, 136
Kawin, Bruce 293, 305, 307
Kee, Joan 138, 140, 151, 152n.7, 153

Keller, James 2, 11n.5, 12
Kelly, Nicholas 51, 62n.9, 63
Kilgour, Maggie 206, 217n.6, 219
knives
  to convey power 140, 157–9
  and predation 42, 83, 123, 158, 163, 215, 228, 231, 239, 241, 244, 315
  sexual inference 159
  and table manners 49, 59, 89, 165 n.17
  trick 241, 247, 249
Korea 138–51, 339, 346
Korsmeyer, Carolyn 279, 289n.28, 291
Koven, Mikel J. 171, 183n.7, 184, 287n.12, 292
Krell, Roberta 205, 216n.1, 217n.2, 218–19, 286, 291
Kristeva, Julia 160, 165n.23, 167, 174–5, 183n.13, 184, 189–91, 202n.1, 204

labor
  alienation of 191, 193–4
  and agriculture 350
  culinary 142, 145, 149
  and discipline 243, 297
  exploited in fast food industry 18, 24–6
Last Cannibal World (1977) 256
Le Boucher (film) 7, 155–67
Lecter, Hannibal (fictional character) 5, 8, 205–19, 294, 301–3, 305
Levi-Strauss, Claude 11n.8, 12, 262
Lewis, Herschell Gordon 221, 225, 227–36
Lindenbaum, Shirley 72, 78n.16, 79
Linklater, Richard 25
liquids 125–7, 132, 345–6
Long, Christian 24, 28n.8, 29
Lu, Tonglin 69–70, 72, 775, 77n.2, 78nn.10,14, 79
Lupton, Deborah 162, 166nn.32,34, 167, 290n.50, 291

M (1931) 9, 294, 296
magical realism 126, 134n.3, 136
Man-Eating Myth, The (book; 1979) 11, 255

Man from Deep River 256
Mangy, Joël 156
Maniac (1980) 300
manners
   social 62, 102, 106, 115, 166n.28, 274
   table 50, 58–9, 62n.20, 64, 111, 113, 165n.17, 167, 274
market
   economics 68–69, 74, 82, 90–112, 145, 327–8, 340
   food 83–6, 88, 139, 142–3, 146, 231, 250n.3, 257, 280–1, 310–12, 349–50
   for human consumption 16, 71, 75, 288 n.22
Marxism 70, 106, 113, 191
masculinity 43, 127, 130, 138, 145, 150, 157, 303–5, 317–43
mass media 1, 192
materialism 68–69, 76, 111
Matheson, Sue 6, 49–64, 93n.5, 358
Mauss, Marcel 162, 166n.30, 167
McDonald, Alzena 294, 306nn.3–4, 307
McDonald's 15, 24–5, 28n.15, 144
"McLibel" case 24
meals
   family 49–50, 60, 86, 91, 210–211, 218n.23, 298, 300, 311, 315
meat
   preparation of 9, 140, 209, 227, 262, 277, 315
   raw 223, 261, 267, 277, 283
meat pies 10, 325, 337
meat-eating
   and sex 9–10, 140, 143, 147, 157–9, 163, 222, 231, 233, 277
   and violence 155, 159
medicine, Chinese 66
Mejia LaPerle, Carol 109, 118n.33, 121
Melies, George 241
mental illness 2, 285
menu 2–3, 22, 26, 100, 103–4, 111, 238, 303–4
Mexico City 10, 310, 314, 316, 322n.18
middle class
   lifestyle 52, 61, 81, 110
   respectability 41–2

rituals 85
   values 49, 86, 302
milk 9, 35, 42, 100, 125, 127, 130–4, 237, 297–8
Miller, Cynthia J. 1–12, 15–30, 237–52, 355, 359
Miller, Sally 342, 352n.11, 353
misogyny 100, 113, 194, 201, 222, 349
modernization 39–40, 138, 151n.1, 152 n.10
Mondo Cane (1962) 257
mondo films 257
Moonlight (2007–2008) 340, 342, 344, 349
morality - ambiguous
Morrison, Toni 7, 123–4, 126, 128, 134n.6, 135–6
Mountain of the Cannibal God (1978) 256–8, 21, 265 n.1
mummies/mummification 255, 234nn.3–4, 235
Murguia, Salvador Jiminez 6, 65–79, 358
"mystery meat" 16, 21–3
mythology
   Egyptian, Babylonian 222, 225–7, 231, 234–5
   Sin-eating 170–2

Nazis
   collaboration with 237–8, 242–5
Neumann, Erich 131
New Zealand 6, 15–29
Newbury, Michael 50, 62n.7, 63, 93n.5, 95
Night and Fog (1955) 245
Night Gallery 8, 173–85
Night of the living Dead (1968) 32, 45, 50
nourishment, 59, 273–4, 287, 291, 311

Only Lovers Left Alive (2013) 339, 344
Ophuls, Marcel 243–4
Other, the 11n.17, 32, 34, 36, 39, 41, 45n.6, 46, 74, 171, 274, 276, 280
ostracism 172, 178, 273, 342

Pachirat, Timothy 262–3, 267n.21, 268
Paglia, Camille 129, 135n.9, 136

Papazian, Gretchen 138, 151n.3, 152n.13, 155
Parasecoli, Fabio 340–2, 346, 352nn.4, 10, 353
Park, Chul-Soo 138, 151n.3, 153
patriarchy 26, 139, 148, 151n.1, 182, 317
Pegg, Simon 51, 58
Pinar, Alex 6, 65–79, 358
Pink Flamingos (1972) 191–2
pink slime 333, 337 n.15
Podalsky, Laura 316, 321nn.12–13, 322
political economy 23–26, 238–41, 247, 351
pollution
  and purity 2, 12, 73, 78
Poultrygeist: Night of the Chicken Dead (film) 2, 6, 15–30
poverty 9–10, 176, 310–20, 350
Powers of Horror: An Essay On Abjection, The 165n.23, 167, 174, 183n.13, 184, 202n.1, 204, 289n.40, 291, 321n.2, 322
Prasch, Thomas 7, 99–122, 358
Primitives (1981) 256
prison 199–201, 243–5, 326
progress 25, 40, 314
progressive horror 32, 36, 38, 40
prosperity 32–7, 77, 225, 332
prostitutes 129, 310–11, 313–14, 319–20
Psycho (1960) 6, 9, 31–6, 40–5, 231, 294, 297–301
Puckle, Bertram S. 172, 183n.9, 184
Purity and Danger 11n.4, 12, 73, 78

Quart, Leonard 111, 119n.42, 121

race 2, 123, 126, 207
racism 119n.51, 194, 201, 271, 287 n.5
Rafferty, Terrence 156, 165nn.7, 9, 167
rape 22, 128, 130, 259, 327 (*see also* abuse)
Rappoport, Leon 4, 11n.9, 12
"Reaganite entertainment" 33, 38
Red Dragon (novel; 1981) 206, 208
religion 329, 339, 351
  Catholicism 171, 180, 346–51
  church 171–2, 183–4, 316
  priests and priestesses 5, 179, 222–3, 227, 231, 328–9, 346
  religious iconography 107–10
Resnais, Alan 245
restaurant
  appearance of 145, 147, 149
  fast food 15, 19, 24, 84
  fine dining 60, 89, 100–4, 113–17, 261, 303–4, 332
resurrection 35–36, 221–2, 225–6
"return of the repressed" 25, 40, 45
Ringdal, Nils Johan 129, 135n.7, 136
ritual
  communion as 171
  dining 103–4, 110, 309, 315, 317, 345
  food as 59, 172, 201–11, 215
  killing 238–9, 244, 310
  purity and pollution 78, 170, 330
  of sin-eating 170–80
  sacrifice 221–7, 255, 259, 318
Rockwell, Norman 272
Rojas, Carlos 70, 78n.13, 79
Rollins, Nita 112, 117n.22, 118nn.25–6, 119n.46, 121
Romero, George 5, 22, 27, 36, 169, 273, 275, 311
  and consumption 50, 61, 274, 276, 278
  post-Romero 6, 278

sacrifice (religious)
Sadist, The (1963) 229–300
Saló, or the 120 Days of Sodom (1975) 191
sanctification 170–1, 179
sandwiches 9, 41–3, 59, 296–8
satire 16, 23, 26, 202, 246, 250 n.6
sausage 54, 159, 211, 326
savagery 56–7, 101, 172, 206–7, 213–14, 314–15, 319
  cannibal-savage films 253–65
Savana Violenta (film; 1976) 257
scapegoat 8, 169–84, 244
Sceats, Sara 278–279, 289nn.37,39–40, 292
Schlosser, Eric 25, 28n.19, 29n.24, 93n.3, 327–8, 336n.5, 337

Se7en (film; 1995) 9, 294, 302
self-reflexivity
  in cinema 103, 106
  in narrative 8, 197, 199, 202, 208, 278, 284
serial killers 9, 205–6, 293–307, 325
sex
  and desire 143, 145
  and dessert 89
  and eating 105
  and food 93, 141, 144, 277
  and pleasure 130
  sacred 222, 225
  (*see also* sexuality, homosexuality)
sexuality
  and exploitation 325
  and horror 8, 10
  and objectification 232–3
  and taste 113
  and vampires 342–4, 349
  as a weapon 310, 318
  (*see also* sex, homosexuality)
Shadow of a Doubt (film; 1943) 85, 294, 297
Shaun of the Dead (film; 2004) 6, 49–63
Silence of the Lambs (film; 1991) 9, 124, 294, 301, 305
Silence of the Lambs (novel; 1988) 206
Silver, Anna 343, 352n.12, 353
Silverman, Kaja 275
sin-eating 8, 169–84
Six, Tom 189, 192, 195–6, 198–202, 203n.16, 204
slaughterhouses 38–40, 257, 261–3, 284
Smith, Gavin 112, 116n.14, 121
snuff film 259–60, 266n.9, 268
soda 19, 299–301
Somos lo que hay (*We are what we are*) (film; 2010) 10, 309–23
Sorrow and the Pity, The (film; 1969) 243, 251nn.16–17, 252
spectator 19–20, 33, 103–4, 106, 276, 301
splatter film 18–20, 221–2, 228–30, 233–4
  splatstick 20, 51–4
Spurlock, Morgan 25

Staats, Hans 6, 31–46, 359
Stam, Robert 51–2, 54, 57–58, 61–3
starvation 5, 70, 141, 174, 176, 178, 244, 311
State, the 198, 317, 319–20
Street Trash (film; 1987) 2–3
Stuff, The (film; 1985) 2–3, 6–7, 81–94
suffering 138, 148, 173, 176, 178, 312, 317, 346
surgery 67, 189, 199, 263
sustainability 328, 348, 350
sustenance 1, 123, 132, 134, 152, 175, 177, 182, 274, 330
Sutton, Donald 69, 78n.12, 79
Sweeney Todd (film; 2007) 2, 4, 10, 325–38

taboo
  and abjection 21
  cannibalism as 4, 10, 55, 61, 70, 74, 167, 209, 213, 215, 227, 244, 247, 256, 325
  cultural 1–3, 54, 65, 86, 138–9, 213, 228, 233, 260–1, 263, 310, 318
Tannen, Ricki Stefanie 129, 135n.10, 136
Targets (1968) 299
Texas Chainsaw Massacre, The (1974) 6, 32–45
Thatcherism (anti) 7, 99–122
Thirst (2009) 341, 346–7
Titus (1999) 10, 325–38
torture 7, 17, 157, 215, 234, 245, 304
"total cinema" 107
trauma 139–44, 146, 174, 330
trickster figure 125, 128–30, 134–6, 215, 241
Trites, Roberta 343, 352n.13, 353
Troma Studios 6, 15, 18, 22, 25, 27
True Blood (2008–2014) 340, 348–9, 352n.21, 353
Twilight franchise (2008–2012) 339, 343–4, 352n.12, 353

vagina dentata 125, 129–31, 134
values
  bourgeois 25, 32, 37, 42

Vampire Diaries (2009–) 340, 344
vampires 3, 5, 10, 54, 125, 276, 286n.2, 339–53
Van Ooijen, Erik 257, 263, 266n.4, 267n.23, 268
Van Riper, A. Bowdoin 1–12, 81–95, 221–36
Vanderschelden, Isabelle 156, 165n.12, 167
vegetarianism 160, 165n.14, 209–10, 239–40, 245, 263, 281, 283–4, 325, 344
Vichy government 9, 242–4, 250–2
Violence and the Sacred (book) 78n.20, 29, 259, 266n.12, 268
viscera 19, 254, 260–1, 274, 315
Visser, Margaret 49, 55, 57, 59–64, 165n.17, 167
vomit 2, 4, 17, 19–21, 27–29, 31, 99, 106, 174, 200, 233–5, 258, 279–82, 302, 311–12

Walsh, Michael 100, 112, 115n.1, 119n.45, 122
Warm Bodies (2010 book) 278, 281, 286, 289n.34, 291
waste, human 8, 189–204, 312
Waters, John 21, 28n.11, 29, 191–2, 202 n.12
Watson, Reginald 131–2, 135nn.18, 21, 136
Welles, Halstead 173
Wheale, Nigel 100, 111, 115n.3, 116n.17, 119n.43, 122
Williams, Linda 20, 28n.7, 30
Williams, Tony 22–3, 45n.8, 47
Willoquet-Maricondi, Paula 106, 117n.18, 118nn.25, 28, 120–2
wine 37, 60, 211, 215, 225, 301, 341, 343, 345, 349
Winfrey, Oprah 124–5, 133, 134n.1, 136
Wolfe, Cary 254, 265n.2, 268
Wollen, Peter 112, 118n.32, 119nn.48, 50, 122
Wood, Robin 25, 29n.25, 30, 36, 44n.3, 46nn.15, 17, 47, 63n.33, 64
World War II 242
Wright, Edgar 50–2, 54–5, 63

Yennie, Ashlynn 193, 197
York, Jonathan David 156, 165n.1, 167

Zheng, Yi 69, 78n.12, 79
Zipes, Jack 242, 250n.11, 252
Zombie Love (film, 2000) 277, 281
Zombieland (film, 2009) 6, 49–64
zombies 5–6, 49–64, 93n.5, 169, 271–92, 311

CPSIA information can be obtained
at www.ICGtesting.com
Printed in the USA
LVHW01s2121210918
590953LV00014B/255/P